CHANGING
HISTORY

CHANGING HISTORY

VIRGINIA WOMEN THROUGH FOUR CENTURIES

Cynthia A. Kierner, Jennifer R. Loux, and Megan Taylor Shockley

Richmond
Library of Virginia
2013

PUBLISHED BY AUTHORITY OF THE LIBRARY BOARD

Library of Congress Cataloging-in-Publication Data will be found on the last printed page of this book.

Standard Book Number: ISBN-978-0-88490-212-6

Library of Virginia. Richmond, Virginia.
© 2013 by the Library of Virginia.
All rights reserved.
Printed in the United States of America.

This book is printed on acid-free paper meeting the requirements of the American Standard for Permanence of Paper for Printed Library Materials.

An endowment from the Virginia Business and Professional Women's Foundation supported the completion of this volume. Any views, findings, conclusions, or recommendations expressed in this publication do not necessarily reflect those of the Virginia Business and Professional Women's Foundation.

The following repositories have generously given permission to use quotations from manuscript collections:

Maryland Historical Society, Baltimore, Maryland, for William Wirt to "My dear Children," 23 May 1829, William Wirt Papers, MS 1011, H. Furlong Baldwin Library, Maryland Historical Society.

American Philosophical Society, Philadelphia, Pennsylvania, for Martha Jefferson Randolph to Ann Cary Randolph Morris, 8 February 1833, Smith Family Papers.

CONTENTS

LIST OF ILLUSTRATIONS

List of Illustrations

LIST OF ILLUSTRATIONS

ACKNOWLEDGMENTS

From its inception, this project has been a truly collaborative enterprise. Current and former Library of Virginia staff members who took part in the planning process, read early drafts of the chapters, checked facts and quotations, edited and indexed the volume include Sandra G. Treadway, Barbara C. Batson, John G. Deal, Matt Gottlieb, Marianne E. Julienne, Gregg D. Kimball, Jennifer D. McDaid, Emily J. Salmon, Brent Tarter, and Sara B. Bearss, who before her untimely death in February 2012 made countless contributions to the book through her extraordinary knowledge of Virginia's women and their history as well as her unparalleled editorial skills. Graphic designer Christine Sisic created an elegant design for the book and dust jacket. Emily J. Salmon expertly copyedited it. Mary Beth McIntire and Dan Stackhouse of the Library of Virginia Foundation supported the editing and publication of the book through their fund-raising efforts.

Many historians, librarians, and archivists have made contributions during the course of this project. Jane Dailey, Marie Tyler McGraw, and Elizabeth R. Varon provided advice and suggestions early in the process. Lorraine Schuyler and Kristin Celello conducted extensive reviews of the literature and compiled fine annotated bibliographies for the authors. Melvin Patrick Ely assisted by reading and commenting on drafts of Chapter 4. At Virginia Commonwealth University, Ray Bonis, archives coordinator, and Wesley Chenault, head of Special Collections and Archives, went beyond the call of duty to unearth valuable sources in the collections at James Branch Cabell Library. Elizabeth B. Dunn, research services librarian at Duke University's David M. Rubenstein Rare Book and Manuscript Library, and Jay Gaidmore, university archivist at the University of North Carolina, Chapel Hill, very graciously located and verified quotations in collections at their institutions. Archivists at the Library of Virginia were unfailingly helpful in locating materials. Senior Accessioning Archivist Jessica Tyree provided assistance with the Virginia Chapter of the National Organization for Women Records, which were still in the midst of being processed.

Staff members at numerous institutions were helpful in securing images: Jamison Davis, Virginia Historical Society; Michele Doyle, Old Salem Museums and Gardens; Meghan Glass Hughes, Valentine Richmond History Center; Marianne Martin, Colonial Williamsburg Foundation; Julie Miller, Library of Congress; Heather Moon, *Richmond Times-Dispatch*; Daisy Njoku, National Anthropological Archives, Smithsonian Institution; Ann Porto, Corbis; Regina Rush, University of Virginia; James Singewald, Maryland Historical Society; Riche Sorensen, Smithsonian American Art Museum; and Ann Drury Wellford, Museum of the Confederacy. Colleagues at the Library of Virginia provided valuable advice and assistance, including Mark Fagerburg, Pierre Courtois, and Paige Buchbinder, of Photo Services, and Dale Neighbors, Dana Puga, and Bruce Rodgers, of Prints and Photographs.

The Jamestown 2007/Jamestown-Yorktown Foundation provided key financial support during the early phase of the project's development.

This project would not have been possible without the help of the Virginia Business and Professional Women's Foundation. Their generous gift led to the establishment of the Library's Virginia Business and Professional Women's Fund, an endowment supporting programs related to the role of women in Virginia history and culture. This book was funded through the endowment, which will continue to enrich our understanding of Virginia women for many years to come.

FOREWORD

In 1982, Virginia's First Lady Lynda Johnson Robb launched the Virginia Women's Cultural History Project, a pathbreaking effort to uncover and document the history of Virginia women across nearly four centuries. Women's history as a field of study was new at the time. So little work had been done on southern women that the project staff started with no clear road map and only a few signposts to point the way. They began by surveying museums, libraries, archives, and historical organizations to identify collections that contained information about women's lives. They appealed to the public for help in locating letters, diaries, images, and artifacts still in private hands. They scoured scholarly journals, unpublished theses and dissertations, memoirs, and the small body of published works about Virginia that mentioned women's activities. As their research progressed, they found a gold mine of material—much of which had never been used before—that provided new information about Virginia women. When they pieced their findings together, a fresh perspective on Virginia's past began to emerge. Virginia history looked very different with women's views and experiences included in the narrative.

The Virginia Women's Cultural History Project tallied an amazing record of accomplishment in the three years of its existence. The project sponsored a documentary film, scores of public programs, and eight regional symposia. It engaged community groups, civic clubs, historical societies, churches, libraries, and universities in lively discussions about women's roles in Virginia's cultural, economic, civic, and political life. The project's most ambitious undertaking was a major exhibition entitled *"A Share of Honour": Virginia Women, 1600–1945*. The exhibition opened at the Virginia Museum of Fine Arts in November 1984 and later travelled to sites in Norfolk and Roanoke, breaking attendance records at each host museum.

Accompanying the exhibition was a 167-page catalog including photographs of many of the artifacts that curator Kym Rice had selected for display and a beautifully crafted narrative history of Virginia women written by historian Suzanne Lebsock. Lebsock's essay provided rich detail about women's participation in and responses to significant historical events such as the American Revolution and the Civil War, but her work paid equal attention to women's daily activities as wives, mothers, laborers, business owners, educators, nurses, community builders, reformers, and volunteers. Her research revealed that across the centuries, women's priorities and values have frequently diverged from those of men. While these differences were usually negotiated privately in family conversations, letters, and diaries, from time to time they surfaced outside the home. Once women had an opportunity to express themselves publicly and affect political decision-making, they often advocated changes in public policy that challenged prevailing male views.

The *Share of Honour* project represented a major step forward in our understanding of women's contributions to Virginia but it also revealed how much we did not know because the requisite research had not yet been done. When the Virginia Women's Cultural History Project ended in 1985, the Library of Virginia (then the Virginia State Library) received permission to reprint Suzanne Lebsock's essay, which was published in 1987 under the title *Virginia Women, 1600–1945: "A Share of Honour."* This reprint was widely distributed and served (as it was hoped) as an inspiration and a catalyst for further research. The public, now more acutely aware of the need to preserve records kept by women, donated many personal collections to libraries and historical organizations. With a newfound appreciation of the importance of documenting women's lives, archivists and librarians placed a high priority on processing and creating finding aids to their women's history materials, which encouraged their use by historians. A generation of scholars took up where *Share of Honour* left off, producing hundreds of articles and books on previously unexplored topics.

The Library marked the twentieth anniversary of the *Share of Honour* project with an exhibition entitled *Working Out Her Destiny*, which opened in August 2004, and a symposium on Virginia Women Through Four Centuries that focused on this new research, held in March 2005. The more than thirty scholars who spoke at the symposium bore witness to how rich the field of women's history had become. Their presentations revealed that women's private and public lives across the centuries were much more complex, intertwined, and nuanced than historians had previously understood. Women, they demonstrated vividly, had been interested in and had influenced public, economic, and social policy long before they obtained the right to vote. Women's political and leadership styles were often different from men's, but these differences did not cause women to be any less effective. Symposium participants shared their extensive research on nonelite women and women who lived at the margins of society, highlighting new resources for capturing their neglected stories. And scholars working on African American history summarized the exciting new work that had been done on black women's activism from the 1870s through the late twentieth century, especially their role in opposing segregation, educational inequality, and the denial of full civil rights to people of color. The consensus of those attending the symposium was that while tremendous progress had been made in recovering women's lives and past experiences, the work was far from over. Planning for a new volume about Virginia women began soon thereafter.

The Library was extremely fortunate that Cynthia Kierner, Jennifer Loux, and Megan Shockley responded enthusiastically to the invitation to undertake this effort. We could not have asked for more knowledgeable or collegial coauthors. An expert on colonial and early national women's history, Kierner assumed responsibility for the first three chapters of the book covering the formative two and a half centuries of Virginia's history. Loux tackled the tumultuous period of the 1850s through the 1870s in the fourth chapter, drawing on her in-depth knowledge of mid-nineteenth-century Virginia society and politics. Shockley, who has written extensively about women in the workforce, civil rights, and the rise of southern feminism, contributed the final three chapters chronicling the expansion of women's participation in Virginia's political, economic, and social life—and the backlash to many of these changes that women still face today. Each author made excellent use of the impressive body of published work about Virginia women now available but also delved deeply into original sources to ensure that the words and voices of women throughout Virginia's past would be clearly heard.

In closing her *"Share of Honour"* essay, Lebsock commented that from the perspective of the mid-1980s, "Virginia women appear to be in a strong position to influence the course of history, both in public policy and in day-to-day living in families and communities." Their activities since then, described in the final chapter of this volume, certainly confirm that observation. Nevertheless, several of the questions that Lebsock posed still remain difficult to answer thirty years later. Has women's increased involvement in the workforce and outside the home made a *lasting* difference in how men and women live their lives? Have women continued to adhere to values they advocated when they first entered public life—compassion, cooperation, nurture, equality, and service— or has their perspective changed as barriers to educational and professional advancement have receded? Are the gains that women have made permanent or fleeting? We may not be able to answer these questions for some time to come, but one thing is clear. With the vast outpouring of scholarship that began with *"A Share of Honour"* and that is so ably woven together with new research in *Changing History*, there can be no excuse for writing or teaching any aspect of Virginia history without including women.

Sandra Gioia Treadway
Librarian of Virginia

CHANGING
HISTORY

CHAPTER 1

"Skillfull in Anie Country Worke": Red, White, and Black in Colonial Virginia

The history of women in what became known as Virginia began thousands of years before the arrival of the first European explorers and settlers. Archaeologists believe that humans inhabited the area by 15,000 B.C. and that distinctive regional cultures emerged over the ensuing centuries. By the Late Woodland Period (A.D. 900–1600), as many as 50,000 people lived in scattered villages in the interior and on the coast. Although the houses, diet, and religious rituals of these native peoples varied, they all developed stable political and social structures, and they all farmed. Women, who tended the crops and reared the children, were visible and valued members of these Native American communities.[1]

In May 1607, three English ships deposited 104 men at the tip of a peninsula that became the site of Jamestown, the first permanent English settlement in America and the beginning of the colony of Virginia. The arrival of these first white settlers set in motion a chain of circumstances and events that would bring together peoples from three continents—North America, Europe, and Africa—each with distinctive cultures and different beliefs about the respective roles and responsibilities of men and women. Generally speaking, native

Virginian and West African women had more influence than their counterparts in early modern England, in part because their work was more visible and more undeniably essential. Nevertheless, peculiarly unstable living conditions in early Virginia made it difficult for English settlers to replicate European family and gender relations in the colony, at least initially, although colonial society gradually became more stable and more conventionally patriarchal. Over time, law and custom circumscribed the activities and roles of women of all races, as Virginia's colonial leaders built a society based on patriarchy and white supremacy.

The history of women in the land the English called Virginia began at least 15,000 years before Jamestown with the arrival of the ancestors of the first people to occupy the Chesapeake Bay region. Archaeological evidence suggests that the Woodland peoples who were the ancestors of a group of Algonquian-speaking tribes, commonly known as the Powhatan, had inhabited the area for at least 1,500 years before the arrival of the English. In 1607, the Powhatan numbered roughly 14,000 people who farmed, hunted, and lived in towns or villages. Their leader, or paramount chief, was the mighty Powhatan, who is best known today as the father of Pocahontas.[2]

Like most other traditional societies, the Powhatan divided work by gender, and both women and men engaged in essential productive labor. Hunting, fishing, and making war were men's most important tasks. All three jobs were physically demanding, though typically seasonal and, at least compared to women's work, not especially time-consuming. Powhatan women were farmers—they planted, harvested, and processed corn—and they were also responsible for building and tending houses, as well as for transporting them if their towns migrated elsewhere. Native women manufactured necessary household items, including pots, baskets, mats, and assorted wooden utensils. They prepared and served meals and offered hospitality, which sometimes included sexual favors, to important guests. They also bore and reared children and taught their daughters and young sons the skills they needed to become contributing adult members of Powhatan society.[3]

English observers often described native men as lazy and native women as overworked, in part because farming was men's work in Europe, and hunting was a favored pastime among Europe's leisured nobility. Indian women, reported the Englishman George Percy, "doe all their drugerie," which included making bread from the corn they grew, a labor-intensive process that provided basic sustenance to their families and communities. "After they pound their [grain] into flowre with hote water, they make it into paste, and worke it into round balls and Cakes, then they put it into a pot of seething water," Percy explained, and "when it is sod thoroughly, they lay it on a smooth stone, there they harden it as well as in an Oven."[4]

In fact, Indian women were not drudges, and, though these women worked hard, the Powhatan people considered women's and men's work reciprocal and probably equal in importance and value. Women's control of corn, which was the main form of wealth and sustenance in Powhatan society, enhanced their status in their families and communities. Powhatan marriage customs attested to the value of women's work and stood in stark contrast to contemporary European practices: while an English father paid his daughter's prospective husband a dowry before the marriage took place, Powhatan men paid a young woman's parents bride-wealth to compensate for the loss of their daughter's labor. Native American religious beliefs, which included at least one goddess among the Patawomeck and possibly among other Algonquians as well, also reflected women's high status and their potential power.[5]

Powhatan society was not matriarchal—in other words, women generally did not rule—but power passed from one generation to the next through the female line. The paramount chief Powhatan had therefore inherited his leadership position through his mother. The immediate heirs to his position as paramount chief were his brothers (his mother's younger sons, in order of age), followed by his sisters, his sisters' male offspring, and then his sisters' daughters, if those sisters had no sons. Consequently, though Powhatan is believed to have had forty-one living offspring in 1610, none of his own children could succeed him as chief. One consequence of this matrilineal system was that Powhatan women had more sexual freedom than their European counterparts, because in Powhatan society biological paternity did not determine the allocation of property and power. In marked contrast, English law harshly penalized women, especially among the nobility, for having sexual relations outside of marriage for fear that a husband's property might be usurped as a result of his wife's bearing another man's illegitimate son.[6]

At the same time, there is some evidence that native women in elite families were controlled and manipulated in ways that may have been comparable to the experiences of aristocratic women in Europe. Like European monarchs, Powhatan used marriage alliances to solidify his authority throughout his chiefdom. Virginia Indians were polygamous, but while most men had perhaps two or three wives, Powhatan had many more. Powhatan's marriages presumably benefited the families of the women he wed, while the ability of the paramount chief to support as many as one hundred women and their children showcased his superior wealth and power. Like European kings, Powhatan also may have been motivated by political and diplomatic considerations when choosing his daughters' spouses. Nevertheless, his favorite daughter, Pocahontas, controlled her own fate when she freely chose to marry the Englishman John Rolfe in 1614, though Powhatan most likely approved her choice in part to improve relations with the English colonizers. Indian women such as Pocahontas served as cultural mediators, or personal links, between Indians and Europeans throughout the Americas during the early stages of colonization, though marriages between Englishmen and native women were uncommon in Virginia from the first and became more so over time.[7]

Although Englishmen praised the young Pocahontas for her marriage to Rolfe and for her conversion to Christianity, they found other native women more alien and off-putting. An early settler described the queen of the Appamattuck, Opossunoquonuske, as a "fatt lustie manly woman" of majestic bearing who, on one occasion, met with English colonists, fed them, and invited them to fire their guns. When they did so, the settler reported, "she shewed not neer the like feare as [chief] Arahatec though he be a goodly man." Like other native leaders, Opossunoquonuske was subject to the authority of Powhatan, the paramount chief, but among her own people she wielded "as greate authority as any of her neighbowr Wyoances," or chiefs. By 1610, alarmed by continuing English demands for food, the queen of the Appamattuck fought back and ordered the ambush of several colonists. The English retaliated the following year by burning her town. The death toll was heavy, and Opossunoquonuske herself probably perished as she tried to escape the conflagration.[8]

Most Englishmen were either unwilling or unable to comprehend the sexual division of labor and status in Native American society. Because clean-shaven Powhatan men neither farmed nor exercised complete patriarchal

Pocahontas, by William Ludwell Sheppard, 1891. This portrait was based on one made in 1616 by Simon van de Passe in London, where the "daughter to the mighty Prince Powhatan" visited with her English husband. Nineteenth-century Virginians idealized a beautiful and assimilated Indian princess, but the original engraving portrayed Pocahontas as dark-skinned, imperious, and exotic, despite her English-style clothes. *Courtesy of the Library of Virginia.*

Noblis Matrona ex Secota (One of the Chief Ladies of Secota), Theodor de Bry, after John White, 1590. Differences in women's roles and status were important measures of the cultural gulf dividing Native Americans and Europeans. Although the Englishman John White portrayed native women sympathetically in his drawings, others regarded the supposed promiscuity and debasement of Indian women as evidence of barbarism. *Courtesy of the Library of Virginia.*

authority over their women and children, bearded English colonizers concluded that native men were idle and unmanly. Because scantily clothed Indian women farmed, wielded influence in their villages, and were not the exclusive sexual property of any single man, the English deemed them licentious and unwomanly—and sometimes less than human. These characterizations enabled Englishmen to cast Indians as savages, which, in turn, helped them to justify the expansion of their settlements and ultimately the imposition of English rule throughout the Powhatan territories.[9]

In the decades following the founding of Jamestown in 1607, a combination of war and imported European diseases (to which Indians lacked physiological immunity) took a tremendous toll on native women and their communities. It became clear to Powhatan's brothers and successors, Opitchapam and Opechancanough, that the English settlements were not only surviving but also expanding, so in 1622 the Indians attacked, killing some 350 settlers, or about one-fourth of the colony's inhabitants. The English retaliated, killing many Powhatan and their allies in the next few years and raiding their corn as well. The Powhatan and their allies attacked again in 1644, but by then the English were stronger and far more numerous, and they soundly defeated the Indians. In 1646, a treaty confined the severely depleted remnant of what had been the Powhatan paramount chiefdom to certain prescribed areas and officially redefined its paramount chief as a vassal of the king of England. In 1669, the colonial government numbered the Powhatan at only 2,900. By then, the English population of Virginia had grown to approximately 35,000.[10]

Of those 35,000, perhaps 10,000 were women.[11] Although the first two English women arrived at Jamestown in 1608—just one year after the first male settlers—Virginia had significantly more men than women throughout the seventeenth century, in part because planters mainly sponsored the transportation of young male indentured servants who, they believed, would be the most productive and cost-efficient workers in the tobacco fields that were fast becoming the main source of income for the colony. A census taken in 1625 reported that there was only one woman for every three men in the colony. Most settlers of both sexes were young and single. Indeed, in 1621 the Virginia Company of London, the joint-stock company that had founded the colony and hoped to profit by it, had actively recruited young, single women to immigrate to Virginia to marry "the most honest and industrious Planters," who would repay the costs of transporting the prospective brides to the colony. Fifty-seven women made the trip. Although most came from socially respectable backgrounds, they apparently had few prospects for marriage or employment in England and therefore opted to try their luck in Virginia. Many came bearing letters attesting to their good moral character and domestic skills. Allice Burges, a husbandman's daughter, was "skillfull in anie country worke." Ann Tanner could "Spinn and sowe ... brue, and bake, make butter and cheese, and doe huswifery."[12]

By the 1620s, Englishmen increasingly idealized "huswifery," embracing a patriarchal family ideal that, at least in theory, circumscribed respectable women and their work within the household. In 1615, the first edition of Gervase Markham's popular and often-reprinted advice book, *The English Housewife*, began by describing the husband as "the father and master of the family, . . . whose office and employments are ever for the most part abroad, or removed from the house," in contrast to his wife, who as "the mother and mistress of the family,...hath her most general employments within the house." The subtitle of Markham's treatise listed the "inward and outward Virtues which ought to be in a Complete Woman" as "physic, cookery, banqueting-stuff, distillation, perfumes, wool, hemp, flax, dairies, brewing, baking, and all other things belonging to a household."[13]

English law reflected the complementary patriarchal assumption that women were best represented in the public world by their male relations. Children of both sexes were their fathers' dependents, but boys grew up to be legally autonomous men, while most girls became wives who were subject— both by law and by custom—to the authority of their husbands. In marriage, according to the eminent English jurist Sir William Blackstone, "the husband and wife are one person in law: that is, the very being or legal existence of the woman is suspended during the marriage, or at least is incorporated and consolidated into that of the husband: under whose wing, protection, and *cover*, she performs every thing." Therefore, wives could not file suit or be sued in court, nor could they control property, including any wages they earned by their labor. Because English jurists and social commentators assumed that women, like children, were weak and dependent on male protection, English law thus radically circumscribed their responsibilities and rights.[14]

Such gender ideals, never entirely attainable in England, were utterly impossible to implement in the Virginia colony, where both settlers and their financial backers in England, who hoped to profit by their venture, settled on tobacco as the commodity that—in the absence of gold or silver—could bring them wealth. A labor-intensive crop, tobacco profoundly shaped the colony's social development in at least three important respects. First, though planters avidly recruited poor Englishmen in large numbers to work as indentured servants in the tobacco fields, prevailing assumptions about women's physical weakness lessened the appeal of female servants to prospective employers (and many poor Englishwomen also may have concluded that employment prospects were less promising in Virginia than in London). Consequently, men outnumbered women in early Virginia by as much as four to one, and this imbalance was not redressed completely until after 1700.[15] Second, women who came to Virginia as servants, especially during the early years, often worked in the tobacco fields—and not in housewifery—because of planters' seemingly insatiable demand for agricultural labor.[16] Third, disease, famine, and brutal working conditions resulted in appallingly high mortality rates in early Virginia. Death dissolved marriages, and many children grew up without parents. All in all, few seventeenth-century Virginians experienced family or domestic life that in any way resembled the idealized English model.[17]

Most of the women who came to Virginia during its early decades were English indentured servants who received transportation to the colony in exchange for service—usually five to seven years—after their arrival. English beliefs about women's bodily weakness, compared to men, did not apparently spare them the physical abuse suffered by their male counterparts in the colony. The servant Elizabeth Abbott received some five hundred lashes with her master and mistress's whip, which left her body "full of sores and holes very dangerously raunckled and putrified both above her wast and uppon her hips and thighes." Elizabeth Nock, of Accomack County, received "blows Kicks & Whipping without any just Occasion given, Only for the pleasure & humor" of her seemingly sadistic master, who brutalized other servant women, too. One Lower Norfolk County mistress beat her maidservant "more Liken a dogge then a Christian" until her head was "as soft as a sponge, in one place," according to one observer. The arms and neck of this unfortunate woman were "full of blacke and blew bruises & pinches," and she also believed that her backbone had been broken as a result of the beating.[18]

Servant women were also vulnerable to sexual abuse and exploitation, though such cases were grossly under-reported because of the vastly superior power and influence of masters (and of white men generally) in the colony. Under English law, rape was a capital offense, but it was extremely difficult to prove. Courts were reluctant to convict a man on the basis of the word of a woman in part because most early modern Englishmen considered women to be innately sexually aggressive and untrustworthy. In Virginia, the relative social positions of male landowners and servant women—who were poor and mostly young and without male protectors in the colony—made recourse for mistreated females even more unlikely.[19]

Generally, Virginia authorities did not punish masters for engaging in either forced or consensual sex with their servants, but female servants typically suffered stiff penalties for illicit sexual activity. Although all sexual relations outside of marriage were technically illegal, courts were more likely to prosecute women than men. Moreover, magistrates' efforts to police sexual behavior focused increasingly on enforcing the laws against the single crime of bastardy, or bearing a child out-of-wedlock, because such children born to poor women would become costly wards of the public, financially dependent on the community. By definition, bastardy was a crime that only women could commit. For servant women, the price of pregnancy was additional years of service added to their labor contract. Although the father of an illegitimate child was deemed liable for its support, this penalty fell comparatively lightly on men in early Virginia, where the scarcity of labor led eager planters to indenture illegitimate children and poor orphans even as infants, with the expectation that these unfortunate youngsters would work for them as servants until they reached adulthood and attained their freedom.[20]

The case of Anne Orthwood, who emigrated from England in 1662, illustrates the potential perils of even a seemingly benign sexual relationship for servant women in the colony. On her arrival, Orthwood's indenture was sold to William Kendall, one of the wealthiest men in Northampton County. She soon began an apparently consensual sexual relationship with her master's nephew, John Kendall, who may have promised to marry her. William Kendall sought to distance his nephew from a woman who was so far beneath him socially by selling her to another master. Nevertheless, Orthwood soon became pregnant by John Kendall, and in July 1664 she gave birth to twins, one of whom did not survive. She herself died soon after giving birth, a common occurrence in seventeenth-century Virginia. Had she lived, Anne Orthwood would have paid a high price—at a minimum, two additional years of servitude—for committing the crimes of fornication and bastardy. Her surviving son, Jasper, was himself a servant until he sued for his freedom at the age of twenty-one. Jasper Orthwood's servitude saved his father the costs of child support. John Kendall married well and lived respectably in Northampton until his death in 1679.[21]

As Anne Orthwood's case suggests, skewed sex ratios, high mortality rates, and the absence of conventional family relationships could variously endanger or empower women. On the one hand, lacking male protectors, Orthwood was vulnerable to Kendall's advances, and, had she survived the ordeal of childbirth, almost certainly no one would have come forward in court either to defend her or to suggest that she be punished minimally for her transgressions. Nor did she have family to whom she could entrust her infant son. On the other hand, without parental oversight young women enjoyed more freedom in choosing their spouses. Perhaps Orthwood believed that she was exercising that freedom when she unwisely consummated her relationship with Kendall.

Unprotected women could be subjected to ongoing intimidation and violence. In one extreme case, Henry Smith, of Accomack County, beat and abused his wife, Joanna Smith, and her four-year-old daughter, raped at least two servant women, and brutalized several others. The full extent of Henry Smith's violence is unknown because many of his victims—and those who witnessed his cruelty—fearing his wrath and perhaps foreseeing that the courts would do nothing to punish him, would not accuse him publicly. In fact, when Joanna Smith and two of the servants, Mary Jones and Mary Hues, lodged complaints against Henry Smith, the magistrates took their charges seriously, indicting him for rape and awarding Joanna Smith a separate maintenance so that she and her daughter could live apart from her notoriously abusive husband. In the end, however, Henry Smith paid no price for his manifold crimes. The higher court (which heard felony cases) dismissed the rape indictment, and the Accomack County magistrates did not enforce its ruling in Joanna Smith's case. Because the justices were ultimately unwilling to interfere with a husband's authority over his wife, Joanna Smith and her daughter received no money, despite the court's ruling. They lived in poverty, dependent on charity, while Jones and Hues were returned to Henry Smith's plantation, ordered to "double there tyme" to compensate him for labor lost during their suit, and instructed by the court to "be Obedient to his just Comands."[22]

Other Virginia women, by contrast, were able to take advantage of the scarcity of females to use marriage as an avenue to upward mobility or to win concessions from their prospective husbands. Sarah Offley's first husband, Adam Thorowgood, came to Virginia as a servant. Less than a year after his death in 1640, Sarah Offley married Captain John Gookin, the son of a great planter in the colony. Gookin died in 1643, and his widow married Francis Yeardley in 1647. The son of a former governor, Yeardley was also significantly younger than his new wife, though he, too, predeceased her. With each successive marriage, Sarah Offley Thorowgood Gookin Yeardley moved farther up the social ladder, accumulating property in her own name from all three of her husbands. When she died in 1657, she was a wealthy woman who included land, labor, livestock, and a diamond necklace among her many possessions. According to tradition,

Sarah Harrison, of Surry County, used her leverage in the marriage market to reject conventional notions of wifely subservience when she married James Blair in 1687. Harrison changed the standard wedding vows, emphatically refusing to promise to obey her future spouse. Three times, the minister asked the seventeen-year-old bride if she would vow to obey her husband, and each time she responded, "No obey." The ceremony eventually continued, and the couple was wed despite Harrison's rejection of the traditional vow of obedience.[23]

Most seventeenth-century Virginia marriages probably were less patriarchal than their English counterparts, in part because the colony's high mortality rates typically resulted in the early death of at least one spouse. Because women were usually younger than the men they married, short life expectancies made widowhood common, even among young women. In early Virginia, widows often exercised significant authority and control over their families' property. Lacking stable family networks and nearby male relations and reluctant to entrust their estates to the management of outsiders, many seventeenth-century husbands appointed their widows to administer their estates and safeguard their children's legacies. Husbands were also far more likely than their counterparts in England to bequeath large portions of their property directly to their widows, who, under the English common law rule of dower, customarily received only a life's interest in one-third of their husbands' estates.[24]

Skewed sex ratios, high mortality rates, and unconventional family structures and relationships were indicative of instability and tension in the wider colonial community. Virginia's early planter elites, most of whose origins were far from aristocratic, were less securely entrenched than England's governing classes. In these unsettled times, lower-class men challenged elite authority by rioting and engaging in other forms of rebellious behavior and (if they had enough property to be enfranchised) by voting against them. But in this relatively fluid social climate, women also found ways to defy authority and claim some public influence and power.

Early Virginia court records suggest that colonial authorities viewed unruly women as a significant threat to their extremely fragile social order. In particular, the words of women from across the social spectrum affected men's reputations and actions in ways that could undermine hierarchical

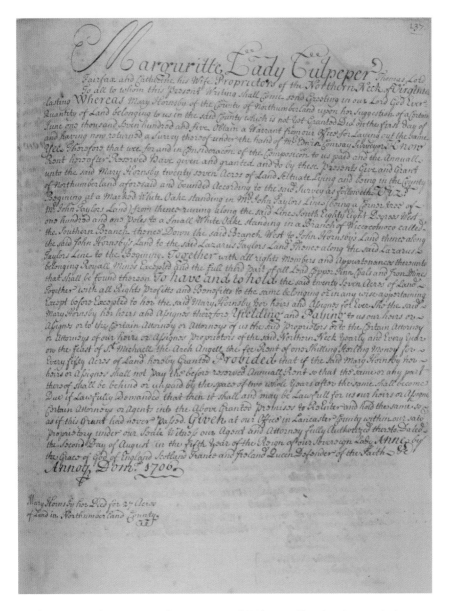

Land patent issued to Mary Hornsby, 2 August 1706. Widows, unlike wives, in many instances retained the right to own and control property under the English common law. This deed records Mary Hornsby's acquisition of 27 acres from Lady Culpeper and two other Northern Neck proprietors. Hornsby and "her heirs and Assignes for Ever" received the rights to the land in exchange for a nominal annual fee. *Courtesy of the Library of Virginia.*

An Overseer Doing His Duty, Near Fredericksburg, Virginia, Benjamin Henry Latrobe, ca. 1798. The vast majority of enslaved women did fieldwork. Contemporary accounts suggest that most labored under conditions that were far harsher than those shown in this eighteenth-century watercolor. *Courtesy of the Maryland Historical Society, 1960.108.1.3.21.*

relationships both in the family and in society generally. When Elizabeth Slate, of York County, shamed her husband and rejected her presumptive role as a subservient wife by publicly proclaiming her right to take a lover, she demonstrated her spouse's inability to control her. When another York County woman, Joanna Delony, publicly denigrated her husband for his illicit sexual relationship with another woman who herself allegedly committed incest and miscegenation, in addition to adultery, she, too, challenged his authority. By publicly criticizing their masters, moreover, servant women sometimes were able to influence the terms of their servitude. When Mary Rawlins petitioned York's county court, the magistrates censured her master for brutally beating her, which led the reprimanded planter to sell her indenture to a man she planned to marry—which perhaps is what Rawlins wanted all along. Elizabeth Cole left her master and mistress, William Clopton and Anne Clopton, without their permission because she believed she had completed her term of service. When the Cloptons forced her to return to work, Cole petitioned the court for her freedom. The justices considered the matter several times before finally finding in the petitioner's favor.[25]

Some black women also may have benefited from the relatively fluid family and social relations that prevailed in early Virginia. The first documented Africans, "20. and odd Negroes," arrived in Jamestown in 1619. At first, their numbers grew slowly. In 1625, a colonial census listed only twenty-one adult Africans—ten women and eleven men—living among approximately 1,200 English colonists; by 1680, though Virginia's black population had grown to about 3,000, people of African descent still accounted for only 7 percent of the inhabitants of the colony.[26] Although it seems clear that African laborers were subject to longer terms of service and in some cases more stringent controls than white servants were, the legal status of black workers in Virginia was ambiguous at first, and the social boundaries between white servants and black slaves were less well-defined than they would become toward the end of the century and especially after 1700.[27] The fact that black women did fieldwork in Virginia—as they had done in West Africa, where agriculture was generally women's work—was not particularly demeaning to them because white female servants performed similar sorts of physical labor in the colony. Both black and white female servants endured harsh working conditions and sometimes brutal treatment. Finally, like white women who managed to survive their terms of service to become free, some determined black women (and men) also won their freedom.

One remarkable story is that of "Mary a Nergro Woman," who arrived in bondage in 1622 but lived most of her life as a free woman in the Chesapeake region. Mary married an enslaved man named Anthony (or Antonio), and together they worked to purchase their freedom. By 1651, Mary and Anthony had adopted the surname Johnson and were living as free people in Northampton County, where they farmed 250 acres of land on Virginia's Eastern Shore. The Johnsons had at least four children, all of whom were free. The family's fortunes declined somewhat in later years, and they left Virginia in search of more-productive land in Maryland in the mid-1660s. When Mary Johnson wrote her will in 1672, she owned livestock, which she bequeathed to her grandchildren, and a 300-acre leasehold, which she passed on to her eldest son.[28]

Conversion to Christianity helped other early black Virginians to escape servitude. For instance, in 1656, Elizabeth Key, of Northumberland County, the mixed-race offspring of a white man and an enslaved African woman, sued for her freedom from indenture in part on the grounds that she had been baptized as a Christian. The English, who justified their dominion over allegedly inferior peoples on the grounds that they were barbaric (and therefore could not be Christian), may have deemed baptism compelling grounds for freedom, at least in the colony's early decades. Elizabeth Key received her freedom and later married her white attorney, William Greensted. In 1667, however, the General Assembly enacted a law that stipulated that the "conferring of baptisme doth not alter the condition of the person as to his bondage or ffreedome," thus effectively closing what may have been a comparatively well-traveled road to emancipation.[29]

This 1667 statute was one of several laws and court decisions by which colonial leaders gradually distinguished black slavery from white servitude and, in so doing, attempted to foster social order by erecting social barriers between blacks and poor whites. Defining the respective status of black and white women was central to this enterprise. In 1643, the General Assembly passed a law that classified black women as "tithable," which meant that the assembly considered their labor—like that of all men, but unlike that of white women—productive and sufficiently remunerative to be taxable. This measure established a legal fiction based on Englishmen's assumptions, however unfounded, that white women did no fieldwork and that their domestic work had little economic value. This distinction also derived from and reinforced incipient white conceptions of black women as uncivilized, sexually promiscuous, and physically robust—in short, the notion that they were not really women at all in the conventional English sense. This law stigmatized black women's work and undermined the ability of free black women to marry because it ensured that any man— black or white—would incur a penalty in the form of taxation for choosing a black wife.[30]

Erecting legal and social barriers between black and white women, and among poor people generally, was part of a more general effort among Virginia's great planters to maintain order in the colony. As mortality rates declined and servants began to outlive their terms of service, the ranks of the colony's impoverished grew, and sometimes the disgruntled poor joined together across

Frances Culpeper Stephens Berkeley Ludwell, ca. 1660. Married to three colonial governors, including Nathaniel Bacon's nemesis Sir William Berkeley, the attractive and intelligent Lady Berkeley was a political force to be reckoned with in the Virginia colony. *Courtesy of the Museum of Early Southern Decorative Arts, Old Salem Museums & Gardens, s-5958.*

racial lines to express their discontent. Civil unrest reached unprecedented heights in 1676, when Nathaniel Bacon, a gentleman-planter, unleashed his insurgent army against the Indians (whose land they wanted) and then incited lower-class Virginians to rebel against Governor Sir William Berkeley (whose high-handed government and political cronyism they resented).[31]

Women were active participants on both sides in Bacon's Rebellion. The insurgents' supporters included the "notorious & wicked" Sarah Drummond, Sarah Grendon, reputedly the "first great incourager ... of the Ignorant Vulgar," and Lydia Cheesman, who later claimed to have "made her Husband joyne in the Cause that Bacon contended for." All three women encouraged the insurgents, furnished supplies to Bacon's forces, verbally attacked Governor Berkeley, and disseminated information about the progress of the rebellion. Bacon and his male supporters, however, did not view these women as their political equals. Bacon's men formalized their participation in the rebellion by signing loyalty oaths, but the women did not. On the other side, wives of Berkeley's leading adherents became unwitting symbols of feminine weakness and dependence when Bacon's troops entered Jamestown, captured the women, and stood them atop fortifications that lay between Berkeley's forces and the rebel militia. Bacon challenged the governor either to fire or to retreat. Berkeley chose the latter course, in order to save the women, who were known as the "white Aprons" because of their fine clothes, which symbolized both wealth and domesticity.[32]

One notable woman played a more prominent and more active role in support of the governor and his policies. Frances Culpeper arrived in Virginia with her parents in 1650, married in 1653, and was widowed late in 1669. About six months later she married Governor Sir William Berkeley. She was about thirty-six years old and he was about sixty-four at the time of their nuptials. Interested in and adept at politics, Lady Berkeley strongly supported her husband's policies. In 1676, she traveled to London as his emissary to seek royal assistance in suppressing Bacon's Rebellion. Her mission was successful, though the rebellion dissipated after Bacon died suddenly, most likely of dysentery, in October 1676, months before the arrival of several armed vessels from England. When William Berkeley died the following year, Lady Berkeley stayed in Virginia, where she remained politically active. Her house, Green Spring, became a gathering place for her husband's former supporters, who joined with her to oppose his successor as governor.[33]

English admitted (together with those of the English) to bee their owne Interpreters.

That the severall Indians concluded in this peace doe forthwith restore the respective English Parents & Owners all such Children, Servants & which they have at any time taken from them & are now remaining with them the said Indians, or which they can make discovery off.

That the trade with the said Indians bee continued Limited, restrained laid open as shall make best for the peace & Quiett of the Country, Vpo which affaire the Governour will consult with the Councell & Assemb & conclude thereon at their next Meeting.

The signe of the Queene of Pamunkey on behalfe of herselfe & the severall Indians under her subiection —

The signe of the [mark] Queen of Waonoke

The signe of the King of the Notto- =wayes —

The signe of the King of the Nancymond Indians.

The signe of Capt John West

sonn to the Queen of Pamunkey.

Convenit cum Originali. Test Tho. Ludwell Secretar

Reproductions of Indian women's marks, 1677. The Treaty of Middle Plantation bore the marks of two female Indian leaders—the Pamunkey chief Cockacoeske and the Queen of Waonoke— along with those of Cockacoeske's mixed race son, Captain John West, and the King of the Nansemond. *Samuel Wiseman's Book of Record (#2582), © The Pepys Library, Magdalene College, Cambridge.*

Another Virginia woman who played an important role in Bacon's Rebellion and its aftermath was Cockacoeske, a Pamunkey chief and a descendant of Opechancanough, who took part in the negotiations leading to the Treaty of Middle Plantation, which clarified the status of Native Americans in the colony. The Treaty of Middle Plantation of 1677 reaffirmed the Indians' subservience to the English king and his government and further circumscribed their landholdings, while at the same time acknowledging that they still retained certain property, land use, and hunting rights. At Cockacoeske's request, the treaty also included provisions that favored her and the Pamunkey exclusively, as a result of her support for Berkeley during the rebellion and her skill as a diplomat after it was over. Specifically, the treaty recognized Cockacoeske's authority over several other tribes, which she hoped to reunite with the Pamunkey into a new confederacy, which she herself would head. Although the other tribes resisted her authority and the new confederation never fully materialized, by maintaining good relations with the English governors, Cockacoeske protected Pamunkey interests until she died, after thirty years as chief, in 1686.[34]

Although most white Virginians probably were unaware of Cockacoeske's continuing influence, Frances Berkeley became infamous as a scapegoat for the corruption and disorder that had plagued the colony. Although her activism drew on a long tradition of political engagement among aristocratic Englishwomen, many in Virginia equated her political influence with misrule and a lack of manly vigor among the colony's elite. Some critics blamed Lady Berkeley for distracting her husband from his responsibilities as governor. "Old Governor Barkly," some believed, had been "Altered by marrying a young wyff, from his wonted publicq good, to a covetous fools-age." Others condemned her political ambition and alleged extravagance. After William Berkeley died in 1677, his successor complained of his widow's "caballs" at Green Spring and the fact that she "acts still in the same maner as if Her Husband were still livinge" and wielding political power. Independent, outspoken, and generally successful, Frances Berkeley had no counterpart among the next generation of Virginia women, who were at best relegated to the fringes of political power.[35]

In the decades following Bacon's Rebellion, colonial leaders used social occasions—such as militia musters, electioneering, and horse-racing—to enhance solidarity among white men of all social ranks and enacted laws to circumscribe the activities of black Virginians and white women. Building on a previous law enacted in 1662, a 1677 statute further regulated female speech, imposing a penalty of twenty lashes on wives who "speake, write, disperse or publish by words, writeing or otherwise, any matter or thing tending to rebellion." This innovation amounted to a legislative attempt to strengthen the authority of husbands by creating a notable exception to the common-law doctrine of coverture (by which husbands were responsible for their wives' public actions) and by prescribing corporal punishment for an offense that under other circumstances was punishable only by a fine and two hours of public shaming. Other statutes and the selective enforcement of existing laws against fornication, adultery, and other sexual transgressions regulated white women's sexuality at a time when prosecutions of white men for sexual offenses were increasingly uncommon. At the same time, slave codes and other laws undermined blacks' potential for autonomy, making slavery more rigid, more demeaning, and typically permanent and heritable for the growing numbers of enslaved people in the colony.[36]

Although Bacon's Rebellion made it imperative for colonial leaders to take steps to promote peace and order in the colony, changes in Virginia's demography made possible the establishment of a relatively stable social hierarchy based on slavery and white patriarchy. The demographic instability that had allowed some flexibility in women's roles in the colony's early decades gradually diminished, as mortality rates declined during the second half of the seventeenth century. Sex ratios became more balanced, and the growing stability of family structures and relationships meant that white Virginians' families became more stable and hence more patriarchal. So, too, did the composition of Virginia's labor force change gradually as a result of declining mortality rates and other factors. After midcentury, as England acquired other American colonies, white indentured servants increasingly went elsewhere, seeking better working conditions and greater opportunity for upward mobility. By then, lengthening life expectancies made slaves better investments for Virginia planters, who imported Africans in growing numbers. By 1700, the colony's labor force, which had been overwhelmingly white in 1676, was predominantly black.[37]

White Virginians increasingly equated blackness with slavery and debasement, despite the continued presence of small numbers of free blacks in the colony. The experience of Jane Webb, a lifelong resident of Northampton

County, illustrates the perils free black women confronted in Virginia's slave society. Although she had been born free, because she was the product of a mixed-race union between an enslaved black or mulatto father and a white indentured mother, Webb spent her first eighteen or twenty-one years in servitude. When she became free and married an enslaved man, however, the law did not recognize their marriage, so Webb agreed with her husband's master to indenture herself for seven years, along with any children she bore during that period—there would be three in all—until they were eighteen years old, in exchange for which her husband, Left, would be freed when Webb's indenture expired. Unlike enslaved women, Jane Webb knew that her children were free and that she could use their labor and her own to negotiate for her husband's freedom. She also had the right, as a free woman, to sue her husband's master when he reneged on their bargain, which she exercised in a series of lawsuits, mostly in the 1720s. Jane Webb eventually secured her children's freedom, but Left remained a slave in part because the county justices decided that, though Webb was entitled to sue in court, a free black's testimony could not determine the outcome of a suit against a white defendant.[38]

One cumulative effect of the changes in Virginia society was to differentiate, in theory and also increasingly in practice, women's experiences along racial lines. Although some Indian women—such as one of Cockacoeske's successors, the Pamunkey chief Ann, who vigorously defended the rights of her people—remained influential after 1700, white hostility and a succession of lopsided agreements and treaties relegated most Native Americans to Indian towns, though some lived on the fringes of white society.[39] Black women, including most free blacks, toiled alongside black men in the fields on both large and small plantations. This increased use of enslaved workers, in turn, made possible the domestication of white women's work in many more Virginia households.

Virginia's population grew steadily in the decades following Bacon's Rebellion. In 1671, the colony had approximately 40,000 inhabitants, of whom perhaps 2,000 were African or of African descent. By 1700, the total population had grown to roughly 58,000, but the black population had increased at a far greater rate to approximately 13,000. Although declining mortality rates were the most important source of white population growth, increasing slave importations, especially after 1700, accelerated the growth of the colony's black population. At midcentury, Virginia had some 230,000 inhabitants, more than one-third of whom were enslaved. By 1776, its population approached 500,000—approximately 300,000 whites and 200,000 blacks—making the Old Dominion the most populous province in British colonial America.[40]

Demographic growth meant territorial expansion, as white and black Virginians moved beyond the tidewater into the piedmont and as Scots-Irish and German settlers migrated southward from Pennsylvania on the Great Wagon Road into the Shenandoah Valley. As planters brought tobacco and slaves from the tidewater into the piedmont and as middling grain farmers populated the West, courts, churches, and other institutions proliferated in the colony. In 1700, Virginia had twenty-one counties; by 1775, there were sixty-one counties, of which Augusta, Botetourt, and Fincastle were the farthest west. The established Church of England also expanded during this period to minister to the growing population though dissenting Protestant denominations predominated in the west.[41]

For most white Virginians, increased longevity and more-equal sex ratios resulted in bigger families, longer marriages, and more conventionally patriarchal households. Seventeenth-century Virginians, who tended to marry late and die young, had relatively few children, many of whom did not live to adulthood. After 1700, as sex ratios became more balanced and as proportionately fewer white Virginians found themselves constrained by indentured servitude, they married at a comparatively early age—men typically were about twenty-four years old and women were slightly younger—and wives bore more children as a result. At midcentury, an average wife in the Chesapeake region bore seven or eight children, of whom five or six usually survived to maturity. Unlike earlier generations of colonists, moreover, eighteenth-century men could expect to live between fifty and sixty years, perhaps longer, and women who survived their dangerous childbearing years had similar life expectancies. For better or for worse, then, eighteenth-century women were likely to have the companionship and protection of husbands, fathers, or even grandfathers for many years, but they were also more likely to be directly subject to male authority.[42]

Parents, especially fathers, oversaw their children's education and social activities, and they influenced the marital choices of both their daughters and their sons. Although Virginia parents did not arrange marriages among virtual strangers to promote their dynastic and economic interests, gentry parents clearly hoped that their offspring would choose mates from families whose wealth and status were at least equal to their own. Young people met during balls, visits, or other carefully orchestrated social occasions, and most sought parental approval before pursuing serious romantic relationships. In elite families, parents could discourage objectionable courtships by threatening to deprive the offending child of economic support. Daughters were more vulnerable to such pressure both because their parents monitored their social contacts more closely and because young women, who had few viable options for gainful employment, were more economically dependent on their families. A young woman's reputation also depended on her family connections, especially because most contemporaries believed that feminine virtue was best preserved within the protective confines of the patriarchal household. Daughters whose parents had comparatively less property had more social freedom. Consequently, premarital pregnancy was common among lesser folk in Virginia and elsewhere in eighteenth-century America.[43]

Some young women risked the loss of both property and respectability in the name of romantic love. In 1773, Judith Carter married her relatively unsuccessful and sickly cousin Reuben Beale in defiance of the wishes of her father, the curmudgeonly Richmond County diarist Landon Carter, of Sabine Hall. Landon Carter warned his daughter that Beale was "a fellow I cannot be reconciled to on any account whatever," and he threatened to disown her if she continued to let him court her. Judith Carter ignored her father's ultimatum, left Sabine Hall for Beale's father's house, and married her lover soon thereafter. Although she remained estranged from her father for months after her nuptials, Landon Carter eventually reconciled with his independent-minded daughter— on her terms—giving her husband a marriage settlement that was comparable to one received by another Carter son-in-law.[44]

Once married, eighteenth-century Virginia women were less likely than their foremothers to control property or to conduct their families' business. Demographic factors largely account for this change, as longer life expectancies and more-stable family networks enabled men increasingly to delegate business responsibilities to their sons, brothers, or other male relations. As men lived longer, fewer women became widows. As more fathers lived to see their children reach adulthood, fathers bequeathed their property to their offspring—especially their sons—and designated their adult sons, in lieu of their wives, to be administrators of their estates. Affluent men also enlisted the services of a growing number of professionally trained lawyers, instead of giving their wives power of attorney, which had been a fairly common practice early in the colonial era.[45]

Of course, there were exceptions, most notably widows whose husbands entrusted them with property and who, along with single women, were exempt from coverture. After William Durley, of Nansemond County, died in 1741, his widow, Mary, managed his far-flung trading interests, which included some unfinished business in Calcutta. As a young widow, Martha Dandridge Custis oversaw the management of more than 17,500 acres of land and the marketing of their produce to English merchants before wedding a second husband, George Washington, in 1759. Mary Dandridge Spotswood Campbell managed the large estate of her first husband, John Spotswood, the son of a governor, along with the lesser holdings of her second, John Campbell, who ran away to Jamaica, abandoning her in the 1760s. After her sons came of age, she fought successfully to retain her dower portion of Spotswood's estate in Spotsylvania County, which included slaves and a plantation that she ran for three decades. At the other end of the social spectrum, wives of tenant farmers, such as those whose names appear on the rent rolls of the great planter Robert Carter, of Nomini Hall, maintained their leaseholds in widowhood, thereby preserving their families' homes and livelihoods for future generations.[46]

Still, the domestication of white women's work was the dominant trend in eighteenth-century Virginia. White families increasingly sought to re-create the gender-based division of labor that idealized men as patriarchs who governed their dependents—women, children, servants, and slaves—and wielded near-absolute authority in their households. According to this view, men were responsible for supporting their households economically and for engaging in business, litigation, politics, and other activities to represent their family and its interests in the public world beyond the household. Women's activities, by contrast, were in theory at least confined to the domestic sphere, where their work included dairying, raising poultry, and tending vegetable gardens, along with childrearing and housewifery. Although male contemporaries and modern historians alike often ignored or underestimated the economic value and

The COMPLEAT

HOUSEWIFE:

OR,

Accomplifhed Gentlewoman's

COMPANION:

Being a COLLECTION of upwards of Five
Hundred of the moft approved RECEIPTS in

COOKERY,	CAKES,
PASTRY,	CREAMS,
CONFECTIONARY,	JELLIES,
PRESERVING,	MADE WINES,
PICKLES,	CORDIALS.

With COPPER PLATES curioufly engraven for
the regular Difpofition or Placing the various
DISHES and COURSES.

AND ALSO

BILLS of FARE for every Month in the Year.

To which is added,

A Colleftion of above Two Hundred Family RECEIPTS
of MEDICINES; *viz. Drinks, Syrups, Salves, Ointments,*
and various other Things of fovereign and approved
Efficacy in moft Diftempers, Pains, Aches, Wounds,
Sores, *&c.* never before made publick; fit either for
private Families, or fuch publick-fpirited Gentlewomen
as would be beneficent to their poor Neighbours.

By *E——— S———*

The THIRD EDITION *correffed and improved.*

LONDON:

Printed for J. PEMBERTON, at the *Golden Buck*, over
againft St. *Dunftan's Church* in *Fleet-ftreet.*

M. DCC. XXIX.

The Compleat Housewife, 1729. This popular English book included hundreds of "receipts" for
foods and medicines "fit either for private Families, or such publick-spirited Gentlewomen as
would be beneficent to their poor Neighbours." In 1742, the Williamsburg printer William Parks
reprinted the book, which was the first cookery manual published in America. *Courtesy of the
Library of Virginia.*

Martha Wayles Skelton Jefferson's thread case. Sewing was a near-constant occupation, even for women in gentry families. This thread case is one of the few surviving personal possessions of the mistress of Monticello, who was only thirty-four when she died in 1782 following the last of many difficult pregnancies. *Courtesy of the Thomas Jefferson Papers, Library of Congress, MS DW.196.4.*

cultural significance of these activities, women's domestic work undoubtedly enhanced both the prosperity and comfort of Virginia's colonial households.

The specific tasks women performed varied by geographic location and social rank, but all eighteenth-century women were in some way involved in the production and preparation of food for their households. In the colony's early decades, the fact that there were few women in Virginia resulted in a scarcity of vegetables, poultry, eggs, butter, and cheese—all of which were traditionally products of women's domestic work—and gave rise to nutritional deficiencies that contributed to the general unhealthiness of the settlers. Better nutrition was one of several factors that helped Virginians live longer after 1700. On her Chesterfield County farm, Elizabeth Dutoy Porter grew vegetables in her garden, kept cows for dairy products, and also raised geese for eggs, meat, and feathers (which she used to make beds). Although some gentry women could entrust domestic servants with the various tasks related to dairying and poultry-raising, many did their own gardening. At Nomini Hall, Frances Tasker Carter grew herbs and asparagus, and she experimented with "Apricot-Grafts," though she relied on enslaved workmen to plant "common garden Peas."[47]

The 1742 publication in Williamsburg of an English recipe book entitled *The Compleat Housewife* suggests the growing availability of and interest in different kinds of food, at least among literate Virginians. Subtitled the *Accomplish'd Gentlewoman's Companion*, this 228-page book was the first cookery manual published in the colonies. Its contents included "several Hundred of the most approved Receipts, in Cookery, Pastry, Confectionary, Preserving, Pickles, Cakes, Creams, Jellies," along with others for wines, cordials, and home remedies. Although Virginia cooks could purchase spices, sugar, chocolate, and some other exotic imported items in shops in Williamsburg and elsewhere, they produced the vast majority of the ingredients in these recipes at home in their gardens, dairies, and households. Although affluent families sometimes had servants to do the cooking, gentlewomen oversaw those servants, and sometimes they did the cooking themselves. In 1771, for example, a young daughter in a Virginia gentry family noted that her mother had made "6 mince pyes and 7 Custards 12 tarts 1 chicking pye and 4 pudings" to serve guests at a ball held at her parents' house.[48]

Sewing, knitting, spinning, and weaving were second only to food-related activities in terms of their importance to women's work and to the domestic economy. "After her knowledge of preserving and feeding her family," wrote the Englishman Gervase Markham, a housewife "must learn also how ... to clothe them ... for defence from the cold and comeliness to the person; and ... for cleanliness and neatness of the skin, whereby it may be kept from the filth of sweat, or vermin." Indeed, so synonymous was sewing and other needlework with women and their prescribed sphere that leather cases containing needles, pins, thread, scissors, and other tools were widely known as "housewives." The Williamsburg milliner Catherine Rathell sold "housewifes for Ladies with instruments" at her shop late in the 1760s.[49]

Sewing and knitting were universal occupations, even for women in gentry families. The fact that the aristocratic Maria Taylor Byrd, of Westover, taught her granddaughter to sew when she was only six years old shows that needlework was considered an indispensable skill for females, even among the highest strata of the colony's elite. Although gentry women studiously practiced ornamental needlework, other work was more practical. At Sabine Hall, in Richmond County, female members of the affluent Carter family knitted stockings, completing one every six days. They also sewed clothing for themselves, for other family members, and for their family's slaves. Sarah Fouace Nourse, of Berkeley County, in western Virginia, who came from a less affluent slaveholding family, spent between sixty-five and seventy-seven days each year knitting, sewing, and mending clothes for her husband, children, and enslaved workers.[50]

Some households also produced cloth, a commodity that colonists consumed in great quantities. While Virginians imported a wide variety of fine and plain textiles from England, women spun wool, linen, and (less commonly) cotton thread, which was woven into coarse "Virginia cloth," either by housewives and their female kin or by domestic servants working in their households. Elizabeth Porter, whose middling household in the Virginia piedmont included her mother, daughters, and two female slaves, owned the implements necessary for making thread, which she then sent to the nearby home of her daughter-in-law to be woven into cloth. A Cumberland County woman, Elizabeth LeSueur, whose husband owned seventeen slaves, directed a bondwoman and two of her daughters in manufacturing cloth from the wool, flax, and cotton produced on their plantation. In both cases, enslaved women were involved in spinning or weaving on a part-time basis, to supplement their work in the fields or in other household tasks. By contrast, enslaved women did much of the work of cloth production on some larger Virginia plantations. For instance, George Washington's enslaved work force at Mount Vernon included both a spinner and a seamstress, and Landon Carter employed three slaves as spinners and another as a weaver at Sabine Hall.[51]

Women's domestic work, so necessary for the sustenance and comfort of colonial families, also constituted an important but often overlooked segment of the family economy. Virginia households consumed eggs, cheese, vegetables, cloth, and other items produced by women at home, instead of having to purchase these goods from outside vendors. In this way, women's domestic work diminished their family's expenditures in cash or credit and thereby benefited the family economy. Some women also contributed to their family's income more directly by selling or trading the goods they produced to neighbors or local storekeepers. Although Virginia women marketed items ranging from cloth to hard cider, eggs and poultry—especially chickens—were the most common goods they sold. The James City County planter Carter Burwell bought chickens, geese, and turkeys from several local women, who traded their poultry for items such as cloth and shoes from his storehouse. Some Virginia merchants kept a special "chicken book" to record transactions with women who brought their poultry and eggs to sell for cash or trade for merchandise or store credit. Married women's participation in such economic exchanges apparently was not controversial, despite their formal legal disabilities under coverture.[52]

Virginia housewives relied primarily on their daughters and other female kin for help with their domestic work, and the overwhelming majority worked without the assistance of enslaved labor. Because enslaved women and men had been brought to Virginia to supplant indentured servants as agricultural laborers and because planters sought to maximize production of their profitable staple crop, most slaves of both sexes were employed primarily in fieldwork throughout the colonial era. In fact, in the eighteenth century, women eventually constituted the majority of enslaved field-workers on Virginia's plantations and farms. As the colony's economy diversified with the spread of grain cultivation and livestock raising to supplement tobacco, some Virginia planters began to train their male slaves to practice various skilled occupations. Male slaves worked as carpenters, coopers, ironworkers, or watermen. By 1776, roughly one-fifth of all enslaved men in the Chesapeake were skilled workers, while roughly four-fifths of the region's female slaves still engaged in agricultural labor.[53]

The small percentage of black women whose work was primarily nonagricultural generally resided on large plantations, which were relatively uncommon in the colony. Before 1740, most enslaved Virginians in both the tidewater and the piedmont lived on plantations with fewer than ten bondpeople. In the closing decades of the colonial period, the proportion of plantations with larger slave populations grew, though in the 1770s more than two-thirds of Virginia's enslaved people still resided on plantations with twenty or fewer slaves. On these smaller properties, female slaves who did nonagricultural work were typically young girls or old women whom their masters considered unfit for field labor. By contrast, the most affluent Virginia planters, who sometimes owned hundreds of slaves, were more likely to divert part of their prime workforce to domestic service or housewifery on their home plantations. In 1757, William Byrd III, of Westover, owned 605 slaves (including children), of whom 142 were working females; some 10 percent of these women worked in nonagricultural occupations on his plantations. Two decades later, the great planters Philip Ludwell, George Washington, and Thomas Jefferson each employed roughly 20 percent of their female slaves in nonagricultural work, mostly as domestic servants or in various cloth-related occupations.[54]

For enslaved women, employment in domestic service or housewifery had both advantages and drawbacks. On the one hand, working conditions were probably better than in the tobacco fields, and planters gave their domestic servants clothing (and possibly food) that was far superior to the meager rations they provided for field-workers. On the other hand, domestic workers interacted closely with white people on a daily basis, which meant that masters and mistresses routinely scrutinized their work and conduct. Residing in the planters' house, moreover, often isolated slave women from their own families and from the larger slave community. For instance, Winney, the enslaved nursemaid at Landon Carter's Sabine Hall, had a room in the great house, where her duties included general domestic service, child care, and caring for sick people, both black and white. She also may have been a wet nurse for Carter's children and grandchildren. Although Winney had a husband, Joe, and eight children of her own on the estate, she spent most of her time and effort caring for her master's offspring.[55]

P. It is rumoured in the city that a large sum of money has
e lately been remitted by government to a certain American
d colony.

TWENTY Gentlemen of the aſſo-
ciation having, by their letters of the 7th of this
inſtant, deſired me to call a general meeting of
the aſſociators on matters of importance, I do hereby re-
queſt the attendance of the aſſociators on Friday the 14th
of December next, at the Capitol, at 4 o'clock in the afternoon.   PEYTON RANDOLPH, Moderator.

To be SOLD at public vendue, for ready
money, on Thurſday the 22d inſtant,
at Williams's warehouſe, in King
William county, for the benefit of the
inſurers,

A BALE of damaged WOOLLENS,
well aſſorted, and imported in the Lord Clive,
Duncan Murray, maſter. And on Monday the
26th inſtant, will be expoſed to ſale in like manner, at Falmouth, two bales of well aſſorted coarſe WOOLLENS,
imported in the ſaid veſſel.   STORRS & ELLIS.

To be SOLD at Prince Edward court-
houſe, on Thurſday the 20th of December next,
ONE HUNDRED AND FORTY
SLAVES,

AMONGST which are ſeveral good
tradeſmen, and ſome valuable houſe ſervants.
Credit will be given till the Oyer and Terminer court in
June next, the purchaſers giving bond and good ſecurity,
and a proper allowance will be made for ready money.
The notes of merchants will be received, and their bills of
exchange, for the greateſt part of the ſlaves, will be
taken in payment. An indiſputable title will be made to
the purchaſers.

To be SOLD at Prince Edward court
houſe, on Thurſday the 20th of December next,
A NUMBER OF
SLAVES,

CONSISTING of men, women, and
lads. The wenches are well acquainted with the
buſineſs of the houſe, &c. and the lads are much accuſ-
tomed to horſes. Credit will be given to the 25th of
April next, the purchaſer (to whom an undoubted title
will be made) giving bond and ſecurity to the adminiſtra-
tors of John Robinſon, Eſq;

this advertiſement, and a ſmall gratuity to the finder,
may have it by applying to
BOLLING STARK.

WHEREAS I hired a mare to one
Peter Brannen, a balancemaſter, for a certain
time and as he has exceeded it, I am apprehenſive he
intends carrying her entirely off: I hereby offer a reward
of TWENTY-FIVE SHILLINGS to any perſon who
will apprehend and convey the ſaid mare to me. She is
a dark grey, has a ſwitch tail, her hind feet white, has
long ears, and paces remarkably well.
WILLIAM GODFREY.
N. B. The ſaid Brannen had on when he went away
a white cotton jacket, and cotton trowſers, bound with
yellow ferret; and wears a ſilver laced hat.

AMELIA county, Nov 1, 1770.

RUN away from the ſubſcriber the
19th of May laſt, a likely Virginia born Negro fellow named TOM, about 26 years of age, 5 feet 6 or 7
inches high, very well made, talks much, has a long
viſage, with a down look, and was cloathed in the uſual
Negro dreſs. He was formerly the property of one
Tompkins of Gloucester, and I am well informed he has
been frequently ſeen lurking about the plantation of Mr.
Hubard, near Poplar Spring church, in ſaid county,
where he has a wife. Whoever will apprehend and ſe-
cure him in the above county gaol, ſhall have FORTY
SHILLINGS reward on notice given to
JAMES HENDERSON.

RUN away from the ſubſcriber,
ſome time in July laſt, two Negroes, who are
huſband and wife, the fellow named TONY,
about 50 years of age, the wench named PHILLIS,
and is about 40. They are both of the middle ſize, he
cloathed in old blue cotton, and ſhe in blue cotton and country cloth. The fellow formerly belonged to Capt. William Payne of Lancaster county, who ſold him ſome years
ago to one Thomas Chilton in Culpeper. The wench was
alſo born in Lancaster, and afterwards belonged to Chilton. They have had ſeveral children, who are ſold and
diſperſed through Culpeper, Frederick, and Auguſta counties, to one of which, if they are not in Lancaster, I ſuſ-
pect they are gone, though I incline to think they are in
the latter, as the fellow always expreſſed an uncommon
deſire to return there. Whoever takes them up, if delivered to either of my overſeers in Fauquier, or to myſelf
in Prince William, ſhall receive 31. reward for each, be-
ſides what the law allows.   CUTHBURT BULLIT.

TAKEN up in Amelia county, about 12 miles above
the court houſe, a black horſe about 4 feet 6 or 7
inches high, a hanging mane and long tail, and is branded on the near ſhoulder W, and on the near buttock C.
Poſted, and appraiſed to 6l.
PHILIP WILLIAMS, ſen.

Slave sales and runaways, 8 November 1770. The *Virginia Gazette* chronicled the pervasiveness of slavery in the colony. Advertisers announced upcoming sales of enslaved women and men, alongside new cargoes of "woollens" and livestock. Some placed notices in hopes of recovering enslaved runaways, such as Phillis and her husband Tony, who fled probably in search of their children. *Courtesy of the Library of Virginia.*

Even for those women who lived in slave quarters apart from their masters, family and community ties were both cherished and tenuous. Because most colonial planters owned relatively small numbers of slaves, their bondpeople often chose spouses from neighboring plantations. Husbands and wives therefore often lived apart, and most children grew up in one-parent households. Because slave mothers usually took care of their young children and because slave women generally were unskilled and less mobile than men, women were far less likely than men to become runaways. Men, who were more likely to live separately from their children, often ran away for short-term visits. Sometimes married couples escaped together, either to preserve their marriages—which lacked legal sanction under Virginia law—or to find children who had been sold, hired out, or sent to work on other plantations. In 1770, a married couple, Phillis and Tony, ran away from Cuthbert Bullitt's Prince William County plantation. According to Bullitt, Phillis and Tony were the parents of "several children, who are sold and dispersed through Culpeper, Frederick, and Augusta counties" in the western part of the colony, and they perhaps had run off in search of them. Despite significant obstacles, African Americans fought hard to maintain their family ties. Some of the more fortunate and resourceful succeeded in establishing stable households, kinship networks, and communities by the closing decades of the colonial era.[56]

When slaves ran away, their masters often advertised for their return, offering rewards for their capture. Such advertisements, which included detailed descriptions of the fugitives, indicate the physical abuse that black women suffered as a result of their bondage. Hannah, who escaped from her master most likely in Dinwiddie County, was "much scarified under the throat from one ear to the other, and has many scars on her back, occasioned by whipping." Annas, a mixed-race woman who fled her master in Northampton County, had been "branded on the right cheek E, and on the left R" as punishment for prior misconduct and had "several cuts on the back part of her neck and a scar upon her left side." Winney had "a lump upon the back of her neck, occasioned by the cut of a switch" when she ran away in 1774 for the second time. Although she was captured and returned to her master in Fauquier County, she ran away again in 1776.[57]

Though they were far from content with their circumstances, the vast majority of enslaved women stayed closer to home, where their work enhanced the quality of life in and around the slave quarters. Virginia planters typically fed their slaves corn—approximately one peck per week—which they sometimes supplemented with small quantities of other vegetables or meat. While slave men hunted and fished to provide additional protein for their families, women raised poultry for eggs and meat. Like white housewives, they also sold or traded chickens and eggs. Slaves also cultivated small gardens that produced potatoes, squash, melons, peas, and other vegetables and fruits to supplement their diet. Slave gardening generally occurred on Sundays because, as one observer noted, masters ensured that bondpeople were "otherwise employed on every other Day."[58]

Industrious slaves and obedient wives and children were essential components in a patriarchal ideal prized by white male landowners throughout the Old Dominion. As William Byrd II declared with evident satisfaction in 1726, "I have a large family of my own, and my doors are open to every body. . . . Like one of the patriarchs, I have my flocks and my herds, my bond-men and bond-women, and every soart of trade among my own servants, so I live in a kind of Independence on every one, but Providence." Yet the reality of Byrd's life was less blissful. His slaves were sometimes ill-behaved or rebellious, and his often gruesome punishments, which included branding and ordering a boy to drink a "pint of piss," belied his imagined patriarchal idyll. Byrd's first wife, Lucy Parke Byrd, was far from docile and obedient. She dispensed corporal punishment to the slaves of Westover as sadistically as her husband did. Besides, although they appear to have loved each other, Lucy Byrd and William Byrd fought constantly about everything from proper medical treatments for their children to whether she should pluck her eyebrows.[59]

Lucy Parke Byrd, like the escaped female slaves, clearly did not conform to the gender ideals of her place and time. Even if the emergence of a demographically stable colonial society had made the attainment of English-style gender ideals imaginable for eighteenth-century Virginians, the continued presence of such recalcitrant women suggests a more complex reality. Despite the enormous power that both law and custom conferred on white men, wives defied husbands, children disregarded their parents, and slaves risked grotesque punishment by disobeying their masters. Nor was the idealized gender-based division of labor, so clearly delineated by custom and prescriptive literature, as starkly dichotomous in real life. Although Virginians increasingly identified women with domestic work, most black women were not domestics, and many white women engaged in a variety of tasks that took them into the marketplace and sometimes into other public venues in the world beyond their households.

There were three ways in which at least some Virginia women became more publicly visible during the last half-century of the colonial era. First, economic growth and diversification generated new demands for goods and services, which, in turn, created opportunities to work in paying jobs or businesses. Second, as Virginia's gentlemen self-consciously constructed an English-style culture of gentility to accentuate and enhance their authority in the colony, women became essential participants in elite civic rituals and social gatherings. Third, some Virginia women were prominent in the evangelical religious communities that emerged in the province in the middle decades of the eighteenth century. Although the rigidly hierarchical established Church of England afforded women no formal voice in its proceedings, evangelical denominations accepted white women, as well as African Americans, as preachers and in certain other activist roles.

Most women who engaged in paid employment worked in occupations that used their domestic skills or fit with prescribed feminine attributes and roles. Women who took in boarders and kept taverns, inns, and coffeehouses marketed their skills as housekeepers, cooks, and hostesses. Others used their putative childrearing and nurturing abilities to secure employment as tutors or governesses. A woman with more specialized skills could work as a midwife, a comparatively well-paid female occupation during the colonial era. The *Virginia Gazette* praised the colony's most successful Virginia midwife, Catherine Kaidyee Blaikley, for bringing "upwards of three Thousand Children into the World" between about 1739 and her death in 1771.[60] Less accomplished women worked as housekeepers, domestic servants, or seamstresses, performing conventional domestic work for pay. Contemporaries regarded all of these jobs as appropriate for women, although most performed these tasks in their own houses, for their own families, and without financial compensation.

Virginia women's involvement in the hospitality business ranged from the nearly invisible practice of renting rooms and selling meals on a casual basis to thoroughly professional enterprises that made their proprietors well-known to the public. In fact, prominent widows and middling women seem to have run most of Virginia's colonial taverns, even if, in the case of married women, the authorities usually issued the official licenses to operate them to their husbands. Taverns sometimes passed in families from generation to generation, from mother to daughter, just as government offices or landed property commonly passed from father to son. Moreover, many men who owned or inherited taverns married women who had experience keeping taverns themselves or who came from tavern-keeping families. In Williamsburg and in other smaller Virginia communities, tavern-keeping offered women a respectable way to earn a living if they had sufficient capital to invest and could persuade the magistrates who issued licenses that they were of good moral character.[61]

The widows Christiana Burdett Campbell and Jane Vobe occupied the apex of the tavern-keeping hierarchy in eighteenth-century Virginia. Both operated taverns in Williamsburg, which, with a population of some 2,000 in 1770, was one of the colony's largest towns and also its capital. Campbell was the daughter of a Williamsburg tavern keeper; she lived in Blandsford, near Petersburg, with her husband and two children until she was widowed in 1752. The next year, she and her daughters moved to Williamsburg, where she opened a tavern, which she operated in at least three successive locations until early in the 1780s. Campbell's chief rival in Williamsburg was Jane Vobe, who was from 1752 to 1784 the proprietor of several taverns, including the King's Arms. Both Vobe and Campbell offered lodging, food, and drink to a clientele that included the leading men of the colony who came to town regularly when the legislature was in session. George Washington patronized both establishments. A French traveler who visited Williamsburg in 1765 lodged at Vobe's tavern, which he maintained was "where all the best people resorted." But Christiana Campbell also promised the "Gentlemen" who patronized her tavern "genteel Accommodations, and the very best entertainment."[62]

Although these establishments provided essentially domestic services, tavern-keeping was a public business, and Vobe, Campbell, and other female tavern keepers were prominent figures in their communities. Tavern keepers placed newspaper advertisements to attract new customers and inform old ones when they changed locations or offered new products or services. They appeared frequently in court to defend their interests and to collect outstanding debts. Susanna Allen, who ran a tavern in Williamsburg early in the eighteenth

Advertisement for Catherine Rathell, 10 October 1771. A successful and well-known businesswoman, Rathell ran several millinery shops in Virginia and Maryland. A regular advertiser in the *Virginia Gazette*, she carried an extensive inventory of imported goods, including textiles, ribbons, ladies' caps, buttons, sewing supplies, and "genuine Dr. Anderson's pills." *Courtesy of the Library of Virginia.*

century, was involved in at least 137 civil cases in York County between 1711 and 1718. At the same time, taverns themselves were the sites of many public activities in colonial Virginia. Dancing lessons, cockfights, art exhibitions, and fancy balls took place in taverns, as did business transactions, including the sale of tobacco and slaves. In taverns, people read newspapers—often aloud—and exchanged political information. Female tavern keepers therefore inhabited an environment that was neither isolated nor domestic. Small wonder that Jane Vobe, whose establishment hosted many political meetings during the imperial crisis, became an avid patriot who incurred considerable expenses supporting the local militia during the American Revolution.[63]

Although the most prominent Virginia businesswomen tended to be widows, wives also conducted business on their own or with their husbands, circumventing the constraints of coverture. The fact that they did so openly suggests that their husbands fully supported their employment and valued the income it brought, and that Virginians, in general, were willing to bend the law to serve the needs of individual families so long as empowering wives did not involve violating the authority of their husbands. As a result, wives were sometimes important players in large-scale trans-Atlantic family trading networks, choosing goods for sale, corresponding with suppliers and clients, keeping accounts, and collecting debts. Other wives shared workspace, if not accounts, with their husbands. The wigmaker Edward Charlton and the milliner Jane Hunter Charlton worked (and advertised) in Williamsburg both separately and as partners during their two-decade marriage. More independent still, Sarah Garland Pitt, a Williamsburg merchant, sustained her business during her eighteen-year marriage to George Pitt, a physician, and gave birth to seven children during that time (in addition to two she had borne during a previous marriage).[64]

Whether married, widowed, or single, milliners were among the most independent and successful businesswomen in the colony. Their business activities were also conspicuously public. Longevity in business, regular newspaper advertisements under their own names, and contacts in the London fashion world gave milliners public visibility and influence at a time when Virginia's gentry were increasingly attuned to English styles and customs, which they viewed as emblems of sophistication and cultural superiority. The prosperity of milliners in Williamsburg and in some other large towns also derived from the growing importance of elite women as consumers of imported finery. Catherine Rathell, one of Virginia's most successful milliners, who had shops in Williamsburg, Fredericksburg, and Annapolis, regularly advertised in the *Virginia Gazette* that she had "*Just* IMPORTED *from* LONDON . . . A GENTEEL Assortment of MERCERY, MILLINERY, JEWELLERY, &c., . . . of the newest Fashion, being chosen by herself, . . . from the eminent Shops" of the metropolis. Rathell's large and prominently placed advertisements typically featured long lists of the mostly fancy and ornamental items she sold for "Ladies and Gentlemen."[65]

Less autonomous than milliners though equally indebted to gentry patronage, printers were arguably the most publicly visible of all female entrepreneurs in early America. Wives of printers commonly worked in their husbands' shops and then as widows took over the family printing business. Like several of her counterparts in other colonies, the widowed Clementina Rind succeeded her husband as public printer, which he owed to the patronage of the colonial legislature, and as publisher of one of two Williamsburg newspapers named the *Virginia Gazette*. Perhaps anticipating criticism of her newfound public prominence, Rind cautiously introduced herself to readers of the *Gazette* when she assumed responsibility for her late husband's affairs in 1773. Invoking conventional images of female debility and dependence, Rind informed Virginians that the fate of her five children—her "orphan Family"—depended on her subscribers' "generous Breasts." When Rind died in 1774, her obituary in a rival newspaper praised her as "a Lady of singular Merit, and universally esteemed."[66]

Clementina Rind, Catherine Rathell, and Jane Vobe were influential public figures, but both their public stature and their ability to earn a living depended on the continued goodwill of their communities. A woman's ability to maintain that goodwill, in turn, depended heavily on her reputation as a virtuous woman, or one who accepted prevailing gender ideals even when the work she did was—as in Rind's case especially—far from conventionally feminine. Countless Virginia women did work that brought them income from and visibility in the world outside their households. Most who did so at least tacitly accepted theoretical distinctions between men's work and women's work, even as they tested the elasticity of Virginians' understanding of women's proper roles.

At the same time, emerging ideas about women's roles and attributes also justified the presence of gentry women in certain public social venues. As Virginia's gentry sought to enhance their prestige and solidify their position atop the provincial social hierarchy, they built fine houses, donned fashionable imported clothing, and orchestrated polite civic and social rituals to display their cosmopolitan tastes and manners both to each other and to their less privileged neighbors. Because eighteenth-century moralists and social critics increasingly viewed feminine virtue as a desirable corrective to masculine vices, wives and daughters were key participants in elite social and civic rituals, where their presence enhanced both the visual display and moral tone of these occasions. Women, one contributor to the *Virginia Gazette* explained in 1738, were both "great Instruments of Good, and the Prettinesses of Society." In 1773, another contributor to the *Gazette* argued forcefully that men's "taste for" women could spur their moral improvement. "Our endeavours to be agreeable to [women] polish and soften that rough severe Strain so natural to us," he noted. "In a Word, if Men did not converse with Women, [men] would be less perfect and less happy than they are."[67]

Sacrifice of Isaac, Elizabeth Boush, 1768–1769. Unlike most girls in the colony, Elizabeth Boush attended school, though the curriculum at her Norfolk boarding school was weighted heavily in favor of fancy needlework and other ornamental accomplishments. The teenaged Boush stitched this elaborate embroidery, in silk, showing the biblical story of the sacrifice of Isaac. *Collection of the Museum of Early Southern Decorative Arts, Old Salem Museums & Gardens, Acc. 2847.*

Elizabeth Boush, by John Durand, 1769. This portrait shows Boush at about age sixteen, when she attended Elizabeth Gardiner's school in Norfolk. Her fine clothes, coifed hair, and erect posture attest to her gentry status. Relatively few females received formal education in colonial Virginia and fewer still had their portraits painted. *Courtesy of the Colonial Williamsburg Foundation, Acc. 1982-271.*

This new appreciation for feminine society and virtue led to improved education for many gentry daughters. Although most women and many men in Virginia remained illiterate, eighteenth-century gentlefolk increasingly sent their sons to college, in Williamsburg or elsewhere, and ensured that their daughters studied various academic and ornamental subjects. Unlike their brothers, however, girls typically learned their lessons at home from family members or hired tutors. Philip Fithian, a young graduate of the College of New Jersey in Princeton, tutored the Carter children at Nomini Hall, where he taught English grammar and arithmetic to all eight of his charges, but only the three Carter sons learned Latin and Greek. The older Carter children of both sexes took dancing lessons, but only the older girls studied music, a polite accomplishment that contemporaries believed could "raise the *sociable and happy Passions*" of those who heard it.[68]

The gentry's quest for cultural distinction, which encouraged educational improvements, also dictated the limits and applications of women's learning. Parents and moralists alike urged young gentlewomen to cultivate their intellects without compromising their sensibility and modesty "lest the sex should lose in softness what they gained in force: and lest the pursuit of such elevation should interfere a little with the plain and humble virtues of life." Women's education, in other words, should make them virtuous and agreeable companions for men at home and in society. Some girls resented the obvious constraints on their intellectual development. In the 1730s, ten-year-old Betty Pratt envied her younger brother's English schooling, observing, "you write [b]etter already than I can expect to do as long as I live," despite her own less formal studies at home. A half-century later, Martha Washington's granddaughter Elizabeth Parke Custis, who learned reading, writing, arithmetic, music, and dancing from her tutors, nevertheless "thought it hard they would not teach me Greek & Latin because I was a girl."[69]

Accomplished, polite, and fashionably dressed women became both ornaments to and participants in an array of civic and social rituals in eighteenth-century Virginia. Most notably, gentry efforts to solidify their claims to political leadership and cultural authority reshaped the colony's civic pageantry, giving rise to new public rituals that included male and female members of the gentry but excluded Virginians of lesser social ranks. In early Virginia, civic celebrations and commemorations typically featured a militia parade and a procession of high officials, followed by a private dinner for the colony's leading men. By the 1720s, however, Virginia's gentlemen had added balls and dancing—and hence women—to the standard format for civic occasions. In 1736, its first year of publication, the *Virginia Gazette* reported that the king's birthday was celebrated in Williamsburg "with firing of Guns, Illuminations, and other Demonstrations of Loialty" followed by "a handsome Appearance of Gentlemen and Ladies, at His Honour the Governor's, where was a Ball, and an elegant Entertainment for them." Civic celebrations adhered to a similar plan in Williamsburg, as well as in some smaller Virginia communities, into the 1770s.[70]

The presence of women also changed the tone of public events ranging from horse races to elections by the closing decades of the colonial era. Elite jockey clubs transformed the social environment of traditionally rowdy men's horse races, adding genteel balls and banquets for ladies and gentlemen to the main events. In 1774, the autumn races in Fredericksburg lasted for five days, with balls and puppet shows featured nightly. Similarly, election etiquette may have been changing in Virginia largely as a result of women's presence at some public gatherings. Traditionally, Virginia's colonial elections had been drunken, sometimes violent, affairs for men only. But in 1768 and again in 1774, George Washington treated both men and women to refreshments after winning election to the House of Burgesses. Although there are no surviving accounts of the 1768 festivities, in 1774 an observer reported that the polling proceeded with "order and regularity" and the postelection ball "was conducted with great harmony." Women's presence fostered order and decorum and, in so doing, reflected well on the taste and virtue of the candidate.[71]

At elections, civic processions, and other public observances, women's participation was informal and extra-institutional. Despite the widespread belief that women were uniquely pious, this pattern persisted in the colony's dominant religious culture, that of the established Church of England. According to the Scotsman John Gregory, author of a popular advice book, women's "natural softness and sensibility" made them "peculiarly susceptible" to piety, but Anglicans nonetheless officially relegated females to unofficial roles. Women could not be ordained as ministers, serve as deacons, or participate in church governance as members of parish vestries, though parishes occasionally made them sextons, paid employees who kept church buildings and their contents clean and orderly.[72]

Most women who participated directly in the affairs of their churches did so by dispensing patronage or benevolence. These activities sometimes made women visible and enhanced their public reputations without conferring formal influence or power. Mary Harrison Gordon, wife of a Lancaster County merchant, provided schoolchildren with pancakes and cider on Shrove Tuesday, the traditional feast day before the start of Lent. Other women routinely offered their hospitality to clergymen as they traveled between their multiple congregations. Elizabeth Stith's patronage was on a far grander scale. This Surry County widow endowed a school for poor children and made substantial donations to her Anglican parish church over two decades. The fact that women and children were prominent among the recipients of poor relief and other charity from churches may help explain the appeal of charitable endeavors among affluent women.[73]

Some dissenting Protestant denominations, most notably the Quakers, afforded women more influential roles. Members of the Society of Friends, or Quakers, had settled in Norfolk and York Counties in the mid-seventeenth century; a second group had established communities in and around Henrico County by 1700. Beginning in the 1720s, other Quakers and Quaker-connected groups migrated southward from Pennsylvania into the Shenandoah Valley. The Quaker tenet that all people were imbued with the spirit of God, or the "Inner Light," led to their belief in human equality. Quaker egalitarianism, in turn, conferred on all members of their meetings license to preach and led some Friends to be early outspoken critics of various forms of earthly inequality, including African slavery. Women were numerous and visible as members of Quaker meetings in Virginia and elsewhere. Hannah Ingledew Janney, who settled with her family in Loudoun County in 1745, was a mother of twelve. She was also an elder and preacher in the Goose Creek Friends meeting, and she spoke out against slavery in her community.[74]

Other dissenting denominations recognized women as preachers or lay exhorters and in some cases allowed them to participate in church governance. Evangelical denominations, particularly the Separate Baptists and Methodists, attracted significant numbers of converts during the religious revivals that swept through Virginia in the 1760s and 1770s. Though generally supportive of patriarchy and unwilling to challenge directly existing social hierarchies, these early evangelicals nonetheless believed in the spiritual equality of church members and were more likely than secular authorities to discipline both women and men for sinful behavior, including sexual misconduct. Neither Baptists nor Methodists ordained women as ministers, but both welcomed white women, slaves, and free blacks as full members of their congregations, sometimes accepting them as lay exhorters or prayer leaders. Both black and white women spoke in Baptist and Methodist meetings, and sometimes women voted on issues of church discipline and policy. Some Baptist congregations also appointed women as deaconesses, who cared for the sick and the poor, and as eldresses, who counseled female members of their congregations. Although both jobs institutionalized women's traditional roles as caregivers and nurturers, they also gave official recognition and approval to women's work within the churches, which was not possible in the established Church of England.[75]

Some Virginia women became prominent in colonial evangelical communities. The most notable of these was the Baptist exhorter Margaret Meuse Clay, who was widely known in Chesterfield County as an inspiring and gifted speaker. Baptist ministers, who recognized Clay's piety and talents, often asked her to lead the congregation in prayer. Like so many other Baptists who publicly defied the established church, Clay was charged with the crime of preaching without a license and ordered to appear in court. Along with eleven male Baptists, Clay was found guilty and sentenced to a public whipping, though an anonymous man offered to spare her the pain and humiliation of the prescribed sentence by paying a fine for her instead. Clay continued preaching after this incident. As her story suggests, religious dissent clearly empowered at least some women to defy convention and question authority.[76]

At the other end of the social spectrum, Baptist religious fervor likewise transformed the life of Hannah Lee, daughter of Thomas Lee, of Stratford Hall, in Westmoreland County. About 1747, this young gentlewoman married her wealthy and prominent kinsman, Gawin Corbin. After he died during the winter of 1759–1760, however, Hannah Corbin's life took an unorthodox turn when she became a Baptist convert, an extremely unusual choice for a member of the gentry, most of whom remained firmly committed to the established Church of England. By 1762, Hannah Lee Corbin had fallen in love with Richard Lingan Hall, a Baptist physician, and the couple lived together on Corbin's lands until Hall's death in 1774. Though they never married, Hannah Corbin and Richard Hall had two children together. Both financial and religious considerations probably led to this unusual arrangement. On the one hand, Gawin Corbin's will had stipulated that his widow would lose control of his property if she remarried. On the other hand, Baptist convictions enabled the couple to justify their choice to forgo marriage because Virginia law recognized only unions solemnized by Anglican clergy as valid and binding. Although the Lees could not have wholly approved of Hannah Corbin's unconventional living arrangements, there is little evidence that either her religious heterodoxy or her relationship with Richard Hall ultimately damaged her standing in her family. She remained a respected and prosperous member of the Virginia gentry and owned sixty-four slaves and more than 1,700 acres of land when she died in 1782.[77]

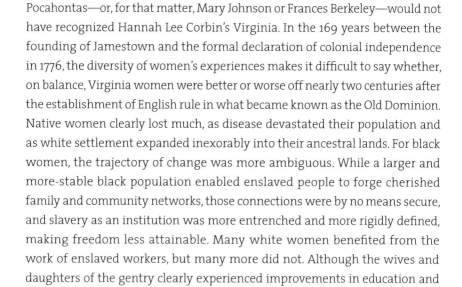

Pocahontas—or, for that matter, Mary Johnson or Frances Berkeley—would not have recognized Hannah Lee Corbin's Virginia. In the 169 years between the founding of Jamestown and the formal declaration of colonial independence in 1776, the diversity of women's experiences makes it difficult to say whether, on balance, Virginia women were better or worse off nearly two centuries after the establishment of English rule in what became known as the Old Dominion. Native women clearly lost much, as disease devastated their population and as white settlement expanded inexorably into their ancestral lands. For black women, the trajectory of change was more ambiguous. While a larger and more-stable black population enabled enslaved people to forge cherished family and community networks, those connections were by no means secure, and slavery as an institution was more entrenched and more rigidly defined, making freedom less attainable. Many white women benefited from the work of enslaved workers, but many more did not. Although the wives and daughters of the gentry clearly experienced improvements in education and in their material circumstances, as the impermanent structures of an earlier era gave way to such splendid mansions as Westover and Stratford Hall, in other respects they enjoyed less independence than had their ancestors in the colony's early decades.

CHAPTER 2

"WE CANNOT BE TAME SPECTATORS": REVOLUTIONARY TIMES

Although Virginians could not have known it at the time, the era of the American Revolution began in their colony in May 1765, when the House of Burgesses adopted several of Patrick Henry's radical resolutions rejecting the Stamp Act on constitutional grounds. Known as the Virginia Resolves, these measures condemned Parliament's attempt to tax colonists in Virginia and elsewhere and contended that the people's right to be taxed only "by Persons chosen by themselves to represent them . . . [is] the distinguishing Characteristick of *British* Freedom."[1] For the next eleven years, Virginia's leaders protested a succession of imperial offenses. They enjoined men and women to protect what they believed to be their rights as British subjects and ultimately committed the colony to independence and war with Britain. The Revolutionary years proved difficult for many Virginia women and their families, who experienced the absence of loved ones and economic troubles, besides the inevitable violence of the war itself.

The return of peace left Virginians to determine the extent to which the Revolution and its ideals would transform the politics and society of their newly independent commonwealth. Once they established a republic, for instance, it remained a matter of contention how democratic and how inclusive their new polity would be. Slavery had to be abandoned or reconciled with a Revolutionary agenda that was allegedly committed to securing liberty and inalienable rights. So, too, was it incumbent on Virginians—as for all other Americans—to reassess the status of women in light of their unprecedented involvement in public life during the Revolutionary era. While the Revolution made the erstwhile subjects of a British monarch citizens of an independent republic, it remained to be seen how Virginia women experienced this transformation.

Women participated in virtually every aspect of the American Revolution, though they were rarely its central actors. During the decade-long crisis that preceded independence, Virginia women joined the consumer boycotts that colonists organized to protest imperial policies, and some contributed to the torrent of essays, pamphlets, and other publications designed to mobilize popular resistance to British tyranny. During the war, women ran family farms and businesses while men served in the army or in government. Some women aided the cause more directly as army nurses, cooks, or laundresses. Surviving letters suggest that the imperial crisis and the subsequent war led many women—and also many others outside the male gentry elite—to think seriously about politics, perhaps for the first time. For some Virginia women, this new political consciousness survived into the post-Revolutionary era.

From the Stamp Act crisis of 1765–1766 through the formal declaration of independence in July 1776, economic sanctions were the colonists' most effective weapon against objectionable Parliamentary laws. Twice during the 1760s, colonial boycotts against British imports led to significant changes in imperial policies. In Virginia, the gentlemen of the House of Burgesses led the fight against what they saw as British tyranny and oppression, but the effectiveness of consumer boycotts depended on broad-based popular support, which necessitated the involvement of those outside the colony's traditional governing elite. As both producers and consumers, Virginia women came to play important roles in these pre-Revolutionary initiatives.

As elite Virginians adapted their fancy balls and other civic and social rituals to changing political circumstances, gentry women became politicized during the 1760s and 1770s. In 1766, the *Virginia Gazette* reported that a "large and genteel company of Ladies and Gentlemen" gathered at the Capitol in Williamsburg to celebrate the repeal of the Stamp Act. On this occasion, as on so many others, Virginia's leading women and men dressed in their most fashionable imported finery. Three years later, however, the "Ladies" of Williamsburg, along with the wives and daughters of colonial legislators, publicly demonstrated their support for nonimportation (in this case, to protest the Townshend Acts of 1767) by joining their spouses and fathers in wearing garments made of homespun cloth when they attended a fancy ball and entertainment in the capital. By 1774, as the estrangement between Virginians and London deepened, balls became occasions for circulating political news, singing patriotic songs, and drinking political toasts. That January, Frances Tasker Carter and her daughters attended a ball where the women toasted the "Sons of america" and sang "Liberty Songs." At another ball in Alexandria, men and women drank punch, wine, coffee, and chocolate but pointedly rejected tea, the "forbidden herb," which, because it carried a Parliamentary tax, had come to symbolize British tyranny.[2]

But longstanding prejudices against women's political activism died hard, and men often trivialized women's capacity for civic-mindedness even as they elicited their involvement in patriotic activities. In 1767, a poem entitled "Address to the Ladies" appeared in the *Virginia Gazette*. This often-reprinted verse was significant in that it was the first published political appeal addressed specifically to Virginia women. At the same time, however, drawing on prevailing gender conventions that identified men with reason and women with emotion, the poem targeted "Ladies" as particularly passionate consumers who, unlike men, needed to be taught to "Love your country much better than fine things." The poet urged women to give up extravagant hairstyles and headdresses, imported ribbons, and "rich dress" in favor of "clothes of your own make and spinning" and to replace their imported tea with infusions of American herbs. In the final stanza, moreover, the author suggested that women's support for nonimportation would come less from their own civic-mindedness than from a coquettish desire to win the admiration of patriotic men. Women who renounced imported luxuries would appear "Fair, charming, true, lovely, and clever," the poet asserted, assuring compliant ladies that "Tho' the times remain darkish, young men may be sparkish/ And love you much stronger than ever."[3]

Although cloth was one of the most important items colonists purchased from British merchants and homespun cloth came to symbolize female patriotism, most early efforts to stimulate local cloth production in Virginia neither addressed women directly nor acknowledged the potential political significance of their domestic manufactures. Part of the reason for obscuring the identity of cloth makers was the ironic and perhaps somewhat embarrassing predominance of enslaved workers in the production of cloth on Virginia farms and plantations. While poor white women worked alone or with other members of their family, many middling women had at least one enslaved girl to assist with the spinning and weaving, and female slaves did most of the spinning and weaving on the colony's larger plantations. Thus, when the British officer Thomas Anburey visited Virginia in 1779 and 1780, he found that "carding and spinning . . . is the chief employment of the female negroes . . . and almost all the families in this Province, both male and female, are cloathed with their own manufacture."[4]

Yet Virginia's patriot leaders did call specifically on free women, as consumers, to support nonimportation and nonconsumption in 1773, when colonists initiated a boycott to protest the Tea Act, which maintained an existing tax on tea and gave the British East India Company a monopoly on sales of that widely consumed commodity. Tea accounted for nearly 8 percent of colonial imports from Britain late in the 1760s, and roughly half of all Virginia households boasted specialized implements for storing, brewing, and serving the fashionable beverage. But colonists especially associated tea and tea-drinking with domesticity and women's sociability, so women's participation in the boycott seemed logical and even essential to its ultimate success. Consequently, the tea boycott posed new responsibilities for women, while also offering them new opportunities to show their patriotism and to participate in civic life.[5]

Most important, the tea boycott resulted in the appearance in Virginia newspapers of the first political writing by and for women. In January 1774, Alexander Purdie and John Dixon's *Virginia Gazette* published a poem entitled "A Lady's Adieu to her Tea Table," in which the female narrator explained her renunciation of "the once lov'd" tea she was accustomed to sharing with her friends "Because I'm taught (and I believe it true) / Its Use will *fasten slavish Chains upon my Country*." In June 1774, another female poet described her

the End of a . . .
Morning; and the Weather being then a little eafier, he hoifted out his
Boat, and took the whole Crew in, eight in Number, and a young
Lady, Mifs Hannah Dempfter, who behaved with the greateft
Refolution, ftanding by the Pumps when moft of the Men gave out.
As it ftill blew very hard, he could not attempt getting out any of the
Cargo, but brought all the People fafe into Norfolk.
[Dublin.] Mrs. ELIZABETH MEADE, the amiable Spoufe of
Richard Kidder Meade, Efq; of Prince George.

A Lady's Adieu to her TEA TABLE.

FAREWELL the Tea Board, with its gaudy Equipage,
Of Cups and Saucers, Cream Bucket, Sugar Tongs,
The pretty Tea Cheft alfo, lately ftor'd
With Hyfon, Congo, and beft Double Fine.
Full many a joyous Moment have I fat by ye,
Hearing the Girls' Tattle, the Old Maids talk Scandal,
And the fpruce Coxcomb laugh at—may be—Nothing.
No more fhall I difh out the once lov'd Liquor,
Though now deteftable,
Becaufe I'm taught (and I believe it true)
Its Ufe will *faften flaverifh Chains* upon my Country,
And LIBERTY's the Goddefs I would choofe
To reign triumphant in AMERICA.

Entered in the Upper Diftrict *of* JAMES RIVER.
January 17. Britannia, George Rapall, from Salem, with 20 Cafks
of Raifins, 6 Cafks of Spanifh Wine, 180 Weight of Coffee, 17 Hhds. of
New England Rum, 3 Dozen of Axes, 4 Barrels of Mackerel, and 9
Quintals of Fifh.

"A Lady's Adieu to her Tea Table," 20 January 1774. This verse, which appeared in Purdie and Dixon's *Virginia Gazette,* was one of several poems and essays that encouraged women to protest British policies and show their patriotism by abjuring tea and other imported luxuries. *Courtesy of the Library of Virginia.*

feelings "on receiving a handsome Set of Tea China," which she regarded as "a SPECIOUS Instrument of Ill," a "ministerial Snare" calculated to corrupt her virtue by tempting her to consume imported luxuries. Both verses presented readers with patriotic female exemplars who sacrificed their usual pleasures and comforts to benefit the common good, encouraging other women to emulate their civic-minded efforts.[6]

Some women published essays that explicitly urged their sisters to exhibit patriotism in this time of crisis. The most notable example of this sort of an appeal to Virginia women appeared on the front page of Clementina Rind's *Virginia Gazette* on 15 September 1774. Like her late husband, William, Clementina Rind was an ardent patriot, and her newspaper gave ample coverage

Masthead of Clementina Rind's *Virginia Gazette*, 15 September 1774. Clementina Rind's solo career was brief but eventful. In August 1773, she succeeded her late husband, William Rind, as printer and editor of the *Gazette*. In May 1774, she became the colony's public printer; she published Thomas Jefferson's influential pamphlet, *A Summary View of the Rights of British America*, two months later. An ardent patriot, Clementina Rind died in Williamsburg in September 1774. *Courtesy of the Library of Virginia.*

to colonial efforts to organize resistance to British imperial policies. But on this date, Rind's *Gazette* was unique in carrying two substantial essays written by and for women. Together, these essays took up roughly one-half of the newspaper's entire front page.

One of these pieces was a letter that a group of unnamed Virginia women addressed to their "countrywomen" in the province of Pennsylvania, where the tea boycott had not succeeded partly because of merchants' opposition to the project. The Virginia women urged the "LADIES of PENNSYLVANIA" to work with their men to support the tea boycott by using instead "some of those aromatic herbs with which our fruitful soil abounds" and by "withstanding luxuries of every kind." Such acts of patriotism, they advised, would enable women to claim a public role and also create a historical legacy. "Much, very much, depends on the public virtue the ladies will exert at this critical juncture," observed these politically minded Virginians, who optimistically predicted that the efforts of American women "will be so far instrumental in bringing about a redress of ... evils ... that history may be hereafter filled with their praises, and teach posterity to venerate their virtues."[7]

Alongside the Virginia women's letter, Rind reprinted an essay written by "A Planter's Wife," which had appeared in a recent edition of the *South Carolina Gazette*. This writer, too, called on women to play a decisive role in the colonial boycott of tea and other imported items. Rejecting pejorative stereotypes of vain and frivolous women, "A Planter's Wife" declared that women must "make it evident to the world that we have some regard for our country, and our offspring" by acting virtuously in defense of liberty. Because tea was "a matter which chiefly respects our sex," she asserted, "surely, my sisters, we cannot be tame spectators, when so much remains for us to do, and may be reasonably expected of us." By renouncing tea and other imported luxuries, women would "disappoint our enemies . . . and greatly assist our husbands, brethren, and countrymen, in their arduous struggle" against tyranny. Individually, "every mistress of a family" could prevent consumption of the tainted goods in her own household. Collectively, women could ruin the East India Company and, more important still, strengthen the patriotic resolve of the men around them.[8]

Many Virginia women responded to such appeals, and men occasionally recognized and publicly praised women's political activism. In June 1774, for example, residents of Fredericksburg observed a day of prayer and fasting to "implore the Divine Interposition for averting the heavy Calamity which threatens Destruction to the civil Rights of America." Women attended the church service and participated in the day's prayers, and whoever submitted the report on the day's events singled his townswomen out for special public praise in the pages of the *Virginia Gazette*. "Credit is due to the Ladies for the Part they took in our Association, and it does Honour to their Sex," he wrote, "for no sooner were they made acquainted with the Resolution to prohibit the Use of TEA . . . they sealed up the Stock which they had on Hand, and vowed never more to use it till the oppressive Act imposing a Duty thereon should be repealed." These Virginia women, he exclaimed, set an "Example" that should "be followed by all the Ladies on this Continent!"[9]

At least one Virginia patriot, however, used the tea boycott as an occasion to question what she saw as men's tyrannical efforts to banish tea from their households. Writing under the pseudonym "Penelope House-Wife," this essayist praised tea for its "soothing" and civilizing properties, while reviling the harsh and "acrid" herbs that patriot leaders promoted as locally produced alternatives. The heart of Penelope's critique was her assertion that men deprived women of their preferred beverage "without so much as our consent being asked" and that in so doing they intruded into woman's "proper sphere," thereby violating her "natural and matrimonial rights." Penelope saw politics as distinct from what she called "matters purely internal" to the family, and, believing that women rightly wielded authority in household matters, she resented what she saw as men's recent usurpation of women's domestic power. "You know, my dear country women, that there are tyrants at the head of little families as well as at the head of great empires," she explained, "and I always thought that our sex, have an undoubted right to carry their resistance [to] as great lengths, if needful, in opposition to domestic tyranny in one instance, as the men pretend to, in their opposition to state tyranny in the other."[10]

By contrast, others who opposed the colonial boycotts cited women's participation in them as evidence that colonial grievances and the resistance movement in general lacked legitimacy. A popular 1775 British cartoon mocked the fifty-one women who had gathered in Edenton, North Carolina, in October 1774 to endorse the Continental Association, a pledge adopted by the Continental Congress to end all colonial imports from and exports to Great Britain in order to pressure Parliament into rescinding the Intolerable Acts of 1774 and other objectionable policies. The artist portrayed the Edenton "ladies" variously as mannish hags, neglectful mothers, and shameless harlots. Another 1775 cartoon, "The Alternative of Williams-Burg," portrayed a menacing crowd, which included at least one masculine-looking white woman and one black man, forcing respectable gentlemen in Virginia's capital to sign the association. In both cases, the general message was clear: critics, which included some conservative Virginians, viewed radical colonial protest as the product of people who, both by law and by custom, lacked legitimate political authority. The cartoons' secondary message, however, was that only base and disreputable women would engage in such overtly political activities.[11]

The virtual stoppage of trade that occurred in 1774 and 1775, which benefited many planters and other debtors, proved fatal to Virginia's milliners, whose goods were virtually all imported and whose stock consisted mainly of luxury items that the Continental Association specifically proscribed. Jane Hunter Charlton, the well-established Williamsburg milliner, shut down her business and left for England with her husband, Edward Charlton, in 1775. Another prominent milliner, Catherine Rathell, who began advertising imported finery and other goods in the colony in 1766, left for England in 1775 and charged her fellow milliner Margaret Brodie with selling off her store fixtures and her entire "stock in trade." Rathell was one of seven passengers who died when the *Peggy* wrecked near Liverpool in the autumn of 1775, about the same time that Brodie, too, departed for Great Britain.[12]

During these transformative years, many women who remained in the colony showed growing awareness of and interest in political issues, which, as war became imminent, increasingly affected their daily lives. The escalation of the "present troubles" alarmed Elizabeth Feilde, the wife of an Anglican minister in Gloucester County. Feilde distrusted Virginia's patriot leaders who, she believed, "brought a Deluge of Calamities on this unhappy Country" by refusing to reconcile with Great Britain. She confided to her friend, the more radically minded Maria Armistead, that she feared both the violence of war and its resulting social upheaval. At the other end of the political spectrum, Martha Washington described ongoing preparations for war as "very terable indeed" when she accompanied her husband to Massachusetts, where he assumed command of the newly formed Continental army late in 1775. Martha Washington was interested in any political news that was not "in the papers," which she promised to share with Elizabeth Ramsay, her friend in Alexandria.[13]

Although comparatively few women left written evidence of their thoughts and concerns as Virginia moved toward war and independence, Anne Dabney Terrell, of Bedford County, may have spoken for many of her countrywomen when she addressed female readers of the *Virginia Gazette* in September 1776. At the time, Anne Terrell was in her mid-thirties, the mother of six children, and the wife of Captain Henry Terrell, who commanded a battalion of Virginia troops in the Continental army. Perhaps drawing on her experience in western Virginia, where settlers had fought Native Americans since the 1760s, Terrell predicted that war would jeopardize both the lives and livelihoods of Virginia women and their families. The British, she warned, were "conspiring with our slaves to cut our throats" and "instigating the savage Indians to fall on our frontiers" to murder "whole families … without regard to age or sex." Their lives endangered, women would also suffer economic hardship as a result of the stoppage of trade and the loss of labor, as men left home to fight the enemy.[14]

Rather than embrace popular stereotypes of feminine weakness and dependence, however, Terrell asserted that women should "support ourselves under the absence of our husbands as well as we can." Although she professed herself "almost ready to start up with sword in hand to fight by [her husband's] side in so glorious a cause," she conceded that women's patriotism was not

A Society of Patriotic Ladies, at Edenton, in North Carolina, attributed to Philip Dawe, 25 March 1775. This British cartoon satirized the 51 Edenton, North Carolina, women who prepared and signed a manifesto in support of the commercial sanctions imposed on Britain by the Continental Congress. *Courtesy of the Library of Congress, Prints and Photographs Division, LC-DIG-ppmsca-19468.*

THE ALTERNATIVE OF WILLIAMS-BURG.

Plate IV.   London Printed for R. Sayer & J. Bennett N°53 Fleet Street as the Act directs 16 Feb 1775.

The Alternative of Williams-Burg, attributed to Philip Dawe, 16 February 1775. By including female images in this cartoon, the artist implied that colonial boycotts and protests were the work of people who lacked a legitimate political voice. *Courtesy of the Library of Congress, Prints and Photographs Division, LC-USZC4-5280.*

best deployed by joining men in battle, but rather that they should devote themselves to "another branch of American politics, which comes more immediately under our province, namely, in frugality and industry, at home," particularly in manufacturing clothing because "although it may not be so very fine, yet we may say we paid nothing for it to Great Britain, and that we are free women." Terrell thus welcomed and encouraged women's involvement in the Revolutionary cause. Though she believed that women and men played different roles in the fight for liberty and independence, she nonetheless saw that Virginia women, like male soldiers and statesmen, could be patriots as well as active participants in the unfolding Revolution.[15]

The War of Independence unfolded in Virginia in three distinct phases, each of which posed new challenges for women and their families. During the first phase, which lasted from 1775 through 1776, the British recruited supporters among slaves and white loyalists, and Virginia patriots fought Native Americans in the West and engaged the British and their allies in and around the borough of Norfolk. The war's second phase, which lasted through 1780, brought no major military engagements to Virginia, whose inhabitants nonetheless suffered economic hardships and the continual departure of men to fight elsewhere. The war's third and final phase began with an enemy attack on Richmond, the new state capital, in January 1781. It effectively concluded with the decisive surrender of the main British army after the Battle of Yorktown nine months later.

The war wreaked havoc on most Native American communities, as Indian nations tried either to remain neutral or to ally with one side (usually the British) in order to protect their interests and preserve their independence. Invariably, Indians lost both lives and land regardless of their choice. In western Virginia, armed conflict between white settlers and Native Americans antedated the War of Independence and began with a series of bloody confrontations early in the 1770s. In April 1774, armed Virginians ambushed a party of Shawnee women and children, killing and scalping them all, including a pregnant woman whose fetus they ripped from the womb and "stuck on a pole." Retaliation led to an all-out war and the defeat of the Shawnee, who lost much of their land in the resulting treaty. In 1776, the Cherokee declared war, in hopes of preserving their land from white incursions, though some Cherokee women actively opposed the war and even aided American militias, perhaps believing that maintaining peace with white Virginians was the best way to ensure the safety of their communities. American militias nevertheless destroyed most of the Cherokee towns. By mid-1777, the Cherokee were officially neutral and the few who remained in Virginia were homeless refugees.[16]

In Virginia, the major military engagements of the war's initial phase occurred in the borough of Norfolk and the surrounding area. With a population of approximately 6,000 and roughly 1,300 houses, Norfolk was Virginia's largest town and the busiest port in the southern colonies. While the town itself was home to a large population of Scots merchants, who ultimately formed the nucleus of a substantial loyalist community, its trade drew on a hinterland of plantations worked by slave labor. On 7 November 1775, Virginia's royal governor, John Murray, earl of Dunmore, issued a proclamation offering freedom to "all *indented servants, negroes,* or others (appertaining to rebels) . . . that are able and willing to bear arms." More than a thousand enslaved people, including some women, answered Dunmore's call to support the king's forces, but the governor's combined force of British regulars, escaped slaves, and white loyalists fell in battle to the patriot militia at Great Bridge, near Norfolk, in December. When the victorious patriots occupied Norfolk, Dunmore ordered a naval bombardment of the borough, to which the Virginia militia responded by burning the homes of local loyalists. When the fighting was over, Norfolk was destroyed—only about a dozen houses remained, according to one account—with American forces having inflicted most of the damage.[17]

For several days early in January 1776, women and other civilians in the Norfolk area witnessed firsthand the violence of war. Some coastal residents fled in advance of the expected attacks. Those who remained behind, either by necessity or by choice, risked physical danger as well as the destruction of their homes and other property. On New Year's Day 1776, the day of the British bombardment of Norfolk, Mary Webley was at home "suckling her Child the youngest of three . . . [and] had her leg broken by a Cannon Ball from the Liverpool Man of War." The Webleys lost their house and "all their Effects," and Mary Webley, whose husband had lost his right arm in an accident some years earlier, sought and received a modest sum in "Aid and Relief" from Virginia's new state legislature in October 1776. Sarah Hutchings, a mother of six, reported the capture of her husband who "commanded a Regiment of Minute men in the County of Norfolk," as well as the destruction of her home in the "general conflagration." She, too, sought relief from the General Assembly after her husband "contracted a disease of which he died." Countless loyalist women, who could not seek compensation from the newly ascendant Revolutionary regime, also lost their homes and other property. Patriots and loyalists alike faced harassment and intimidation by soldiers on both sides, who seized food, supplies, and buildings from the embattled civilian populace.[18]

The patriot militiamen who occupied Norfolk and its environs depended on civilians to supply them with food and lodging, and they also relied on women in particular to care for sick and wounded soldiers. Margaret Rawlings nursed a soldier in her home for sixteen days before he recovered from "the Flux." Maria Carter Armistead boarded sick prisoners in her Williamsburg home, where one died under her care. Although these women dispensed their services informally and in response to specific requests for help, other women took up nursing as a more formalized occupation in the coming months. As early as July 1776, the newly established Continental Hospital in Williamsburg placed a notice in the *Virginia Gazette* to recruit *"some* NURSES *to attend the sick."* Poorly paid, overworked, and usually inexperienced, women served as nurses in Virginia and elsewhere throughout the war.[19]

In August 1776, military action effectively ended in coastal Virginia with the departure of Dunmore and the British fleet, accompanied by many escaped slaves. Although single men had predominated among the runaways who had responded to Dunmore's proclamation months earlier, enslaved women also began to flee to the British with their children, and family members who worked on separate plantations reunited to seek their freedom. Violet and her son Nathaniel fled Princess Anne County to Dunmore's fleet, where they joined Violet's husband and his brother, both of whom had escaped slavery in Norfolk County. Black refugees included those escaping not only from patriot masters, but also some belonging to loyalists because Revolutionary officials threatened to seize slaves from loyalist slave owners and sell them to new masters. Mary, who worked on a plantation that belonged to a suspected loyalist, escaped to Dunmore with her daughter Patience; Mary's Revolutionary odyssey took her first to New York—where she met and married Caesar Perth, who had escaped from slavery in Norfolk—and then to Nova Scotia and the British West African colony of Sierra Leone in the post-Revolutionary era. Although many of the slaves who fled Virginia in 1776 succumbed to smallpox and other diseases, some 300 black women survived this exodus to resettle elsewhere as free people after the war was over.[20]

Many white women also became refugees as a result of the destruction of Norfolk and its surrounding area. Some families who chose to stay, perhaps to protect their remaining property, lodged in the few surviving buildings—which included Mary Ross's tavern—or in temporary shelters. Of those who left the area, some were homeless, like Mary Webley and her children, while others sought refuge with relatives who lived elsewhere. Wealthier refugees could retreat to their plantations or country houses. Although some eventually returned to Norfolk, the town rebuilt slowly. By 1779, when young Jenny Steuart visited Norfolk, she found that only about fifteen houses had been rebuilt, though there were "a great many small huts" sheltering townspeople who "cannot be happy anywhere else."[21]

White loyalist women faced especially tough choices after 1776, as the state's Revolutionary government began to implement a series of laws designed to punish those Virginians who refused to swear allegiance to the state and thereby renounce royal authority. Shortly after the Continental Congress declared independence, Virginia's General Assembly required all merchants to swear allegiance to the new Revolutionary regime and prescribed the penalty of banishment for those who did not. In 1777, all free males over the age of sixteen were required to take the oath; though those who refused were not banished, they were disarmed, disenfranchised, and prohibited from buying land or filing suits in state courts. In addition, Virginia's government, in need of financial support for the ongoing war, began to sequester loyalist estates, but the state granted wives of loyalists a one-third dower right—the equivalent of a widow's portion—in any sequestered property. As a result, some women stayed behind in Virginia when their loyalist husbands left in order to preserve at least a portion of their family's estate.[22]

Legislators probably voted to protect the dower portions of the wives of loyalists at least in part because they assumed that the women themselves were apolitical and therefore should not suffer for the political transgressions of their spouses. In fact, some Virginia women were committed loyalists. Elizabeth Feilde, the clergyman's wife who had distrusted the patriots from the start, remained a loyal subject of King George III. She and her husband left for New

York with Dunmore in 1776. The wife of the Reverend John Agnew, another Anglican minister, was less fortunate. When Agnew became a chaplain for Dunmore's troops, his wife hid in the swamps for three years rather than remain among unfriendly patriots. Most loyalist women who stayed in Virginia to protect their family's property after their husbands fled were probably careful to avoid offending their volatile patriot neighbors, who vastly outnumbered them. Still, county authorities occasionally punished loyalist women for passing information to British forces or for otherwise not cooperating with the Revolutionary government.[23]

Women on both sides of the Revolutionary conflict showed their level of commitment—and sometimes their desperation—by traveling with the armies. The vast majority of Revolutionary camp followers were women and children who found themselves impoverished or even homeless once their men left home to fight the war. Army life afforded these women and their families meager military rations and tents to shelter them, in return for which they cooked, washed, did laundry, and nursed diseased and wounded soldiers. Although General Washington repeatedly complained about the large numbers of civilians who accompanied his troops, the labor these women performed was essential to the army's survival. So, too, did the more genteel wives of officers contribute to the soldiers' well-being when they visited army encampments. Martha Washington left the comforts of Mount Vernon each year to spend the winter with her husband at army headquarters. While she and other officers' wives lived far more comfortably than the kin of common soldiers, the ladies' presence lifted the troops' spirits and, according to one observer, "inspired fortitude" among the suffering at Valley Forge and elsewhere.[24]

Other women disguised themselves as men and joined the army. Because the penalties for these cross-dressing soldiers could be severe, they tried hard to avoid discovery. As a result, historians will never know precisely how many women actually fought as soldiers in the War of Independence. The most famous female soldier was Deborah Sampson, of Massachusetts, who served in the Continental army for more than a year, came under fire at least twice, and was wounded in battle. In 1783, after her sex was discovered, she received an honorable discharge and eventually was awarded a pension from Congress. Perhaps some Virginia women served in the army without revealing their true identities. Anna Maria Lane, a Connecticut native who probably enlisted with

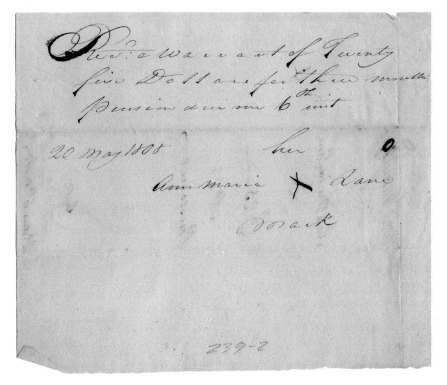

Receipt for pension signed by Ann[a] Maria Lane, 20 May 1808. Virginia's only known female veteran of the American Revolution, Anna Maria Lane had to prove that she had been a soldier and that she was destitute in order to get a government pension. In 1808, she acknowledged receipt of her pension by making her mark. *Courtesy of the Library of Virginia.*

her husband John Lane, was Virginia's only acknowledged female veteran of the Revolution. Anna Maria Lane wore "the garb . . . of a soldier" when she was severely wounded at the Battle of Germantown in 1777. As the war was ending, the Lanes settled in Richmond. In 1808, the General Assembly publicly recognized Anna Maria Lane's military service and gave her a generous annual pension.[25]

During the war, though perhaps as many as 20,000 Virginia women left the state for various reasons, the overwhelming majority stayed home, where they did important work for their families and communities.[26] When men left their plantations or their workshops to serve in the military or in government, patriot leaders appealed to women to supply the labor necessary to sustain their families and produce commodities to aid the Revolutionary cause. As early as September 1776, the *Virginia Gazette* exhorted its female readers to follow the example of patriotic women in Pennsylvania who were "determined to put in the crop themselves" if their "fathers, brothers, and lovers, be detained abroad in the defence of the liberties of these states."[27]

Women's work on the homefront became especially crucial as the disruption of trade by British naval blockades resulted in shortages of cloth and most other manufactured items, leading housewives and plantation mistresses to augment the productivity of their households. At Monticello, Martha Jefferson oversaw the production of cloth during the war. Rebecca Ellegood Aitchison and her sister Margaret Ellegood Parker, both of whom were wives of loyalists, fled the destruction of Norfolk for a cottage in Northampton County, where they spent the war years making cloth, dairying, and raising poultry, with the help of their daughters who now had few opportunities for reading, writing, and "polite company." In Berkeley County, Sarah Nourse, whose patriot husband James Nourse held various political offices, repeatedly patched her family's old clothes, perhaps knowing that they would need to last until after the war was over.[28]

Other women oversaw enterprises that were essential to the war effort but were not necessarily the sorts of work that contemporaries considered appropriate for women. Mary Marshall Tabb Bolling, a Petersburg widow who owned several plantations and many slaves, also operated a gristmill that processed grain that fed Virginia's soldiers. After her husband died, Catherine Park ran her family's Richmond tannery, which supplied leather goods to the state government. Park's tannery was capable of processing up to 2,000 hides annually. She assumed her added responsibilities with gusto, confidently informing Governor Thomas Jefferson that, if the state supplied her with sufficient bark necessary for tanning, she would "Exert every Ability I am Mistress of" to secure able workers to get the requisite work done.[29]

By late in the 1770s, shortages worsened and inflation soared as both Congress and the state issued paper money to finance the war and called on civilians to pay increasingly higher taxes. Although even gentry families faced financial hardships in wartime, soldiers' families were especially vulnerable. At best, such families exchanged their men's labor for meager military wages paid—if at all—in virtually worthless paper currency. At worst, soldiers died of disease or in battle, leaving their families bereaved, impoverished, and often dependent on public relief. Margaret Irvine, of York County, sought help from the state after her husband enlisted in the Continental army in January 1777 and died of disease a few months later. In her petition to the General Assembly, Irvine explained that her husband had died "much in Debted & having but very small property, not enough to satisfie . . . his Crediters," and that she was left with four young children "& Pragnant with the fifth" to pay his outstanding debts. Not surprisingly, even some women who avidly supported the Revolution dreaded the potential consequences of their husbands' enlistment in the army.[30]

Somewhat better off than Irvine was Martha Hodges, of York County, who nonetheless struggled to make ends meet after her husband, a militiaman, caught "a cold that brought on a disorder which occasiond his death" early in the war. The "principle support" for herself and her children was a "Waggon & Team," which Hodges rented to generate income. In September 1777, however, a militia colonel commandeered her wagon and draft animals to haul his soldiers' supplies to Williamsburg. The colonel kept the widow's property for eight days, paid her only half the negotiated price, and did "great damage to the Team" before returning the horses to her, only to have another militia officer a short time later press the wagon and team into service for nineteen days, at a similarly low price. As a soldier's widow, Hodges surely understood the importance of the war effort, but she also needed to rent her wagon at a fair price to provide food and shelter for her children during these troubled times.[31]

The case of Frances Seayers and her family suggests that the loss of a male breadwinner could have dire consequences even among the gentry. John Seayers, who rose to the rank of lieutenant colonel and was considered a gentleman in his neighborhood, died in battle at Germantown, Pennsylvania, in 1777. Seayers had supported his wife and children comfortably until 1776, when his patriotism inspired him to leave his family, enlist in the army, and fight for American liberty. According to his widow, Frances Seayers, "his death was as fatal to his family, as it was Glorious to himself." Before 1776, John Seayers had "formed a Plan for Educating his sons, in the best manner that the circumstances of the country would allow, and their Genius's would admit of," but Frances Seayers now worried that her husband's death would leave her "indigent" and unable to fulfill his "benevolent and truly Paternal designs" for the future of her children. Frances Seayers, who in 1776 had considered herself the wife of

Two-pound currency note, 1775. Virginia began printing paper currency even before the colonies declared independence, switching from British pounds to Spanish dollars in 1776. Because the state government had almost no specie to back its paper money, inflation was rampant throughout the war, bringing economic hardship to many women and their families. *Courtesy of the Library of Virginia.*

a Virginia gentleman, a few years later found her own prospects and those of her children hopelessly diminished.[32]

Wartime inflation posed special problems for widows and orphans who lived on fixed incomes from estates or government pensions. Elizabeth Crowley, of Henry County, received a public pension after her husband had died fighting the western Indians in 1774. Although the pension had initially contributed "towards the Relief of her Self and her numerous Family of small Children," the "extraordinary & unexpected Depreciation of the Money" in wartime rendered the sum, in her words, "quite inadequate to that benevolent & charitable Purpose." A group of men in Brunswick County echoed Crowley's concern, which also affected those dependent on income from private estates. The Brunswick men urged state legislators to consider the plight of the state's orphans who "had been comfortably provided for by their Deceased Parents,

[who] are now reduced to that State of Indigence & Poverty as to depend solely ... on the charitable Assistance of their Friends and Relations" as a result of rampant wartime inflation.[33]

Although most Virginia families suffered economically during the war years, households headed by women may have been the most vulnerable. In 1783, when the fighting had stopped, authorities in Princess Anne County settled accounts with local tax delinquents, seizing and selling their lands and using the proceeds to pay the taxes they owed. Because the common law doctrine of coverture deprived married women of property rights, women constituted a small minority of the landowners in Princess Anne, as in other Virginia counties. Nevertheless, of the sixty-one tracts county authorities confiscated for nonpayment of taxes on this occasion, twenty-two were owned by women, one belonged to the guardian of a woman or female minor, and six were part of the unsettled estates of deceased men, who ordinarily left the bulk of their holdings to their wives and children. In other words, women headed nearly half of the households that owed arrears in taxes and lost property as a result.[34]

At least two Virginia women employed the logic and rhetoric used by colonists during the imperial crisis to express resentment of what they deemed unfair and onerous taxes. In 1778, Hannah Lee Corbin, of Westmoreland County—the widowed Baptist sister of Richard Henry Lee, a prominent member of the Continental Congress—complained to her brother that "widows are not represented, and that being temporary possessors of their estates ought not to be liable to the tax" recently imposed on property-holding Virginians.[35] In two remarkable letters to Governor Thomas Jefferson and his successor Thomas Nelson, Mary Willing Byrd, of Westover, even more pointedly invoked the Revolutionary dictum of "no taxation without representation." The widow of William Byrd III, a member of the colonial governor's Council whose debts and political indecision led him to commit suicide in January 1777, Mary Willing Byrd counted both patriots and loyalists among her family and friends, though she maintained that "no action of my life has been inconsistent with the character of a virtuous American." Byrd characterized herself as a property-holder, taxpayer, and stepmother of a Continental soldier "who had lost his life in the Service of my Country." More important, however, she protested, "I have paid my taxes and have not been Personally, or Virtually represented" because

Mary Willing Byrd, by Matthew Pratt, ca. 1773. This Philadelphia native married William Byrd III and went to live with him on his Virginia plantation. William Byrd committed suicide in 1777, leaving his wife to protect his estate and her many children from armies on both sides. Mary Willing Byrd disliked paying taxes to support the war effort, in part because she resented women's lack of political representation. *Courtesy of the Library of Virginia.*

of her sex. Lacking the right to vote or other means by which to influence government policies, she declared, "my property is taken from me and I have no redress."[36]

Taxes, inflation, and other economic problems became secondary considerations for most Virginians, however, as the war entered its third and final phase, known as the Southern Campaign. After fighting the Americans to a virtual stalemate in the Middle Atlantic states, the British decided to invade the southern states, where they hoped to find support among white loyalists, restive slaves, and Native Americans. Although the British vastly overestimated the extent to which local whites and Indians would flock to the king's standard, thousands of slaves sought freedom by joining the British, as they had several years earlier in response to Dunmore's proclamation. The British seizure of Savannah in December 1778 initiated a military campaign that, after nearly three years of sustained warfare in the southern states, ended triumphantly for Americans and their French allies with the decisive surrender at Yorktown in October 1781.

Wartime violence returned to coastal Virginia in spring 1779 with the arrival near Norfolk of a fleet of twenty-eight ships carrying 1,800 enemy soldiers. Sailing up the Elizabeth River, the British plundered Portsmouth and burned Suffolk, leaving many homeless. Although atrocities against women and other civilians appear not to have been widespread during this engagement, the *Virginia Gazette* reported an instance in which four members of the invaders' party visited the home of one Nansemond County woman, where they "plundered her money, clothes, and most valuable furniture," and tore her rings off her fingers. Patriot women and their children tried to escape the area on foot, though the *Gazette* informed its readers that enemy soldiers "forced three young Ladies on board their ships," where they presumably were sexually violated, noting that one of the Portsmouth victims was a young woman "on the point of being married."[37]

Although few people said so explicitly, most women knew that the presence of soldiers brought the possibility of rape or sexual assault. That so few rape victims came forward to seek justice continued to be less a measure of the actual frequency of rape than a consequence of cultural norms that, even in peacetime, afforded rape victims little recourse in the courts or elsewhere. Indeed, contemporary accounts of real and fictional rapes portrayed the sexual

The able Doctor, or, America Swallowing the Bitter Draught, 1774. In this cartoon, a female representing America is forced to drink tea by the British prime minister, Frederick, Lord North, while the libertine John Montagu, earl of Sandwich, plans his sexual assault as others look on. *Courtesy of the Library of Congress, Prints and Photographs Division, LC-DIG-ppmsca-19467.*

assault of women primarily as a crime against the rights and reputations of their fathers, husbands, and brothers. Hence the significance of noting that one of the Portsmouth women who was forced to board the British vessel was betrothed, making her imminent ruin a violation of her fiancé's right to exclusive sexual access to his prospective wife.[38]

Revolutionary Americans also conceived of rape metaphorically, as in the well-known political cartoon in which America (represented by a forcibly restrained and obviously vulnerable female) was abused by leering male Britons, one of whom lifted her skirt (implying his intent to ravish her) while another force-fed her dutied tea. While such images clearly recognized the possibility that real women could be—and often were—raped in times of political and military confrontations, those who created and consumed these cartoons were less interested in the violation of women's bodies than in the infringement of men's rights.[39]

Probably more common than rape and in some respects nearly equally ruinous was the seduction of girls and young women by seemingly honorable soldiers. Unscrupulous men preyed on vulnerable females even in peacetime, but splendid uniforms, impending danger, and the constant movement of armies in wartime created more opportunities for illicit sex, with less risk for the men involved. One instance of wartime seduction and betrayal involved Rachel Warrington, the orphaned daughter of a prominent Yorktown family, who bore a child out-of-wedlock in 1782 while living in Williamsburg. The child's father was Donatien Marie Joseph de Vimeur, vicomte de Rochambeau, son of the commander of the French land forces in America, who seduced and impregnated Warrington and then returned home alone after the war was over. Though mortified, Warrington's wealthy aunt accepted and provided for her niece's son. Neither Rochambeau's wealth nor his reputation suffered as a result of his seduction of Rachel Warrington, who paid dearly for her transgression. Her eventual marriage to a poor and obscure man reflected her public disgrace and the limited options available to unchaste women, whatever their social origins.[40]

On the frontier, where military engagements often pitted patriots against local loyalists and Native Americans, the line between soldiers and noncombatants, battlefield and homefront, was even more thinly drawn. Social exchanges and violent confrontations between soldiers and civilians were common. In some instances, Virginia women joined the fighting on the frontier to defend themselves and their homes. The widow Anne Trotter became a local legend (usually remembered as Mad Anne Bailey) in western Virginia for supposedly fighting Indians who had allied with the British and reporting their movements to white settlers. Another westerner, Betty Zane, helped to defend Fort Wheeling from an Indian attack in 1782.[41]

In October 1780, British forces under Major General Alexander Leslie returned to coastal Virginia, but by early in 1781 the fighting had also spread to the interior, as Brigadier General Benedict Arnold, the turncoat who was now an officer in the British army, arrived in Richmond, the new state capital. The British invasion of central Virginia brought war-related violence to large numbers of the state's civilians for the first time since 1776. Some families fled their homes in anticipation of enemy raids, while others braved the onslaught in hope of protecting their families' property. Widow Mary Willing Byrd, who lived with her children and stepchildren at Westover, her plantation in Charles

City County, was poorly treated by soldiers on both sides. In January 1781, British troops under Arnold, whose wife was Byrd's cousin, commandeered Byrd's house and confined her and her family to its upper floors. The troops knocked down her fences and butchered her milk cows, and when they left, they took forty-nine slaves, three horses, and two ferryboats with them. In February, American troops, who suspected Byrd of aiding the British, arrived at Westover, where they seized her papers, made her entire family prisoners in their home, and, she later asserted angrily, inflicted "*savage* treatment" on them. Another wealthy widow, Mary Marshall Tabb Bolling, of Petersburg, was more fortunate. She persuaded the British to return her slaves and let her keep her warehouses and her gristmill, though they burned her tobacco crop, confiscated several horses, and seized her house when they occupied Petersburg briefly in 1781.[42]

Unlike Bolling and Byrd, who chose to remain at home to protect their property, other patriot women and their families fled the approaching enemy. The wartime odyssey of Elizabeth Jaquelin Ambler and her family took them initially from their hometown of York to Richmond, where Betsey's father, a prosperous merchant and government official, chaired Virginia's Board of Trade. When the British assault on Richmond was imminent, the family traveled from there to Louisa County, then to Charlottesville, and then back again to Louisa. Ambler found wartime conditions both horrifying and inspiring. "What an alarming crisis is this," the sixteen-year-old Betsey wrote to a friend from Louisa County in 1781. "War in itself, however distant, is indeed terrible, but when brought to our very doors—when those we most love are personally engaged in it, when our friends and neighbors are exposed to its ravages, when we know assuredly that without sacrificing many dear to us as our own lives, our country must remain subject to British tyranny, the reflection is indeed overwhelming."[43]

Similarly, the wife and children of Governor Thomas Jefferson spent the first half of 1781 moving from place to place to escape the advancing enemy. In January, rumors of the planned British attack on Richmond led Governor Jefferson to send his wife and their three young children to Tuckahoe, the nearby home of his friend, Thomas Mann Randolph. The next day, the family moved to Fine Creek, a Powhatan County property that Jefferson had inherited from his father. The family then returned to Richmond, where they mourned the death of its youngest member, the infant Lucy Elizabeth, in April, before again leaving the capital. In May and June, Martha Jefferson and her children lived in at least six different places—Richmond, Tuckahoe, Monticello, Blenheim and Enniscorthy (both plantations in Albemarle County), and Poplar Forest (roughly sixty miles from Monticello in Bedford County)—sometimes with and sometimes without the governor.[44]

The British invasion also mobilized black Virginians, though generally for different reasons. For example, when the Jeffersons and other politically prominent patriot families fled Richmond in 1781, they left most of their slaves there, perhaps hoping that they would protect their homes and property from British depredations. Within ten minutes of Arnold's arrival, recalled Isaac Jefferson, a young slave who had stayed at the governor's residence, "not a white man was to be seen in Richmond." When the British withdrew from Richmond, ten of the Jeffersons' slaves left with them. The three women, two men, and five children who left included Ursula, one of the family's most valued domestic servants, who, with her husband and son, attached themselves to the British in hopes of attaining their freedom. They accompanied the army to Yorktown, where, according to Isaac Jefferson, the British "treated them mighty well," though American forces eventually recaptured them and returned them to slavery at Monticello. Some of George Washington's slaves were more fortunate. A group of Mount Vernon slaves, including three young women, escaped with a British raiding party on the Potomac River in April 1781. One of the young women, Deborah, went first to New York and then resettled in Nova Scotia as a free woman after the war was over.[45]

In October 1781, the final and decisive major battle of the War of Independence occurred at Yorktown, where some 8,000 British, Hessian, and loyalist troops and the camp followers that accompanied their army occupied and fortified the peninsula, which they sought to defend against a juggernaut of American and French troops—including a naval force—totaling more than 18,000 men. When the battle was over, the British were defeated, and the town itself was in ruins. When young Mildred Smith returned home to Yorktown after the British surrender, she was shocked to see that "more than half our much loved little Town is intirely destroyed, and many of those elegant Edifices that to our youthful minds appeared magnificently beautiful are leveled with the dust [and] others that remain are so mutilated . . . as to grieve one's very soul."[46]

While Smith and other displaced patriots made their way home after the surrender, escaped slaves crowded onto departing British ships, hoping to thwart the efforts of victorious patriots to retrieve their slave property. In all, thousands of black Virginians escaped bondage during the Revolution, though many of those who fled to the British died of disease at Yorktown or elsewhere before they secured their freedom. Meanwhile, white loyalists who had remained in Virginia during the war had to decide whether to abandon the state or finally to accept defeat and acknowledge the legitimacy of the Revolutionary government. Loyalist families who had stayed in the commonwealth during the war generally remained afterward and made their peace with the new regime once it was over.[47]

By contrast, families and individuals who chose exile or active service to the Crown after 1776 were not welcome in Virginia in the postwar era. Sometimes they and their heirs risked losing significant amounts of property as a result of their political choices. After the merchant Archibald McCall left Virginia in 1775, following his daughters to Scotland, state authorities confiscated his Essex County estate. McCall's mother-in-law, Elizabeth Flood, fought valiantly to regain the property for her granddaughter Catharine McCall, maintaining that the conduct of her son-in-law had been "manly, liberal, [and] paternal," and that he had sent his daughters abroad in 1773 only because he had "resolved to give them an Education which might add dignity to their fortune." Flood wanted her granddaughter to return home, but she contended that "the tenderness of her age and sex" necessitated paternal protection during the potentially hazardous trans-Atlantic voyage. Therefore, in 1782, Flood petitioned the legislature to allow Archibald McCall to accompany fifteen-year-old Catharine to Virginia, where she might reclaim her patrimony, which her father could oversee until she reached adulthood. The legislators rejected Flood's plea that they "befriend the youth, the innocence and weakness of a young Virginian of the fair sex," though Archibald McCall was allowed to retain his property after he returned to Virginia in 1783.[48]

Wives of exiled loyalists who remained in Virginia after the departure of their spouses faced the biggest dilemma of all as the war came to a close. When Humphrey Roberts, a prominent loyalist merchant, left Norfolk for Britain in 1776, his wife Ann Roberts stayed. Humphrey Roberts returned briefly in 1783 but soon went back to England. His wife did not go with him. Although the couple remained legally married, they lived on separate continents. Other

America Triumphant and Britannia in Distress, 1782. Female figures often represented nations or ideals—such as Liberty—in Revolutionary-era iconography. Here, Britannia, on the left, weeps for the loss of American trade; a triumphant America, on the right, offers an olive branch. Some historians argue that generic female figures were ideal representations of political values in part because contemporaries assumed that real women could not be political. *Courtesy of the Library of Congress, Prints and Photographs Division, LC-DIG-ppmsca-24328.*

wives of exiles chose differently. Margaret Goodrich, who had lived with her children on a portion of her husband's property in Nansemond County while he served the British as a privateer, reunited with him in Great Britain, where they settled as a family in the 1780s.[49]

Meanwhile, jubilant patriots marked their great triumph with balls, parades, and other festivities that had been rare in wartime. Two months after the American victory at Yorktown, Mary Burwell observed that Williamsburg was the site of many weddings and that, for the first time in many years, students at the College of William and Mary staged a play for the town's inhabitants. By the spring of 1782, the dancing master had returned even to remote Berkeley County, after a two-year absence.[50]

In celebrating their victory, Virginians revived the public balls and dinners of the colonial era, but they made these events more inclusive to accommodate the Revolution's somewhat more egalitarian political and social values. Although African Americans and poor white Virginians did not participate in these celebrations, at least one observer believed that "all ranks and sexes" joined the "elegant and plentiful" celebration at Spotsylvania Court House in April 1783 to commemorate the preliminary treaty of peace between the United States and Great Britain. Organizers of some celebratory public balls determined the order of dancers by lot, instead of by social rank, as had been customary before the Revolution. Later that year, when people in Richmond held a public ball to celebrate the official peace treaty a shoemaker's daughter drew the honor of dancing first. Although most who attended the ball approved of this democratic innovation, the wife and daughters of Governor Benjamin Harrison, who were members of an old and prominent gentry family, reportedly resented their loss of precedence.[51]

In 1783, it remained to be seen how Virginians—and Americans in general— would sort out the democratic implications of a revolution that had been inspired in part by a manifesto, penned by a slaveowning Virginia gentleman, that boldly declared "that all men are created equal, that they are endowed by their Creator with certain unalienable Rights." Virginia women of all social ranks had participated in various ways in the Revolutionary movement, and many had made profound sacrifices. In Virginia, as elsewhere, the Revolution had led to important changes in political institutions, legal codes, and other areas that tended to enhance the rights and liberties of white men. Despite this reformist political climate, however, few Americans systematically addressed the issue of how, if at all, the ideals and experiences of the Revolution would affect women's rights, identities, and roles.

Many Virginia women undoubtedly emerged from the Revolutionary era with a new political consciousness. The hardships of the war years, in particular, had led Hannah Lee Corbin and Mary Willing Byrd to question, albeit privately, the fact that even property-owning women lacked a political voice in the new republican regime. Other women expressed themselves publicly through both words and actions. One signal development was the participation of some elite Virginia women in a fund-raising campaign to benefit poorly supplied Continental soldiers. Following the example of prominent women in Pennsylvania, New Jersey, and Maryland, and responding to a personal appeal from Martha Washington, Martha Wayles Skelton Jefferson wrote letters during her husband's governorship, urging Virginia gentlewomen to support the efforts of the Philadelphia-based Ladies Association to raise money to support the troops. "I under take with chearfulness," she averred, "the duty of furnishing to my country women an opportunity of proving that they also participate of those virtuous feelings" of patriotism. This initiative set an important precedent for women organizing collectively to pursue a public agenda. Perhaps in part because of this precedent, women's associations of various sorts became increasingly common in the post-Revolutionary era.[52]

Wartime circumstances also prompted women to interact directly with government officials to an extent unprecedented before 1776. Because women could not vote, petitioning was the only formal political channel through which they could address their governors or legislative assemblies. The right to petition, which assumed an unequal relationship between the individual or group seeking favor and the official empowered to grant it, was medieval in origin and came to Virginia with its English colonizers. Although Virginia women had the right to petition both the governor and the legislature in the colonial period, they were far more likely to do so during the Revolution, when more women lived on their own and when many faced unusual war-related problems. Like their counterparts elsewhere, Virginia women petitioned for relief from taxes and other financial obligations. Others, including some members of the Pamunkey and Mattaponi tribes who resided in King William County and whose husbands had fought in the Revolution, sought to recover the back wages of soldiers and other public debts. Women sometimes also requested official intervention in property disputes. Wives and widows of loyalists appealed to the legislators for leniency toward male loyalists and preservation of at least a portion of their estates.[53]

Women's petitions were often deferential and self-effacing, but the mere act of petitioning led them to venture into an alien political world. Unlike Hannah

To the Honourable the Speaker and Gentlemen of the House of Delegates

The Petition of the unfortunate Mary Webley late a Resident of the Borough of Norfolk humbly sheweth.

That your Petitioner on new Years Day last, while suckling her Child the youngest of three now dependent on her, had her Leg broken by a Cannon Ball from the Liverpool Man of War

That her Husband from the Loss of his right Arm upwards of twenty Years since is scarcely able to maintain himself.

That She hath at present no Ways or Means to procure Shelter or acquire Subsistence for herself and miserable little Children, her Husband and Self having had all their Effects totally destroyed in the Flames of Norfolk from whence they have been drove in most distressful Circumstances

Therefore prays this Honourable House will on Consideration of the Premises grant unto her such Aid and Relief as in their justice and mercy shall seem right. And your Petr. &c. &c. &c.

Petition of Mary Webley, 1776. Petitioning was the most common way for women to interact formally with their government. In this petition, Mary Webley asked the legislature for relief after her house was destroyed during the bombardment of Norfolk. *Courtesy of the Library of Virginia.*

Lee Corbin and Mary Willing Byrd, female petitioners did not dramatically assert their liberties or rights. But while Corbin and Byrd expressed their potentially radical ideals in private letters, the petitioners' requests were public and some, in their own way, were truly unprecedented. In June 1777, a Northumberland County African American named Rachel petitioned Virginia lawmakers on behalf of herself and her infant daughter, also named Rachel, in order to prevent Zachariah Barr from keeping them enslaved, despite the fact that Barr's deceased brother had emancipated both mother and daughter in his will and had set aside a twenty-five-acre plot for their benefit. In 1783, Ann Rose and her daughter Margaret, both of whom also were freed by their master's will, sought the legislature's formal verification of their freedom. Although the Halifax County Court already had recognized the women as free, they worried that "Doubts have arisen, with respect to the Legality of the order of the said Court" and therefore they asked the legislators to "Enact a Law that shall secure to us our Freedom." Upholding the validity of white men's wills, the General Assembly granted both petitions.[54]

Petitioning signified women's growing awareness of their relationship to their government. By definition subordinate, petitioners were nonetheless members of political society and among those whose interests political leaders ideally protected and represented. The republican rhetoric of the Revolution inspired some free women—both white and black—to prod Virginia legislators to take that responsibility seriously. At the same time, however, these women clearly were not citizens of the Republic in the same sense as men—or, more specifically, propertied white men. In Virginia and elsewhere, American republicans identified citizenship with independence, but both law and custom continued to presume that females were necessarily dependent.[55]

Despite their ambiguous public status, however, some women pursued their interests and showed an enhanced political consciousness by their involvement in the increasingly partisan politics of the post-Revolutionary era. In the 1780s, Virginians and Americans generally divided over whether the United States should have a stronger central government than that which existed under the Articles of Confederation, with proponents of change emerging victorious with the ratification of the United States Constitution. Within a few years of the installation of the new government, partisan divisions emerged both in the Congress and among the general population, pitting Federalist followers of George Washington and Alexander Hamilton against the Republican Party of Thomas Jefferson and James Madison.

Virginia women participated in the vigorously partisan politics of the early American Republic. Some were "female politicians" who actively championed their own party and disparaged its opponents. "I am becoming an outrageous politician, perfectly *federal*[ist]," reported Eleanor Parke Custis, Martha Washington's granddaughter, in 1798. After the Federalists lost the election of 1800, Custis and her friends wore white plumes to balls and other public functions to show their opposition to President Thomas Jefferson and their continuing loyalty to the defeated Federalist Party. In 1801, Federalist Elizabeth Gamble, of Richmond, complained that the Jeffersonians had "by Intrigue, & Falshoods, raised their *Idol* to a station, of which He is . . . very unworthy." At the opposite end of the political spectrum, the Randolph sisters, of Cumberland County, addressed their correspondents as "Citizen" to show their support for Jefferson and the Republicans, who sympathized with the French revolutionaries who had adopted that title to signify a new political equality. Years later, in 1815, Nancy Randolph, who was still an ardent Jeffersonian (though she had married a prominent Federalist), initiated an ultimately unsuccessful letter-writing campaign to prevent her anti-Jefferson kinsman John Randolph of Roanoke from regaining his seat in Congress.[56]

Some women clearly cared deeply about partisan politics and the outcome of elections in the early republican era. Elizabeth House Trist, Jefferson's Albemarle County neighbor and frequent guest at Monticello, was a committed partisan who proclaimed that "no event of a publick nature ever afforded me half the *pleasure*" as her friend's elevation to the presidency in 1801. "After felicitateing my Country on its choice believeing that we shall now have a fair experiment of What a Republican Administration can effect as to the happiness of the people," Trist went on boldly to warn Jefferson of continuing Federalist "machinations" that might undermine his presidency. Yet even Trist acknowledged the limits of women's political reach. "The only privilege our sex injoy is that of freely communicating our sentiments," she wrote. Although the opinionated Trist showed little restraint in confiding her political sentiments to Jefferson, she also slyly—and, one suspects, only half-seriously—distanced herself from her own strident (and seemingly unfeminine) political rhetoric. "We [women] are generally thought of little consiquence in the Political World," she observed, adding, "but if we are incompetent to decide properly on these subjects, we certainly can revibrate the opinion of others."[57]

Politically conscious women were avid consumers and purveyors of political news and information. Fanny Bassett Washington relished reading the weekly newspapers at Mount Vernon. Elizabeth Preston Madison, who lived in western Virginia, eagerly awaited the arrival of the papers from Richmond. "I . . . dislike living in the World & knowing so little of, or about it," she explained to her brother, who sent her "News Papers" from the capital. Women whose husbands held political office often pumped them for the latest news. Dolley Payne Todd Madison, who normally remained in Washington while her husband served first as secretary of state and then as president, was "extremely anxious to hear . . . what is going on in the Cabinet" when she left the capital to visit Philadelphia in 1805. The shrewd and personable Dolley Madison, in turn, often shared with her spouse her own political information, which she mostly gained via her frequent social interactions with politically influential women and men in the nation's capital.[58]

Dolley Madison, who is generally regarded as America's prototypical "First Lady," was not an average Virginia woman, but her remarkable public career as the president's wife suggests that gender profoundly shaped the political activities and influence of even the most elite women in post-Revolutionary America. Unlike men who may have sought political power to advance their own personal policies or interests, Dolley Madison used her influence primarily to promote the policies of her husband and his party. She used traditionally feminine rites of sociability, which she adapted to post-Revolutionary republican circumstances, to cultivate political connections and influence. While her male contemporaries delivered orations, wrote newspaper essays, and even fought duels to conduct political business and shape public opinion, Dolley Madison pursued the same objectives by orchestrating visits, dinner parties, and polite drawing room conversations. Even so, some of James Madison's political adversaries criticized his wife's social leadership and her undeniably political activities. In time, men in both parties grew increasingly wary of women's partisanship and of female politicians generally.[59]

Unlike Dolley Madison, most other politically conscious Virginia women inhabited the fringes of political life. After 1776, Virginia law still required ownership of either twenty-five acres "with a house and plantation" or one hundred acres of unimproved land to qualify to vote, thereby limiting suffrage to roughly 60 percent of the state's white men, which meant that a significant minority of Virginia's white women belonged to families in which even the male household head could not vote. Even nonvoting white men, however, might actively participate in civic celebrations, the most important of which occurred on the Fourth of July to commemorate American independence. By the 1790s, militia parades had replaced more elitist balls as the dominant civic rituals in Virginia and elsewhere. While women had been equal participants in balls and other genteel public celebrations, these new republican civic rituals literally relegated them to the sidelines, where they lined the streets as passive witnesses to these patriotic public spectacles. Nevertheless, women's presence was essential to the central message of this militarized performance of citizenship, which showcased patriotic, brave, independent, and vigorous male citizen-soldiers protecting virtuous but vulnerable women as part of their staunch defense of republican liberty.[60]

Virginia men sometimes acknowledged the significance of the presence of female spectators on civic occasions. One observer described a "numerous concourse of ladies" whose presence at Petersburg's Independence Day festivities in 1808 "infused an additional joy in the feelings of every citizen and soldier, and emphatically impressed on their minds this truth, that in the hour of danger and distress, it is on THEM, the virtuous fair reposed for their safety and protection." Similarly, in January 1814, at a festival planned to celebrate Petersburg's "gallant VOLUNTEERS" who had mobilized during the War of 1812, participants choreographed their movements to dramatize this ideal of vigorous men protecting the town's vulnerable and appreciative women. After the militia paraded, the soldiers and other male "Citizens" arranged themselves into a protective circle "around the Ladies" who had gathered to hear the day's patriotic oration.[61]

Whatever its effects on women's political consciousness, with the very significant exception of those African American women who became free via escape or manumission, the Revolution brought Virginia women no new civil or legal rights. The libertarian ideals of the Revolution led some prominent Virginians to question the acceptability of slavery and helped lead to the enactment of a statute, in 1782, that allowed slaveholders to emancipate their bondpeople.[62] Legislators, however, never seriously considered changing women's legal status. Barred from voting, sitting on juries, and serving in the militia, Virginia women lacked the chief rights and responsibilities of republican citizenship. Perhaps more important, the English common law doctrine of coverture remained in force, despite Thomas Jefferson's extensive revision of Virginia's colonial legal code to make it more consistent with the political values of a now-independent commonwealth. Indeed, one of Jefferson's most significant reforms, the abolition of entail and primogeniture, by which he aimed to make inheritance more equal among male siblings, may have diminished the property that daughters from wealthy families inherited in the post-Revolutionary era. In 1848, New York became the first state to enact legislation allowing married women to own and control property—thereby eradicating coverture—but Virginia wives did not receive such rights until after the Civil War.[63]

Although laws governing marriage generally did not change as a result of the Revolution, the ideals and circumstances of the Revolutionary era may have contributed indirectly to some Virginians' willingness to consider divorce as a remedy for intolerable unions in certain rare instances. In the colonial period, civil divorce was available only in New England, but most states grappled with the issue of divorce during and after the Revolution, with most northern states enacting general statutes by 1800 that codified permissible grounds for divorce and the procedures for requesting one. In Virginia, legislators did not enact a general divorce statute until 1827, but individuals had begun to raise the issue decades earlier.

One notable early effort to dissolve a Virginia marriage via legislative enactment occurred in 1744, when both houses of the colonial legislature enacted a special statute in response to a petition from Susannah Sanders Cooper, of New Kent County. Cooper's husband had abandoned her more than twenty years earlier and since his departure she had worked as a tavern keeper and merchant, accumulating an estate that included both land and slaves. Cooper petitioned the legislature for a legal separation from her husband so that she could control her property and shield it from his creditors. The legislators granted her petition, though the statute recognizing Cooper's separate estate never formally took effect because it did not receive the approval of the King's Privy Council, the final step in the process of colonial law-making.[64]

The earliest-known effort to procure an all-out divorce in Virginia, which occurred decades later, proceeded from vastly different circumstances and premises. Early in the 1770s, lawyer Thomas Jefferson prepared to argue before the colonial legislature in favor of what would have been the first divorce in Virginia history. He represented Dr. James Blair of Williamsburg, whose nineteen-month marriage to Kitty Eustace, he claimed, had never been consummated. In the absence of explicitly defined grounds for legal dissolution of a marriage, Jefferson invoked the Enlightenment ideals that were so widely accepted by colonial gentlemen and that he himself later used to justify American independence. Jefferson based his assertion of the "liberty of divorce" on a Lockean contractual theory that deemed the origins of civil marriage analogous to those of civil government. In both instances, he maintained, partnerships were freely joined and thus might be dissolved when they ceased to protect the rights of their constituents. Jefferson's client died while he was preparing his case, so the General Assembly never heard these arguments. Since Virginia's legislature granted no petition for divorce until 1802—allowing a white man to divorce a white woman who bore a mulatto child—it seems unlikely that Jefferson would have won his case.[65]

When post-Revolutionary Virginians petitioned the legislature for divorce, unlike Jefferson, they invoked prevailing gender stereotypes rather than social contracts and theoretical natural rights. In 1786, Susanah Wersley of Hanover County, the first Virginian known to have petitioned for a formal legislative dissolution of her marriage, described herself as an innocent victim of seduction whose utter ruin occurred in the wider context of the danger and disruption of the American Revolution. Wersley's story had all the drama of a popular sentimental novel. In 1781, she informed the legislators, her family had offered lodging to John Wersley, a sick soldier who claimed to be an officer from North Carolina. While John Wersley recovered, he courted Susanah, and she fell in love with him. They married the following spring, but he abandoned her within a month. Five years later, Susanah Wersley unsuccessfully sought a divorce on the grounds that her husband had been "actuated by a principal of convinience and deception alone in Marr[y]ing" her. Like many fictional sentimental heroines, Susanah Wersley had been seduced and deceived by a dashing and seemingly honorable man and was left alone to face the consequences.[66]

Although the Revolutionary experience did not impel legislators to grant divorce petitions or even to devise more efficient procedures for those seeking divorces, Virginians continued to submit divorce petitions in the post-Revolutionary era. Susanah Wersley was the first of eight women who sought divorces between 1786 and 1800; twelve Virginia men and two couples also filed divorce petitions during this period. Despite the expense and inconvenience of the petitioning process, in all 242 women, 218 men, and 5 couples submitted a total of 583 petitions through 1851, when the courts finally assumed jurisdiction over divorce cases in the commonwealth. Roughly one-third of these applicants eventually obtained a divorce by special legislative acts, most of which granted what amounted to a legal separation—known as a divorce *a mensa et thoro*—which allowed spouses to maintain separate households and property while prohibiting them from remarrying. While men sometimes obtained divorces if their wives committed adultery, legislators were most likely to grant women's petitions if they had been physically abused by their spouses. Wives were expected to be chaste first and foremost, and husbands were supposed to protect their wives and other dependents. Virginia legislators reluctantly granted divorces in rare instances when spouses radically deviated from these prescribed gender roles.[67]

Post-Revolutionary Virginians also continued to use less formal means to resolve the problems posed by unhappy marriages, as they had done throughout the colonial era. As one historian has noted, unsanctioned separation agreements amounted to "a kind of do-it-yourself divorce" at a time when legal divorce was nearly impossible to obtain. Spouses entering into separation agreements remained legally married, but they contracted to renounce their rights to each other's property and services and to act as if they had never wed. Occasionally, women who sought independence from incompatible or abusive spouses tried to obtain formal separation rulings from the courts in order to regain the property rights they lost on marrying, but this strategy was not always successful. In 1792, Elizabeth Pinckard Yerby turned to Lancaster's county court when she sought a legal separation from her husband, having left his plantation the previous year. Yerby publicly accused her husband of battery and also of having a slave mistress and several mixed-race children, but her neighbors judged her sharp tongue and supposedly bad housekeeping as harshly as her husband's shortcomings. The court denied Yerby's request for a formal separation and the resulting recognition of her right to control her own property and thus to live independently of her estranged husband.[68]

As Yerby's case suggests, the Revolution did not weaken gender conventions that idealized women as modest, moral, and nurturing, and often penalized those who behaved otherwise. In language that revealed how little the Revolution had affected his thinking about women's proper role and status, Thomas Jefferson enjoined his own newly married daughter to embrace what he saw as an appropriately subservient domestic role. "Your new condition will call for abundance of little sacrifices," he wrote to Martha Jefferson Randolph in 1790, adding that the "happiness of your life depends now on the continuing to please a single person," namely her new husband. Many Virginia women probably took such admonitions seriously. Elizabeth Foote Washington, of Fairfax County, believed that most men who were "fond of going abroad" to gamble and carouse were driven to vice by their overbearing wives. Washington resolved that her own husband "should court my company," and she vowed "never to hold disputes" with him in order to please him and to conform to religious precepts that, from Eve's time on, taught woman that "her husband should rule over her."[69]

Outside the household, there was only one arena in which Virginia women arguably wielded more acknowledged influence after the Revolution than they had during the colonial era. The Revolution transformed Virginia's religious landscape as a result of the enactment of the Statute for Religious Freedom in 1786. Written by Jefferson and supported by an alliance of secular-minded liberal reformers and also by Baptists and other evangelicals, the statute dismantled the Anglican establishment and freed Virginians of all legal disabilities arising from their religious affiliations (or lack thereof) and eliminated discriminatory church taxes. For Virginia women, disestablishment had two important consequences. First, though still overwhelmingly Protestant, Virginia's religious landscape became increasingly diverse, with the biggest growth occurring in the evangelical denominations—notably the Baptists and Methodists—which were more accepting of female activism and influence, even as they became more conventionally male-dominated in the post-Revolutionary era. Second, the severing of ties between Church and State resulted in a decline in the public influence of the erstwhile Anglican establishment—which became the Protestant Episcopal Church—that, in turn, led men to invest their energies in other institutions, especially political parties. As newly politicized men increasingly embraced the creeds and rituals

of partisanship, women assumed primary responsibility for promoting piety and religion, both at home and in society.[70]

In the end, then, the effects of the Revolution on Virginia women were mostly ambiguous or negligible. No one systematically pondered the status of enslaved or Native American women, whose lot was presumed to be essentially unchanged as a result of the Revolution. For white women, especially those from elite and middling families, there was a mixed message. Most Americans envisioned patriotism and public spirit as masculine virtues, while they still deemed private moral traits—such as piety, modesty, and chastity—the chief attributes of virtuous women. Yet women exhibited patriotism during the Revolution, and, though their contributions were often forgotten, Virginians occasionally revived the specter of female patriotism in times of crisis during the post-Revolutionary era.[71]

In 1807, when Congress enacted a commercial embargo to punish warring European powers for harassing American shippers, patriotic women like Martha Jefferson Randolph responded by increasing domestic production of cloth, as their mothers had done in the 1770s. In 1808, the "ladies" of Richmond and of Goochland County wore dresses made of homespun to their local Fourth of July festivities. Lamenting the seeming decline of public spirit on the eve of a second war with Britain, one Virginia patriot mused hopefully that the *virtues of this country are with our women,* adding that *the only remaining hope of the resurrection of the genius and character of the nation rests with them.*[72]

CHAPTER 3

"The Uncertainty of Our Prospects": Antebellum Perils and Possibilities

The worlds of Virginia women changed dramatically early in the nineteenth century, during the decades that historians, with the benefit of hindsight, have come to call the antebellum era. Between 1800 and 1860, the state's population nearly doubled as a result of natural increase and immigration, despite the fact that thousands of white and black Virginians left the commonwealth. Although it remained overwhelmingly rural, Virginia developed a network of towns and cities, the largest of which, Richmond, had a population of more than 27,000 by midcentury. Virginia was home to factories and mines, as well as plantations and farms. Reflecting the spirit of religious and secular improvement that swept the nation in the antebellum era, the Old Dominion also boasted a growing array of newspapers, schools, churches, and charitable associations.

For Virginia women, the nineteenth century's early decades brought new opportunities, which paradoxically co-existed with both old legal and customary constraints and increasingly strident assertions of patriarchal power. On the one hand, moralists and social critics throughout the United States idealized women's devotion to—and isolation within—the domestic sphere, and Virginians and other southerners particularly emphasized the need for all women to submit to the authority of white men. On the other hand, female Virginians in the antebellum era were far more likely than their foremothers to attend school, work for wages, write for publication, and engage in other public activities. Though few Virginia women openly defied the existing order, many tacitly stretched the bounds of respectability, invoking widely held assumptions about female virtue to justify an impressive range of unconventional activities.

Changes in the lives of Virginia women were fundamentally rooted in the social, economic, and demographic trends of the post-Revolutionary decades. Perhaps the most notable of those trends was geographic mobility, which began with the loyalist exodus during and after the Revolution and continued as post-Revolutionary Virginians left home in search of fertile land or urban opportunities. Virginians were on the move in the half-century after Yorktown. While some women clearly embraced the prospect of beginning life anew elsewhere, more resisted the disruption of cherished family relationships and communities.

Although the movements of white and black Virginians are comparatively well-documented, those of Native Americans are more difficult to follow. In *Notes on the State of Virginia*, Thomas Jefferson claimed that there were few Native Americans left in Virginia by 1780, but his account focused primarily on the eastern Indians who constituted the remains of the once-powerful Powhatan paramount chiefdom and those who, like the Tuscarora, had left Virginia before the end of the colonial era. Moreover, perhaps because whites thought of Native Americans primarily as obstacles to be conquered, Jefferson was mainly interested in counting Indian men as potential warriors, so his estimates often neglected women entirely. The Pamunkey, Jefferson thus reported, "are reduced to about 10 or 12 men," while the Mattaponi had "three or four men only, and they have more negro than Indian blood in them." Worse off still were the Nottoway who, according to Jefferson, had no men left at all. "A few women," he wrote disparagingly, "constitute the remains of that tribe."[1]

Because diminishing numbers and intermarriage with white and black Virginians promoted real or imagined Indian assimilation into the social mainstream, Jefferson and others often underestimated or distorted Native

Americans' presence in the commonwealth. In 1808, a special commission reported that the Nottoway actually consisted of seventeen people, including six adults—three women and three men—none of whom was married to or cohabiting with another adult Indian. One of the Nottoway women was Wané Roonseraw, or Edith Turner, the tribal leader, whose life illustrates ways in which Native Americans strove to preserve their culture and traditions while in other respects adapting to white society. Turner embraced white agricultural methods and promoted the division of the Nottoway's dwindling Southampton County lands among individual Indians, becoming a prosperous farmer in her own right. As the only contemporary Nottoway known to have written a will, she disposed of her property on her death in 1838. But Turner also sought to preserve the Nottoway as a distinctive people by educating the next generation. She was both a foster mother and a teacher to tribal youth, whom she taught the Nottoway language and traditions, along with strategies for surviving in Virginia's white-controlled society.[2]

The seeming elasticity of Indian identities makes it difficult to find Native Americans even after 1860, when the federal census began to count them as a separate category. Nottoway population grew slowly, reaching twenty-seven by the mid-1830s, but the sale of their reservation lands, by their own request, led to their dispersal and disappearance, mostly into Southampton County's free black community. Other tribes who never had reservations, such as the Monacan in Amherst County, intermarried with white settlers and lived as whites. In 1860, the census reported no Native Americans living in either Southampton or Amherst Counties—the homes of the Nottoway and Monacan, respectively—though census-takers found twenty-two Indians in Southampton and twelve in Amherst in 1870. In all, the 1860 census listed only 112 Native Americans living in six Virginia counties; the next census found 229 Native Americans in the state, but their geographical distribution suggests errors in either the 1860 or 1870 figures, and possibly in both. Most notably, King William County, whose inhabitants are known to have included descendants of the Powhatan, was credited with 117 Native American residents—by far the most of any county—in 1870, though census-takers had reported not a single Indian there ten years previously.[3]

When Native Americans assimilated into the dominant white culture, women lost status and power. In communities where Indian women married white men, both families and tribal governments became more patriarchal. As Native Americans adopted more sedentary agricultural practices, women's work seemingly lost its economic significance and women themselves lost status and influence as a result. As Native Americans gradually converted to Christianity, their new religion, too, reflected white ideals of male dominance. For that reason, in many tribal cultures, women were far more likely than men to resist acculturation because they realized that white laws and customs would deprive them of both their land and their customary power.[4]

Although marriages and sexual liaisons between Native American and white Virginians produced mixed-race progeny whose racial identities also were ambiguous or even changing, African American women generally could not escape the legal and customary disabilities that white society imposed on them, even if they were mixed-race and free. Virginia, unlike the northern states, adopted no plan to bring about the statewide abolition of slavery during or after the Revolution, but influential Virginians who believed that slavery was immoral, antirepublican, and in some respects detrimental to the prosperity and safety of the state's white population spearheaded an effort that, in 1782, resulted in the passage of a statute making it easier for individual slaveholders to manumit their bondpeople. Some did so, especially in northern Virginia, where planters increasingly grew wheat instead of the more labor-intensive tobacco. Aside from the attainment of American independence and sovereignty, this challenge to slavery—however limited—in Virginia and elsewhere was arguably the Revolution's most significant long-term consequence.[5]

The combined effect of wartime escapes, emancipations, and natural increase was a tenfold rise—from roughly 2,000 to more than 20,000—in Virginia's free black population in the quarter-century following independence. By 1800, however, manumissions had waned, and in 1806 the General Assembly, wary of the destabilizing influence of free African Americans in their slave society, passed a law requiring freed slaves to leave the commonwealth within a year of their emancipation. Still, by 1850, Virginia's free black population was second only to that of Maryland. That year, the federal census recorded the presence of more than 54,000 free African Americans in Virginia, of whom 28,331 were female.[6]

Free black women resided in all but five Virginia counties, but they were most numerous in urban areas and in rural places where the black population

Registration of Lucy Jarvis as a free person, 19 June 1848. Born free in York County about 1801, Lucy Jarvis Pearson Scott registered with local authorities to obtain this paper, which she could use to certify her status as a free person if someone tried to enslave her. Beginning in 1793, the General Assembly, fearing the growth of the free black population, required free African Americans to register every three years with their local county courts. Lucy Jarvis Pearson Scott and her family later migrated to Canada. *Courtesy of the Library of Virginia.*

overall was large. In 1850, the twenty Virginia jurisdictions with the largest free black populations included four of the state's largest cities—Richmond, Norfolk, Petersburg, and Alexandria—and also eleven rural counties where African Americans constituted the majority of residents. These counties were located primarily in southeastern Virginia and on the Eastern Shore. While many free black women probably stayed in these rural areas to maintain ties with family and friends who remained enslaved, others moved to towns and cities in search of employment. In both town and country, free black women who acquired property were usually long-standing members of their communities.[7]

Free African American women typically worked in the most menial and poorly paid occupations. In Loudoun County, although some worked as seamstresses, nurses, or midwives, the overwhelming majority were either unskilled general laborers or laundresses, who earned only a few cents a day and occupied the lowest rung of the county's occupational hierarchy. Although cities and towns offered more opportunities for paid employment, there, too, free black women labored disproportionately in low-status and low-paying occupations. In Petersburg, some worked as seamstresses and others found employment in the city's tobacco factories beginning late in the 1820s, but most worked as laundresses or domestic servants. Most of Richmond's free black women were employed as house servants or cooks. Many of Norfolk's were working as laundresses by 1860. In Alexandria, free black women from neighboring counties found seasonal employment cleaning fish in the shacks of "Fishtown"—a harsh, dirty job that left them "covered from head to heels with scales," according to one observer.[8]

Although Virginia's free black women were less likely than their counterparts in Charleston or New Orleans to run their own businesses, some clearly did so, but most of these enterprises were probably precarious and marginal. For instance, an African American woman named Nancy sold "all fruits in their season" every day in the same spot outside a Richmond shop. Though she had "a monopoly" on fruit sales in that neighborhood, she was also vulnerable to harassment by white schoolboys who routinely stole her goods "without fear of arrest." A longtime resident of Richmond recalled that a "skilful mulatto woman" operated a far more substantial concern, a restaurant on Main Street that served oysters, steaks, and "other refreshments," but this establishment eventually closed, despite the "canvas backs, soras and other delicacies of the season that attracted many customers." In 1860, the census listed only two free black women in Norfolk who engaged in nondomestic work. One was a peddler, and the other was a shopkeeper.[9]

Although they were generally the poorest of poor, free black women were more likely than white women to own property and to be heads of households. Almost one-quarter of all free black households in antebellum Loudoun County had female heads; women headed nearly half of Norfolk's free African American households and more than half of both Richmond's and Petersburg's. This preponderance of female-headed households says more about the impact of slavery and racism on black families than it does about black women's success or power. Free African American women were more likely than white women to head households and control property because they were more likely to remain legally unwed and thus not subject to the law of coverture. Free black women were less likely to marry both because they slightly outnumbered free black men in most Virginia locales and because the law recognized neither interracial marriages nor unions between free persons and slaves. So, free black women who considered themselves married either to white men or to slaves retained their property rights because they were not wives in the eyes of the law. Other free black women, however, purposefully avoided marriage, which gave men control over both property and children, while arguably affording the wives of poor men few tangible benefits.[10]

In part because even free African American men earned so little, free black wives were far more likely to work for wages than their white counterparts. In 1860, at least one-quarter of Norfolk's free African American wives held paying jobs. Most were married to poorly paid unskilled laborers. The economic circumstances in these families—and the resulting division of labor—resembled that of Sally Roberts and her family, who lived in antebellum Richmond. Sally Roberts was the wife of a free black factory worker and mother of four young children. To supplement her husband's income, she worked as a laundress, besides caring for her children and her household, which included a young male boarder. Both Sally Roberts and her husband were illiterate and very poor. Despite their hard work, tax records indicate that the Roberts family owned no taxable property in 1860.[11]

While most free African Americans struggled to make ends meet, some accumulated enough capital to purchase the freedom of their enslaved loved ones. Men, who generally earned better wages, secured more emancipations overall, but free black women also played the role of liberator. Indeed, Jane Minor, of Petersburg, was probably Virginia's most successful black emancipator. Born a slave and known in slavery as Gensey Snow, Minor was an accomplished healer who was emancipated for her "most unexampled patience and attention in watching over the sick beds" of prominent citizens during a lethal epidemic in 1825. Minor's medical skills enabled her to prosper as a free woman, and by 1838 she had saved enough money to purchase the freedom of several slaves. Over two decades, she effected the emancipation of sixteen people—all women and children, who, as she must have known from her own experience, were especially vulnerable to the horrors of slavery.[12]

Emancipation, however, came with more strings attached after 1806, when the General Assembly required the newly freed to leave the state or obtain legislative permission to stay, and then again after 1831, when a major slave uprising led by Nat Turner resulted in more-rigorous enforcement of this statute and the imposition of draconian new restrictions on the rights of free African Americans. For example, when Caesar Hope, a free black barber whose clients included many state legislators, died in 1807, he left a will directing his executor to purchase his enslaved daughter, Judith Hope, and manumit her. Aware that emancipation would require Judith to leave the state, her mother purchased Judith, who then petitioned the legislature for permission to remain in Virginia if her mother freed her. "Your Petitioner is not insensible to the blessings of liberty," she explained in 1820, "but to be driven even for this great possession to a separation from every friend and natural connexion upon earth, to sunder every habit and association which years have fostered and matured, she regards as a condition for which even life or freedom can scarcely constitute an equivalent." Freedom, under such circumstances, she asserted, was "little better than a cruel mockery." Judith Hope ardently wished "to live and die in the land of her nativity." The General Assembly denied her request three times between 1819 and 1822, but in 1831 she successfully petitioned the Richmond City Hustings Court to remain in the city after being freed by her mother's will.[13]

Former slaves who owned property or had dependable employment were often reluctant to leave their communities in Virginia to start anew elsewhere. Over many years, Elvira Jones saved enough money to purchase first herself and then her children, as well as a "humble habitation in the suburbs of the City of Richmond." Because Jones's master let her pay for her children in small installments, however, by the time they were free they were subject to banishment under the 1806 residency statute. Jones petitioned to remain in Virginia to enjoy the "small pecuniary resources" she had amassed through "great frugality" because "the endearments of kindred and of home" were perhaps even more precious to the "humble and obscure . . . than they are to persons more elevated in life." Fifteen white men who supported her petition described Jones as "highly meritorious, and becoming her station in life." So, too, did Harriet Cook claim the support of white neighbors when the authorities threatened to expel her after she had lived and worked for twelve years as a free woman in Leesburg. In 1850, ninety-three white men and women attested to Cook's "gentility, trustworthiness and skill" as a laundress. They insisted that she posed "no possible injury" to the community and that "it would be a serious inconvenience . . . to be deprived of her services as a washerwoman and in other capacities."[14]

Although many free African Americans abandoned Virginia for the northern states, especially after 1831, single men and two-parent families were more likely than single women to leave. Of those who left, either forcibly or voluntarily, some thrived, but many regretted their separation from family and friends who stayed behind. Lucy Jarvis Pearson Scott and her husband, William Scott, were prosperous and free after they immigrated to Canada West (after a stop in Ohio) early in the 1850s. Their daughter Elizabeth, they noted proudly, was attending school, where she learned to write as well as "any of our ladys in old virginia." The Scotts departed voluntarily, accompanied by a group of relatives. Still, they clearly missed other members of their family whom they tried to coax into joining them with promises of "butiful schools" and good wages in Canada. There were "very few blacks in this city," the Scotts lamented from Brantford, Canada West, in 1854, adding, "thar is such a few that some times I think I left them all behind in old virginia."[15]

While many black and white Virginians left their native state for the free soil of Ohio and other states of the Old Northwest, others expanded slave society westward and southward. Between 1780 and 1810, Virginia and Maryland planters moved approximately 75,000 enslaved people into the area that became Kentucky and Tennessee; during these years, they transported an additional 15,000 Chesapeake slaves to South Carolina, Georgia, Alabama, and Louisiana to toil on cotton planatations. After Congress outlawed slave importations in 1808, some Virginia slaveowners chose to make money by selling enslaved people to the growing ranks of labor-starved planters in the cotton states. Between 1810 and 1820 alone, some 137,000 Chesapeake and North Carolina slaves were sent to the faraway cotton frontier. This domestic slave trade did irreparable damage to black families and communities.[16]

Although the law defined enslaved people as chattel, some clearly resisted their masters' efforts to dictate their place of residence. When a portion of the

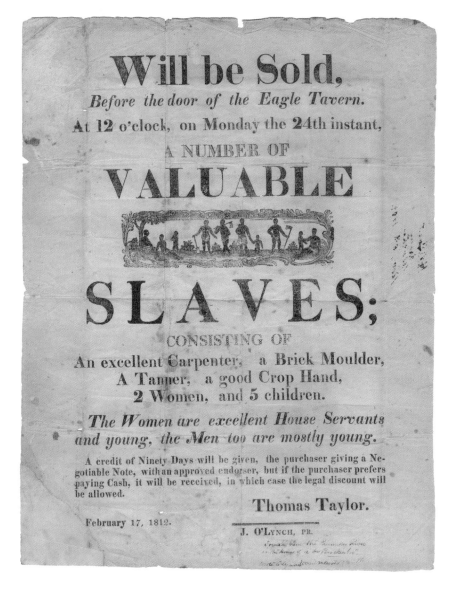

Will be Sold . . . A Number of Valuable Slaves, 17 February 1812. This broadside advertised an upcoming sale of men, women, and children at Richmond's Eagle Tavern. Sales and auctions were humiliating and often traumatic experiences for enslaved people, who especially feared being sold away from their families and communities. *Courtesy of the Library of Virginia.*

Kidnapping, by Jesse Torrey, 1817. Slave kidnapping became a lucrative business with the growing demand for labor on the cotton frontier, but free African Americans were also vulnerable to kidnappers who could force them into slavery. *Courtesy of the Library of Virginia.*

Cabell-Breckinridge family migrated from Albemarle County to Kentucky, taking a corps of enslaved workers with them, a slave woman named Violet simply refused to go, unless her husband and daughter Sarah went with her. Although such defiance could have resulted in severe punishment for Violet or her family, the Cabells allowed the woman, her husband, and daughter to stay with them in Virginia for nearly a decade after the departure of the Breckinridges, who nevertheless took Violet's son, Bill, and another daughter, Jenny, with them. Eventually, Violet's husband, Stephen, went to Kentucky, too, whereupon Violet herself decided that she wished to join him at the Breckinridge plantation. But this time Violet's efforts to control her own destiny were doomed to failure. Despite five years of pleading and an unsuccessful attempt to establish her legal right to freedom Violet remained unhappily in Virginia.[17]

White women also resisted the severing of family ties and they, too, often had little influence over men's decisions to pack up their households and resettle them elsewhere. Laura Wirt unhappily deferred to the wishes of her fiancé,

Slave trader, Sold to Tennessee, by Lewis Miller, ca. 1853. The artist, a Pennsylvania native, recorded the tearful beginning of a forced march from Staunton to Tennessee, where these enslaved people would be sold. Virginians, he found, sold their slaves "in droves." Other slaveholders who did not sell their bondpeople sometimes forced them to move with their masters to new plantations in other states. *Courtesy of the Abby Aldrich Rockefeller Folk Art Museum, The Colonial Williamsburg Foundation. Gift of Dr. and Mrs. Richard M. Kain in memory of George Hay Kain, Acc. 1978.301.1.*

father, and uncles by moving to Florida, where the newly married couple was expected to prosper as cotton- and sugar-planters, though she preferred the company and support of family and friends at home to the promise of great wealth. "I cannot endure the thought!" she exclaimed on hearing the plan, adding, "The very prospect breaks my heart!" Laura Wirt Randall was, indeed, lonely and despondent in Florida, where she bore four children and died at the age of thirty, just six years after her arrival. The middle-aged Jane Randolph, whose large family had occupied the pinnacle of Virginia's colonial society, was able to delay—but not avoid—following her husband to Florida after debt forced him to sell his Albemarle County plantation and its slaves in the 1820s. Polly B. Glover, of Buckingham County, moved to the Alabama Territory with her husband, but she returned to Virginia after he died, not wishing to remain "in a strange land, without Father, brother, or any relation to look to for protection, or even acquaintances, on whose friendly advice she might have derived some consolation."[18]

To be sure, some Virginia women came to see migration as a signal opportunity. In April 1827, Mary Elizabeth Randolph Eppes, eagerly anticipating her departure, explained that she was "weary of . . . the state of things" in Virginia, where "tobacco is the only thing which can be made . . . and after vast labour and expense, in raising and manufacturing the vile weed . . . to find still that no profit must be expected, is disheartening indeed." A year later, however, Eppes, who was still in Lynchburg, worried about "the uncertainty of our own prospects, the dread of taking a false step, the fear of incurring risk for our children in going to a new & untried country & the deep grief to go & leave so many . . . dearly loved friends." But when Eppes and her sister Harriet Randolph finally left Virginia with some other relatives in May 1829, they regaled their mother with letters about their adventures en route to Florida and the beauty of their situation once they arrived there. Soon Harriet Randolph and her sisters were excitedly planning for the opening of their new school, where they would teach English, French, Spanish, drawing, and other subjects to prosperous rustics on the Florida frontier.[19]

If some white women looked to the frontier for economic opportunity, many more gravitated toward towns and cities in the antebellum era. Indeed, while pundits advised young men to "go west . . . and grow up with the country," women generally found more opportunities to support themselves and to establish mutually supportive networks with other women in more densely populated urban settings. Like their free black counterparts, poor white women in rural areas were hired to work with slaves doing fieldwork or other agricultural tasks, and planters also hired white women to spin, weave, or sew. Cities offered more options, both in terms of the types of jobs open to women and the numbers of prospective employers. Another advantage was that most urban employment, unlike agricultural work, was not seasonal.[20]

Virginia's cities and towns were home to nearly 10 percent of the state's population by 1860. Growing urban communities attracted newcomers from the surrounding countryside and from northern states, along with European immigrants, most of whom were Irish or German in the antebellum era. Although Richmond attracted the most immigrants, Alexandria, Lynchburg, Norfolk, Petersburg, Portsmouth, Wheeling, and some other towns had significant foreign-born communities. Many Germans emigrated as families, but Irish emigrants were disproportionately young and male. Single Irish women found work mainly as domestic servants. By 1860, almost all the white domestic workers in Richmond were Irish women, who also were displacing African American women as servants in Norfolk homes.[21]

Cities offered more attractive alternatives to women who had property, education, or marketable skills. Those who owned houses sometimes took in boarders, as was the case of Mary Randolph, who converted her family's large house on Cary Street in Richmond into a successful boardinghouse as her husband sank under the weight of debilitating debt. On a smaller scale, the seamstress Mary Taylor, probably a widow, rented a room to a male boarder to augment her income and that of her fifteen-year-old daughter, who also took in sewing (though her younger brother attended school). Other women turned their houses into schools, accepting both boarders and day scholars. Mary Randolph's sisters, Jane Cary Randolph and Harriet Randolph Hackley, ran schools in Lynchburg and Norfolk, respectively. Women who were genteel and educated, but who lacked the means to open schools themselves, could nonetheless earn a modest living by teaching in one of the growing numbers of schools and academies for girls and young women.[22]

As they had done since colonial times, townswomen worked as tavern keepers, milliners, midwives, shopkeepers, or prostitutes—all jobs that employed skills and attributes that women used as wives, mothers, caregivers, and domestic workers and all occupations whose practitioners found customers more readily in cities than in sparsely populated rural areas. Some Virginia cities also afforded women the option of less traditional forms of employment in newly established factories, whose owners recruited female workers, who they could pay far less than men. White women worked long hours in the cotton

Amelia Heiskell Lauck, by Jacob Frymire, 1801. The daughter of German immigrants who settled near Winchester, Lauck had borne nine of her eventual eleven children by the time she sat for this portrait at about age 41. Lauck was an accomplished quilter whose works are today considered important examples of early American folk art. *Collection of the Museum of Early Southern Decorative Arts, Old Salem Museums and Gardens, Acc. 3406.*

factories of Petersburg and in the textile mills of Wheeling, where they earned between one-third and one-half of the wages of male workers and accounted for more than 70 percent of the labor force in 1850.[23]

Besides the options for employment that city life offered, urban women across the social spectrum enjoyed certain social benefits. Rural women often complained of loneliness: Anne Nicholas was typical, if overly dramatic, in describing herself as "absolutely as far removed from every thing like intercourse with my own species, as If I was an inhabitant of a solitary tomb" at her plantation in "the dreary woods of Fluvanna." Women who lived in towns and cities, by contrast, could visit each other more readily to socialize or—in the case of working women—to share household work and childrearing responsibilities. In towns, there were theatrical performances and other forms of public amusement. Urban women also could gather more frequently for church-related events and other collective activities. Indeed, as Martha Jefferson Randolph learned, her sister-in-law, having endured misery as a plantation mistress, thrived as a widow in Norfolk, where "her afternoons are devoted to walking, she visits the pensioners of the Dorcas society, the Orphan Asylum, and indeed has something to do with, or for, all the charitable schemes on foot in our town." The Monticello-bound Randolph was perhaps envious that in her new urban milieu her sister-in-law "can spend her leisure time abroad with propriety."[24]

For some, urban life also featured the pleasures of an annual social season, an essential part of the courtship ritual for elite young Virginians. Affluent parents often sent marriageable daughters to visit relatives in nearby cities, where they could meet eligible young men and learn proper social etiquette. Although public scrutiny in such formal surroundings made some young women feel bashful or uncomfortable, others clearly relished the rites of sociability. When Ellen Randolph, Thomas Jefferson's granddaughter, spent one season in Richmond and then another in Washington, she sent her family appreciative letters describing the sumptuous clothes she wore, the elegant balls she attended, and the interesting and important men she met during her urban adventures. During six months in 1837–1838, eighteen-year-old Mary Greenhow, of Richmond, spent a season with her brother in Washington, where she attended nearly forty parties, including two at the White House. In 1842, Greenhow, who was still single, enjoyed flirting and socializing in

Williamsburg. Harriet Randolph may have spoken for legions of young Virginia ladies when she correctly predicted that once she and her companions "became habituated to . . . the etiquette" of urban society, "our time will pass very pleasantly indeed."[25]

Many women fondly recalled their days as belles, when they enjoyed social and intellectual stimulation and temporarily escaped the isolation, responsibilities, and constraints of rural domestic life. Perhaps no Virginia plantation mistress pined for her youth as much as Eleanor Parke Custis Lewis, Martha Washington's granddaughter (and George Washington's stepgranddaughter). Young Nelly Custis had reveled in the elegant, erudite, and highly partisan society of Federalist Philadelphia during Washington's presidency. In 1797, however, the Washingtons retired to Mount Vernon, and Nelly married Lawrence Lewis, a nephew of Washington, in 1799, settling at Woodlawn, his plantation in Fairfax County. Nelly Custis Lewis often reminisced about her time in Philadelphia, when she had enjoyed the city's urbane and fashionable society. In 1817, she knowingly advised a newly married friend not to "give up music & painting, for pickling, preserving, & *puddings* although I have done so in great measure." Fifteen years later, as Americans marked the centennial of George Washington's birth, Nelly Lewis remembered her time in Philadelphia as her "*happiest* days," adding wistfully, "I like to recall them altho' it saddens me."[26]

Most Virginia women, of course, never got a chance to savor a season in Philadelphia, Washington, or even Richmond. Instead, they spent their entire lives on farms or plantations. The vast majority of Virginia's African American women were slaves who worked as agricultural laborers. Most white women lived in rural areas, first as daughters and then as wives. Even more so than urban women, they had few viable options for gainful employment and overwhelmingly conformed to social pressures to marry, thereby submitting themselves to their husbands' legal and customary authority.[27]

Although antebellum America was in most respects a patriarchal society, it was most markedly so in the Old South, especially in rural areas, where women had few opportunities to become self-supporting and lived far from other women who might offer advice, help, or protection in troubled times. Although divorce was uncommon everywhere in the United States, southern legislators and magistrates granted fewer divorces than their northern counterparts and, though authorities were most likely to grant women's divorce petitions if they could prove abuse, Virginia courts (and southern courts generally) also upheld husbands' right to inflict physical injury if they did so in the process of disciplining disobedient or unruly wives. White men claimed unfettered authority over their wives, children, and slaves, and state law, as well as a widely accepted interpretation of Scripture, largely supported these claims. Slavery provided a rationale for a more extreme version of patriarchy in the Old South, where white men contended that both women and slaves were in different ways inferior and therefore inherently dependent. Indeed, white men justified slavery in part as a means to protect allegedly frail and chaste white ladies from sexual assault by black men—which was, in fact, extraordinarily rare—even as law and custom gave them unlimited authority over the bodies of their female slaves.[28]

Unless they were elderly, ill, or in the advanced stages of pregnancy, most enslaved women worked in the fields alongside men. Although proslavery apologists later celebrated the beloved and contented Mammy as the female face of a supposedly benevolent institution, visitors to Virginia and to other southern states routinely noted that enslaved women did fieldwork, often performing the same tasks as enslaved men. When Frederick Law Olmsted toured Virginia in the 1850s, he found the slaves there "very ragged, and the women especially, who work in the field with the men, with no apparent distinction in their labor." Though white southerners insisted that women were delicate and dependent, as one Swedish visitor observed sardonically, black women "are not considered to belong to the weaker sex."[29]

Just as race and slavery distinguished black women's status from that of their white counterparts, so, too, did gender differentiate the experiences of black women in bondage from those of enslaved men. Female slaves were uniquely vulnerable to sexual exploitation and abuse at the hands of white men, especially their masters and masters' sons. Some sexual relationships between white men and slave women were long-lived and possibly affectionate, as was probably the case of Thomas Jefferson and Sally Hemings at Monticello. But sex between slaves and their masters was never consensual in the modern sense because enslaved women, who were legally the property of their masters, could neither consent freely nor legitimately defy the authority of their owners. For that reason, the law did not hold masters accountable for the rape of their bondwomen.[30]

Because slave children inherited the status of their mothers, slaveowners had a financial stake in enslaved women's reproductive labor. While some masters merely encouraged their female slaves to procreate, sometimes offering gifts or privileges to those who bore children, others forced slave women to have sex with men specifically to make them pregnant. Forcible mating of slaves may have been more common in Upper South states, such as Virginia, where masters and slave traders prospered by selling slaves to the cotton states after Congress outlawed the trans-Atlantic slave trade in 1808. According to Olmsted, while planters in the cotton states judged the value of slave women on the basis of both their ability to toil in the fields and their capacity to bear offspring, the latter was much more highly valued among masters in Virginia and other "slave-breeding States." In Virginia, he surmised, "a slave woman is commonly esteemed least for her laboring qualities, [and] most for those qualities which give value to a brood-mare."[31]

Motherhood fundamentally shaped women's experience in slavery. Although many Virginia slaves lived in two-parent households by the early nineteenth century, women assumed primary responsibility for children, who typically stayed with their mothers if their parents lived in separate quarters. The physical demands of motherhood for enslaved women could be staggering. Slave women gave birth roughly every two years—a slightly longer interval between births than that of planters' wives. But unlike elite women, who could rest if they needed in the months before childbirth and sometimes lived as invalids for months thereafter, slave women toiled well into their pregnancies, if not in the fields, then at sewing or other domestic work. They also returned to work soon after giving birth, either carrying infants on their backs and nursing young children while they labored or leaving their tasks several times a day to breastfeed their infants. In the slave quarters, their responsibilities as mothers and caregivers continued after the long hours of fieldwork were over. Motherhood also imposed unique emotional burdens on women, who saw their children sold, whipped, and otherwise exploited. Caroline Hunter, whose mother had watched her children beaten until they bled, recalled that "during slavery it seemed lak yo' chillum b'long to ev'ybody but you."[32]

Enslaved people sometimes went to extraordinary lengths to preserve their families. Lucinda, who was emancipated by the will of her mistress in 1814, offered to "become a slave to the owner of her husband" in King George County if by so doing she could avert "such a heartrending circumstance" as being separated from her spouse. Equally poignant were the efforts of Maria Perkins of Charlottesville to prevent her marriage and her children from falling victim to the slave traders. In 1852, Perkins, an enslaved woman who was literate, wrote an anguished letter to her husband, Richard—enslaved in Staunton—to inform him that one of their sons already had been sold to a trader and that Maria herself and their other child would be sold shortly. "I want you to tell dr Hamelto[n and] your master if either will buy me they can attend to it know and then I can go after wards," she explained hopefully, adding "I dont want a trader to get me."[33]

The survival of slave families rested precariously on the financial interests of slaveowning whites, who routinely acquired or discarded slaves by sale or rental or by including them in marriage settlements or bequests. When John Cowper Cohoon Jr. began his career as a planter in Nansemond County about 1813, he acquired one slave from his father and eight from his father-in-law, besides the twenty-eight men, women, and children he bought from twelve different owners or estates. Cohoon purchased no young married couples or complete families; the movement of these thirty-seven people to his plantation, Cedar Vale, therefore must have separated many wives from husbands and parents from children. As Cohoon succeeded as a planter, his labor force grew and individuals intermarried with other slaves at Cedar Vale and in its vicinity. Two enslaved couples, Fanny and Jacob and Margaret and Tom, all four of whom lived at Cedar Vale, produced a total of eighteen children. Of these, however, an aging Cohoon sold two and gave another two to his sons, as part of a large-scale process of divestiture that dispersed his black workforce to at least fourteen different white households, dismembering slave families as Cohoon consolidated his property and transmitted resources to the next generation.[34]

Some enslaved people moved with kin, but many others did not. Elizabeth Keckley, who later became successful and famous as Mary Todd Lincoln's favorite dressmaker, recalled that "in a majority of instances wives were separated from husbands and children from their parents" when her master liquidated his slaveholdings in the 1830s.[35]

ELIZABETH KECKLEY.

Elizabeth Keckley, 1868. Born into slavery in Dinwiddie County, young Lizzy endured brutal beatings and sexual assaults, as well as the loss of her family. After earning her freedom, she became a successful dressmaker. This portrait of Keckley was the frontispiece to her 1868 autobiography. *Courtesy of the Library of Virginia.*

Keckley's dramatic life shows how slavery undermined family ties and subjected African American women to physical and sexual abuse. In some ways, her lot was better than most—she was literate and a skilled seamstress—but in other respects it may have been fairly typical. Born of an apparently forced union between her mother, Agnes, and her master, Armistead Burwell, young Lizzy considered her mother's enslaved husband, George Hobbs, to be her father, and she experienced "fearful anguish" when Hobbs's master forced him to move to Tennessee. Lizzy Hobbs—as she was known—was whipped for the first time at the age of four. When she was fourteen, Burwell sent her away from her mother to live with his married son, first in Chesterfield County and then in Hillsborough, North Carolina. There, for weeks, she endured beatings that aimed to—in her words—"subdue my proud, rebellious spirit." By 1838, when she was twenty, a white man named Alexander Kirkland was raping her regularly, and she eventually became pregnant. Lizzy Hobbs returned to Virginia with her child and later was given to Burwell's daughter and her husband, who took them both to Saint Louis, where she became a dressmaker and earned her freedom. In her autobiography, she wrote tersely that Kirkland "persecuted me for four years," protected by "the edicts of that society which deemed it no crime to undermine the virtue of girls in my then position."[36]

While Lizzy Hobbs defied her abusers by verbally questioning their authority and physically fighting their efforts to inflict violence on her, enslaved women typically used more subtle—and ultimately more effective—means to resist the terms of their enslavement. Some attacked their tormentors covertly by setting fires or poisoning food. Others feigned illness or ignorance to avoid onerous work. Still others exploited special skills or talents to win privileges for themselves and for others. Mildred, an enslaved woman from Hanover County who took the surname Graves after emancipation, was a healer and a midwife whose master considered her "valuable." Because of her skill, he treated her well, hired her out, and let her keep a small portion of the money she earned for delivering white babies. Aunt Rebecca, an elderly Powhatan County slave, was a religious leader who ministered to blacks and whites alike and, as a bridge between these two groups, wielded influence and even power. Sometimes slave preachers invoked religion to encourage their listeners to resist the authority of their masters. In the 1850s, a slave preacher known as Old Aunt Ann empowered

Horrid Massacre in Virginia, 1831. Accounts of Nat Turner's insurrection emphasized blacks' brutality toward white women and children and the heroism of white men who defended them. Here, a white mother begs for the lives of her children, sword-wielding African American men attack a gentleman, and another white man takes on an ax-bearing insurgent to abet the escape of his wife and child. The print's lower panel shows a company of "mounted Dragoons in pursuit of the Blacks." *Courtesy of the Virginia Historical Society, 1831.2.*

her flock by teaching that it was permissible for slaves to appropriate "whatever of de wite folk's blessins de Lord puts in our way."[37]

At the same time, women were notably absent from the ranks of those implicated in Virginia's two major slave conspiracies. Family responsibilities afforded them few opportunities to plot and many reasons to avoid violent confrontations with whites, while lingering West African traditions also may have led to women's exclusion from such openly militaristic activities. Twenty-six men were tried, convicted, and hanged for their involvement in Gabriel's Conspiracy, an abortive slave uprising planned for Richmond in 1800; more men were arrested and later acquitted, while still others whom the courts deemed guilty were sentenced to be transported outside the commonwealth. Forty-nine men and one woman stood trial for conspiracy and insurrection related to the uprising led by Nat Turner in Southampton County in 1831, which resulted in the deaths of at least fifty-five white people. Lucy, the lone woman implicated, prevented her mistress from fleeing when Nat Turner's men arrived, purposefully endangering her life. Tried, convicted, and hanged for her offense, she was one of the very few women among more than 250 slaves who were tried for insurrection in Virginia between 1785 and 1831. Yet some enslaved women surely sympathized with the insurgents and quietly abetted their efforts. Gabriel's wife, Nanny, helped get information to his allies. During Nat Turner's uprising, a slave woman named Charlotte taunted her mistress and did nothing to assist her as insurgents approached her house.[38]

More prominent in white Virginians' accounts of slave revolts were white women, whom they portrayed, along with white children, as the primary victims of black men's brutality. In 1831, newspaper reports from Southampton repeatedly asserted that the "helpless classes," meaning white women and children, bore the brunt of the violence. "What strikes us as the most remarkable thing in this matter, is the horrible ferocity of these monsters," mused the *Richmond Enquirer*, in that "nothing is spared; neither age nor sex respected—the helplessness of women and children pleads in vain for mercy." Likewise, the commander of the troops who suppressed the uprising praised his men "for the interest you have taken in behalf of our wives and children" by defeating the insurgents. Despite this rhetoric, however, white women were not subject to sexual "outrages" during the revolt and they were only slightly more likely than white men to have been killed by the insurgents, who murdered seventeen or eighteen women, compared to thirteen or fourteen men. Less because they were specially targeted than because they outnumbered adults in most households, children constituted the largest number of casualties. Although contemporary reports varied, insurgents killed between twenty-four and thirty white children at the Southampton houses they raided in August 1831.[39]

White men generally lumped women and children together as passive dependents, who required both protection and governance, and women themselves sometimes accepted or even promoted that view. In 1828, Virginia Randolph Cary, of Fluvanna County, published *Letters on Female Character, Addressed to a Young Lady, on the Death of Her Mother*, which was the first advice book written by a southern woman for the women of her region. Cary idealized the authority of benevolent men and—as both an educated woman and a committed evangelical—she cited both the laws of nature and Scripture to argue that women should be subordinate to men both at home and in society. Better a woman be "pitied as a submissive wife to a strict husband, than applauded as having usurped the government [of a family] from the hands of an incompetent [man]," she asserted, because "both reason and religion prompt us to choose that which is approved by God. . . ." Should women "grasp at more than their allotted portion of power," she argued, "misrule and disorganization" ensued, and women inevitably suffered, too, losing the protection of both God and man.[40]

Notwithstanding Cary's idealized view of white male patriarchy and popular stereotypes of frail and leisured southern ladies, plantation mistresses worked hard even at the pinnacle of Virginia's social hierarchy. Plantation households were productive households, and slaveholding women, including Cary herself, supervised domestic servants who scrubbed, laundered, sewed, and cooked, while they themselves performed a myriad of household tasks, as their foremothers had done since the colonial era. Lucy Hopkins Johnston Ambler, wife of a slaveholding planter in Fauquier County, was in many respects typical. She married at eighteen, bore eight children in sixteen years, and oversaw a corps of domestic workers. Ambler did all of her family's sewing, which included the production of clothing for their enslaved workforce. She raised poultry and ran a dairy that produced more than sixty pounds of butter a year to sell, in addition to what was consumed in her own household.[41]

Most rural women were farmers' wives who lived far less genteelly and worked even harder. Virginia's white farm families typically lived in two- or

Letters on Female Character, by Mrs. Virginia Cary, 1828. The illustration on the title page of Cary's book reflected her idealized view of virtuous womanhood. Her circumstances as a widowed and impoverished mother of a large family probably led her to romanticize patriarchy as a source of security and protection. Cary earned $1,000 for this book, and she wrote at least three others. *Courtesy of the Library of Virginia.*

four-room houses that one English visitor described as "wretched." When he traveled from Washington, D.C., to Richmond, Frederick Law Olmsted found that the houses of common white farmers' families "are either of logs or loosely-boarded frames . . . everything very slovenly and dirty about them." Like their more affluent neighbors, these farm women tended gardens, poultry, dairies, and children; they also did fieldwork, when necessary, though white men did not admit their occasional dependence on their wives' and daughters' work in the fields, which belied their status as autonomous male patriarchs and protectors. The Englishwoman Frances Trollope called these farm women "slaves of the soil," whose lives, she concluded, were far harder than those of poor women in contemporary Britain. "One has but to look at the wife of an American cottager, and ask her age," she wrote sympathetically, "to be convinced that the life she leads is one of hardship, privation, and labour."[42]

Even as they insisted on wifely subservience, however, some Virginia men recognized the economic significance of women's domestic work and effective household management. Thomas Jefferson, who advised his daughter Martha that "all other objects must be secondary" to her husband's wishes, nonetheless considered wives crucial partners in the economy of plantation households. In 1808, perhaps reflecting on his own family's deteriorating finances, he counseled Martha that "a wife imbued with principles of prudence, may go far towards arresting or lessening the evils of an improvident management," which led so many "unthrifty" Virginia planters to financial ruin. Evangelical ministers, like Richmond's John Holt Rice, a Presbyterian, championed humane and loving marriages in which wives should be submissive, "exemplifying the meekness, the patience, the humility, the charity, the fervent piety, which characterize true religion." But he, too, appreciated the economic value of women's domestic work. "Active industry and habits of economy," he advised his readers, "constitute an important part of the good works with which women are to be adorned." Contributors to southern agricultural journals generally shared this perspective. For farmers' wives, one such author in *Farmer and Planter* contended in 1852, "Industry and toil make all the difference between the useless and the useful." Without women's work, he added, men "must all perish for want of the common necessaries of life."[43]

Even as they expected subservience from females of every social rank, white male patriarchs thus praised and idealized virtuous mothers, wives, and housekeepers. Women's obituaries, which were increasingly common in antebellum newspapers, served primarily to celebrate the lives of virtuous women who embodied this feminine ideal and accordingly could be role models for female readers. One such woman was Elizabeth Y. Vaughan, of Goochland County, who died peacefully in 1860 at age sixty-eight "after a short and painful illness." A committed member of the Baptist Church, Vaughan was also celebrated as "an affectionate wife and mother, an indulgent mistress, and a good neighbor" who helped the needy. These qualities—piety, resignation, domesticity, and benevolence—ensured that she "died beloved and lamented by all who knew her."[44] That Vaughan left barely a mark on the historical record besides her obituary (which, significantly, was penned by someone else) is utterly in keeping with the logic of the gender conventions of antebellum Virginia. Yet this feminine ideal, which aimed to circumscribe the ambitions, activities, and voices of even the most-privileged women, however virtuous, paradoxically could also inspire and empower some to test the limits of patriarchal power.

Although Virginia women rarely defied or rejected outright the prevailing gender ideals that mandated female submission and subservience, they did increasingly participate in the affairs of the world beyond their households. Necessity motivated most Virginia women who entered the paid labor force to work outside the home in the antebellum decades, but other women purposefully chose to undertake other public activities during this period. Virginia women, like their contemporaries elsewhere, formed religious and charitable associations. They cautiously entered the political arena where, like men, they favored one political party over another and, as civil war seemed imminent, they expressed opinions on the deepening sectional crisis.

Improvements in female education, especially but not exclusively for elite and middling Virginians, made these changes possible. Although Virginians and other southerners lagged behind their northern contemporaries in terms of literacy and education generally, circumstantial evidence of improvements in female education is nonetheless compelling. Antebellum women left behind far more manuscript documents—letters, diaries, petitions, and so on—than did earlier generations. Publications by Virginia women were rare before 1800, but antebellum women wrote advice books, novels, and devotional works, mostly for female readers. Finally, although Virginia had few public schools before the Civil War—and none that accepted female pupils—private schools and academies proliferated early in the nineteenth century. Elite and middling girls were most likely to attend school, but some poorer girls did, too. Even some African American girls learned to read and write, despite laws that criminalized the instruction of slaves and free blacks.[45]

Religion was women's main avenue to involvement in public life. Although mainstream denominations still denied women formal authority in church affairs, women vastly outnumbered men in most congregations and some became important lay leaders whose ecclesiastical contributions were increasingly public. Elizabeth Henry Campbell Russell, the sister of Patrick Henry, was an important Methodist lay leader in southwestern Virginia, where she was famous for living simply, freeing her slave, and exhorting men to repent and be saved. Susan Catharine Spotswood Bott, a Petersburg Presbyterian, organized fairs and other fund-raising efforts to support the Female Education Society, which paid for the training of needy candidates for the ministry. The patronage of Mary Lee Fitzhugh Custis and her circle of mostly female kin was largely responsible for reviving the Episcopal Church in Virginia and for spawning an array of denominationally based Sunday schools and missionary societies. A few women went even further, becoming missionaries themselves. Although most female missionaries accompanied their husbands abroad, in 1850, Lydia Mary Fay, an Episcopalian who had lived at various times in Essex, Fairfax, and Loudoun Counties, traveled as a single woman to China, where she taught a Bible class and English for nearly three decades.[46]

Closer to home, piety inspired most of those who taught slaves and other poor Virginians to read in the antebellum era. As evangelicalism became the predominant religious force in the commonwealth, Virginia Protestants increasingly emphasized the need for individuals to tend to their own souls by praying and reading the Bible. Some also believed that religion would make the sometimes unruly poor more virtuous and governable. In 1803, ninety-eight women and twenty-two men from Fredericksburg and Orange intimated as much when they petitioned the legislature for permission to hold a lottery to raise funds for a charity school for the "many young and Indigent Females who were exposed to ignorance, Vice, and Infamy without a Friendly hand . . . to save them from the worst and deepest State of Ruin." Religious education, reading, and writing were the top priorities of charity schools for girls in Fredericksburg, Richmond, and Norfolk, but most of these schools excluded slaves and free blacks. Some pious white women, however, persisted in their efforts to teach African Americans to read. Women like Mary Berkeley Minor Blackford professed to "obey a higher law than the laws of man" by teaching blacks to read the Bible in her Fredericksburg home. A more notorious case was that of Margaret Douglass, a Norfolk resident who provided religious instruction, including reading, for free black children for about eleven months before local authorities prosecuted her. The jury assessed a fine of $1, but the judge sentenced Douglass to one month in jail, which she served before leaving Virginia for Philadelphia.[47]

Pious rural women also taught slaves to read on plantations across the commonwealth. Jane Hunter, of Essex County, taught a Sunday school for slaves with her sisters in the 1820s and 1830s, while Louisa Cocke, of Fluvanna, cleverly bent the law by allowing literate slaves on her plantation to instruct the others. In the 1850s, Martha Hancock Wheat taught a "large & interesting sabbath school consisting of young Men & Ladies in addition to many children" in a schoolhouse her husband built for her on the grounds of his Bedford County plantation. Although her students were initially local whites, she also taught some of her slaves to read the Bible.[48]

Less spiritual concerns also motivated Virginians who supported education for poor females, who needed to become self-supporting in order to avoid dependence on public relief. Besides religion and morality, charity schools therefore emphasized manual training in skills that would be useful to poor women either as employees of others or as mistresses of humble households. Students learned practical lessons, especially sewing and general housekeeping skills, reflecting the disproportionate demand for female workers as domestic servants and seamstresses. In rural areas, local authorities paid literate women (and sometimes men) to teach poor girls and boys the basics of reading, writing, and arithmetic. In 1850, Jane Bumgardner offered a session of at least four months for seven Augusta County children—five girls and two boys—who ranged in age from eight to thirteen. Martha A. Walker, who described herself as "very poor, and dependent upon her own exertions for her support," provided a similar service in Brunswick County in the 1840s.[49]

Far more expansive was the course of study that educators offered to elite and middling students whose parents paid tuition at boarding schools and day schools to prepare them for courtship, marriage, motherhood, and managing genteel households. Ornamental accomplishments like music, painting, drawing, and dancing continued to have a place in the female curricula, as they had during the colonial era, but most educators increasingly regarded these polite accomplishments as optional additions to the main course of study and often charged extra for them. Students at the Richmond Academy for Female Education could not enroll in music, dancing, or drawing classes without taking an academic course. Tuition at the Roanoke Female Seminary was $50 per term, which included the standard English curriculum, along with lessons in either French or Italian, but music lessons cost an additional $50. Nevertheless, parents who could afford to provide their daughters with instruction in music, drawing, and other polite accomplishments usually did so at least in part because many men valued these accomplishments in their prospective wives.[50]

In the minds of parents, even the most highly educated Virginia daughters were preparing for marriage and domesticity. As a result, educators who promoted ambitious academic curricula reassured sometimes ambivalent parents that learning arithmetic, history, French, and even Latin would make young women better daughters, wives, and mothers. James Mercer Garnett, a former congressman who, with his wife, ran a highly regarded academy in Essex County in the 1820s, urged students to read and study diligently, but he also disparaged "learned ladies," lauded women's calling as men's "best comforters" and "most beloved friends," and maintained that "to render married life even tolerably comfortable, qualities for *use*, rather than for *show*, should always be preferred." Most parents agreed. The attorney and author William Wirt, who ardently encouraged his daughters' education, nonetheless condemned the "*ostentatious* display of intellect in a young lady," which he deemed "revolting." Henry W. Wood told his daughter, Julia, that he hoped she would merit "applause from your tutors and associates" at school, which he believed was best attained not through stellar academic displays but rather "by courteous affability and a kind deportment to every one."[51]

In their efforts to persuade parents that education was consistent with domesticity, proprietors of early Virginia schools often portrayed their establishments as surrogate homes. Virtually all advertisements for women's schools and academies included the proprietors' promise to safeguard the morals of their charges. Most stipulated that students would participate regularly in religious observances and that there would be no unsupervised interactions with members of the opposite sex. Some small town educators boasted not only a healthful physical environment but also a situation—in the words of one Lynchburg schoolmaster—"desirably removed from the intrusion of dissipation, and yet sufficiently accessible to agreeable and improving society." Proprietors of boarding schools likened these institutions to extended families that afforded students much the same discipline and guidance they received at home. "Having daughters of their own to educate," explained one Williamsburg couple, they sought to "render an acceptable service to society, in forming a seminary where polite literature and the arts of personal improvement may be equally cultivated" in a family setting. The operations of some boarding schools replicated the conventional gender-based division of labor, with husbands tending to administrative matters and academic instruction, while their wives oversaw the students' progress in domestic skills and moral development.[52]

By all accounts, young women cherished the opportunities for learning and personal growth that education afforded, and many made lasting friendships during their time as students. The sisters Rebecca Beverley and Jane Beverley, who left their Essex County home to attend schools in Pennsylvania, overcame their initial homesickness and eventually took great pride in winning academic prizes. In 1852, Caroline Clay Dillard, the daughter of a prosperous Lynchburg planter, went with her sister Mary to Greensboro, North Carolina, to attend the Edgeworth Female Seminary. Dillard spent four pleasant years at this "very popular and flourishing institute," where she studied the usual academic and ornamental subjects and followed a daily regimen that included rising before dawn, making her own bed, and exercising before beginning classes at 8:30 A.M. Students attended church three times a week, but they also participated in carefully monitored social gatherings. In the security of this self-affirming female community, Dillard, like many other schoolgirls, developed a taste for independence and skepticism about marriage, resolving to remain unwed until she was at least twenty-one.[53]

Most girls eventually married and their parents believed that education, in various ways, prepared them for their future domestic lives. Thomas Jefferson, whose extensive plans for public education in Virginia excluded females

Alphabet in German and English, by Ambrose Henkel, ca. 1810. German immigrants settled in the Shenandoah Valley in the colonial period, and more came to Richmond and other towns during the nineteenth century. German-American mothers might have used this broadside, published in New Market, to teach their children the alphabet in two languages. Educating young children, especially daughters, was a maternal duty and an increasingly common justification for improvements in female education. *Courtesy of the Library of Virginia.*

completely, nonetheless wanted his own daughter to be well-educated because he feared that "in marriage she will draw a blockhead ... and ... the education of her family will probably rest on her own ideas and direction without assistance." Decades later, the Reverend John Holt Rice expressed a more common argument in favor of female education when he asserted that virtuous and well-informed women would be better companions for men. Educated women, he explained, would "encourage the zealous pursuit of knowledge in the other sex ... and countenance ... [those] who endeavour to prepare for the able and faithful service of their country, in any department to which they may be called." Virginia Randolph Cary, the generally conservative author of *Letters on Female Character*, agreed, although she worried that education was "liable to abuse" by "aspiring females [who] are not content to retain any vestige of subordination to the anointed lords of the creation." Cary hoped "to see women highly cultivated in mind and morals, and yet content to remain within the retirement of the family circle."[54]

As sectional tensions increased, some Virginians also argued that the daughters of the commonwealth needed schooling designed specifically to reflect and reinforce the values and culture of their region. In 1850, school trustees in Spotsylvania County sought to incorporate the purposefully named Southern Female Institute. The main goal of this school, as they explained in their petition to the state legislature, was to shield Virginia schoolgirls from "that sickly-sentimentalism which seems to be becoming epidemical at the North, and which generates such monsters as the . . . Anti-slavery societies, and womens' rights conventions," which they declared undermined the family, Christianity, and social order, and led to the disintegration of civilization into "the mire of a Barbarian licentiousness."[55]

By the 1840s and 1850s, growing numbers of young women attended colleges offering both traditional and classical curricula that was comparable to—and perhaps even better than—the typical male college curriculum in the Old South. Virginia's first women's college, the Female Collegiate Institute, in Buckingham County, received a charter from the legislature in 1837 and had ninety-two students, all from Virginia, by 1839. Students boarded at the Institute or with local families. The classical curriculum, in which roughly one-third of the antebellum alumnae enrolled, included ancient and modern languages, in addition to the regular English curriculum that featured algebra, political economy, natural history, and other subjects. Lessons in music, drawing, and painting were available at extra cost. When the Female Collegiate Institute encountered financial difficulties in 1843, thirty students—twenty Virginians and ten from the Carolinas—petitioned the state legislature for aid. "Impressed . . . with the justice and importance of our cause itself, and knowing the character of Virginia for liberality and gallantry," the petitioners declared, the legislators could not "disregard the necessities and earnest petitions of her daughters, while she is so lavish of her benefits to her more favored sons." After the General Assembly rejected the students' petition, the Female Collegiate Institute closed for about five years, but it began offering classes again in 1848 and continued until 1863. Comparable institutions in Danville, Farmville, Roanoke County, and Staunton, all founded before the Civil War, survived as institutions of higher learning into the twenty-first century.[56]

Buckingham Polka, drawn by the Rev. Henry Brown, ca. 1852. The Female Collegiate Institute in Buckingham was Virginia's first women's college. The school boasted a serious academic curriculum and charged extra for the ornamental accomplishments that many families still valued. This image appeared on the cover of sheet music composed by Arnaud Preot, who taught at the college and "respectfully Dedicated" the piece to its students. *Courtesy of the Library of Virginia.*

Although Virginians who championed female education never expected women to use their schooling to enter public life or to become self-supporting, some women did just that. Paradoxically, the same generations that included such vocal proponents of male patriarchy and female domesticity also produced women whose public activism and visibility were unprecedented. Virginia women tacitly used their widely lauded feminine attributes—piety, modesty, compassion, and their supposedly innate maternal feelings and virtues—to justify public endeavors. Women educators marketed their learning and their virtue when they solicited students for their schools. Women writers became public figures chiefly by pursuing subjects and genres that were in some respects extensions of their domestic roles. Virginia Randolph Cary, who strenuously opposed women's seeking equality or influence beyond their family circle, wrote advice books and novels with evangelical Christian themes; her sister, Mary Randolph, penned *The Virginia House-Wife*, America's first regional cookbook, in which she asserted that "the mistress of a family" was responsible for managing money and other aspects of the "grand arcanum" of household management.[57]

The career of Anna Hickman Otis Mead, a Richmond educator and author, though more successful than most, was in some ways typical. A native of the Michigan Territory, Mead came to Virginia as the wife of an Episcopal clergyman, who died in 1840, leaving her a widow with four young children from two marriages. Mead, who had assisted her husband as editor of the *Southern Churchman*, continued to work with his successor, but in 1841, with the support of local clergymen, she opened a successful school for girls, which she ran for twelve years while she also continued writing. Mead published a collection of short fiction and devotional works—which also appeared in a second edition—as well as articles and essays for various periodicals, including the *Southern Literary Messenger*. When her children were grown, she gave up her school and remarried. In 1860, she published an adaptation of six chapters of Thomas Hughes's popular novel *Tom Brown's School Days*. Teaching and publishing enabled Anna Mead to support her family, but these activities also made her a public figure in Richmond and beyond.[58]

Antebellum women, especially those who lived in cities, also came together to establish organizations to aid the poor and promote virtue in their communities. Inspired by a combination of compassion, noblesse oblige, and awareness of growing urban problems, the earliest women's associations, in Virginia as elsewhere, were benevolent societies that provided food, shelter, and alms for the poor. Evangelical women later founded other organizations whose objectives were more plainly religious and that often were affiliated with a specific church or denomination. Women's associations met regularly, raised money, and sought (and received) charters of incorporation from the state legislature. Some men criticized the women who "to the neglect of their domestic duties, and many to the injury of their reputations, are . . . forming themselves into clubs of one sort or another . . . to gratify the love of selfishness and notoriety." But the influential clergyman John Holt Rice commended "female charitable societies," which "call forth the best affections, and promise the best results" in terms of helping others and spreading "the blessings of

A number of Females of the Town of Portsmouth, assembled at the house of Josiah Fox, on the 4th of May, 1804, and agreed to form themselves into a Society, under the name of the

FEMALE CHARITABLE SOCIETY,
OF PORTSMOUTH.

The sole object of which, is to extend relief to all White Female sufferers, particularly children within the Town of Portsmouth.

THEY THEN AGREED TO THE FOLLOWING

RULES.

I. MEMBERS shall be admitted into the Society by a vote of a majority of the Members present, at any quarterly, or annual meeting of the Society.

II. EVERY Member exclusive of the donation their benevolence may bestow, shall pay twenty-five cents, at every quarterly meeting.

III. THE following Officers shall be chosen annually, by a majority of votes of the Members present at the quarterly meeting in May, from amongst the resident Members, viz. a First Directress—a Second Directress—a Secretary—a Treasurer—six Solicitors, and Six Visitors.—N. B. The number of Solicitors and Visitors, may be increased if thought expedient by the Society.

IV. THE First Directress, shall preside at all meetings of the Society and Board of Managers, preserve order, state questions for discussion, and declare the decision ; in all divisions she shall have a casting vote : with the advice of the Board, she shall call special meetings of the Society, she shall see that its regulations be duly observed, and shall take an active superintendance of its general welfare—in case of her inability to perform the duties of her station, they shall devolve for the time being, on the Second Directress ; if both be absent from any meeting of the Society or Board, a Directress shall be chosen for that meeting.

V. THE Secretary shall keep a register of the Members' names, collect the quarterly payments, and pay the money into the hands of the Treasurer; shall notify the meetings of the Society, record their proceedings, and render at every stated meeting, a regular account of the money received by her, and paid to the Treasurer, and of monies due ; she shall attend the meetings of the Board, and examine their accounts.

VI. THE Treasurer shall take charge of the money collected for the Society, make all their disbursements, attend the meetings of the Board, examine their expenditures, and render to the Society at every stated meeting, an account of its funds, and of her receipts and payments.

VII. THE Solicitors shall ask donations for the Society of well disposed persons, and pay what they may receive into the hands of the Treasurer.

VIII. THE Visitors shall seek amongst the distressed, for suitable objects to partake the benefit of the institution.

IX. ALL the official Members shall constitute a Board to manage the business of the Society ; which Board shall meet quarterly, viz. on the first Monday in May, August, November and February. at 3 o'clock, P. M. and at such other times as the First and Second Directresses may think necessary on any emergency, and seven Members shall be competent to transact business.

X. THE Directress, at the request of two Visitors, may draw on the Treasurer for money to relieve the distressed.

XI. THE meeting in May, shall be considered as an anniversary, at which all the Members be present, and a full statement of the affairs of the Society, be laid before them.

XII. EVERY meeting shall be opened with reading a portion of the word of God and prayer, and closed with prayer.

XIII. NO partiality for religious sects or country to be observed, either as to membership in the Society, or objects of their benevolence.—The only consideration as to the objects must be—she is in distress—we must help if we can, if we cannot do all we would, let us do what we can.

N. B. IT is recommended to every official Member, to make notes of their transactions and notable circumstances that may turn up, relative to the concerns of the Society, and lay the same before the Board.

Female Charitable Society, of Portsmouth, 1804. Benevolent women established Virginia's first formally organized women's associations. The Female Charitable Society, of Portsmouth, one of the earliest, was founded to *"extend relief to all* White Female *Sufferers, particularly children within the Town of Portsmouth." Courtesy of the Library of Virginia.*

the gospel." The many men who donated money to women's associations presumably shared Rice's views.[59]

By 1813, elite women in Virginia's leading cities—Richmond, Norfolk, Petersburg, Fredericksburg, and Alexandria—had established benevolent societies. One of the chief founders of the Female Humane Association of the City of Richmond, probably the earliest of these efforts, was Elizabeth Jaquelin Ambler Brent Carrington, whose father had been an official in Virginia's Revolutionary government. As a teenager, Betsey Ambler had fled British troops as they marched on Richmond; as an adult she married twice, but both husbands died, leaving her widowed and childless at forty-five. A committed Episcopalian who was related by blood or marriage to many of the state's leading families, Carrington became a community leader in Richmond, where she joined with some other prominent women to establish the Female Humane Association for the relief of orphans about 1805. Among the association's cofounders were Mary Spear Nicholas, the wife of the state's attorney general, and Jean Moncure Wood, the wife of a former governor. Carrington served as secretary of the association from its incorporation in 1811 until at least 1833. When she died in 1842, the *Richmond Enquirer* recognized and honored her public activism in a flattering obituary that described her as one of the state's most "distinguished women," and one who was notable for her "intelligent and cultivated mind; her generous heart; her active and diffusive charity."[60]

Women's benevolence focused primarily on helping girls and women. The stated objectives of the founders of Richmond's Female Humane Association were "the general purposes of charity and benevolence, the relief and comfort of distressed females, and for the maintenance and instruction of destitute white female children residing in the city of Richmond, or its suburbs," though its orphanage eventually accepted poor girls from across the state. The Richmond women raised money by holding charity fairs to augment their income from donations and bequests. Their school taught poor girls reading, writing, arithmetic, and domestic skills—especially sewing and knitting—and, after 1811, the association bound out girls as servants or apprentices to generate money for the school and orphanage and to ensure that their charges would be brought up well in a family environment. The Norfolk Female Orphan Society operated along similar lines. Such organizations were part of a national phenomenon, addressing the needs of the poor at a time when local poor relief was limited and there was no welfare system at either the state or federal level.[61]

There is some evidence that benevolence work was changing by the 1840s and 1850s. On the one hand, women became more ambitious in their undertakings: in Richmond, for instance, the Union Benevolent Society, founded in 1835, sent members to the homes of poor families and tried to find work for needy women. On the other hand, men—who had previously left charity work to women—became increasingly involved in benevolence, either because they now believed that the job of helping the poor and training them to become self-supporting was too big to be left to women alone or because they feared or resented women's growing public activism. Regardless of their motives, men formed their own benevolence groups, founding an orphanage for boys in Richmond, for instance, to complement the efforts of the Female Humane Association. In Lynchburg, when a long-established women's Dorcas Society, which provided assistance to the poor, collapsed because of a lack of funds, men founded their own Relief Society to take its place. In Petersburg, women's benevolent enterprises survived, but men, who generally could raise more money, assumed control of one organization and created others in the 1850s that relegated women to supporting, auxiliary roles.[62]

A more prominent trend in women's organizations, beginning as early as the 1810s, was the proliferation of denominationally based evangelical groups, formed by religious women who tended to be of middling social rank. Generally overseen by clergymen, church-based groups raised money to help the poor, establish domestic and foreign missions, and fund church-building projects in both cities and rural areas. Although most were Protestant—Virginia, after all, remained an overwhelmingly Protestant state—Jewish women in Richmond established a religious school for Jewish children, which they supported by holding a series of balls patronized by Jews and Gentiles alike. In 1849, German immigrants established the Ladies' Hebrew Association, which dispensed benevolence in Richmond. The state's Catholic population left most of its benevolence work to the Sisters of Charity, who came from Maryland in small numbers to run orphanages, schools, and infirmaries in Richmond and Norfolk, and also (briefly) a school in Martinsburg for whites and another for African American women. Some female parishioners also occasionally participated in fund-raising events, such as the ladies' fair that raised $1,200 for Petersburg's

Catholic congregation in 1859. Some free black women formed their own church-based philanthropic associations. In Fredericksburg, for instance, a charitable organization called the Sisters of Zion helped organize and pay for funerals in the African American community.[63]

One group of white women in Petersburg banded together to protect themselves in the troubled economic times of the late 1850s. Founded in 1859, the Female Benevolent Society of Petersburg was less a charitable organization than a mutual aid society, a type of organization that had been popular for decades among immigrants and other working-class men in American cities. Unlike the elite women who had created organizations that addressed the physical and moral needs of poor females, or the evangelical women who dispensed alms to convert the impious, these women sought to "unite ourselves together for the infusion of virtue, and the suppression of vice, and immorality among our own class, and for the inculcation of every honest and correct principle that can render woman respectable, good and happy." Members paid a $2 initiation fee and 12¢ per month in dues. In exchange, each member received "one dollar per week during sickness" and "eight dollars toward her funeral expenses." Members of a seven-woman standing committee "wait[ed] on sick members." Like men's mutual aid societies, this Female Benevolent Society sought to create a safety net for working women who could afford neither the loss of wages as a result of illness nor the cost of a proper funeral. They thus joined together to help each other, individually and collectively.[64]

Religion, benevolence, tending the sick, caring for children—all of these activities squared well with the feminine ideals of antebellum Virginians, but some women also became more visible in other public venues that were seemingly at odds with prevailing sentiments about women's proper place and role. Women attended civic and patriotic events ranging from Fourth of July parades to festivals at which German immigrants honored the memory of Friedrich von Steuben, the Prussian hero of the American Revolution. At such civic observances, conventional gender ideals typically circumscribed women's participation, as had been the case since the post-Revolutionary era. Nevertheless, strong antebellum beliefs about women's unique virtue and the importance of motherhood justified modest expansions of women's roles on some public occasions. Women still gazed admiringly at marching militia on the Fourth of July, but they now also sometimes presented flags to soldiers, whom they publicly praised as chivalrous protectors of their families and communities. The German-American Steubenfest in 1857 featured the obligatory militia parade, but there were also social activities that women organized, including dancing and children's games.[65]

Some Virginia women managed to play more unconventional public roles and, on rare occasions, even sought political rights. In October 1829, as Virginia's constitutional convention debated extending the right to vote to all white men, an essay appeared in the state's leading newspaper demanding the enfranchisement of women. "Are *we* not as free as the Lords of Creation?," asked Virginia Freewoman. "Are *we* not as much affected by the laws which are passed, as the Lords of Creation themselves? What just reasons can be given for this unjust exclusion?" Men, she argued, unfairly disparaged women's intellects, while purposefully keeping them ignorant. "You make us embroider for you; thrum upon the guitar or piano; draw sketches of your lordly faces; . . . but you exclude us from your best schools." Moreover, if women lacked the independence allegedly necessary to "exercise the right of suffrage, firmly and freely," so, too, she asserted, did the propertyless men whose right to suffrage many now advocated. "We call upon the Convention, then, in the name of Justice and of Truth," the essayist declared in vain, "to listen to our Claims, and secure our rights."[66]

Another bold criticism of the status quo came from nine black Fredericksburg women who, in 1837, addressed a petition to Congressman John Quincy Adams, of Massachusetts, thereby joining the cacophony of petitioners—many of whom were northern women—seeking the abolition of slavery in the District of Columbia. Accompanying the petition was a cover letter, in which Susan Loushing (possibly a pseudonym) informed the former president that the women "could have obtained a great many names but had no time having heard that the Petitiones must all go up now," and expressed her wish that "you good men would do something in this business, but it seems all talk up with you in Congress." Loushing also correctly predicted that John Patton, a congressman from Richmond, would be "mightily against all such doings as this business." Indeed, when Adams attempted to present the petition of the "nine ladies" in the House of Representatives, Patton disparaged one petitioner, whose name he recognized, as being "of notoriously infamous character and reputation" and asserted that none of the others were "ladies" either. Like most other antislavery petitions, as Loushing had intimated, this one did not receive serious consideration in Congress.[67]

Not surprisingly, few Virginia women followed the examples of the Fredericksburg petitioners or VIRGINIA FREEWOMAN by publicly championing abolitionism or woman suffrage. Unlike a small but vocal minority of their northern contemporaries, Virginia women generally remained aloof from the most radical antebellum reform efforts, the related movements to abolish slavery and to promote women's rights. In Virginia, as in the other slaveholding states, the two most ambitious reform movements to attain some success and thereby seemingly to threaten the status quo were temperance and a less egalitarian version of antislavery known as colonization. Virginia women were avid participants, with men, in both of these important efforts.

Evangelical men, who founded approximately 250 local temperance organizations in Virginia in the 1820s and 1830s, actively solicited female members because—in the words of leaders of the Prince William County Temperance Society—"intemperate use of ardent spirits . . . have resulted primarily from the uses made of it in private families," where women might use their influence to discourage drinking. Temperance men also recognized women and children as those most likely to suffer as a result of men's drinking, and they relied on women as mothers of future generations to instill in their children the virtues of temperance. For all these reasons, men sought women's support and many women happily gave it. In 1835, roughly half of the 35,000 members of Virginia's temperance groups were women. By then, however, many white male southerners were increasingly critical of the temperance movement because of ties between northern anti-liquor leaders and radical abolitionism. Many also worried that restricting white men's access to alcohol conflicted with the ideal of autonomous masculinity that lay at the heart of southern patriarchal values.[68]

Despite growing criticism, temperance advocates persisted, mounting a series of petition drives late in the 1840s and early in the 1850s in which women participated, not only by signing men's petitions but also by producing and submitting their own. For instance, twenty-six "Ladies" from Cabell County used the language of female dependence to mask their thoroughly political—and arguably antipatriarchal—intent when they petitioned the General Assembly for temperance legislation in 1849. Acknowledging that "we have no right to a voice in the affairs of Government," the petitioners nonetheless called on the legislators to "enact such laws, as will protect virtuous females, and innocent children from degradation, poverty, and wanton cruelty, inflicted by men who should . . . be our friends." Four years later, fifty-six women and forty-nine men in Hancock County submitted two nearly identical anti-liquor petitions. A comparison of the signers' surnames suggests that for many women and men temperance was a family commitment. But the fact that thirty-one of the female petitioners had surnames that did not appear on the men's petition also suggests that some women publicly worked for temperance on their own, without the encouragement or assistance of male relatives.[69]

Women were equally prominent in white Virginians' efforts to resolve the dilemma of slavery. The main thrust of antislavery sentiment in nineteenth-century Virginia derived from three essential points made by Thomas Jefferson in *Notes on the State of Virginia*. First, the most basic assumption in Virginia antislavery circles was that slavery was evil. Second, though antislavery Virginians believed that African Americans suffered as a result of their enslavement, most were far more concerned about the ill effects of slavery on whites. Virginia Randolph Cary, who penned an antislavery petition in the wake of Nat Turner's revolt, echoed Jefferson when she warned that slavery encouraged a "habit of despotism" among slaveholding whites and that enslaved people—those "unfortunate beings who surround our homes, and constitute a portion of every family"—were "by nature and habit the fosterers of moral evil." Finally, because they believed that, for various reasons, whites and blacks could not coexist peaceably as free people, antislavery Virginians insisted that emancipation had to be coupled with the expulsion of freed African Americans from the commonwealth. Under the auspices of the American Colonization Society (ACS), they therefore worked to resettle both manumitted slaves and free blacks in the west African colony of Liberia, which the ACS established for that purpose in 1822.[70]

Women were among Virginia's leading supporters of the ACS and, though their stance was not nearly as egalitarian as that of northern abolitionist women, their position was comparatively humane and courageous for their place and time. While concerns about the safety and security of white people seem to have motivated most male colonizationists, many female members of the ACS—most of whom were committed evangelicals—genuinely abhorred the injustice of slavery and sympathized with the plight of African Americans. These women worked to promote manumission, immigration to Liberia, and the spread of Christianity. Louisa Maxwell Holmes Cocke, a devout Presbyterian who taught her slaves to read the Bible and donated money to the ACS, probably helped persuade her husband, the Fluvanna County planter and reformer John Hartwell Cocke, to manumit an enslaved couple and their six children, whom they resettled in Liberia. Ann Randolph Meade Page, of Frederick County, who referred to slaves as her "fellow-creatures in bondage," believed that God summoned her to minister to the spiritual and physical needs of her bondpeople. From 1810 until her death in 1838, Page sought to improve the material conditions of slaves and taught religion to her family's enslaved workforce. Forced to sell more than one hundred slaves to pay the debts of her late husband, Page worked hard to save others from sale and to prepare them for freedom. She sent more than twenty emancipated people to Liberia in the 1830s.[71]

Nat Turner's revolt shocked white Virginians and galvanized their leaders to consider seriously a plan for the gradual abolition of slavery in the state, which coupled emancipation with the subsequent expulsion of freedpeople from the commonwealth. Both humanity and fear led some white women to embrace this vision of a future without slavery. On the one hand, Mary Berkeley Minor Blackford, who drafted a petition on behalf of the "Female Citizens of Fredericksburg" in support of this conditional termination plan, emphasized "the interests of an unfortunate people" in bondage and sought to "supplicate for them . . . attention to their welfare and happiness." On the other hand, female petitioners from Fluvanna and Augusta Counties called on legislators to end slavery to ensure the safety and prosperity of white Virginians. A petition signed by 215 "Females" from Augusta County pointedly noted that "very many of our sisters & brothers have fled to other [free labor] lands from the evils which we experience. And they send us back the evidences of their contentment & prosperity." Abolishing slavery in Virginia, they averred, would free white people from the fear of slave insurrections and other "perilous circumstances," allowing them to "enjoy our exultation in the land of our nativity."[72]

In 1832, the proposed conditional termination of slavery failed in the General Assembly by a vote of 73 to 58, but some Virginia women continued their active support for manumission and colonization, even as the emergence of radical abolitionism as a mass movement in the northern states made opposition to slavery on any grounds increasingly unpopular in Virginia. Arguably the state's most notable colonizationist was Blackford, who in 1829 founded the Fredericksburg and Falmouth Female Auxiliary to the ACS, Virginia's most-successful antislavery association for women. A deeply religious woman who decried the suffering of the enslaved, Blackford kept a private journal chronicling the horrors of slavery and her own efforts to secure the manumission of bondpeople and their resettlement in Liberia, where in 1837 her organization helped fund a school for girls run by Presbyterian missionaries. Though her husband, like virtually all other white male Virginians, became increasingly committed to preserving slavery, Mary Blackford remained a staunch colonizationist. So, too, did Mary Lee Fitzhugh Custis and her daughter, Mary Anna Randolph Custis Lee, who continued to raise money and prepare enslaved families for emigration, despite their husbands' growing coolness toward the colonizationist cause.[73]

Ultimately, roughly one-third of the emigrants who left the United States for Liberia between 1820 and 1860 were Virginians, of whom 521 were part of a fear-induced exodus in 1832 and 1833, in the wake of Nat Turner's insurrection. Most emigrated as families, but some, like Adaline Southall, who came from Albemarle County with her son, Horace, left enslaved spouses behind in Virginia. Emigrants who were urban, educated, and free before their departure tended to prosper in the African colony, while recently freed slaves often languished, especially if they were uneducated and came from rural areas. Perhaps the most upwardly mobile female emigrant from Virginia was Jane Rose Waring, the daughter of an educated free black preacher from Norfolk and Petersburg who became a wealthy merchant after settling with his family in Liberia in 1824. Jane Rose Waring married Joseph Jenkins Roberts, another free black Virginian who eventually became Liberia's first president and most important statesman. In 1892, Jane Rose Waring Roberts, by then a widow, represented her country at Windsor Castle, where she had an audience with Queen Victoria.[74]

White women who worked for colonization, temperance, or other reformist causes drew on the ideals and networks of Protestant evangelicalism, consciously avoiding involvement in the seemingly amoral—and maybe even immoral—partisan politics of the antebellum era. Eventually, however, at least some came to see party politics as a possible means by which they might

Henry Clay Monument and Gazebo, ca. 1860. Led by Lucy Barbour of Orange County, Whig women spent sixteen years raising funds to erect this monument in Richmond's Capitol Square, which was dedicated in 1860. *Courtesy of the Library of Virginia.*

pursue their reformist ends. By the 1840s, such women were gravitating toward the Whigs, who were more sympathetic than the Democrats toward reform initiatives, especially temperance. Recognizing the prominence of women in temperance and moral reform efforts generally, beginning with the 1840 presidential campaign, Whig leaders urged them to bring their uniquely feminine virtue to the often raucous political arena. Civic-minded women responded enthusiastically to their call. As a ten-year-old Augusta County girl who was a self-described "Whig" reported, "the Ladies here thay all say if thay had to vote thay would all vote for [William Henry] Harrisson," the Whig presidential candidate. Women gave speeches at Whig political rallies, and in 1844 Lucy Barbour of Orange County formed an organization to raise money to erect a statue in honor of the party's greatest leader, Henry Clay, of Kentucky.[75]

This effort to pay tribute to Clay illustrates both the extent and the limits of women's political participation in the antebellum era. Women could not vote, but Whig men, who were themselves disproportionately members of elite families or committed evangelicals—sometimes both—welcomed the support of pious women from prominent families, whose presence, they believed, reflected well on their party's reputation for wisdom, virtue, and morality. Whig women came mainly from the upper classes; many were involved in benevolence work and other civic or philanthropic organizations. Even so, some Democratic men criticized the women of the Virginia Association of Ladies for Erecting a Statue to Henry Clay for their partisanship. In the end, the Clay Association organized a network of auxiliaries throughout the state and collected donations from more than 2,500 contributors in Virginia and elsewhere in 1845 and 1846. Clay died in 1852 and the Whig party perished amid the sectional conflict of the 1850s. But in April 1860 the completed statue of Clay was unveiled with much fanfare in Richmond with some 20,000 spectators in attendance.[76]

Commemorating Clay, who had been known as the Great Compromiser, on the eve of the Civil War, was entirely in keeping with women's generally conciliatory approach to the sectional crisis in the 1850s. Indeed, one historian has described Virginia's politically minded white women as "sectional mediators" who hoped for reconciliation between North and South, at a time when most white male southerners were becoming increasingly intransigent. Some Virginia women entered the political debate, taking positive steps to encourage mutual understanding across regional boundaries, and wielding their pens to defend their state, their region, and the southern way of life—specifically, the institution of slavery—from increasingly hard-hitting northern criticism. Virginia women penned two of five novels that southerners wrote in response to Harriet Beecher Stowe's influential antislavery novel, *Uncle Tom's Cabin*, which elicited near-unanimous outrage from white southerners—colonizationist Mary Berkeley Minor Blackford was a notable exception—when it appeared in 1852. *Aunt Phillis's Cabin: Or, Southern Life as It Is*, generally regarded as the best southern response to Stowe's critique of slavery, was the work of Mary Eastman. Martha Haines Butt, who described herself as "a warm-hearted Virginian," wrote *Antifanaticism: A Tale of the South*. Both novelists defended slavery as a sometimes regrettable but generally benevolent system. Invoking a common conceit of proslavery apologists, both also maintained that most southern slaves were better off than poor white workers in the northern states.[77]

Women's most visible attempt to promote national unity, however, came via the effort to preserve Mount Vernon, the Fairfax County home of George Washington. What began in 1853 as a regional appeal from a self-described "Southern Matron," South Carolinian Ann Pamela Cunningham, quickly became

Mount Vernon, Home of Washington, Representing Two Hundred Acres purchased by the Ladies Association, 1859. The Mount Vernon Ladies Association of the Union attained its objective of preserving Mount Vernon as a shrine for future generations. Their massive undertaking showcased women's organizational abilities, as well as their patriotism, on the eve of civil war. *Courtesy of the Library of Virginia.*

a national movement among elite women whose twin objectives were to buy and preserve Mount Vernon and—in the words of one admiring male Virginian—to further "the cause of extinguishing, in our country, sectional feelings and sectional asperities, and reviving those fraternal sentiments which in by gone days constituted [Americans] in interest and feeling . . . [as] one people." Ultimately, the Mount Vernon Ladies' Association of the Union (MVLA) attained only its first goal, purchasing the historic house in April 1858.[78]

The white women of the Mount Vernon Ladies' Association represented the cream of Virginia society. The national scope of their fund-raising, the money they amassed, and the visibility their organization enjoyed both in Virginia and nationwide made it in many respects the most ambitious of women's public undertakings in the antebellum era. Men, including the famed Massachusetts orator Edward Everett, publicly praised the efforts of "ladies" who sought to "soften the asperity of sectional feeling, by holding up to the admiration of all parts of the country, that great exemplar [Washington] which all alike respect and love." But their enterprise also drew criticism from those who questioned women's ability to raise and manage money, as well as their readiness to navigate the stormy political waters that in the eyes of some skeptics threatened to make Mount Vernon property of the Union and thus captive to the interests of the increasingly "obnoxious" northern states.[79]

Defenders of the MVLA invoked powerful gender stereotypes to insist that women were uniquely suited to rise selflessly above politics to save Mount Vernon for all Americans. For men like Beverley R. Wellford Jr. who addressed the organization's Virginia supporters in 1855, women's efforts to preserve Mount Vernon were logical extensions of their roles as wives and mothers. Unlike some northern women, Wellford explained, Virginia ladies happily did not seek "an equal participation with man in the labors and burthens, the honors and rewards of active and public life." Wellford applauded the "daughters of Virginia," who, "in the quiet and unobtrusive walks of private life, shut out from the public gaze and removed far from the arena of conflict," nonetheless indirectly guided the "current of events" through their virtuous influence on their husbands and their sons. Though MVLA members clearly moved beyond the domestic sphere to engage in both politics and fund-raising, Wellford nonetheless praised the organization as "in itself the proudest memorial to manly worth the world has ever known." Like many of his contemporaries, he tacitly accepted women's public activism because he believed that women were essentially different from—and not equal to—men. "It is [man's] ambition— it may be his destiny to be great," he concluded, but "it is woman's higher ambition—her heaven-born mission to be good."[80]

The most notable trajectory of Virginia women in the antebellum era was to venture out, either literally or figuratively, into the wider world beyond their households. Women and their families left long-established communities, resettling in growing cities and in other states. More women than ever before were visible members of a paid labor force—a development that signaled both new economic opportunities for women and, for many more, dislocation born of social change and economic instability. Educational improvements afforded many girls and young women knowledge of and contact with the outside world, even if they lived on plantations, far removed from society. Some girls left home to pursue their education. Virginia women exchanged letters with family and friends. They read newspapers and religious and secular books and magazines. Some even wrote and published their own essays, books, and poems.

To be sure, gender profoundly limited women's options, as well as the ideals and images they invoked to justify their public activities, but the case of Julia Gardiner Tyler shows how the juxtaposition of rhetoric and reality could at times be downright jarring. The wife of President John Tyler, this transplanted New Yorker embraced southern ways and women's prescribed domestic role, insisting that most American women knew "nothing of political conventions, or conventions of any other sort than such as are held under suitable pastors of the Church." Tyler asserted that Virginia women in particular lived contentedly as domestic beings and had little interest in woman's rights. Nevertheless, Julia Gardiner Tyler herself was an undeniably public woman, both as the most prominent "Lady Presidentess" since Dolley Madison and as the author of an 1853 letter to Harriet Sutherland-Leveson-Gower, duchess of Sutherland, in which she defended slavery and slaveholders—a letter that she had published in the *Southern Literary Messenger*. Tyler's well-publicized letter, roundly praised in Virginia newspapers, made her a heroine throughout the South.[81] Like many of her contemporaries, though on a somewhat grander scale, she stretched the limits of feminine respectability, embracing and expertly manipulating the gender conventions of her time and place to justify playing unconventional public roles.

CHAPTER 4

"A Constant State of Hopes and Fears": Women in the Secession Crisis, Civil War, and Reconstruction

Home to the capital of the Confederacy and neighbor of the United States and its capital, Virginia was the central battleground of the Civil War. The state's landscape suffered widespread destruction, and its people witnessed horrific carnage. Motivated in large part by a desire to defend their homes and families, and at the same time to vindicate slaveholders' rights, slightly more than two-thirds of white men in Virginia between the ages of 15 and 50 fought for the Confederacy. Ironically, fulfilling the male role of "protector" meant leaving female relatives to take care of themselves during a period of massive upheaval. White women took control of farms and shops as the state's economy fell into disarray, and they assumed management of slaves as the institution began to crumble. For enslaved women, the diminished presence of white men created more space for resistance, and the arrival of Union troops offered a pathway to freedom. Gender and racial roles shifted unpredictably, leading women and men to question their very identities. Secession, a political act designed to defend the social order of the South, led to an all-consuming war that produced profound *dis*order.[1]

———————◆———————

During the 1850s, a series of political clashes over the future of slavery soured relations between North and South. John Brown, already famous for employing violent tactics against proslavery settlers in Kansas, brought the escalating sectional crisis to Virginia soil on 16 October 1859, when he and a small group of black and white associates took possession of several federal buildings, including the armory and the arsenal, in Harpers Ferry. Their objective was to spark a sustained war of slaves against Southern slaveholders, but the plot collapsed when United States Marines captured Brown and his surviving comrades on 18 October. News of the raid alarmed and infuriated white Virginians, particularly when it became evident that many Northerners sympathized with Brown's cause. Perceiving that their way of life was under attack, some white women began to reassess their commitment to the cause of sectional reconciliation.[2]

Amanda Edmonds, a young woman from a wealthy Fauquier County family, wanted revenge; she wrote privately of her desire to see the invaders "singed and burnt until the last drop of blood was dried within them."[3] A young woman in Norfolk found satisfaction in the knowledge that Brown would pay for his "numerous crimes" on the gallows. Other white women focused less on vengeance than on securing adequate protection for the South. In a letter to the editor of their local newspaper, several elderly ladies in Harrisonburg denounced Northern "fanaticism" and asserted the need to "defend our institutions from outrage," proclaiming that "true women, genuine women" would be more than willing to send their husbands and sons to fight. Across the state, women supplied uniforms and flags to new volunteer companies organized in the wake of Brown's Raid. Many women also vowed to boycott Northern goods. In several cities they formed "Homespun Clubs" to keep their money out of the hands of merchants from a region they now regarded as hostile.[4]

Yet elite and middle-class women's anger at Northerners did not signify a desire for immediate secession or an abandonment of the idea that sectional compromise was possible. As the nation's attention turned to the presidential election of 1860, most white Virginians hoped for a political solution that would protect slavery and keep the Union intact. Since the 1840s, women had found ways to participate in political campaigns despite their inability to vote, and the tumultuous canvass of 1860 captured their avid interest. The four major parties competed for female support because prevailing ideology held that respectable white women were exemplars of morality and patriotism; endorsement by the ladies brought legitimacy to political platforms and might influence the voting behavior of their male relatives.[5] Partisan newspapers boasted when women presented flags to local political clubs or rewarded campaign speakers with bouquets of flowers. In Princess Anne County (later Virginia Beach), supporters of Southern Rights Democrat John C. Breckinridge hosted a barbecue at which "some four hundred ladies" were treated to a "sumptuous feast" and "stirring appeals . . . for the safety of the South."[6] In the northwestern corner of the state, the only region to sustain an active Republican organization, women cheered from the sidelines at campaign parades and on at least one occasion spoke at a rally for Abraham Lincoln.[7]

Constitutional Unionist candidate John Bell defeated Breckinridge by a small margin in Virginia, while Lincoln, with little or no support in any slaveholding state, won the presidency. In response, a small but vocal group of Southern Rights partisans in Virginia argued that the state should leave the Union immediately rather than submit to Republican rule; these men and women applauded the secession of South Carolina on 20 December. At the same time, Congress debated compromise measures that proved acceptable to neither Northern nor Southern representatives. Among women as well as men in Virginia, the prospect of secession dominated conversation. One woman recalled that in Winchester, "nothing was talked of but secession, in every company, at every street corner." A proponent of immediate disunion apologized to her friend for writing at length about political developments, explaining that "I am so much interested in politics, that I forget myself when ever I get on the subject." Elite women reiterated their willingness to sacrifice luxuries and to wear inexpensive, homemade clothes until the crisis ended. Acknowledging women's prominence as consumers, the editor of the *Fredericksburg News* told his readers to "let the ladies set the example of encouraging the manufactures at home, and men will gladly follow."[8]

In January 1861, after three additional Southern states had seceded, the General Assembly called for a state convention to determine Virginia's course. Early in February voters elected delegates, less than one-third of whom favored immediate secession, and the convention opened in Richmond in the middle of the month. Held at the hall of the Virginia Mechanics Institute, where a gallery was set aside for women, the proceedings attracted large crowds.[9] Sarah Ann Brock, of Richmond, reported that the convention hall became the "favorite place of resort" for local women, who sometimes "engaged in political discussion" while waiting for the members to assemble.[10] Women consistently filled their gallery hours before the morning session opened. One delegate had trouble crossing a lobby on his way to the convention floor because the room was so crowded with ladies, who granted him passage only after he assured them that he was a secessionist. Unionist women were also present in the throng. In March they rewarded one pro-Union delegate with a floral wreath and another with a gold watch.[11]

As secessionism gained popularity late in the winter of 1861, a new ideal of women's civic duty—one that envisioned women as nurturers of Southern nationalism rather than as soothers of sectional tension—quickly took shape. Virginians who believed that Northerners had corrupted the Union transferred their patriotic devotion from the nation as a whole to the South, which they saw as the true repository of the freedoms bequeathed by the nation's founders.[12] In private correspondence and in public pronouncements, men glorified the purity of women's patriotism and held women up as exemplars for men to follow. In a letter to his cousin Mary Berkeley Minor Blackford, John B. Minor, of the University of Virginia, praised women's "magnanimous unselfishness," which equipped them to inspire the same in men, thus "diffus[ing] an aroma of virtue through Society."[13] The *Richmond Examiner* asserted that women were endowed with a "clearer view of the true state of the great questions now before the world than any lawyer's logic or politician's power of calculation can ever afford," and the *Staunton Vindicator* agreed that "the ladies are always quicker in their apprehension tha[n] the men." One Alexandria man offered others of his sex some pithy advice regarding the ladies: "What they endorse, subscribe to."[14]

Some women embraced the role of ideological leaders. In March, forty female residents of Essex County submitted an address and resolutions for publication in the *Daily Richmond Examiner*. Though the editor withheld their names for reasons of "delicacy," and the writers humbly referred to themselves as "weak women," the message they advanced was bold and forceful. Citing their "bursting indignation" at Virginia's hesitancy to secede, they urged Virginians to "hurl back in the faces of our enemies, all insulting compromises" and promised "infinite scorn" for men who failed to defend the South against "the traitorous inhabitants of the North." They rallied their female counterparts across the state to "nurse in the temples of men's hearts the sacred fire of patriotism."[15]

Women from Petersburg quickly responded with an enthusiastic letter to the *Examiner* in which they declared their refusal to "submit to the ignominious rule of Lincoln." They admitted their fears that Virginia men might not remove the state from the Union but expressed hope that "woman's prayers" would be effective in bringing about disunion.[16] In another public letter, more than a hundred women in Gloucester County joined the chorus of frustration at men's failure to achieve immediate secession. Having "heard so much to excite our womanly scorn and grief" during the deliberations over Virginia's future, they agreed with the Essex ladies that it was women's responsibility to "influence some who hold the destiny of our State."[17]

Though secessionist women expressed anger and disgust at the way men were handling the crisis, neither they nor the men who shared their political opinions criticized the legal bar against women having their say at the ballot box. Instead, women found a variety of other ways to take political action in the early months of 1861. In Staunton, a group of ladies planned a fair to raise money for the purchase of tents and knapsacks so that the local militia would be prepared if called on to fight. Women in Alexandria made overcoats, bedding, and cartridges. Late in March, a group of women in Harrisonburg sewed a Confederate flag and had it raised over the Exchange Hotel.[18]

Unionist women, too, sought to influence their male relatives and friends—sometimes with little success. Mary Berkeley Minor Blackford, an opponent of slavery who belonged to a slaveholding family, regretted her failure to instill devotion to the Union in her five sons. To see them "arrayed against one part of their Country, our own 'Star spangled banner,' and *in such a cause*, is a sorrow that makes me feel that the grave is the only place for me," she wrote to her cousin in January. Blackford considered her voice "drowned," as did some of her fellow Unionists who decried the influence of rash and greedy politicians.[19] Other Unionist women, however, found satisfying ways to assert their views. Women in Alexandria presented an American flag to militia troops in March, and a group in Charlottesville proudly raised the Stars and Stripes. Unionism was most entrenched in the state's northwestern counties, where women participated in mass meetings by presenting ceremonial flags and, occasionally, by delivering patriotic addresses.[20]

On 4 April, the Virginia Convention defeated a motion to secede by a vote of 90 to 45. On the 12th, Confederate artillery in Charleston, South Carolina, opened fire on Fort Sumter, a federal installation that Lincoln intended to resupply. The garrison at the fort surrendered the following day, and on 15 April Lincoln called on the states to provide 75,000 troops to put down the rebellion. Given the choice between fighting the Union and fighting fellow Southerners, a great majority of white Virginians now embraced the cause of immediate secession. "Those who had been calm and moderate," Winchester resident Cornelia Peake McDonald remembered, "were now furiously indignant at the insult to Virginia." In Alexandria, Judith McGuire expressed approval that Virginians had spent the preceding months seeking compromise and maintaining peace, but she resoundingly rejected the Union after Lincoln ordered Virginia to stand against her "brethren of the South." Ida Dulany, of Fauquier County, agreed, writing that "Lincoln's war proclamation" had turned her into "a Secessionist from the bottom of my heart."[21]

By a vote of 88 to 55, the convention passed an ordinance of secession on 17 April. Jubilant men and women crowded the streets of Richmond. Cornelia McDonald remembered that everyone she encountered in Winchester was "full of joy."[22] Private feelings—even among those who had come to favor disunion— were often more complicated. Sally Taliaferro proclaimed secession "glorious news," but she also evinced apprehension about the future and described herself late in April as "too disturbed in mind to enjoy anything."[23]

Even after the clash at Fort Sumter and Lincoln's call for troops, a minority of white Virginians shared the opinion of Barbara Miller, a resident of Rockingham County and member of the pacifist Church of the Brethren, who declared the breakup of the Union "wrong and uncalled for."[24] Simply by maintaining their loyalty to the federal government, Unionists embarked on a precarious existence in which they and their families suddenly found themselves in hostile territory. Powerless in the face of events that had upended her life, Mary Brenneman of Rockingham complained that she was "opposed to secession but could do nothing."[25] Frustratingly little is known about the opinions of black women, free and enslaved, during the secession crisis. Many had access to news reports and understood that the political commotion was intimately related to their status. With every other Virginian, they now peered into the unknown.

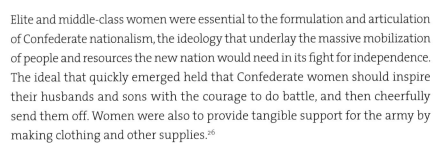

Elite and middle-class women were essential to the formulation and articulation of Confederate nationalism, the ideology that underlay the massive mobilization of people and resources the new nation would need in its fight for independence. The ideal that quickly emerged held that Confederate women should inspire their husbands and sons with the courage to do battle, and then cheerfully send them off. Women were also to provide tangible support for the army by making clothing and other supplies.[26]

Because such self-sacrifice and effort were understood to flow from patriotism, discussion of and praise for women's love of their new country abounded. Comparisons to women's support for the War for Independence were especially popular. "The spirit that animated the 'Women of the Revolution' still lives in the hearts of the lovely and accomplished daughters of Virginia," boasted the *Alexandria Gazette*, while the *Lynchburg Daily Virginian* pronounced local ladies "worthy descendants of the matrons of the revolution."[27] With women so devoted to their country, Confederate ideology held, men must follow their example and stand steadfast for the protection of home and nation, two institutions that became inseparable in the minds of many white Southerners. "The man who would not lay down his life in defence of [women's] honor is a wretch," asserted the *Staunton Vindicator*. Gender roles thus lay at the heart of ideological preparations for war.[28]

Some Virginia women, particularly young members of the elite class, adhered closely to the prescriptive ideal of Confederate womanhood. It may have helped that many of them also subscribed to the prevailing belief that the military campaign would be a brief, romantic adventure. Confident in the justice of their cause and scornful of the enemy—"those low contemptible ruffians from the North," sneered Pattie B. Cowles of Petersburg—these women urged their male relatives and friends to take up arms.[29] No task could be more honorable for a man, Front Royal resident Lucy Buck told her cousin, than "repelling the insolent invaders of your sacred rights, fighting for your homes, defending your fire sides, protecting brothers, sisters and mothers!"[30] While some mothers lamented that they had no sons to send to the army, others expressed pleasure that they had boys who could fight. One widow in Harrisonburg remarked on how "cheerfully and gladly I have given all my sons to the cause of Southern Rights, Liberty and Independence."[31] The departure of volunteer companies attracted crowds of women, who presented the units with flags, gave flowers to the recruits, and cheered as the men marched off.[32] Confederate women expressed great disdain for men who did not volunteer. In Petersburg, "no man in citizen's dress dares to visit ladies now," Pattie Cowles reported to a friend in June. A group of young women in Rockingham County, refusing to socialize with men who stayed behind, resolved to remain unmarried until the soldiers returned home.[33]

Despite ideological pressure, however, many Confederate women—while they supported Southern independence and understood that men must fight for it—were not able to live up to the ideal of cheerful self-sacrifice. Some women soberly predicted that the war would be long, difficult, and bloody, and they looked to the future with anxiety. Even wives and mothers who had thoroughly internalized the precepts of Confederate womanhood were fearful of sending their loved ones to meet unknown fates. Though Ann Catron, of Washington County, encouraged her seventeen-year-old boy to enlist "not with grief, but thanking God that I have a son to offer," she also admitted to "trembling" as she contemplated his departure.[34] In Fauquier County, Ida Dulany wrestled with her mixed feelings in her diary. Though she believed her husband "should be" in the army, his departure had left her "miserable and desolate."[35] Isabella Woods, a Confederate sympathizer who lived in divided Barbour County, in northwestern Virginia, described her feelings bluntly in a letter to her husband. "I find I am much more selfish than patriotic," she wrote. "What good would all the honor, glory and independence of the Southern Confederacy do me, if . . . your life had been sacrificed for it?"[36]

Preparations for war dominated Virginia society in the spring and summer of 1861, and most white women—with all their complexities and personal idiosyncrasies—worked to aid the cause of Southern independence. They were certain that the sanctity of their homes and the survival of their way of life now depended on the successful defense of the Confederacy, and women perceived themselves as partners in the struggle for military victory.[37] "While men are making a free-will offering of their life's blood on the altar of their country, women must not be idle," Judith McGuire wrote in Alexandria.[38]

"Making clothes for the boys in the army," by John Adalbert Volck, ca. 1862. Confederate women gather to make clothes for soldiers. *Courtesy of the Library of Virginia.*

Some women's contributions were as simple as making clothes for their own husbands, sons, or brothers who served in the army. Many others, however, brought their private, domestic endeavors into the public sphere. Drawing on their experience in antebellum aid societies, elite women across the state organized local voluntary associations to produce clothing and equipment for men in the field. In churches, courthouses, and town halls, women gathered day after day to make pants, shirts, coats, caps, sheets, towels, bandages, knapsacks, and other items. By the first week in June, a society in Charlottesville had produced more than 2,000 articles.[39]

Some wealthy women, unused to such labor, had much to learn. "Except for fancy work, I had never sewed a stitch in my life," recalled the wife of a cavalry officer, who learned during the war to "make clothes out of next to nothing." In Winchester, Cornelia McDonald remarked that "even tents were made by fingers that had scarcely ever used a needle before."[40] Women's typical prewar domestic duties had rarely included the production of sandbags, which they now turned out in high quantities for use in military fortifications. In some cases, soldiers' aid societies offered elite women the novel experience of interacting with poor women. Several Petersburg ladies founded an association that paid wives of enlisted men, who struggled for income in the absence of their husbands, to make clothing with materials delivered by the Commissary Department in Richmond. One of the group's organizers noted that she "became well acquainted with a class of women I had not known before."[41]

Having in many cases bidden farewell to men from their own households, women lavished attention on the soldiers from other Southern states who had begun to arrive in Virginia. These interactions had political meaning, as their effect was to bolster the resolve of men who had set out to protect the South. Women socialized with the soldiers in their encampments, cheered for them at parades and drills, and gave them flowers. In Petersburg, Pattie Cowles reported that she had spent the previous evening "with some of the Alabama soldiers quartered at the 'Fair Grounds,'" and that her friend had "lost her heart with one."[42] When illnesses broke out in camps, women were called on to care for sick soldiers. In Lynchburg, a group of ladies held daily meetings in a church basement to coordinate their efforts. The "delicate attention" of "tender hands," which women had cultivated as mothers, wives, and sisters, now became a tool in the fight for Southern independence.[43]

Some women, not content with the roles their gender allowed them to play as Virginia prepared for war, wished they could volunteer for military service. Feeling stifled by her inability to do more for the cause, one disgruntled female in Winchester voiced her regret at "being only a woman."[44] Those who shared her opinion fantasized about the opportunities being male would give them. "If I was a man I would take none of the Negro Lovers prisoners I would do my best to kill the last one of them," Maggie H. Berry, of Augusta County, wrote to her cousin, a soldier.[45] In Petersburg, some young women cast gender conventions aside and, eager to learn drilling and shooting, organized a "ladies home guard" in May. The company was short-lived, one of its disappointed members explained, because local men "talked about it in an outrageous manner."[46]

While Confederate women helped Virginia mobilize for war in the months following secession, Unionists in the northwestern counties worked in similar ways to promote the cause of the federal government. Women organized Union

Aid Associations to equip local volunteers and, in ceremonies almost identical to those in which Confederate recruits left home, they presented flags to departing military companies.[47] Yielding nothing to their Confederate counterparts, they claimed to be the true patriots and employed language that reflected the direct connection they saw between themselves and the Revolutionary generation. "We've not forgotten seventy-six," went the lyrics of a song favored by a group of young women in New Martinsville. "We're for union with the men / Who love our glorious Union," the song continued, to the tune of "Yankee Doodle." As with Confederates, women's affections became a tool in political discourse.[48]

At the same time they articulated their identity as Americans, Unionists made it clear that they felt deeply devoted to Virginia and did not want to concede the state to the Confederacy. "We expect to be able to point to you proudly and say, they are our countrymen and they are Virginians!" Sarah Grafton told the Hancock Union Guards after presenting them with an American flag in May.[49] A woman who wrote to the Wheeling *Daily Intelligencer* spoke for many when she voiced her desire to remain in the United States as a Virginian. Characterizing the secessionist takeover of Virginia as an illegitimate "reign of terror," she called for "a new Virginia . . . one that will shine upon our national banner as a star of the first magnitude."[50]

Preparations for war quickly gave way to the harsh realities of armed conflict. The war placed great psychological demands on Virginia women, who were acutely aware that its outcome would shape the future course of their lives. Uncertainty prevailed: "We live in a constant state of hopes and fears," wrote Laura Lee, a Confederate sympathizer in Winchester, in 1862.[51] Certain basic emotions transcended the color line, even as women's specific worries depended partly on race. Enslaved women pondered whether freedom might finally be at hand, allowing them to reunite with loved ones from whom they had been separated, or whether they and their family members would remain in bondage for years to come. White women, who shouldered unaccustomed responsibilities at home while contending with inflation, shortages, and poverty, wondered whether they would be able to sustain their families. All the while, the desperate, wrenching fear that their men would be killed loomed over all women who had male relatives in the military.

Many women began keeping journals as a means of coming to grips with their feelings; these diaries, along with personal letters, frequently exhibit great courage and fortitude, but they also abound with expressions of vulnerability and deep anxiety. Early in the war Ida Dulany wrote that she could "never feel safe" until her husband returned. She worked hard to appear calm as she took charge of their substantial plantation in Fauquier County, but her diary is replete with references to her "mental exhaustion," and she admitted that she was "often weak and nervous from the constant pressure of an anxiety that I cannot speak of."[52] "I cannot see how such a strain of anxiety and struggle can be borne much longer," wrote Cornelia McDonald in Winchester in 1863. Enslaved women, Unionists, and Confederates each expressed faith that God was on their side and would offer protection, but the magnitude of their earthly concerns prevented many from finding lasting comfort.[53]

Because uncertainty and fear of the unknown were at the root of much of their disquietude, women hungered for information that might put their minds at ease. They eagerly sought war news from fronts both near and distant and were able to discuss recent military developments in great detail.[54] Frequently, however, women were left in suspense when newspapers were scarce or delayed. Even when fresh dispatches were available, readers could not be sure they were getting accurate information. In the aftermath of battles, diarists often complained about the "contradictory accounts" to be found in the papers.[55] "We have heard so many results from the battle that we scarcely know which one to believe," wrote Maggie H. Berry, of Augusta County, following a skirmish in July 1861.[56]

Even more nerve-wracking than the quest for reliable military news was the wait for letters from husbands, sons, and brothers fighting in the field. Knowing their men were alive and perhaps even temporarily out of harm's way provided welcome relief, while the absence of communication gave rise to fearful speculation. "Was so uneasy at not hearing from the boys," Lucy Buck noted in her diary in 1862.[57] Black women and poor whites, who were much less likely to be literate, had even fewer opportunities to receive assurance that their men were safe.

The war forced many Virginia women to face their deepest fears. Perhaps as many as 30,000 of the state's white men died while serving the Confederacy, ensuring that very few women endured the war without being touched in some way by death.[58] The loss of a dear one was a stunning, crushing blow. The "screams of agony" emitted by one Fauquier County woman when informed of the death of her only son were replicated thousands of times across the state. Neighborhood boys, sons and brothers of friends, nephews, cousins, and acquaintances all left home never to return. "Day after day, one after another, the young and the strong, the good and the lovely fall around us," wrote Ida Dulany.[59]

Women who lived in areas of the state where Union and Confederate troops engaged in battle were confronted not only with the loss of men they knew; they also encountered death on a grand scale. Female hospital volunteers frequently witnessed the end of life, and in some cases they gave the deceased personal attention by preparing bodies for burial, reading from the Bible at quick services, and writing letters to assure relatives that their loved one had been cared for at the end of his life. Women's roles in the rites of death were memorialized in *The Burial of Latané* (1864), an immensely popular painting that depicted Virginia ladies presiding over the graveside service of a fallen cavalry captain.[60] While men who were killed early in the war often received individual burials and elaborate funerals, the sheer number of deaths soon required a more impersonal treatment of corpses. Those who died on the battlefield were typically buried in hastily dug mass graves, which occasionally became exposed. Traveling from Mechanicsville to Richmond, Fannie Gaines Tinsley recoiled at the sight of dead soldiers "strewed on every side" of the road. In Winchester, Cornelia McDonald's young sons found a severed foot in her garden.[61]

For every man who died, many more were wounded or contracted disease, and Virginia was home to more military hospitals than any other state. Though the image of genteel women tirelessly nursing soldiers back to health would be cherished by later generations, only rarely did members of the elite class find long-term employment in hospitals.[62] Contradictory social impulses prevented the development of a consensus about whether public nursing was proper for a lady. On one hand, the desire to promote widespread mobilization for the Confederate war effort led Virginia newspapers to emphasize the patriotism and respectability of female nurses.[63] At the same time, male hospital officials frequently resented women's presence and tried to limit their responsibilities. Most middle-class and elite women themselves did not consider such work appropriate or desirable; few wished to contend with the grisly aftermath of battle. Instead, poor and immigrant women and conscripted slaves performed most of the hands-on work that kept hospitals running. They cared for the wounded men, mopped soiled floors, laundered bloody sheets, and prepared food.[64]

Some elite and middle-class women, of course, were exceptions. Though not assigned to perform menial labor, they nonetheless did difficult work. Overcoming their aversion to mangled bodies, they washed and bandaged wounds and assisted doctors during surgery. When one would-be volunteer at a Winchester hospital could not bring herself to wash the face of a man whose eyes and nose had been destroyed by a bullet, another white woman stepped in and expertly did the job.[65] Some elite women, having won the respect of the doctors in charge, became supervisors of hospital wards. These matrons oversaw the poor white and enslaved workers and won a reputation for cleanliness and low mortality rates. Acknowledging their success, the Confederate Congress formalized arrangements that were already in place in the fall of 1862 when it authorized women to serve in military hospitals.[66] In December of that year, Phoebe Yates Pember, a native of South Carolina, arrived in Richmond to take charge of a division of Chimborazo, the largest Civil War hospital. She faced a daunting job of administration, made more challenging because many of her male colleagues thought the post inappropriate for a woman.[67]

A handful of women in Virginia established private hospitals. In the rail hub of Lynchburg, where more than twenty buildings were turned into hospitals to accommodate wounded men evacuated from the front, a group of women founded the Ladies' Relief Hospital in a hotel late in 1861. They solicited donations of food, clothing, bedding, and cash, and they sold charitable subscriptions to pay the salaries of hired nurses. Though the women's work benefited the war effort, some men treated them as intruders. The surgeon in charge of all the military hospitals in Lynchburg repeatedly tried to close the Ladies' Hospital, and the Confederate government denied its directors the privilege of purchasing goods from the city commissary.[68] Sally Louisa Tompkins, a native of Mathews County, had more luck with Confederate officials. The Robertson Hospital, which she founded in Richmond not long after the First Battle of Manassas in July 1861, established a record of returning a great many former patients back to active duty; to make the institution eligible for public funds, Jefferson Davis appointed Tompkins a captain of cavalry. She was the only woman to hold a Confederate commission.[69]

Most white women who entered hospitals did so not as employees but rather as providers of informal volunteer support. These contributions did not inspire controversy, as they constituted extensions of women's traditional roles as mothers and nurturers. At the beginning of the war, when resources were still plentiful, women sent milk, meat, fruit, vegetables, bread, and items such as books, towels, and bandages to local hospitals, sometimes by the wagon load.[70] Some middle-class and elite women became regular visitors at hospitals, where they spent time with recuperating men in an effort to lift their spirits. The men "are always ready to be amused, or to be instructed," wrote Judith McGuire, an upper-class woman who often read the Bible to soldiers at a Richmond hospital. At Christmas in 1864, the only festive event in which Laura Lee and her Winchester friends participated was a party they organized for hospitalized Confederates.[71]

Just as the war relentlessly produced casualties, it created profound economic hardships. The demands of the Confederate war effort, coupled with the Union blockade of Southern ports, resulted in shortages of essential goods as the war dragged on. Even such basic items as toothbrushes and combs were difficult to obtain. Poor women had no choice but to do without, while middle-class and wealthy women had to make radical adjustments to their patterns of consumption.[72] Materials for clothes and shoes became exceedingly scarce by 1863. That winter Isabella Woods, then in Waynesboro, informed her husband that their son "doesn't have dry feet one hour in the day."[73] Some women made clothing and blankets out of carpets or cotton mattresses. Others devoted many hours to repairing clothes, which they had no way to replace. Many slaveholding women, struggling to outfit themselves and their families, were unable to provide the enslaved with adequate clothing.[74]

The demands of the Confederate and Union armies made it difficult for families to hold on to goods they managed to acquire. The Confederate government commandeered for military use (and underpaid for) much of the food produced on Virginia farms, even as many soldiers remained undernourished. Union troops frequently emptied the storehouses of farms in their path, particularly after July 1862, when the commander of the Army of Virginia directed his men to subsist off the countryside.[75] Shortages fueled inflation; as prices skyrocketed and purchasing power eroded, hunger became common. Early in 1865, Cornelia McDonald reported that $100 bought her one pound of bacon, one pound of "bad" butter, and three candles. Her daily diet was a cup of coffee and a roll, while her children subsisted mostly on beans and sorghum.[76] Judith McGuire and her upper-class friends, waiting out the war in Richmond, were reduced to two plain meals a day by 1864. Rural areas that had not seen military action fared a bit better, as they had direct access to such milk, produce, and livestock as the army did not impress for its use.[77]

The war caused city populations to swell; order became more difficult to maintain, compounding the problems caused by poor food distribution networks and astronomical prices. In Lynchburg, the presence of large numbers of soldiers sustained numerous bars, dancehalls, gambling establishments, and houses of prostitution.[78] Richmond overflowed with soldiers, government workers, refugees, entrepreneurs, and impoverished laborers, free and enslaved. The police force could not curb increasing lawlessness, and the streets were noisy and dirty. "Tis a horrible place," Richard Watkins told his wife in July 1862. "A refined lady is seldom seen now on Main Street."[79]

In the aftermath of an unusually heavy snowstorm that made it difficult for farmers to bring their produce into Richmond, a group of working-class women met on the night of 1 April 1863, and resolved to demand food from the governor. They also decided to resort to force if they could obtain food no other way. Armed with axes, clubs, pistols, and knives, women from the city and surrounding counties converged on Capitol Square early the next morning. The governor addressed them but offered no food from government storehouses, and the growing crowd moved downhill toward the business district. Locked doors and police with fire hoses were unable to deter the angry mob. Women and men broke into stores and carried out groceries, clothing, shoes, and other goods. The crowd dispersed only when members of the Public Guard received orders to load their weapons and prepare to fire. Refusing to admit that hardworking, native women were capable of lashing out in such a manner, journalists and government officials falsely characterized the women responsible for the riot as foreigners and prostitutes.[80]

Across the state, the military service of men from poor families created dire economic conditions for the wives and children they left behind. Some indigent women sought assistance from private charitable organizations. Frequently operated by upper-class women, these groups solicited donations of food, clothing, and fuel from the community and distributed them to those

Bread Riot, 23 May 1863. *Frank Leslie's Illustrated Newspaper*, published in New York, depicts participants in the Richmond Bread Riot, which occurred on 2 April 1863, as both desperate and defiant. The presence of middle-class ladies alongside ragged and rough-hewn women trumpets the supposed breakdown of Confederate society to a Northern readership. *Courtesy of the Library of Virginia.*

in need.[81] Other impoverished families turned to city and county governments, which scrambled to find funds for poor relief during the first two years of the war. Occasionally wives wrote in desperation to Confederate officials, asking that their husbands be discharged from the service because their families needed them at home. Such requests were almost always denied.[82]

In 1862, to alleviate some of the suffering on the home front and thus remove a major incentive for desertion, the General Assembly of Virginia created a formal system of relief for disabled soldiers and sailors, widows and children of deceased soldiers and sailors, and impoverished families of men in service. County and corporation courts were authorized to borrow money, impress supplies, compile and maintain lists of people eligible for aid, and, beginning in 1864, to levy taxes. Typical of those who appeared on such registers was "Mrs James Minor 1 child 2 years no support wants corn and leather." Almost every war widow in Henry County received assistance in 1863. During the next two years, as more women fell into poverty, and as goods became more difficult to procure, local governments were forced to turn away many of their petitioners. The state government attempted to provide additional relief in 1864 by appropriating $1 million for families in counties controlled by the Union army and by setting prices for cotton, cloth, and salt, but no policy was able to stem the deepening economic distress.[83]

Some poor white women made ends meet by following the army and working as cooks, clothes washers, and seamstresses. Some turned to prostitution in cities and in military camps. Others found jobs that, while "respectable," were nonetheless arduous. Hundreds of women operated sewing machines at the Confederate clothing depot in Richmond, while many more waited in line for hours to obtain precut fabric, which they sewed at home. The pay for piecework was meager, and shortages of cloth sometimes limited the amount of work that was available.[84] Black women and poor whites labored for long hours in uncomfortable conditions at factories that equipped the Confederate army. The Confederate States Laboratory in Richmond, for example, employed white women and girls, some as young as nine years old, to assemble ammunition. On 13 March 1863, a massive explosion at the factory killed almost fifty workers and injured another twenty. Some victims, burned beyond recognition, died instantly, while others ran from the building with their clothes and hair on fire. Richmonders were deeply disturbed by the tragedy.

"Virginians going to commissary for rations," by Edwin Fobes, 18 February 1864. A family of upper-class women, unable to provide enough food for themselves, travel to the commissary for rations early in 1864. Despite experiencing newfound privations, they are still more fortunate than most, as they possess livestock, a sturdy cart, and the assistance of an enslaved man and a white man. *Courtesy of the Library of Congress, Morgan Collection of Civil War Drawings, LC-DIG-ppmsca-20662.*

Nonetheless, women who were desperate for work lined up for jobs when the factory soon reopened.[85]

Even women from wealthy backgrounds sometimes found it necessary to engage in paid work during the war. Educated women sought employment at various state and Confederate government agencies. Lucy Parke Chamberlayne Bagby, who came from a prominent family, worked at the Confederate Treasury office, where she and her colleagues signed, clipped, and numbered currency.[86] Judith McGuire, wife of an influential minister, applied several times for a clerkship and finally obtained a position at the Commissary in December 1863. She found her duties agreeable but averred that "no lady would bind herself to keep accounts for six hours per day without a dire necessity." Most of her fellow workers, she wrote, had been driven to work there by "fallen fortunes and destroyed homes."[87]

Women who took over the management of farms and plantations in the absence of their husbands or fathers confronted work of a different kind. In yeoman households, white women devoted most of their time and energy to the daily struggle for subsistence, performing heavy physical work formerly done by men.[88] Rural women of the upper class did not have to spend their days in the fields, but they were confronted with many strenuous duties for which they had not been prepared. Under chaotic circumstances, they had to handle the disposition of produce and livestock and manage household finances. They decided how much wheat and corn to send to the mill, when to sell livestock and what price to accept in an unstable economy, and how to allocate money that was becoming ever scarcer. "I am so unaccustomed to care and anxiety of this kind, that it troubles me, and you may be sure that I miss my provident husband," Isabella Woods wrote when contemplating whether to sell her family's cattle late in the summer of 1861.[89] Husbands in the service advised and instructed their wives from afar, often in response to questions, and they offered encouragement and expressed respect for the work women were doing. "I think you did excellently well with your cattle," Hal Dulany assured his wife, Ida Dulany, in the fall of 1861. Just as Hal Dulany indicated his recognition of his wife's new role by using the word "your" when referring to their common property, Ida Dulany used "my" when discussing the items now under her purview.[90]

Slaveholding women assumed management just as the institution of slavery was breaking down. Their duties included making sure slaves had adequate food and clothing even in the midst of shortages, planning work schedules, imposing discipline, and sometimes hiring out laborers to generate income. Taking advantage of wartime disorder, slaves began to mount overt challenges to the authority of their female owners, who, they realized, were more acutely dependent than ever on the labor enslaved blacks performed.[91] Enslaved men and women increasingly ignored orders, chose which tasks to do, left work unfinished, refused to be hired out, or spent days away from home.[92] In Lynchburg, a woman named Maria was sold after declining to do any work while her mistress was sick; in Winchester, a black woman called Emily left home temporarily after her mistress offended her; in Fauquier County,

Lucy A. Cox, after 1865. Lucy Ann White Cox traveled with her husband's unit, the 30th Virginia Regiment, Company A, as a vivandiere. Her duties likely included cooking, washing clothes, and nursing the wounded. The relatively few white Southern women who worked in this capacity endured the hardships of military life and generally earned the respect and affection of the soldiers they served. *Courtesy of the Museum of the Confederacy, Richmond, Va.*

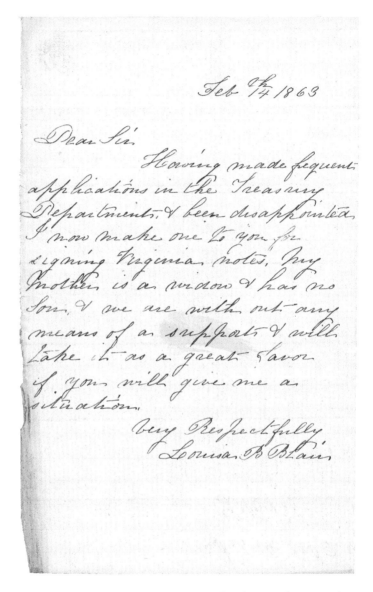

Louisa B. Blair letter, 14 February 1863. With men away from home and money in short supply, Louisa B. Blair and other women from privileged backgrounds sought employment for the first time. Clerkships in government offices offered a steady income but were difficult to come by. *Courtesy of the Library of Virginia, Applications of Ladies for Clerkships on Virginia Treasury Notes, 1861–1864, Auditor of Public Accounts, Administration of State Government: Public Debt–Treasury Notes (Entry 454).*

one Patsey refused to move into the house that her mistress ordered her to occupy.[93] What Ida Dulany in 1862 called "the arrogant triumphant insolence of the slaves" deeply frustrated elite white women, some of whom began to question whether slavery was worth maintaining. By undermining order on the home front, enslaved blacks made a tangible contribution to the Union war effort that complemented the service of many blacks in the United States armed forces.[94]

Though slavery was eroding, the institution continued to function in many regions of Virginia for the duration of the war. On small slaveholding farms, the absence of white men meant that enslaved women were given new chores and often had to perform more heavy labor in the fields than they had before the war. When enslaved men escaped, women who stayed behind were confronted with additional work.[95] The demands of the Confederate war effort also shaped black women's experiences during the conflict. The government drafted slaves and free black men and impressed free black women to work in military camps and hospitals, separating family members and subjecting them to difficult labor

"Waiting for Dinner," by Edwin Forbes, ca. 1864. Enslaved women and children gather in a plantation kitchen. *Courtesy of the Virginia Historical Society, 1996.190.2.*

on behalf of a cause that few if any blacks supported. Other enslaved women were hired out when their owners could no longer afford to support them.[96]

Sales of slaves continued throughout the war, even as prices increased dramatically, reflecting the purchasers' unwillingness to admit that the South's labor system was falling apart. Because so many enslaved men had escaped or been impressed into Confederate service, those who faced sale late in the war were mostly women and children.[97] Sales conducted amid the chaos of war were especially likely to tear black families apart, as the death of an owner or the financial collapse of a slaveholding family frequently necessitated the disposal of human property without regard for kinship ties. In Winchester, the owner of an enslaved woman named Lethea sold her in 1862 because he was afraid she would leave with the Union army. Weeping and wringing her hands, Lethea departed with her daughter after bidding farewell to her sleeping son, who was not to join them.[98]

As Lethea's owner realized, enslaved men and women were presented with a straightforward means of attaining freedom in areas where Union forces appeared. Even in regions untouched by Federal troops, home front disorder made escape seem more feasible. Because men often fled from slavery first, women and children frequently faced the dangers of escape on their own in the later stages of the conflict.[99] Along the Pamunkey River in the tidewater region, slaves seized their opportunity to leave when Northern troops arrived in July 1862. In Lynchburg, slave departures became commonplace after the Union army established itself in the Shenandoah Valley and the Blue Ridge Mountains in the spring of 1863; in Winchester, which changed hands many times during the war, groups of blacks left town each time Federal forces evacuated.[100] Union soldiers encouraged blacks to leave their masters but frequently failed to provide much assistance to them. Catherine, an enslaved woman who left Winchester with Union forces, turned back because she did not have enough food and because she had seen other starving, raggedly dressed black women collapse by the side of the road. Some escapees equipped themselves for their journey by taking horses, clothes, food, and valuables from their owners when they left, exacting a further economic toll on Confederate Virginia.[101]

By taking the risks necessary to obtain their freedom, enslaved people forced changes in federal policy and helped ensure that a Union victory would mean the end of slavery. At Fort Monroe near Hampton early in the war, General Benjamin F. Butler declared escaped slaves who reached Union lines to be contraband of war, explaining that the army was within its rights to harbor them because they were a species of property that could otherwise be used against the United States. By July 1861, about 900 black men, women, and children had arrived at the fort. Though the federal government's policy toward fugitives quickly evolved—the Confiscation Acts of 1861 and 1862 and the Emancipation Proclamation, which took effect in 1863, were all designed to weaken and eventually destroy slavery—the Union army was ill equipped to care for the rapidly growing population of refugees, and many Federal soldiers regarded the blacks with contempt.[102]

Life was precarious for women in the refugee camps that sprang up around Hampton Roads. When possible, women were put to work preparing food, washing clothes, and assisting in hospitals, but military commanders generally

Contrabands at Cumberland Landing, Virginia, 1862. African Americans across Virginia escaped slavery by making their way to Union lines. James F. Gibson photographed this group of "contrabands" on 14 May 1862, at Cumberland Landing, New Kent County, where Union forces were stationed during the Peninsula Campaign. *Courtesy of the Library of Congress, Prints and Photographs Division, LC-DIG-cwpb-01005.*

considered them a drain on resources. A few became prostitutes; others were victims of rape by Union soldiers. Black refugees endured inadequate housing and clothing, overcrowding, hunger, and disease.[103] To alleviate these conditions, the Bureau of Negro Affairs, established by General Butler in 1863, set up government farms on abandoned lands. Women did a substantial amount of the agricultural work because able-bodied black men were engaged in military labor.[104] One of the most stable refugee communities was the Freedman's Village, established on a portion of Robert E. Lee's Arlington plantation in May 1863. Its more than 1,000 inhabitants had access to sturdy houses, two churches, a hospital, and a school. They attended general education classes and received instruction in trades.[105]

Not all escaped slaves lived in refugee camps. Some black women—often those who had husbands serving in Union regiments—followed the army, where they worked as peddlers or as cooks and laundresses for individual soldiers. Frustrated by their presence, officers sometimes accused black women of undermining the discipline of their troops and ejected them from their lines, or, in a few cases, sent them back to their masters in defiance of federal policy. A minority of refugees avoided any contact with the Union army. After escaping from their masters, they formed self-sustaining maroon communities near their former homes, perhaps in an effort to remain near relatives.[106]

While black women who escaped slavery went about the difficult work of forging new lives, the owners they left behind had to make psychological and practical adjustments to their absence. Early in the war, white women frequently expressed faith in the loyalty and affection of their slaves, believing that blacks were contented with their station in life. Slaveholding women therefore felt shocked and betrayed when they discovered that their slaves had left. Lucy Buck, after realizing that her family's slaves had departed one night in June 1863, voiced "indignation at their ingratitude in taking the horses when they knew they were our main dependence of support."[107] Many white women were convinced that blacks who left did not know what was best for them and would deeply regret having traded the "many comforts" of their life in bondage, as Judith McGuire put it, for the "hard work" that awaited them in freedom. "Poor, deluded creatures!" she exclaimed.[108]

The departure of enslaved women meant that their former mistresses, unaccustomed to washing clothes, ironing, cooking, baking bread, and cleaning the kitchen, now had to turn their attention to these and other essential chores. Several days after her family's slaves ran away, Lucy Buck described her activities: "Finished ironing, got dinner and did some cleaning up. In the afternoon there were pies to make for tomorrow, salt rising to bake, and supper to get besides milking, and washing the children. Oh such a weary time we had of it—the children were sleepy and fretful, the stove *wouldn't* get hot, the bread would not bake and the cows *would* run. . . . I felt almost crazed."[109] Slavery had provided the basis for white Southern beliefs about the nature of black womanhood and white womanhood. As black women claimed their freedom and white women took over work formerly done by the enslaved, members of each group came to see the world in new ways.

In addition to the erosion of slavery, the war brought about other major changes in the composition of Virginia households that altered the substance of women's daily lives and reshaped their self-perceptions. Many households headed by men in the antebellum era became female-centered after the war began. White women frequently moved in with relatives to find companionship and to pool resources, creating tightly knit female kin groups. Many of these units achieved self-sufficiency; those that did not tended to turn to female friends for assistance.[110]

Particularly in areas near Washington, D.C., in counties that became part of West Virginia in 1863, and in the Hampton Roads region, the arrival of Union troops forced some Confederate families to abandon their homes in great haste and move elsewhere; they left behind most of their possessions, including objects of great sentimental value that reflected important events in their lives and anchored their identities. Judith McGuire, whose family fled from Alexandria at the beginning of the war, deplored the need to part with "so many relics—hair of the dead, little golden memorials, etc.—all valueless to others, but very dear to our hearts."[111] Vacated homes and the items inside them often met harsh fates. Some houses were occupied by Union soldiers, used as hospitals, or dismantled to obtain construction materials.[112]

Finding a new place to live in unfamiliar surroundings was a daunting task, and one that women often had to accomplish without the help of men, a radical departure from prewar life. Many women found themselves for the first time traveling unescorted, driving wagons, handling money, and negotiating for lodging.[113] After leaving Winchester and traveling to Amherst

Brandy Station, Va., photographed by James F. Gibson, February 1864. Officers and a lady pose outside the headquarters of a horse artillery unit in Brandy Station, Culpeper County. *Courtesy of the Library of Congress, Prints and Photographs Division, LC-DIG-cwpb-04066.*

County with her eight children in the summer of 1863, Cornelia McDonald and one of her adult stepdaughters had to settle in an abandoned hotel, which she described as "rather doleful, with the paper streaming down off the walls, the hearths sunk, and rat holes all around." In Richmond, where many refugees congregated, housing was scarce and expensive, and long-term quarters were especially difficult to find. Families had to split up when quarters large enough to accommodate them were unavailable or unaffordable.[114]

Women who did not leave their homes when Union troops appeared faced challenges of a different kind. For African Americans, the arrival of Federal forces could be a mixed blessing. Some soldiers made off with the possessions slaves and free blacks had managed to accumulate, just as they did with the belongings of white Virginians, and some soldiers considered black women fair game for violent abuse. Most of the time, however, the presence of Northern troops offered a gateway to freedom, even when the soldiers provided little material assistance. When troops camped nearby, black women volunteered to cook meals for them and passed along information about local Confederates. In one extraordinary case, Mary Louveste, a black employee of Gosport Navy Yard in Portsmouth, traveled to Washington, D.C., in February 1862 with documents describing the ironclad *Virginia*, intelligence that was of great use to the secretary of the navy.[115]

Among Confederate women, the arrival of Union forces generated widespread fear and uncertainty. "The women seem terribly alarmed at the thought of the Yankees coming here, as if they were monsters in human form," Unionist Julia Chase wrote from Winchester in 1862.[116] Daily life was disrupted in a variety of ways. Union troops prevented residents from crossing picket lines without passes, which stifled mobility and cut off communication with those beyond the lines.[117] Because Federal troops were under orders to arrest men who refused to fight for the Union or to take a loyalty oath, male Confederate sympathizers often went into temporary hiding, returning when the soldiers had moved on. Women who maintained too high a profile as Confederate stalwarts also faced arrest; some were banished to places beyond Confederate lines.[118]

It was not unusual for rural women and children, unaccompanied by men, to encounter enemy forces. Union soldiers marched past their farms and sometimes camped or even skirmished with Confederates on their property. Soldiers and civilians engaged in bitter confrontations: as Union troops crisscrossed the state, they trampled crops, dismantled fences to use as firewood, helped themselves to corn, wheat, and vegetables, took livestock (and shot animals they could not transport), destroyed mills, and carried away farm implements. Some of the most concentrated destruction of the war took place during the autumn of 1864, when Union troops under General Philip Sheridan, moving up the Shenandoah Valley with the objective of total destruction, left many burning houses and outbuildings in their wake.[119] A group of women in Harrisonburg, distressed by the Confederate army's inability to turn the Federals away, petitioned the War Department for permission to "raise a full regiment of *ladies*—between the ages of 16 and 40—armed & equipped to perform regular service." The signers pledged to "leave our hearthstones—to endure any sacrifice—any privation for the ultimate success of Our Holy Cause."[120]

"Your men bin stealing my hogs," by Alfred R. Waud, 17 June 1863. Whimsically labeled a member of the "F.F.V" (First Families of Virginia) by artist Alfred R. Waud, a correspondent for *Harper's Weekly*, this barefoot woman in Loudoun County wields a harvesting tool in defense of her hogs. Across Virginia, wealthy and poor women alike attempted to keep their livestock, food, and valuables out of the hands of Union soldiers. *Courtesy of the Library of Congress, Morgan Collection of Civil War Drawings, LC-DIG-ppmsca-20129.*

Most women did not propose to leave the hearthstone, however, and many across the state suffered invasions of their domestic space. In Barbour County, Isabella Woods opened her door one morning in 1861 to find six men with drawn swords and daggers. "I told them there was not a man in the house," she reported. "They merely walked in and waited for breakfast."[121] In addition to demanding meals, Union officers sometimes selected conveniently located houses to serve as temporary quarters, forcing residents to confine themselves to one or two rooms. "They use all the furniture, house linen, kitchen utensils and everything as if all was their own property," Laura Lee wrote from Winchester in 1864.[122] While some Union soldiers who arrived on Confederate doorsteps were polite and respectful—an officer encamped at one plantation consulted the lady of the house about how best to protect her French china— others seemed bent on humiliation and destruction.[123] Soldiers forced their way into homes, searching for valuables and for Confederate-sympathizing men. Ida Dulany described a raid on her house in 1864: "They would not wait for me to unlock any drawers, but with their heavy boots kicked and broke open my handsome furniture. . . .[They] broke the liquor case all to pieces and took every thing they could carry off . . . they broke open the oak book case, threw everything out of it over the floor . . . they kicked open the trunks, pulled open the drawers, opened the wardrobes, ransacking every thing." Known Unionists in Virginia faced similar attacks by Confederate troops.[124]

Raiders sometimes made special efforts to humble the women whose homes they targeted. One strategy was to bring slaves inside to assist with the search or to consume refreshments.[125] Another common tactic was to destroy women's clothing and that of their families. Soldiers trampled women's dresses, smeared them with bacon grease, or ordered female slaves to put them on.[126] One woman in Middleburg had carefully filled a camp chest with the clothes worn by her two recently deceased daughters; though she pleaded with raiding soldiers not to break open the chest, they reached inside and tossed the contents about the room. The bereaved mother "bore it in silence until the sight of a half worn little shoe held up by one of them prov[ed] more than she could bear." Shrieking, she collapsed to the floor, while the soldiers "walked off laughing at the whole affair as a good joke." Because clothing was such an intimate possession that in many ways represented the self, attacks on garments grieved Southern women deeply.[127]

Virginia women, many of whom were thrust for the first time into the role of defender of the household, did what they could to protect their belongings. Many female Confederates took care to hide jewelry, silver, and important papers, often by burying them.[128] Some tried to defend their property rights by traveling to Union camps and lodging complaints with commanders about the actions of their men. Though frequently ineffectual, such missions occasionally yielded a small measure of satisfaction.[129] Women with bold personalities overtly resisted the demands of soldiers who showed up at their houses. While nothing could stop bands of armed men who were intent on searching a residence and stealing or destroying its contents, most Union soldiers were interested in foraging rather than in gratuitous violence, and persistent refusals to accommodate them could sometimes dissuade those looking for easy targets. Some women saw resistance as a political act. "My tongue being my only weapon," Ida Dulany wrote, "I determined when I came in contact with the enemy to use it in the service of my beloved country."[130]

Many Confederate women employed strategies of resistance that fell squarely within prescribed gender conventions. Some treated Union soldiers with silent contempt, turning their backs when they approached or crossing the street to avoid meeting them. Others displayed their opposition through the use of personal adornments. They attached small Confederate flags to their dresses, proudly wore calico and gingham "secession bonnets," or donned veils to prevent enemy soldiers from seeing their faces.[131] When Union soldiers were within earshot, women sometimes sang or played Southern songs such as "The Bonnie Blue Flag" and "Dixie." Protected to some degree by their gender, women could be more openly disrespectful of Federal troops than Confederate men dared to be. Some women took further advantage of the cover offered by their femininity to smuggle mail or other items, which they sewed inside their skirts.[132]

A few Confederate women became spies. Maria Isabella "Belle" Boyd, a young native of Martinsburg, signaled the depth of her resistance in July 1861, when she shot and mortally wounded a Union soldier who had insulted her mother as he attempted to hang a Union banner over their house. Sent to live with relatives in Front Royal, Boyd informed Confederate officers about Union troop positions and in October 1861 became a courier for Generals Thomas J. "Stonewall" Jackson and P. G. T. Beauregard. She was arrested in July 1862 and spent a month in Old Capitol Prison in Washington, D.C.[133] Antonia Ford, a young woman who lived in Fairfax Court House, learned of Union troop activity from Federal officers quartered in her house and reported the information to General J. E. B. Stuart, who gave her an honorary commission as aide-de-camp in October 1861. She also passed intelligence to partisan ranger John Singleton Mosby and was implicated in his raid on Fairfax Court House in March 1863, after which she was confined to the Old Capitol Prison for seven months. In Tazewell County, Molly Tynes became aware of Union troops' plans to attack the Virginia and Tennessee Railroad near Wytheville in July 1863. She is credited with riding more than fifty miles on horseback to warn Confederate forces, saving the railroad and nearby lead and salt mines.[134]

The most important female spy was a Unionist, Richmond native Elizabeth Van Lew. Her Northern-born parents owned slaves and had become part of the Richmond elite, but Van Lew and her mother developed antislavery convictions and worked in the decades before the war to ameliorate the system from within, all the while conforming in public to social conventions. During the war, Van Lew—casting herself as an exemplar of Christian ladyhood and taking advantage of Southern men's belief that elite Southern women were by definition Confederate patriots—delivered food, supplies, and money to Union prisoners of war and hospital patients and hid escapees in her mansion on Church Hill. At great personal risk, she became the leader of a network of Union spies that included clerks in the Confederate military bureaucracy (probably in both the Adjutant-General's and War Departments), a railroad superintendent, the clerk of Libby Prison, a handful of white women, and some black Richmonders of both sexes. One of Van Lew's former slaves, Mary Elizabeth Richards, also known as Mary Elizabeth Bowser, was a member of the ring and may even have worked for a time as a servant and spy in the Confederate White House, though the evidence is sparse. In 1864 Union general Benjamin F. Butler recruited Van Lew as an official federal agent, and she passed sensitive military information to him in coded letters written with invisible ink. She shrewdly evaded detection for the duration of the war.[135]

The creation of West Virginia in 1863 removed the majority of Unionists from Virginia's borders, but a few of them remained scattered throughout the state. The origins of Union sympathy were diverse. Some women, like Van Lew, despised the Confederacy because they abhorred slavery; others— such as Julia Chase in Winchester—supported slavery but valued the Union more. Whatever their motivation, Unionist women assisted Federal troops when they were nearby, just as secessionist women aided Confederate forces. They brought soldiers food, took care of sick men, and shared information about the surrounding countryside. In Rockingham County, Margaret Rhodes baked bread for Northern soldiers, hid Confederate deserters in her home, and operated an underground mail route that allowed Unionists to communicate.[136]

The benefits of Union sympathy were scant. When Federal troops conducted raids, Unionists frequently fell victim alongside their Confederate neighbors. In 1864, Northern soldiers took more than $1,000 worth of personal property from Margaret Rhodes, despite her record of material assistance to the Union cause.[137] Caroline Bradby Cook, a resident of the Pamunkey Indian Reservation in King William County, averred that she had opposed the Confederacy "from first to last." She cooked and washed for Union soldiers, while her male relatives served as river pilots and scouts. But in May 1863, Federal soldiers camped on her property and dismantled her fence and house (then unoccupied, as Cook had moved into her father's nearby home). After the war, Cook and some of her fellow Unionists received compensation from the federal Southern Claims Commission, but most such applications were denied.[138]

In communities that were home to substantial numbers of both Unionists and Southern sympathizers—most of which were located in the northern part of the state—neighbors quickly turned against one another. In Winchester, which each army occupied at various points during the war, Unionist and Confederate residents reported their adversaries to the opposing forces. "The citizens in town have become demons almost," wrote Unionist Julia Chase in May 1862. In Barbour County, Confederate sympathizer Isabella Woods wrote of her "bitter enemies" in the town of Philippi in 1861, and her mother reported in 1862 that pro-Southern friends were afraid to help each other "lest their houses

Caroline Bradby Cook and family, 1899. During the Civil War, Caroline Bradby Cook and her family assisted Union troops encamped at the Pamunkey Indian Reservation in King William County. Cook appears in this photograph from 1899 with the family of her son, George Major Cook, who was chief of the Pamunkey tribe from 1902 to 1930. *Courtesy of the National Anthropological Archives, Smithsonian Institution, NAA INV 6196100 OPPS NEG 880.*

be burned by the Abolition party." The war ruptured some of Virginians' most intimate relationships, as churches and even families divided.[139]

For a minority of Confederate women, the relentless demands of a drawn-out war eventually created personal interests that outweighed their commitment to victory. With their slaves gone, their wealth eroded, and perhaps one or more male relatives dead, these women saw nothing left to fight for. Some poor women wanted their husbands to desert the army, come home, and save their families from destitution. By late in 1864 many considered it futile to expend any more effort on the war.[140]

The majority of white Virginia women, however, did not give up on their new nation; they maintained a deep conviction that the Confederacy must win the war. Though they grumbled about government policies, complained of weariness, and yearned for an end to hostilities, they invested themselves wholeheartedly in the Confederate cause. Only by turning away the Union army could life ever go back to normal, they believed.[141] Cornelia McDonald hoped for peace in 1863, but wrote that she did "not want it at the expense of our honour or independence."[142] Tremendous hardships created bonds of shared anger and a common desire for revenge against the United States that reinforced devotion to the cause. "I am more of a Rebel every day I live," Jane Woods Holt declared in 1863, not long before her town of Philippi became part of the new state of West Virginia.[143] These women held on to their faith that victory was possible and considered desertion an appalling abandonment of duty. In March 1864, a woman brought her deserter husband back to his military unit and begged that he be forgiven. In Culpeper County that year, neighborhood opinion still held that desertion was a disgrace.[144]

On 2 April 1865, the Confederate government fled Richmond, and Confederate forces set fire to supply stores in the capital, producing a conflagration. Union troops entered the city the next day. While women devoted to the Confederate cause shed tears of anguish, African American women ran into the streets to celebrate. Several fell at the knees of Union soldiers—some of them black—and embraced even their horses.[145] On 9 April, General Robert E. Lee surrendered his Army of Northern Virginia at Appomattox Court House. For some white women, the end came as a relief. But for most, defeat was a shock and a humiliation. "My brain refuses to grasp the idea of this great calamity," Mary Washington Early, en route from Buckingham County to Lynchburg, wrote.[146] "I cannot *cannot* believe we are whipped," lamented Mary Goodwin in Wythe County.[147] In Richmond, a Confederate officer's wife expressed the thoughts of many other white women: "Was it to this end we had fought and starved and gone naked and cold? to this end that the wives and children of many a dear and gallant friend were husbandless and fatherless? to this end that our homes were in ruins, our State devastated?"[148]

In cities and towns, on farms and in refugee camps, African American women greeted the news with joy. Shouting and singing, they celebrated their freedom. On one Virginia plantation, former slaves sat together contemplating their new status when an elderly woman began to speak: "Tain't no mo' sellin' today/ Tain't no mo' hirin' today/ Tain't no pullin' off shirts today/ Its stomp down freedom today/ Stomp it down!" Setting the words to music, the other men and women "shouted dat song all de res' de day," former bondwoman Charlotte Brown remembered. It was, she declared, a "glorious time!"[149]

The Civil War left deep scars on Virginia's landscape and gave rise to profound social disruption. One-third of the state's territory had been lost. Virginia's once-profitable agricultural economy was in tatters—barns and fences lay in ruins, livestock was scarce, and fields were empty. The armies had destroyed roads, bridges, and railroads. Industrial output, which had burgeoned during the 1850s, ground to a halt. Towns and cities, especially the capital, had sustained severe damage. Land values plummeted, and Virginians struggled to obtain credit and cash. Enslaved labor, the foundation of Virginia's antebellum economy and social order, was gone forever.

The task of rebuilding fell on a population whose energies were all but exhausted. More than thirty thousand Virginians had died while serving in the Confederate and Union armies, leaving widows and orphans to devise strategies for survival. Many soldiers returned with permanent physical disabilities or psychological wounds that left them unable to provide for their families. Even Confederate men who emerged from the war without major injuries were defeated and demoralized. Two of the responsibilities that once had stood at the center of their identities as white men—the mastery or potential mastery of slaves, and the protection and sustenance of white women—had been obliterated or severely undermined, raising questions

Ruins, photographed by Alexander Gardner, April 1865. Two women in mourning clothes walk through the ruins of Richmond in April 1865. The fire set by evacuating Confederate troops devastated much of the city. *Courtesy of the Library of Congress, Prints and Photographs Division, LC-DIG-cwpb-00434.*

about the meaning of masculinity. White women, many of whom had faced great hardships and wielded newfound authority while their male relatives were absent, had in the process demonstrated the limitations of antebellum ideas about femininity, setting up a postwar need for white men and women to renegotiate gender roles.

Black women surveyed the postbellum world with joy, hope, and a certain amount of trepidation. They struggled daily to shape freedom so that it did not resemble slavery. Their paramount goals were to bring their relatives together, care for their families, strengthen the black community through churches, schools, and benevolent societies, and exert some control over the terms of their labor, but limited resources and dogged opposition from many white men and women threatened to subvert their aspirations.[150] The large number of freedpeople who crowded into refugee camps and tidewater cities—a situation exacerbated by the postwar arrival of former slaves from other states—made employment difficult to find, particularly as war-related jobs disappeared.[151] The federal government's decision to return abandoned lands to their white owners rather than distribute them to newly freed slaves displaced many blacks who had settled on farms during the war, depriving them of the opportunity to become independent producers.[152] Meanwhile, enslaved women who had remained on their owners' farms and plantations during the war faced a different set of challenges. Many did not know where to go now that they had their liberty, and rural travel was difficult once they decided on a destination. Those who worked for their former owners often found them reluctant to admit that emancipation need change anything about the way labor functioned.[153]

In March 1865, the federal government established the Bureau of Refugees, Freedmen, and Abandoned Lands to oversee the transition to free labor in the South. Once the war ended, Freedmen's Bureau agents set up shop in communities across the former Confederacy. Their first order of business was to provide food, clothing, and medicine to the thousands of destitute former slaves who needed immediate assistance. During the summer of 1865 the Bureau developed more-stringent standards for eligibility, and by October 1866 aid was officially available only to orphans, the physically infirm and elderly, and family members of black Union soldiers. Averse to creating a culture of dependency, agents were adamant that able-bodied blacks must not receive handouts but should support themselves by working; those who did not find jobs could even be arrested and hired out. Though no less insistent that women should find paying work, agents sometimes made exceptions and provided rations to impoverished women, especially if they were unmarried or had small children.[154]

In its effort to ensure the gainful employment of as many former slaves as possible and to establish order amid postwar chaos, the Bureau strongly encouraged freedmen and women to stay with their old masters and to work under yearlong contracts. In cases where Bureau officials doubted that black parents could care for their children, they supported the placement of the youngsters as apprentices to white employers. These policies contradicted blacks' ideas about what freedom should be.[155] At the same time, however, the Bureau made it possible for blacks to claim their rights as citizens. Among its many functions were to help separated family members find one another, to legalize marriages contracted informally under slavery, to establish schools, and to help families of black Union soldiers prepare applications for pensions. Freedmen's courts adjudicated disputes among blacks and between blacks and whites. By lodging complaints and filing suits with the Bureau, black women worked to protect their families, their property, their labor, and their physical safety, though the very need to seek such extensive government intervention gives some indication of the obstacles that littered the road to freedom.[156]

For most former slaves, freedom meant first and foremost the ability to define for themselves who constituted their family and to reunite with those people if they had been separated. Black women went to great lengths to find their husbands and children, with whom they established households unencumbered by the fear that a relative could be sold away. Yet the legacy of slavery complicated the formation of many postemancipation black families, engendering bitter disputes and forcing people to make difficult decisions. Some former masters kept black children in their custody and denied mothers their parental rights. Many women confronted with such resistance lodged complaints with the Freedmen's Bureau, which had the authority to order the release of illegally detained children.[157] The complainant was responsible for delivering such orders to the white offender, however, which sometimes resulted in violent reprisal. In 1866, a former master threatened the life of a woman who repeatedly attempted to reclaim her granddaughter from him; after finally giving his word that he would return the child, he rescinded his promise and knocked the grandmother down, choked her, and whipped her.[158]

Even when tracking down children did not result in confrontation, the path to family unification could be rocky. Sometimes women who regained custody of sons or daughters after a long period of separation discovered that the children no longer regarded them as parents, and in some cases did not remember them at all.[159] Older children occasionally resisted being returned to their mothers. In August 1866 Margaret Wesendonck sought the assistance of a Freedmen's Bureau agent in Christiansburg when her thirteen-year-old daughter, Jane, refused to leave Richmond, where she had been taken by her former mistress. Despite Margaret's insistence that "I have a good Home here, where I can take care of her," the Bureau allowed Jane to stay where she wished. Some relationships simply could not be picked up where they had left off.[160]

Relations between black spouses were also reconfigured in the postemancipation years. Many black marriages received legal recognition through Virginia's Legitimization Act of 1866, which declared couples who were cohabiting by 27 February of that year to be regarded officially as husband and wife.[161] On the other hand, men and women who had been subjected to unwanted spousal relationships while enslaved dissolved those unions after they were emancipated. Some freedwomen emerged from slavery with more than one husband, their first spouse having been sold out of visiting range. Those who were involved in such relationships faced heart-wrenching situations when they encountered one another as free people. One unidentified woman described a brief reunion with her first husband as "like a stroke of death to me. We threw ourselves into each others arms and cried. His wife looked and was jealous, but she needn't have been. My [current] husband is so kind, I shouldn't leave him, but I ain't happy."[162]

Children born to enslaved women sometimes became the focus of custody battles between parents when the father, separated from his offspring under slavery, sought them out after Emancipation. At stake were emotional bonds as well as control over children's labor. To resolve such disputes parents often turned to the Freedmen's Bureau. In 1867 John Burbridge filed suit in Yorktown to gain custody of the two teenage children he had fathered with Mary Winder. Though he had played little part in raising the children, he wished to be their guardian now that they were old enough to work. Winder defended her parental rights, arguing that "I have worked hard to raise these children," and that "they are now at an age that they can help me." The Bureau, which tended to support the claims of mothers but also took into account the character and financial stability of each parent, ruled that the children should stay with Winder.[163]

Initially in flux, gender roles began to take distinct forms as many black men asserted themselves as protectors of and providers for their families. Men increasingly took it on themselves to represent their wives to the outside world—for example, by making labor contracts for them or by going to court to recover money owed them. Black preachers and politicians encouraged women to respect their husbands' authority and devote themselves to home and family. Reinforcing this turn toward male dominance were white missionaries and educators, who idealized the middle-class notion of husbands as providers and wives as homemakers, and the Freedmen's Bureau, which emphasized the duties and responsibilities of black manhood. When black women complained about husbands who shirked their obligations, the Bureau often responded by granting divorces and ordering the payment of child support. In Suffolk, a Bureau agent recommended that a man who had deserted his wife be arrested and forcibly returned to their household, as the woman had an infant child she could not support on her own.[164]

Emerging ideological prescriptions regarding gender roles did not always dictate the way real men and women lived their lives. Though black women had a considerable interest in building men up after the degrading experience of slavery, they were equally intent on making freedom meaningful to themselves. For some, freedom meant the ability to cease working for wages and to focus instead on the domestic concerns of their own families. Establishing a private life outside the oversight of whites was of paramount importance. The ability to labor for the benefit of their own households—through such activities as raising garden produce and poultry, making clothes, and cooking—was for them a privilege of freedom, not a relegation to a separate sphere. Rather than accept submission to whites or to men, many black women looked for ways to control the terms of their labor and thus have a say in balancing their work and family life.[165]

The vast majority of black women, whether married or single, could not make ends meet without working for pay. The quality of their freedom, therefore, depended on their ability to serve notice that they would no longer be treated as slaves. Many women reinforced their status as free people by refusing to work for their former owners or by switching employers frequently. They often pursued part-time or task work, such as clothes washing, which allowed them to devote a significant portion of their time and energy to the upkeep of their own households and communities. Even those who had no practical option but to work for their old masters understood the value of their labor and tried to shape the nature of their employment accordingly. Domestic workers, for example, performed only the work they were hired to do and rejected additional tasks; cooks refused to iron clothes, and housekeepers declined to prepare meals. Those who did not work by the task clearly defined the number of hours per day they would be at their employer's disposal and negotiated for days off. Field laborers bargained for similar concessions, sometimes by conducting work slowdowns or strikes, though many black women avoided fieldwork altogether after emancipation.[166]

Black women's self-assertion led to clashes with whites, who wanted to maintain an inexpensive, deferential, permanent labor force. Many white women of the former slaveholding class complained bitterly that servants had become disobedient and demanding. Planters disparaged the "idleness" of black women who withdrew from field labor.[167] Frustrated employers showed their disregard for blacks' freedom by withholding wages, ignoring the provisions of written labor contracts, forcing employees' children to work without pay, and lashing out violently when servants or other employees declined to follow their orders. Black women countered by lodging voluminous complaints with the Freedmen's Bureau, making it clear that they were determined to protect their rights as free people. The ability to bring charges against whites signaled a radical shift in the status of black women, yet reliance on the efforts of a government bureaucracy could be a chancy proposition. While Bureau agents strove to adjudicate individual claims fairly in order to make free labor meaningful in the South, they were unable to help everyone, and, in the end, they failed to effect widespread changes in white attitudes toward black labor before the Bureau ceased most of its functions in 1868.[168]

By about 1870, agricultural labor contracts—which satisfied neither planters nor freedpeople and consequently gave rise to many disputes—were largely replaced by sharecropping and, less frequently, by tenant-farming arrangements. Planters divided their lands into parcels to be worked by black families; sharecroppers almost always received a fraction—usually a fourth—of the crop they raised, while tenants paid landowners an annual rent in crops and sometimes in cash. Tenancy yielded a greater measure of independence for black men and women because they were able to make their own decisions about what to grow, but both sorts of arrangements allowed blacks to live and work together as family units removed from the supervision of whites. Most white landlords welcomed the reprieve from having to oversee labor and find enough cash to pay wages. Though sharecropping appeared to be mutually beneficial, the system very often led black families into perennial debt.[169]

As black women reshaped their family and work lives, they also participated in community events and institutions that reinforced their identity as free people. Particularly in cities, many black women took an active interest in politics. In Richmond shortly after Emancipation, women attended mass meetings and rallies that protested municipal codes designed to deny blacks the rights of citizenship. One such gathering, attended by more than 3,000 people, called on the governor and the president to intervene, resulting in an immediate reorganization of the city government.[170]

Though the federal Reconstruction Acts of March 1867 gave the franchise only to black men, women took part in meetings organized by the radical wing of the Republican Party, which was in favor of black officeholding, disfranchisement of former Confederates, and the protection of civil rights. At

"A Visit from the Old Mistress," by Winslow Homer, 1876. Winslow Homer's painting *A Visit from the Old Mistress* depicts what appears to be an uneasy postwar encounter. Though the black women's ragged clothing reflects their poverty, particularly in comparison with the white woman's lace-adorned dress, they look their visitor in the eye without a hint of deference. Formerly enslaved women often defined freedom in ways that differed sharply from the expectations that whites harbored, leading to tense relations. *Courtesy of the Smithsonian American Art Museum, Gift of William T. Evans, 1909.7.28.*

a Republican convention in Richmond in August 1867, black women cast votes and spoke from the floor.[171] Likewise, women in the capital and in the Hampton Roads area made their opinions known at political meetings held between December 1867 and April 1868, when the state constitutional convention was in session in Richmond. Required by the United States Congress to frame a new state constitution before Virginia could be readmitted to the Union, the convention—which included 24 black delegates among the total of 105—drew black spectators of both sexes. Though many black women saw politics as a path to racial justice—a meeting in Nansemond County attended by both sexes passed resolutions calling for the franchise to be extended to black women—

few women actually agitated for the right to vote.[172] Instead, they regarded black men's votes as community property. In Richmond, women established the Rising Daughters of Liberty to raise money for political campaigns and encourage men to vote, and across the state women accompanied men to the polls and influenced their decisions.[173]

Black men and women also staked out their freedom by appropriating public spaces for large-scale civic celebrations. Former slaves marked such occasions as Republican presidential victories, the adoption of the Fifteenth Amendment (which granted the vote to black men), and the anniversary of Emancipation Day with barbecues, games, political speeches, and festive parades featuring bands, banners, and black military organizations. In Richmond, blacks instituted an annual celebration of Emancipation on 3 April 1866, the anniversary of the Confederate capital's surrender. Ignoring the opposition of angry white officials, thousands of blacks paraded through the city to Capitol Square, which had been off limits to black gatherings in the days of slavery.[174] Throughout the state, black men and women asserted their identities as American citizens by engaging in public observances of the Fourth of July. Such celebrations were typically peaceful, though white men disrupted a Norfolk parade marking the passage of the Civil Rights Act in April 1866, leading to a violent interracial confrontation.[175]

To promote economic security while reducing their dependence on whites, black city dwellers formed hundreds of benevolent societies in the postwar years. Often affiliated with churches, these associations raised funds and pooled resources to aid orphans, widows, and the destitute. Many such groups were open to both sexes, and women served alongside men as officers, sometimes even assuming leadership while men played supporting roles. In Richmond, for instance, a group of women directed the Golden Rule Society, established in 1872.[176]

All-female charitable organizations also operated in cities. Lucy Goode Brooks, whose enslaved husband had earned enough money operating a livery stable to purchase her freedom in 1862, convinced the black Ladies Sewing Circle for Charitable Work, of which she was a leader, to join with a congregation of Quakers to support an orphanage; the building was completed in 1871, and the General Assembly incorporated the Friends' Asylum for Colored Orphans in March 1872.[177] In Danville, black women founded the True Friends of Charity to help the elderly and the ill. Blacks also established mutual aid societies, sometimes segregated by gender, in which members paid dues and received specific benefits, such as monetary support during periods of unemployment, accident insurance, or burial services. In 1872 a group of Richmond mothers, many of them unmarried, organized the Mutual Benevolent Society to provide for their children in case of misfortune, and in Norfolk the Grand United Order of Tents emerged as an influential women's lodge.[178]

Next to families, churches were the most important institutions in the lives of most black Virginians. In the aftermath of emancipation, blacks formed their own congregations, many of them Baptist, throughout the state. Liberation from slavery had confirmed their spiritual convictions, and religious commitment was strong. Churches hosted social events, offered evening classes and Sunday schools, enforced moral precepts, and often became incubators of political leadership. Women participated extensively in church activities, including service as Sunday school teachers, but they very rarely became preachers.[179]

Black Virginians, understanding that literacy would be crucial to their success as free people, eagerly sought schooling for themselves and for their children in the postwar years. In so doing, they delivered what one Freedmen's Bureau agent called "a knock-down argument to the old masters cherished . . . notion, that the mind of the Negro was not susceptible of receiving an education."[180] By May 1865, about 2,000 black children in Richmond were already attending classes conducted by Northern missionary societies. The Freedmen's Bureau was quick to establish schools throughout the state, frequently relying on male and female missionary workers to staff them. While these institutions thrived in cities and in the tidewater region, many rural schools were forced to shut down because of virulent opposition from local whites, a dearth of necessary supplies, and the disinclination of Northern teachers to accept positions in potentially hostile areas. Occasionally black communities held fairs or other events to raise money for public schools, but widespread poverty limited the efficacy of such initiatives.[181]

Where free schools did not take root, blacks refused to abandon their educational aspirations; men and women who could read and write offered private courses, and churches hosted classes for their members. In 1869, with the adoption of the new state constitution, Virginia established a statewide, albeit racially segregated, public school system. Blacks welcomed this development but reaped limited benefits from it during the 1870s, when funds were diverted

GLIMPSES AT THE FREEDMEN—THE FREEDMEN'S UNION INDUSTRIAL SCHOOL, RICHMOND, VA.—FROM A SKETCH BY OUR SPECIAL ARTIST, JAS. E. TAYLOR.

"Freedmen's Union Industrial School, Richmond, Va.," published in *Frank Leslie's Illustrated Newspaper*, 22 September 1866. At the Freedmen's Union Industrial School in Richmond, white women oversee former slaves who are learning to be seamstresses. During Reconstruction, the Freedmen's Bureau and Northern missionary associations established schools throughout the South to instruct African Americans in reading and writing and to provide vocational training. Freedpeople also set up their own schools to meet the great demand for education. *Courtesy of the Library of Virginia.*

to pay off Virginia's antebellum debt. A brighter spot for blacks who cared deeply about education was the establishment in 1868 of Hampton Normal and Agricultural Institute (later Hampton University), which taught trades and industrial skills and trained men and women as teachers. Graduates such as Jennie L. Ivy, who left the institute in 1874 and went on to teach school in Halifax County, fulfilled the institute's mission by improving themselves and passing on their knowledge to others.[182]

As black women went about the business of enhancing their freedom, white women worked to rebuild their own lives. Many common whites had sunk into desperate poverty during the war and had few prospects for bettering their situations in its immediate aftermath; in May 1865, impoverished and hungry women in Henry County depended for survival on supplies handed out by the Union army, and six months after the war about 25,000 Virginians still relied on federal rations.[183] Thousands of women faced the prospect of forging ahead without the labor of husbands or sons who had been killed or disabled. Some widows made their way to cities in search of work, but the unsettled economy meant that jobs, particularly for women, were scarce. In Lynchburg, for example, the postwar availability of ready-made clothing from the North undermined the local seamstress trade, depriving many women of a respectable way to make a living. Ordinary white women who tried to make a go of it on farms often found themselves performing heavy labor in the fields, even when their households included able-bodied men. The difficulties of pooling enough cash to retain or purchase their own land meant that more white families became agricultural tenants.[184]

White women without resources sought assistance from various entities. City and county governments, themselves financially strapped, had little to offer. The state government likewise failed to provide appreciable relief; not until 1888 did the General Assembly authorize appropriations for Confederate widows. White churches stepped into the gap by providing the needy with food and sometimes with cash. When male church officials oversaw these charitable donations, they often assumed a paternalistic stance by, for example, managing money for female recipients rather than allowing them to make decisions about its use.[185] In other cases, however, church-sponsored women's benevolent associations took responsibility for distributing aid. The Dorcas Society, affiliated with Court Street Methodist Church in Lynchburg, operated a Sunday school for poor white children and handed out clothes and shoes to pupils who could not afford them.[186] Rather than seek assistance from an organization, some needy women applied to local elites for help finding a job, or for money that would allow them to retain their land or to buy essential supplies. Because the upper classes deemed the respectability of common white women questionable, petitioners had to demonstrate that they were hardworking and deserving of assistance.[187]

Many elite white women had difficulty accepting the defeat of the Confederacy. With the social and economic underpinnings of their way of life destroyed, they remained bitterly antagonistic toward the federal government even as white men largely acquiesced in the project of sectional reconciliation. "I am an alien enemy of the United States & always shall remain such," declared Chloe Tyler Whittle, of Norfolk, about six weeks after Lee's surrender. Women who had provided tangible support for the Confederate war effort were not prepared to cease contributing their labors, and they found an opportunity for further service in the institutional vacuum created by the disintegration of the Confederacy.[188]

Since there were no Southern government agencies equipped to memorialize the vanquished cause and the men who had died in its defense, women quickly met the need by reconstituting local Soldiers' Aid Societies as Ladies' Memorial Associations. Because Northern and Southern men alike understood mourning to be an apolitical, feminine activity, women were able to organize events honoring the Confederacy without, in the vast majority of cases, provoking accusations of treason from Northerners. The ideological work of keeping Confederate identity alive during the early years of Reconstruction thus fell to them. Women directed the recovery of Confederate soldiers' remains, established cemeteries, decorated graves, erected monuments, and planned Memorial Days, which drew large crowds to cemeteries. They created far-flung networks of like-minded individuals and raised money for their projects from across the South, tapping into and reinforcing an unrepentant sense of Southern nationalism.[189]

Women's objective in honoring the Lost Cause was not so much to shore up the masculinity of defeated white men as to fulfill their own patriotic impulses. Men played supporting roles in the early years. By 1870, however, when Reconstruction ended in Virginia and federal authority no longer loomed to discourage male leadership in commemorating the Confederacy, men began to seek control of memorialization efforts. After Robert E. Lee's death in October 1870, for instance, the Ladies' Lee Monument Committee (LLMC) in Richmond clashed with the Lee Monument Association, led by former general Jubal Early and composed of veterans, over plans to erect a monument for Lee. Refusing to submit to men's arguments that women should withdraw to auxiliary roles, the LLMC raised its own funds and declined requests to contribute its resources to the monument as the male groups envisioned it.[190]

With emancipation, slaveholding families lost much of their wealth and their ability to secure credit. Real estate prices declined and debts mounted. Smaller labor forces cultivated fewer crops, and poor weather contributed to planters' woes by depressing agricultural output between 1865 and 1868. The national financial panic of 1873 imposed another setback. "The hard times with us and throughout this area are perfectly appalling," Maria Louisa Wacker Fleet, a widow from an elite family in King and Queen County, informed her son, who was attending college in Missouri, in 1870. "The people about here are getting poorer and poorer and I hope you will never think of coming back here to live—or starve."[191]

Downward economic mobility frequently affected the composition of elite white households and altered relationships within families, continuing a trend that had begun during the war. The patriarchal model, in which the husband served as protector and provider, became less viable. Particularly when headed by widows, families relied more than before on extended kin networks for emotional and financial support. Adult siblings lived together more often, and parents depended on the labor of their children. While these strategies for maintaining solvency could bring relatives closer together, they also had the potential to undermine family unity. Physical separation resulted when grown children moved away from their families in search of employment that would allow them to send money home. Emotional estrangement also ruptured families, especially when members balked at the contributions they were expected to make. Children whose work was needed at home, for instance, sometimes expressed resentment at being deprived of an education, and intergenerational tensions flared.[192]

These clashes over schooling could be particularly explosive because parents felt humiliated by their inability to invest in their children's future. For boys, education in the postwar period was valuable because it imparted important skills and forged social connections that could enhance one's career, which was likely to be in an occupation other than farming. For upper-class girls, who studied such subjects as music, French, Latin, algebra, and natural philosophy, knowledge and refinement were prized as markers of elite status, which families wished to project even in straitened times. On a more practical level, women who had received an education could seek jobs as teachers. Because of these benefits, elite families sacrificed in other areas of life in order

VIRGINIA FEMALE INSTITUTE,
STAUNTON, VIRGINIA.

Miss *L. Staples* ____ Monthly Report for *May* ____ 1866.

HIGHEST NUMBER, 6.

| CONDUCT, | 6 | DILIGENCE, | 6 | NEATNESS, | 6 | ATTENDANCE, | 6 |

STUDIES.		STUDIES.		STUDIES.		EXTRA STUDIES.
Orthography,..............		Elocution,.............		Science of Things Familiar,.		FRENCH. Ollendorf's System,........
Definitions,................		Rhetoric,...............	5.	Political Economy,.........		French Grammar,.........
Reading,.................		Philosophy of Nat. History,		Intellectual Philosophy,....		French Literature,........
Writing...................	4.	Rom. & Greek Antiquities,.		Physical Geography,.......		LATIN. Grammar,............. ...
Geography,..............		Town's Analysis,........ ..		Elements of Criticism,......		Exercises,..............
Drawing Maps,............		Trench on Words,........		Butler's Analogy,..........		Literature, ...
History,..................	6	English Synonymes,.......		Geology, ...		Spanish,...............
English Grammar,.........	6	Algebra, ...		Logic,.................		Italian,..... .....
Ancient Geography,........		Geometry,..............		Principles of Taste,........		Drawing,........ ....
Natural History............		Natural Philosophy,......		Study of Poetry,........		Oil Painting,...........
Book of Commerce,........		Chemistry		Burke's Subl. & Beautiful,.		Grecian,...............
Arithmetic,...............	6	Botany		Book Keeping,..........		Ornamental Needle Work...
Parsing and Punctuation,..		English Literature,........		Trigonometry............		MUSIC. Piano,..............
Parker's Eng. Composition,.		Evidences of Christianity,..		Moral Philosophy..........		Guitar,................
Mythology,..............		History and Chronology,....		Weekly Composition,.....	4	Organ,................
Physiology,..........		Natural Theology,........		Biblical Literature........		Melodeon,.............
Astronomy,..............	6	*1st Book Hist.* 6				Vocal Music,...........

Very Respectfully,

R. H. PHILLIPS, PRINCIPAL.

Virginia Female Institute, *June 5th* 186*6*.

Grade report, 5 June 1866. Laura Staples, a student at Virginia Female Institute in 1866, received monthly report cards documenting her academic progress. In the postwar years, upper-class families placed a high value on education for girls. Many different subjects of study were available, from ancient geography to astronomy to political economy. Female students often went on to become teachers. *Courtesy of the Library of Virginia, Smith Family Papers, Acc. 40502.*

to send their children to school. "Virginians will educate their children if they possibly can even if they have money for little else," observed Maria Fleet, who, with several of her daughters, opened an academy for girls in King and Queen County in 1873.[193]

Many women had taken over the management of their families' farms and plantations during the war, and some retained those responsibilities after hostilities ceased. Widows and single women who had inherited property from their fathers were responsible for conducting business, balancing accounts, and obtaining supplies, as were many women whose husbands worked full-time in salaried jobs to supplement the family's agricultural income. Some women thrived in their supervisory roles. Elizabeth Munford, who ran her family's plantation in Gloucester County while her husband worked at the Office of the Superintendent for Public Buildings in Richmond, informed him in 1875 that "we are so used to be[ing] without a gentleman now, that it never occurs to us to be afraid." Other women, reluctant to take charge, sought extensive advice from male relatives and yielded to their judgment.[194]

Of all the duties that fell to female plantation managers, the one they found most onerous was hiring and overseeing black agricultural workers and domestic servants. Both the concept of free labor and the process of negotiating contracts were unfamiliar to white women. They complained about the difficulty of retaining workers; even blacks who committed to yearlong contracts frequently moved on when the year was over, forcing employers to search for replacements among a pool of laborers they did not know or trust. White women accused field hands of being lazy, inefficient, and prone to stealing, and grew angry when domestic servants refused to be on constant call. While the turn to sharecropping attenuated many of the problems that arose between agricultural workers and their employers, white and black women continued to contest the meaning of freedom in the domestic realm.[195]

With black men no longer under the direct supervision of white households, white women increasingly perceived them as a threat. Newspapers highlighted crimes committed by blacks, and rumors about arson and physical violence contributed to white women's unease. Frustrations with the quality of blacks' labor and fears of social unrest prompted planters to consider hiring white workers. To broaden the pool of such laborers, agricultural societies and the state government recruited European immigrants to settle in Virginia. In the end, substantial immigration did not materialize during the 1870s and experiments with white labor typically failed.[196]

Many former slaveholders could afford only part-time domestic help, when they could afford any at all. Whether or not they had access to a servant, most women from elite families had no choice but to perform a wide variety of domestic tasks, from cleaning their kitchens, to caring for their own children, to harvesting eggs and vegetables. Many supplemented their family's income by selling their produce.[197] Sallie Turner, of Goochland County, informed her brother in 1867 that, "I feel most too tired to do anything, we are still without a cook, and I have everything to do. ...[M]y arms are so sore from drawing water and cutting wood." Though women increasingly purchased appliances such as stoves and sewing machines to make their work less cumbersome and to diminish their reliance on hired servants, they regularly worked so hard that they could not find the time to engage in social events outside the home.[198] While older elite women had a great deal of trouble adjusting to this new way of life, many of their younger counterparts came to take personal satisfaction in their work. They embraced a new conception of femininity that upheld vigor and usefulness as admirable traits. Their attention to housekeeping brought them in line with the culture of domesticity then ascendant among the Northern middle and upper classes.[199]

In the decades following emancipation, the economic survival of plantation families depended as much on white women's work as it did on men's. Within marriages, gender roles that had been firmly held in place by slavery began to shift. Husbands, understanding that they could not keep their households solvent without their wives' help, increasingly expressed appreciation for the work women performed. This recognition of partnership undermined patriarchy as an organizational principle for marriage and raised questions about the meaning of masculinity. While the result never approached gender equality, many women did come to relate to their planter husbands on a basis that more closely resembled mutuality than deference. These changes were evident in public as well as in private. Agricultural organizations, which became important dispensers of practical advice in the difficult postwar years, championed women as essential to the rebuilding and expansion of the state's agrarian economy. Women were eligible to hold some lower-level offices in the Patrons of Husbandry (better known as the Grange), which arrived in Virginia in 1872.[200]

Postwar economic difficulties forced some elite and middle-class women to obtain employment outside the household. Many younger women left farms and plantations for cities. As during the war, government clerkships were desirable but relatively rare. In Richmond, the wife of a dentist implored the governor for a job in 1871, explaining that "unless relief comes in some form, I see no prospect but starvation."[201] The majority of women who sought paid employment, however, were single or widowed. Those who later married left the workplace. Some women—also typically unmarried—made a living by operating their own businesses. The number and variety of these enterprises increased during and after the war, particularly as widows took over proprietorship from deceased husbands. While most businesswomen were milliners or retail grocers, others ran bakeries, butcher shops, shoe stores, and cigar stores.[202]

Teaching was by far the most popular option for elite women who needed to earn money. Most teachers were young, single women who retired upon marriage, but widows and women who never married—categories that grew as a result of the war—could make long and respectable careers in education. In far greater numbers than their antebellum counterparts, women taught at private academies, tutored students in their homes, opened their own small schools, and, after 1870, worked in Virginia's nascent public school system. Teaching allowed women to support themselves, assist their extended families, and engage in intellectual activity, pursuits that had not been expected of genteel white women before the war. The job offered both rewards and challenges. "Sometimes I think of my schoolroom as my studio where I may mould immortal minds for immortality," Maria Fleet told her mother in 1873. "Then again it assumes the form of a gigantic crucible in which I have been placed by the Master Chemist to be *tried*, & TRIED, & TRIED."[203]

Unmarried women who owned property—whether obtained from a deceased husband, inherited from parents, or earned in the workplace—were at liberty to dispose of it as they wished. In 1873, for instance, Eliza Beale, of Fauquier County, took in $17,000 when she sold to a railroad her interest in the farm she had inherited from her parents. She then spent the next decade buying and selling tracts of land.[204] Married women, however, did not have the right to control property; legally, everything a married couple possessed belonged to the husband, and his creditors could lay claim to property a wife brought to a marriage. During the antebellum decades, it had become commonplace for wealthy parents to draw up deeds and marriage settlements that established separate estates for their married daughters. The purpose of these maneuvers was not to endow women with more independence, but rather to protect their inheritances for transmission to future generations.[205]

Virginia tardily enacted a Married Women's Property Act on 4 April 1877; almost every other state in the Union had already passed laws—and most of the former Confederate states had adopted constitutional provisions—giving wives the right to acquire and manage their own property.[206] "No one will contend that radical changes as to woman's position in the community have not been brought about within the last fifteen years, and particularly so in domestic matters," asserted the author of the bill, state senator Charles Smith, of Nelson County.[207] Even so, Smith was not an advocate of expanding rights for women in general. He argued paternalistically that the state must protect female property holders from being victimized by unscrupulous men. Opponents charged that the legislation would damage domestic harmony and drag women into the aggressive world of business, tarnishing all that was pure about femininity. In the end, the bill passed because the ability to keep some family resources out of the hands of creditors during a time of economic instability made financial sense to many men. The new law was a boon to blacks as well as whites; black businessmen sometimes deeded property to their wives to protect it from creditors.[208]

Even as he promoted his bill, Smith insisted that women "do not, and should not, under any circumstances, vote," and he contended that women "do not ask nor want such privilege."[209] Indeed, women in postwar Virginia did not mount a widespread or sustained campaign for suffrage. In January 1868, John C. Underwood, a Republican from New York who had lived in Virginia during the 1850s and who served as presiding judge of the United States District Court for Virginia from 1864 to 1871, offered a rare voice in favor of extending the franchise. As president of the state constitutional convention, at the end of a long speech advocating universal suffrage, he argued that society would benefit from having "the finer moral instincts of our mothers, sisters, wives and daughters made available in raising our codes, our habits and our lives to a higher and nobler plane of civilization, by giving them a voice, influence and vote in shaping our political affairs."[210] Underwood's proposal to give women the vote did not even generate debate; the convention enfranchised Virginia's black men but ignored its women of both races. One of the few women who spoke publicly about the right to vote was Elizabeth Van Lew, the former Union spy. In 1869, President Ulysses S. Grant appointed her postmistress of Richmond, an important position because its occupant had control of significant political patronage. Though she served for eight years, her inability to vote or hold office prevented her from using her post as a springboard to greater political influence, a circumstance she regarded as bitterly unfair.[211]

Van Lew's convictions were shared by fellow Richmonder Anna Whitehead Bodeker, a native of New Jersey who had moved to Chesterfield County with her family at the age of ten. Bodeker was impressed by the National Woman Suffrage Association, founded in 1869, and in January 1870 she arranged for several of its leaders to meet at her home with a handful of her sympathetic Richmond friends. In March, Bodeker and some associates published a "Defence of Woman Suffrage" in the Richmond *Daily Enquirer*, a newspaper that opposed their efforts. The authors argued that women should have the right to make a living in any way they chose—they should "invent machinery, sketch architec-[t]ural plans, illustrate and elucidate scientific principles"—and that the only way to secure such equality of opportunity was to exercise the vote. On 6 May, a small group of men and women met in Underwood's courtroom and organized the Virginia State Woman Suffrage Association, of which Bodeker was elected president. On several occasions over the next two years, Bodeker invited nationally prominent suffrage activists, including Susan B. Anthony, to give public lectures in Richmond while the General Assembly was in session. Few legislators or women attended the speeches, however, and the small audiences did not respond to fund-raising appeals. By 1872 Bodeker ceased her public activity. When Virginia women next founded a suffrage organization in 1909, they did not even remember that Bodeker's had ever existed.[212]

Most Virginians of both sexes believed electoral politics to be the domain of men. Opponents of woman suffrage denied that female participation would purify the political system; on the contrary, they argued, direct involvement in political confrontations and competitions would corrupt women.[213] In the wake of military defeat and financial reversals, many white men felt insecure about their ability to live up to traditional conceptions of manhood. They therefore placed great value on the all-male nature of the political world, seizing on politics as the realm in which they could reassert themselves as protectors and providers.[214]

After 1870, when Virginia was restored to the Union and elite white males resumed control of the state government, the disposition of the state's antebellum debt emerged as the salient political issue. Funders, who favored paying the debt in full, largely by diverting state funds from public schooling, rallied voters essentially by offering restored masculinity as a reward for their support. Nothing less than the defense of Virginia's honor was at stake, they argued, and the only "manly" course was to make sure the state fulfilled its financial obligations. Leaders of the Readjuster Party, a biracial coalition of white farmers from the western region, small businessmen, and African Americans, that won control of the General Assembly in 1879, also employed the discourse of masculinity as they worked to convince voters that their policy of renegotiating the debt downward would rescue Virginia's economy and better allow men to protect their families.[215]

Alongside the widespread conviction that electoral politics was the domain of men, Virginians continued to believe—as they had before the war—that women could exert a positive influence on the political system by means other than voting. During the presidential campaign of 1876, Virginia Democrats applauded the organization of women's clubs, and in 1878 a pro-Funder newspaper in Warrenton called on local women to form an association through which they could influence men to support the cause of debt payment.[216] Though the Warrenton group fizzled after one meeting, many women paid attention to politics, and some spoke out in an attempt to shape public policy. Members of the Women's Association for the Liquidation of the Virginia State Debt asked women across the commonwealth to encourage their male relatives to support funding the debt. Virginia newspapers reported that the state's women—after "economiz[ing] in their dress or household expenses"—had contributed a total of $107 for reduction of the debt during the month of June 1878.[217]

Most elite women were disdainful of the Republican and Readjuster parties. In 1871 Lavalette Dupuy labeled a Republican electoral victory in Prince Edward County "mortifying," but voiced relief that, as a whole, "the Old State is redeeming itself and has given a large Conservative Majority" in the General Assembly.[218] Following the Readjusters' takeover of the Assembly in 1879, Maria Fleet told her brother that "we can't help feeling very gloomy when we think of Va's future in the hands of such men." Yet the Readjusters reminded women that renegotiating the debt would allow the state government to allocate money to public schools, and they invited "every Mother" to "determine for herself who are the friends to the Children." For black and nonelite white women, the argument was convincing.[219]

———— ◆ ————

By offering incontrovertible evidence that women could be strong and adaptable, that men could not necessarily protect women from disaster, and that black skin did not imply servility, the Civil War destabilized ideas about gender and race that had provided the foundation for antebellum Virginia society. Despite this rupture with the past, however, white women did not push for equality with men in the postwar years. Women's activities outside the home expanded, to be sure, and men more frequently acknowledged the value of their economic contributions, but femininity was still considered grounds for subordination. African American women worked to make freedom meaningful for themselves and for their families, but most whites refused to accept blacks as equals, and many black men asserted themselves as heads of their households. Though Virginia's women of all races had seen their lives profoundly transformed by sectional animosity, war, and Reconstruction, they would have to wait many years for true liberty and equality.

CHAPTER 5

"Lifting as We Climb": The Progressive Era

From the 1880s to the 1920s, Virginia women from all socioeconomic backgrounds, black and white, worked to claim places in the increasingly urbanized and industrialized state. While many white women embraced the changes and took advantage of new educational, vocational, and ultimately, political opportunities, others chose to retain a traditional view of womanhood, based on idealized conceptions of antebellum gender norms. Elite white women reacted to the growing modernization of 1880s Virginia in two general ways. Some took advantage of new opportunities, while others idealized and glorified their own version of what they had lost after the Civil War. Those who embraced modernity were among the first women in Virginia to engage in professional occupations. Still more took advantage of the power they gained through leading reform movements to lead the fight for woman suffrage. Middle-class African American women used their professional status to push back against the racism and sexism of Virginia society, becoming leaders in the struggle to uplift their communities. Some rural and working-class women who were often marginalized by the "New South" industrialization process acted to help themselves and their families in any way they could.

Virginia emerged from Reconstruction a very different place from many other southern states. It experienced much political turmoil during the 1870s and 1880s over issues of race, education, and paying off the state's antebellum public debt. Democrats regained control of the assembly from the Readjuster Party in 1883 and beginning in 1885 elected every governor until 1969.[1] By early in the 1900s, Democrats had successfully adopted a new constitution that disfranchised the majority of the voting population and passed laws that segregated African Americans in many areas of society. For all of its political turmoil in the period, Virginia's rich natural resources boosted its business enterprises. Virginia became the model of a New South state, in which government and local business leaders touted the region's climate, natural resources, and nonunionized workforce to attract numerous industries. Coal, iron, and timber interests dominated the western region, while Danville became a center of tobacco and textile manufacturing. Real estate speculators brought money to Lynchburg, Norfolk, Petersburg, Portsmouth, and Roanoke. Richmond became the second-largest manufacturing center in the South with its tobacco, iron, and flour mills. More than 2,000 new miles of railroad track carried raw and finished goods to the market.[2]

Some Virginia cities experienced rapid population growth. Most of these migrants came from the North and rural areas of Virginia, rather than from overseas. The percentage of the foreign-born population in Virginia was only 1 percent in 1900, as compared to 13.6 percent in the nation as a whole. Nevertheless, the influx of rural migrants and northerners joined with the approximately 19,000 immigrants of mainly German, British, and Irish descent to bring a new cosmopolitan tenor to such places as Roanoke and Norfolk.[3] Among these immigrants were Jews of German and increasingly Russian descent, who opened dry goods stores, manufactories, and tailor shops, or who worked in mills and factories.[4] Perhaps the greatest diversity in the commonwealth was exhibited in the coalfields of the west. Such places as Craig and Tazewell Counties saw an influx of Italians, Hungarians, Welsh, and Germans who moved from Pennsylvania and newly arrived immigrants hired just after they entered the United States to work in foundries and coal mines. Catholic churches sprang up to minister to hundreds of these immigrants, who were mostly men who had come to the region for work without their families.[5]

Virginia's New South economic plan enhanced the visibility and political power of upper- and middle-class urbanites, but leaders' focus on industrialization belied the reality of most Virginians. More than 80 percent of the state's population was rural at the end of the nineteenth century, and many farmers suffered from agricultural depressions that were particularly bad in the 1890s and 1920s. Virginia's per capita wealth was higher than other southern states but lower than those outside the region, in part because its industries were often built on the backs of nonunionized, poorly paid workers—including many women and children—who put in long hours under dangerous conditions to produce such commodities as tobacco products, clothing, and cloth that defined Virginia's modernization.[6] Under these conditions, black and white

"Group of adolescent spinners in Washington Cotton Mills, Fries, Va. The youngest ones would not be photographed," photographed by Lewis Wickes Hine, May 1911. Textile mills hired numerous young women and children to work in many areas of factories, including on the spinning machines, which are pictured. Employers paid them far less money than men, considered them a tractable labor force, and laid them off in the slow periods of the year. Despite the poor conditions, long hours, and exploitative wages, many young women enjoyed earning their own money for the first time, as it gave them a level of independence. *Courtesy of the Library of Congress, National Child Labor Committee, LC-DIG-nclc-02059.*

rural women and poor city-dwelling women struggled to survive by doing what they could to make their lives better.

New reform impulses sweeping the nation inspired thousands of women to action in Virginia. Beginning in the 1880s, middle-class "progressives" began to address the problems they perceived as caused by modern society. Women were extremely active in reform efforts during the Progressive Era. Claiming to have the authority and mandate to make the world better and safer for their children, women involved themselves in "social housekeeping" projects. They worked to ameliorate the problems they often linked to urbanization and industrialization, including poverty, child labor, dangers posed to young women coming to cities for work, and excessive alcohol consumption.

Progressive women began taking a scientific approach to show how dirty homes, crowded cities, and child labor contributed to such social problems as poverty and disease. They also enlisted, or became, social workers and nurses to assist in aiding the poor. These professions developed in earnest during and after the Civil War and signaled a shift away from the philanthropic "moral suasion" techniques of the nineteenth century and opened up new employment opportunities for white and black professional women.[7] In Virginia, many middle-class women participated in the Progressive movement, which culminated in the woman suffrage movement and the passage of the Nineteenth Amendment in 1920. This reform enabled many women to be politically active in a way never before witnessed in the commonwealth and helped move women closer to claiming the full rights of American citizenship.

Elite women born between 1820 and 1869 were largely responsible for redefining the roles of women in their class, as well as the limits of respectability during this period. Many parents encouraged their daughters to get an education to be self-sufficient if necessary. More upper- and middle-class white women also took jobs out of necessity, which challenged the traditional view of a "woman's place." In 1873, when Mary Howard made her debut in Richmond society she was a schoolteacher, which vexed her future mother-in-law greatly. Like women all over the country and for a variety of reasons, fewer elite women in Virginia married than their counterparts in other social classes. Some preferred not to leave their parental homes, while others did not want to have children.

Some women were disappointed with the availability of potential spouses within their social circles and refused to marry men beneath their status. Some, however, did not want to diminish their own autonomy and preferred to rely on themselves to maintain their socioeconomic status. Society in general did not look kindly on married women's working outside the home; many school boards, for example, fired or refused to hire married women. Some women chose their careers over marriage in the 1880s and 1890s. On the whole, Virginia's elite white women in the 1880s and 1890s were more-formally educated, less likely to get married, and far more likely to work for wages at least some point in their lives than their antebellum counterparts.[8]

Wealthy white women in the post-Reconstruction period continued to perform household labor that elite antebellum women would have given to slaves, and many took on even more responsibility for finances than before. Continuing a trend that had begun in the antebellum period, particularly with widows, women bought property through their male relatives and financed it with their own capital. Women appeared to become much more comfortable securing credit and managing their own money, particularly after the passage of the Married Women's Property Act in 1877. Nannie Tunstall, a writer from Lynchburg, borrowed $1,000 from the bank of a friend in 1884 to finance her trip to Europe with Virginia Clay. The banker provided her with a letter of credit to his bank in London in case she also needed money there.[9]

Moreover, as more landowners embraced sharecropping and tenancy over wage labor, more elite women from landowning families became land managers. The widowed Emma Carrington, of Charlotte County, wrote of preparing to receive a new tenant in 1882 to raise wheat on her land. She regularly corresponded with—and dismissed when necessary—her tenants, which reveals her comfort level with managing farm business. Other socially prominent rural women began to do what yeoman farmers' wives had done for centuries—raise farm products for profit. Many turned to poultry and livestock to earn money. Sally Watson, of Louisa County, was almost entirely responsible for the success of her family's poultry business and raised 100 turkeys and 300 to 400 chickens in 1883.[10]

Many women chose teaching for their career path, a profession that northern women had long embraced and that was open to more women in Virginia after the public school system was created in 1870. In 1884, Virginia established the State Female Normal School (later Longwood University) in Farmville in response to the need to provide adequate education and preparation for white women to teach.[11] Taking advantage of greater educational opportunities, many young white women saw teaching as a way to retain their social status and earn a living. Elite women viewed it as a respectable and flexible occupation that did not require a four-year degree, but for other Virginia women teaching became an avenue to gain higher status and better-paying jobs than were generally available. By early in the twentieth century, the majority of teachers were women. Teachers wrote about their enjoyment of teaching, not necessarily because of the activity itself, but because of the influence they had over their pupils and the lifestyle it afforded.[12]

For poor but talented African American women, teaching was a critical way to serve their communities, while also enabling them to improve their own status and that of their families. In 1882, the Readjuster-controlled General Assembly established the Virginia Normal and Collegiate Institute (later Virginia State University), near Petersburg, to train black women and men for a variety of professions, including teaching. In Virginia's segregated school system, African Americans faced overcrowded and unsanitary schools that were in poor condition and often lacked basic classroom supplies. Private institutions frequently filled the void, and by 1900, Virginia had more than thirty black colleges and industrial schools, about half controlled by African American boards. Among them was the Manassas Industrial School for Colored Youth, which was founded in 1893 by Jennie Serepta Dean, a former slave who raised funds for the school from local supporters and northern philanthropists. Like other industrial secondary schools it provided education and training for girls and boys who did not have access to public high schools. Given the economic and social circumstances of the black community in Virginia, it is not surprising that many prominent black women reformers began their activist careers as teachers, including educational reformer Janie Porter Barrett, banker Maggie Lena Walker, and community organizer Ora Brown Stokes.[13]

Virginia Estelle Randolph, the eighteen-year-old daughter of a former slave, began teaching in Henrico County in 1892. Believing that "the destiny of our race depends, largely, upon the training the children receive in the schoolroom," she improved conditions at the dilapidated school. She developed a curriculum that included manual training for boys and girls in addition to academic instruction and involved parents and the local community in funding and undertaking school improvement projects. Her techniques attracted the attention of the county's school superintendent and led to her appointment in 1908 as the first industrial supervisor by the Anna T. Jeanes Foundation, which had been established the previous year to fund educational opportunities for African Americans in the South. Randolph supervised the organization of School Improvement Leagues at the county's twenty-two segregated public schools, and the program's success led to its adoption across Virginia and throughout the South. Known as Jeanes Teachers, the supervisors, who were usually women, served as community activists as they implemented programs to improve public health and living conditions, started canning, sewing, and gardening clubs, sought more opportunities for teacher training, and encouraged students to further their education. As the Jeanes Supervisor for Cumberland County from 1913 to 1920, Matilda V. Mosley Booker lobbied her community for a longer school year, encouraged the construction of eight new schools, and raised money for higher salaries for teachers.[14]

White women enjoyed greater opportunities to find their calling in other professions. Katherine Harwood Waller Barrett came from an elite family that had suffered economically as a result of the Civil War. She married a young Episcopal minister from Wytheville and ultimately settled in a parish in Butchertown, one of Richmond's roughest neighborhoods in Shockoe Valley, where she became an activist for poor women during the four years she lived there. Despite having six children in twelve years, Barrett studied at the Woman's Medical College of Georgia and received her M.D. in 1892. She started the first home for unmarried pregnant white women in Atlanta, Georgia, before moving back to Virginia and becoming the president of the National Florence Crittenton Mission in 1909.[15] Just a decade later, Ethel Madison Bailey Carter Furman became one of the first practicing women architects in Virginia. She studied in New York and returned to Richmond to practice in 1921. As a black woman, she often had to submit plans through male colleagues to get her work approved by city planners, but she persisted and her career lasted for decades. One of the first Virginia women to hold a license was Mary Brown Channel, of Portsmouth, who received her architecture degree from Cornell University in 1933.[16]

Some women broke barriers in the legal profession and law enforcement fields. Several women filed lawsuits in unsuccessful attempts to reverse state legislation barring women from becoming licensed attorneys. Annie Smith, of Danville, wanted to enter into a partnership with her husband, but the General Assembly denied her petitions between 1889 and 1892. Prominent and successful Washington, D.C., lawyer Belva Lockwood moved to the commonwealth to fight for entry to the bar, but the Virginia Supreme Court of Appeals denied her that right in 1895. It was not until 1920 that Virginia allowed women to become licensed attorneys. That same year both the University of Virginia and the University of Richmond began accepting women into their law schools. Richmond's Rebecca Pearl Lovenstein and Lynchburg's Carrie Gregory were the first women in Virginia to pass the bar, and in 1925 Lovenstein was the first woman to argue a case before the Virginia Supreme Court of Appeals.[17] Pauline Haislip Smith, of Arlington County, became one of Virginia's earliest women law-enforcement officers after the Organized Women Voters in 1923 demanded a female deputy sheriff to deal with women offenders. Like subsequent women officers, Duncan worked mainly with youth and female offenders.[18]

Other women sought their fortunes in the literary world. Albemarle County's Amélie Rives, Lynchburg's Jane Lathrop Stabler and Nannie Tunstall, Winchester's Mary Tucker Magill, and Nelson County's Mary Greenway McClelland were all published and widely recognized authors of short stories and novels. Mary Johnston's novel *To Have and to Hold* was a national bestseller in 1900. These women often focused on heroines fighting against the constraints of traditional societal expectations. As Mary Johnston wrote in *Hagar* (1913), "If you couldn't write—couldn't earn, you'd trot along quietly enough! The pivotal mistake was letting women learn the alphabet." Some women published their work commercially because they needed the money, while others explained that they were embracing their literary ambitions by living as artists. Although these authors gained appreciative audiences, much of their work failed to make it into the canon of southern literature. Many contemporary critics viewed their work as hackneyed, popular pulp that was not worthy to stand the test of time, written by badly educated women. Institutions of higher learning did not support women authors late in the nineteenth and early in the twentieth centuries, so women lacked the same academic or institutional support as men. Still, these women were the progenitors of a literature about southern women confronting change, a point that the well-regarded and widely read author Ellen Glasgow made in 1913 in her first novel. Glasgow's work is well-known for its critique of southern society, and although a bit younger than her writing companions, she was friends with and benefited from the work of these pathbreaking women writers.[19]

Many wealthy and well-connected white women sought to take advantage of economic opportunities late in the nineteenth century. Others sought to rectify traditional gendered ideologies of "southern womanhood" by institutionalizing their idyllic version of the Old South. Women continued to participate in the memorial associations established in the 1860s and 1870s, and as the nineteenth century came to an end, many of these women turned to even more concrete ways of publicly commemorating the past.

Mary Jeffrey Galt, of Norfolk, and Cynthia Beverley Tucker Coleman, of Williamsburg, officially founded the Association for the Preservation of Virginia Antiquities in 1889. Not unlike the Mount Vernon Ladies' Association begun in the 1850s to conserve Washington's home, these women saw the preservation of historic structures as a way to promote the cultural traditions of Virginia's elite society. The first private statewide preservation society in the South, the APVA focused specifically on acquiring and preserving buildings from the colonial period and on maintaining graveyards. Largely composed of women, the organization's leadership believed that it was a woman's duty to maintain ties to the past. These mostly elite, white women were concerned with securing the homes of prominent families and government buildings, but their efforts helped to save such important historical structures as the Williamsburg Powder Magazine, the Mary Ball Washington home in Fredericksburg, and the church ruins at Jamestown.[20]

In 1890, the Ladies' Hollywood Memorial Association, which had been established after the Civil War to raise funds to care for the graves of Confederate soldiers in Richmond's Hollywood Cemetery, turned its attention to saving the White House of the Confederacy. After learning that the city could deed public property only to educational or literary associations, Richmond civic leader Isobel Lamont Stewart Bryan created a new group, the Confederate Memorial Literary Society. Other prominent women, many married or otherwise related to former Confederate officers, joined the movement. They included Lora Hotchkiss Ellyson, who had moved to Richmond from the Shenandoah Valley and was the niece of Stonewall Jackson's famous mapmaker, Jedediah Hotchkiss; Janet Weaver Randolph, whose father and husband had served in Virginia's forces during the Civil War; and Mary Maury and Lucy Maury, daughters of the famous Confederate naval officer Matthew Fontaine Maury. Women controlled the society's finances, property, and legal issues on the board. They raised more than $30,000 for the purchase and restoration of the house and for erecting a Soldiers and Sailors Monument by sponsoring a bazaar. They named regents for each room from different states that were responsible for contributing Confederate artifacts from their state to the museum. The museum opened in 1896 with an all-female officer board. The museum later became the Museum of the Confederacy, which is known for the largest collection of Confederate artifacts in the world.[21]

The United Daughters of the Confederacy emerged in 1894 as the preeminent Lost Cause memorial association. Virginia created the first state division a year later, and its leaders soon took prominent roles in creating monuments to the past. Janet Weaver Randolph established Richmond's chapter in 1896 and devoted herself to the cause of assisting Confederate women. In 1903, Randolph energized the Jefferson Davis Monument Association in Richmond after the United Confederate Veterans had failed to raise enough money for a statue and turned the effort over to the UDC. She organized a Confederate bazaar that raised $20,000 in two weeks and continued to solicit funds from Confederate veterans' groups and UDC chapters. By 1907 the association had raised enough money to complete monuments to Davis and J. E. B. Stuart.[22]

The UDC sought to perpetuate its version of the idyllic Old South of genteel belles and cavalier beaux, happy and well-cared-for slaves, and lavish plantations by sponsoring essay contests and scholarships, and by providing materials and even pictures of Robert E. Lee to classrooms around the country. At Roanoke College, the UDC challenged the adoption of an American history textbook that called the Civil War a "slaveholder's rebellion" and discussed the slave-owner relationship in stark contrast to the ways the UDC wanted it remembered. To be sure that the memories of the Old South and Lost Cause would not die with the original members of the UDC, the Alexandria chapter founded the first Children of the Confederacy chapter in 1896. Under the tutelage of Emma Frances Plecker Cassell, the Staunton chapter had the largest enrollment in the state, which included two children who were enrolled the day they were born. Children learned the ideology of the UDC and participated in parades and other memorial rituals, and the children's chapters continued to flourish alongside the UDC late in the nineteenth and early in the twentieth centuries.[23]

By memorializing and institutionalizing their version of the Old South, the women involved in memorial associations like the UDC registered their rejection of the New South and the change in gender norms it brought. Ironically, many of the women involved in the UDC were, in fact, married to men who were very much involved in Virginia's New South industries. Isobel Lamont Stewart Bryan, for example, who was a leader in several statewide organizations, was married to Joseph Bryan, one of the state's wealthiest and most-influential industrialists and financiers. For these women, it was a way to maintain status and a connection with the preindustrial Virginia they idealized.[24]

Some prosperous and socially connected white women accepted and embraced or noted their displeasure with the new Virginia, but wealthy African American women dealt with a far more complex and ambiguous commonwealth. The defeat of Virginia's interracial Readjuster Party by the Democrats in the 1883 election made clear to African American women that they would need to work together to organize and provide basic necessities to their communities. As more black women achieved middle- and upper-class status through education, they lived in an increasingly restrictive and segregated society. Moreover, they continued to deal with the stereotype of African American women as sexually available and inherently deviant, which threatened their ability to be regarded as respectable community leaders. To counter the racism and sexism of the politically and economically dominant white society late in the nineteenth century, upper- and middle-class African American women worked to help their communities as they fought to preserve their own social standing. In short, they put into action the motto of the National Association of Colored Women to which many Virginia women belonged through their association with the Virginia State Federation of Colored Women's Clubs: "Lifting as We Climb."[25]

Colleges and universities in Virginia led the charge to mold African American students into responsible, respectable community leaders. These colleges, universities, and institutes fostered an elite black culture that stressed maintaining respectability at all times and focusing energy and attention on serving less fortunate people. In addition to providing an education, Hartshorn Memorial College, founded in Richmond in 1883, trained young black women to be leaders in their communities. As at other black institutions, Hartshorn's administrators urged students to act responsibly and respectably. They also eased concerns about interactions with Virginia Union University's male students by noting that "our girls will be cared for, and not subjected to excessive exposure."[26] Hartshorn's first principal, Carrie Victoria Dyer, was a model for students. She had supervised women students at the Nashville Normal and Theological Institute before moving to Richmond. She served as treasurer of the Rachel Hartshorn Education and Missionary Society from 1886 to 1915 and managed daily operations on the campus when the school's male president was incapacitated by poor health. Money bequeathed by Dyer at the time of her death in 1921 enabled the Women's National Baptist Convention Auxiliary to establish five years later the Carrie V. Dyer Memorial Hospital in Liberia.[27]

Training to work as community leaders began early in students' college careers. Hartshorn sponsored two major mission groups. One raised money for black women missionaries to Africa, while the Hartshorn Home Workers engaged the female students in visiting the poor and sick residents of Richmond. The home workers distributed food and clothing and read from the Bible during their visits. In 1900, Hartshorn added a sewing program for boys and girls and began visits to the city's public almshouse. Some people, though, slipped away when they learned the Hartshorn women were coming, possibly because the visits included healthy doses of morality lessons. At Hampton Normal and Agricultural Institute (later Hampton University), every female student automatically became a member of the Circle of King's Daughters, which focused on philanthropic efforts in the community at large. These lessons were absorbed by students, such as Sarah J. Parker Courd, an 1878 Hampton graduate who later wrote from her home in Accomack County "that a true Hamptonian's work does not end at the school-house, but it must be in every step that he or she takes."[28]

Black institutions of higher education trained their students to become community leaders and activists in part because state and local governments did not provide nearly the same amount of funding for segregated black public education and community infrastructure as it did to white neighborhoods. It was clear by the end of the nineteenth century that African American women were prepared to take responsibility for filling the gap created by this fundamental inequality. Hampton graduate Amelia Perry Pride began teaching in 1882 at a black-funded community school in Lynchburg and became its principal in 1890. Her community activism extended far beyond her job title. In a survey for Hampton, she described her job duties as gardener, housekeeper, poultry and hog rearer, dressmaker, Sunday school worker, temperance advocate, and construction supervisor. Pride took black orphans into her home because Lynchburg did not allow them into its white-only orphanage early in the 1880s. She also cared for (and financed the funerals of) five elderly women who lived in her rented home. In addition to teaching classes in morals and etiquette, she taught night classes in cooking and sewing to help women gain employment and aid their families at the same time. Janie Porter returned to Hampton from Georgia and married Harris Barrett in 1889. After watching some young girls playing in the street, Barrett used her life savings to create the Locust Street Settlement House, which became a central feature of the community. The center provided classes in homemaking, child welfare, poultry raising, and canning. It also held a night school for adults.[29]

In 1895, black women in Richmond began what became a statewide effort to free three African American women convicted of murder in Lunenburg County. Schoolteachers Rosa Dixon Bowser and Marietta Chiles created the Richmond Women's League to raise money for the defense of Pokey Barnes, Mary Barnes, and Mary Abernathy, two of whom sat on death row after being convicted of murder on the sole evidence of the testimony of a man also convicted of the same murder. The other woman, Mary Barnes, had received a ten-year sentence in the state penitentiary for the crime. Bowser and Chiles called a meeting at the First African Baptist Church, and 200 women showed up to help. They pledged to raise $500 for the women's defense. By the end of the first week, the group had raised $100 and supported the women through visits to the jail and gifts of clothing, food, and sewing materials. One member of the group went to Philadelphia and returned with $50. Chiles organized another Women's League in Hampton, which raised $175. After meeting her, the staff at a Hampton hotel was so moved that they raised $68. The Women's League eventually raised $700 and helped with financial and housing assistance after the women were finally freed. The Richmond Women's League became the Richmond Mothers' Club, which eventually joined the Virginia State Federation of Colored Women's Clubs, a chapter of the National Association of Colored Women. The Mothers'

Club advocated educational and health initiatives, interracial cooperation on public projects, and prison reform.[30]

It was not only African American women who worked for uplift in their communities. Like the efforts of black women, white women's charitable activities late in the nineteenth century fell directly in line with the national Progressive movement. The religious convictions of many Protestant women in Virginia led them to embrace the promotion of social reforms to reduce poverty and disease in their communities. In 1877, an interdenominational group of middle-class white women concerned about the plight of Richmond's poorest residents founded the City Mission, which housed a soup kitchen and provided food, clothing, and fuel during visits to those in need of help. It had a sewing school by the 1880s and had raised enough money to hire a matron who directed the mission's operations. Their efforts were so important to the city that the women received money and coal directly from the city council to support the mission. The City Mission pledged to help anyone "regardless of any fact, save that the recipient of its charity be needy and helpless," understanding that the costs of consumer goods, not personal financial failings, were often responsible for many families' sinking into poverty. The mission later became part of Richmond Associated Charities, a central organization designed to coordinate charitable efforts to aid clients it deemed worthy of help.[31] Jewish women in Richmond also worked to alleviate the poverty of Eastern European Jewish families who had recently arrived. Beth Ahabah's Ladies' Hebrew Benevolent Association handled several hundred charity cases each year, and the National Council of Jewish Women established a settlement house in a predominantly immigrant Richmond community in 1912.[32]

White women also worked to help poor women secure financial futures, and while the outward focus was on charitable efforts, the organizations helped poor women find autonomy through boosting their incomes. In 1883, a group of Presbyterian women opened the Richmond Exchange for Women's Work, which sold white women's crafts and baked goods. The exchange operated until 1956. Similar exchanges emerged in Charlottesville, Lynchburg, and Staunton.[33] Perhaps inspired by these earlier attempts to help poor women become economically independent, Laura Lu Scherer Copenhaver followed the model of these earlier groups and built a veritable industry in Marion. As a prominent lay member of the United Lutheran Church in America, Copenhaver was involved with mission efforts. By the 1920s she had begun hiring women to produce textiles in order to help the economy of the region and, more directly, the Appalachian women she saw who needed employment and economic opportunities. Working out of Copenhaver's home, the women used local wool and traditional patterns to craft rugs, bed canopies, and other household decor. Copenhaver marketed Rosemont Industries by advertising nationally "in magazines read by women who want the sort of things we make," and its products became popular throughout the world. Renamed Laura Copenhaver Industries, Inc., in 1960, the corporation produced household textiles into the twenty-first century.[34]

Concerned about the influx of young women into Richmond looking for jobs, in 1887 a group established the South's first Young Women's Christian Association, an organization dedicated to assisting women of all socioeconomic levels secure jobs, safe housing in cities, and cultural and educational opportunities. Emily Fairfax Whittle, the wife of the bishop of the Episcopal diocese, served as its first president, along with seven vice presidents from other church denominations. The city's YWCA opened with a six-room flat for white women workers. The following year they rented a house to hold nineteen women, and in 1891, the YWCA board purchased two houses on East Franklin Street to serve forty-five women. By 1893, they housed sixty regular and twenty-four transient residents. The YWCA held educational classes, prayer meetings, and entertainments. It provided medical care in the 1880s and 1890s, and daily child care for more than thirty children with its day nursery and kindergarten, both established in 1890. The Employment Committee found jobs for forty women in 1893. By 1894, the YWCA boasted 669 members, and it became a charter member of the National YWCA in 1906. This YWCA was for white women only, however; the Phyllis Wheatley branch, named after the colonial-era African American poet, opened in 1912 and served Richmond's African American community.[35]

White women throughout Virginia were active with the Woman's Christian Temperance Union late in the nineteenth century. Although women had participated in the temperance movement early in the century, the WCTU's scope of activities eclipsed antebellum efforts. By early in the 1880s, Richmond, Alexandria, Charlottesville, Staunton, Harrisonburg, Dayton, Winchester, and Henrico County all boasted chapters of the WCTU. Women disseminated literature, sponsored coffeehouses as an alternative to saloons, established Board of Hope chapters for children, visited jails and almshouses, and obtained pledges from Sunday School children not to drink. Although it got a later start, in 1887 the Norfolk–Princess Anne Bi-County Chapter was particularly active. It established the *Virginia Call*, which became the official organ of the state WCTU. During the 1890s the chapter started a home for unwed mothers that was later affiliated with the National Florence Crittenton Mission, and it also started a boardinghouse for elderly African Americans. In the 1900s it opened a boardinghouse for young women and established a day nursery. The WCTU in Virginia made some attempts to reach out to African Americans, but left most temperance efforts in the black community to black women. Many embraced the effort and established local WCTU chapters and temperance societies, often in conjunction with their Sunday school classes. Mary C. Robinson Steward reported in a survey of Hampton graduates that she belonged "to a Temperance Club that is doing all it can," because she feared that "Intemperance is one of the evils that help to keep our people back."[36]

At first, WCTU chapters tended to focus on less political activities to address what the members perceived to be societal problems caused by excessive alcohol consumption, but Virginia's WCTU shifted its tactics to achieve its goals. Its efforts to change society through coffeehouses and Sunday Schools proved successful at the local level—by 1905, many of Virginia's 100 counties were dry as a result of a local option law the General Assembly had passed in 1886. During the first decade of the twentieth century, the WCTU began advocating a statewide prohibition law. Chapters all over the commonwealth collected signatures on petitions and worked with the Anti-Saloon League of America for stronger antiliquor laws. By 1914, a total of 79 Virginia counties had banned alcohol through local elections. That year a bill to prohibit alcohol consumption statewide came up for a referendum vote. Women activists sponsored parades, established rooms that were stocked with comforts and prohibition literature near factories, and canvassed locally. On election day, WCTU women served lunch and coffee to poll workers. The referendum passed by a 3 to 2 margin, and the prohibition of the sale and distribution of alcohol became law in 1916.[37]

Upper- and middle-class white women, and even some wealthy black women, had the means to carve out a new social and economic place for themselves in late-nineteenth-century Virginia. Poor urban dwellers and

Telephone operators, ca. 1890. In the 1880s and 1890s, clerical and service work opened up to women across the country. These Virginians took advantage of the new jobs in technology as telephone operators. This job required dexterity, concentration, and a good memory, as switch operators had to connect callers manually. Although these jobs were higher paying than mill work, they were available only to white women who generally held a high school education. *Courtesy of the Valentine Richmond History Center, Cook Collection 1030.*

farm women had fewer options. By 1900, more than 125,000 Virginia women worked outside the home, but the majority of women—about 58 percent—were engaged in service work, mainly in the domestic realm. Only 6 percent were employed in professional positions, and most of those were teachers. Another 3 percent of women were saleswomen and secretaries, 10 percent were farmers, 8 percent were agricultural laborers, 6.5 percent were seamstresses, and 5 percent worked in factories. Richmond boasted many women factory operatives. In 1890 a shirt factory employed 500 black women who each made $3 a week. Many tobacco factories in the city, including the Allen and Ginter company, employed hundreds of black women to sort, pick, and stem tobacco. White women rolled cigarettes. Women factory workers received approximately half the salaries of men in the 1890s. At Allen and Ginter, the maximum weekly wage for women tobacco rollers was $9 a week, based on their ability to roll 15,000 to 18,000 cigarettes in that time.[38]

Virginia had little union activity, but it was not devoid of worker activism. The presence of Knights of Labor women's assemblies in twelve cities indicates that working women organized for better working situations late in the nineteenth century. Richmond's Knights of Labor had 10,000 members, black and white, male and female, many of whom worked in the tobacco industry. The more exclusive American Federation of Labor had a few chapters in the city, but it represented only about 10 percent of Richmond's workforce. With or without union help, fifty women went on strike in 1899 when Allen and Ginter attempted to cut women's wages. Their strike forced the company to restore the original wages.[39]

Beyond striking, however, women in factories and mill towns worked to create mutually supportive communities both at and away from work. When the average worker, such as Anthelia Holt at the Matoaca Manufacturing Company, in Chesterfield County, worked ten-to-twelve-hour days, six days a week, late in the nineteenth century, it meant that women did not get home until 7 P.M. They then started the chores expected of women, including washing clothes, cooking, and child care. In 1880, about 23 percent of women were mill workers in the town of Matoaca, as opposed to only 9 percent of the men. In 1900, only 8 percent of women in the town worked outside the home, more than 85 percent of them at Matoaca Manufacturing Company. Women created support groups for each other based on their kin, neighbor, and work relationships as they worked in the carding, weaving, and spinning industries. Women looked after friends' looms to provide each other with rest breaks, and they took care of sick relatives and neighbors and supported bereaved families. They also created social networks around chores and held cooking and quilting parties. They relished church social events, which allowed them courting opportunities and recreational pleasure in their time off. These women created solidarity by building strong community ties, despite the 70-hour workweek they endured in the factory.[40]

Some white women created institutions to help poor women, but many working poor had to rely on public assistance to survive. In Richmond, poor black and white women moved in and out of the almshouse, called the City Home. They did the domestic work for the house—sewing, cooking, cleaning, laundry, and caring for their own and the other residents' children. In addition, pregnant women, most of them unwed, used the almshouse as a maternity home. Black women who were unaffiliated with one of several religious denominations did not have any private institutions of support, and white women often could not afford to pay for services at private maternity homes. Some maternity homes also had poor reputations for high infant mortality rates and unsafe conditions. The majority focused on redemption and social control, and they discouraged adoption. Approximately one-third of the 1,519 women who gave birth at the Richmond almshouse between 1874 and 1914 left their children for adoption. Of these births, 329 were white, 1,106 were black, and the rest were not identified.[41] Poor women's use of the public relief late in the nineteenth and early in the twentieth centuries suggests that they had to cobble together multiple strategies in order to survive.

A large majority of all the women in Virginia, nonelite farm women led lives that more nearly resembled those of their antebellum ancestors than the lives of urban women did. Often their only political role late in the nineteenth century was to sign petitions for or against saloons trying to open in their communities.[42] Middle-class and poor farm women had little free time to organize in any formal way, because they performed many agricultural duties on the farm. In the tobacco region of Virginia's Southside, black and white women were involved in every process of cultivation. It took an estimated 430 hours of labor per acre to produce a successful crop. Women planted seedbeds and moved the plants to the fields, pulled suckers off the top of plants to generate better-quality leaves, pulled and killed the hornworms that could devastate the crop, and harvested alongside the men, often sharing labor with neighbors at harvest time. Women grouped, tied, cured, and graded the tobacco leaves. Women did this work in addition to raising vegetable gardens and livestock. Women worked extremely hard on tobacco farms and took pride in their work and productivity.[43]

When cultivating a crop did not bring in enough money, rural women often made up the shortfall. Farmers' wives took in boarders, washing, or sewing, and they produced butter, chicken, and eggs for the market. Rural black women often served as domestics in addition to working their own farms. As Amelia Perry Pride noted, many black women in Lynchburg attended her canning and preserving classes in the 1880s and 1890s, but she avoided referring to them as servants.[44] Pride understood that the women came to the classes to learn how to help their own families, not their employers. Farmers late in the nineteenth century were often gripped by agricultural depression, so it is not surprising that rural women had their hands full with traditional farming responsibilities.

In the twentieth century many women became political activists, radicalizing their calls for reform. The emergence of urban white women's political voice came at a time when African American women saw possibilities for equality wither before an increasingly segregationist government. From 1900 to 1920, progressive white women activists fought to expand their voice in Virginia society, while African American women continued to struggle for the betterment of their own communities in the face of growing segregation and disfranchisement. Rural women and poor women also took advantage of increasing numbers of private and public programs designed to benefit themselves and their families.

The new state constitution of 1902 allowed conservative white Democrats to consolidate their power by severely restricting the right to vote. In the elections of 1902 and 1903 a voter had to pay at least one dollar in property tax a year, be a Civil War veteran (or the son of one) on either side, or read and interpret any part of the Constitution. Beginning in 1904 applicants for voter registration had to be able to fill out their own application, answer any questions to the satisfaction of the registrar, and have paid a cumulative poll tax for each of the three previous years six months in advance of election day. The Democratic Party was in control of most localities and registrars had total discretion over giving the constitutional literacy tests. Nine-tenths of African American men lost the franchise, and the poll tax disfranchised about half of the white male population.[45]

Between 1900 and 1906, the General Assembly passed a series of laws that segregated public transportation. At first the laws were voluntary, but the General Assembly quickly passed legislation that made transit segregation compulsory. Noted black community leader Maggie Lena Walker joined the editor of the *Richmond Planet*, John Mitchell Jr., in leading boycotts of Richmond's streetcar company in 1904. The state's only public institution of higher learning for African Americans lost some of its autonomy during this period. The assembly purged its board of black members in 1890, removed the four-year degree option in 1902 and changed its name to Virginia Normal and Industrial Institute (later Virginia State University). The new state constitution also did not allow the school to nominate a faculty member to serve on the Board of Education, as was the case for the state's white public colleges and universities. These new legislative efforts ensured that Virginia's white wealthy class would retain dominance over the government and public services in the state.[46]

The Virginia court system further enforced a racial hierarchy. Virginia boosters boasted of the "rule of law" in the state, citing a lower lynching rate than other southern regions. In fact, the courtrooms themselves were stacked against black defendants as racism affected all conviction decisions. The threat of mob violence outside the courtroom doors often leached into the court itself. The assembly made rape a capital offense in 1894, enabling Virginia judges to feed whites' need for aggressive retribution and elites' desire to look superior to other state leaders who could not control "mob rule." Lynch mobs were unnecessary if judges could sentence black defendants to death.[47]

While these changes challenged African American women to work even harder in their struggle for equality and the uplift of their communities, other twentieth-century realities stirred active clubwomen to reform their society. In 1900, only about half of Virginia's school-age children were enrolled, and most attended one-room schoolhouses. The number of public high schools was limited, and the illiteracy rate was 11 percent for whites and 45 percent for African Americans. The school year in Virginia averaged only six months, with 80 percent of teachers holding only high school diplomas. Virginia's public health record was not much better. Richmond's mortality rate early in the 1900s was higher than all but three other American cities. In Jackson Ward, a black neighborhood, about half of all children died. Tuberculosis outbreaks were common in all cities at the turn of the century. Neither urban nor rural poverty had been alleviated through existing programs. These dire conditions, often ignored by Virginia's political leaders, led many progressive clubwomen to call for change. Through the work of their clubs and associations, in which they acquired new business, money, and oratorical skills, women expanded boundaries of appropriate behavior and increasingly took up new roles in the public sphere, where they fought for a stronger voice, more power, and new public policies in Virginia.[48]

Many black and white clubwomen pursued aggressive public health initiatives in the first two decades of the twentieth century. The relatively staid Woman's Club of Richmond, founded in 1894 as a literary and arts society, ended its policy of not participating in public projects when it invited Nannie J. Minor, a settlement nurse, to give a talk on the Nurses' Settlement house program in 1901. Minor had established the Nurses' Settlement house with Sadie Heath Cabaniss and Agnes Randolph, co-workers at the Old Dominion Hospital. They and seven other nurses rented a house on Seventh Street and modeled their programs after other prominent settlement houses such as the Hull House in Chicago and Lillian Wald's house in New York. The settlement offered classes in cooking, child care, and hygiene in addition to providing visiting nurse services to the poor, regardless of race, but facilities and programs were segregated. The nurses had visited more than 2,600 whites and 1,400 African Americans by 1916.[49]

Motivated by the work of the Nurses' Settlement, the Woman's Club joined other clubwomen and nurses in 1902 to organize the Instructive Visiting Nurses' Association, which was under the direction of a board of female clubwomen and staffed by nurses and ultimately, social workers. The IVNA established the first tuberculosis clinic in Richmond, sponsored a juvenile officer in the police force, placed nurses in schools and factories, and staffed a home for the elderly. Nine of the IVNA's fourteen board members were also members of the Woman's Club. Women in Richmond were often willing to cross denominational and religious boundaries in their charitable endeavors, and the longtime president of the Ladies' Hebrew Benevolent Association, Zipporah Michelbacher Cohen, served on the IVNA board for forty-two years. In 1913, the IVNA hired a black nurse, who was funded by the Richmond Council of Colored Women, and by 1930, there were seven black nurses on staff. The association's social work component was split off in 1923 to form the William Byrd Settlement House. The IVNA became an extremely influential statewide organization as it helped to start programs in Charlottesville, Danville, Lynchburg, and Newport News. It also provided instructors for the School of Social Work and Public Health (later Virginia Commonwealth University), in Richmond, when it opened in 1917.[50]

Maggie Lena Mitchell Walker galvanized black women to support public health and other initiatives to aid Richmond's black residents. The daughter of a former slave who worked as a washerwoman, Walker attended the Richmond

Clerical workers, ca. 1910. African American women could find clerical jobs only in black-run businesses. As leader of the Independent Order of Saint Luke, Maggie Walker established several businesses, including a department store and a bank, that hired African American women. These workers are pictured in the Independent Order of Saint Luke's office about 1910. *Courtesy of the Valentine Richmond History Center, V. 88.20.23.*

Colored Normal School, became a teacher, and by the age of thirty-two had taken over the Independent Order of Saint Luke, a benevolent fraternal association. Under her leadership it opened the Saint Luke Penny Savings Bank of Richmond, Virginia, in 1903 and a retail center called the Saint Luke Emporium in 1905 to provide job opportunities for the black community. She was one of the most influential leaders in Richmond's black community by early in the twentieth century, and she used Saint Luke's children's program to educate youth about the importance of hygiene and public health. She also founded the Richmond Council of Colored Women, which funded the first black nurse in the Instructive Visiting Nurses' Association and established a tuberculosis clinic.[51]

In Roanoke, a small effort ultimately became a strong force for change in the city. A railroad boomtown, Roanoke's population grew from about 1,000 at the time of its incorporation in 1882 to more than 21,000 in 1900, and it suffered from haphazard development. A group of women formed the Educational League in 1906 after learning from a local physician that the student-teacher ratio in the schools of 58 to 1 reflected the city's dangerous and overcrowded conditions. The women demanded that the city council provide better garbage removal and hire a milk inspector to uphold the city's 1904 pure food ordinance, inspected and recorded sanitation problems at local schools, and fought for a strong board of health. Employing the language of social housekeeping to justify the group's political activism, Sarah Johnson Cocke, the wife of a prominent lawyer, argued that if the city council would make improvements, the women would be happy to return to their traditional duties. In the meantime, however, league members successfully lobbied the council to appropriate more money for the city's overcrowded white schools.[52]

Building on their success, the women established the Woman's Civic Betterment Club of Roanoke later in 1906 to oversee health and welfare initiatives in the city. By 1910, the organization's 152 members included members of patriotic societies, the Woman's Christian Temperance Union, and the wives of councilmen and prominent local businessmen. The club's organizing force and its second president was Willie Walker Caldwell, who in 1908 declared that "the aims of the club are wide in scope" in order to "make Roanoke healthful and a beautiful city" as well as to "raise the standard of her citizenship...." The group sponsored lectures on city health and beautification projects, held a festival to raise money for betterment projects, and funded and backed urban planning projects. The organization successfully lobbied for the establishment of a large park, a new food ordinance that made vendors comply with health department inspectors, and sewer improvements.[53]

Progressive women worked to reform Virginia's educational system at all levels. A leader in the movement for better schools was Mary-Cooke Branch Munford, a well-connected Richmonder whose mother had denied her the college education she desperately wanted. Along with several other Woman's Club members, including Lila Meade Valentine and Landonia Minor Dashiell, she initiated a program to expand kindergarten for children in Richmond. When they learned of the deplorable conditions of Richmond's white high schools, the women helped organize the Richmond Education Association in 1900 to lobby the city government for better facilities, bigger school budgets, and higher teacher salaries. The association also worked for new buildings with playgrounds, literary and vocational training, and improved curricula. It raised private money and secured city funding for a new industrial department for African American students in Richmond. In 1904, the group joined forces with the Co-operative Education Association of Virginia, which lobbied local and state governments to create nine-month school terms, more four-year high schools, and better training for teachers. The General Assembly's spending on education rose 900 percent between 1900 and 1920, although it was still only half that of the national average. In 1920, Munford became the first woman to serve on the Richmond School Board, on which she sat for eleven years.[54]

Munford was also a driving force in opening up higher education to women of Virginia. In 1903, only 2 of 140 southern colleges offered four-year programs for women, and only one of these had a top national rating—Randolph-Macon Woman's College (later Randolph College), in Lynchburg. Virginia had only one publicly funded normal school for teachers, in Farmville, but in 1908, the General Assembly established two more normal schools for women, one in Harrisonburg (later James Madison University) and one in Fredericksburg (later the University of Mary Washington), and in 1910 it authorized the last regional normal school in Radford (later Radford University), which opened in 1913. Munford founded the Co-ordinate College League in 1910 to advocate for a coordinate institution for women at the University of Virginia. A college education for women was "of tremendous importance," Munford and Virginia S. McKenney declared in 1914, "and a wrong decision on the subject would undoubtedly be a calamity to Virginia's women, to her public school system and to her great state university." League members included members of the Young Women's Christian Association, the Virginia Historical Society, the Virginia division of the United Daughters of the Confederacy, and the State Board of Charities and Corrections. The CCL also received formal support from the Farmers Union, the Virginia Federation of Labor, the State Teachers Association, the Woman's Christian Temperance Union, and most major state newspapers. Nevertheless, the House of Delegates defeated a final bill to establish a coordinate college in 1916 by a vote of 48 to 46.[55]

Other prominent women worked not only to secure education for women, but also to help college-educated women make their way in the business world. In 1914, Orie Latham Hatcher, a Richmond native and an English professor at Bryn Mawr College, solicited the assistance of clubwomen to establish the Virginia Bureau of Vocations for Women. Organizers included Virginia S. McKenney, president of the Richmond chapter of the Southern Association of College Women; Mary Keller, dean of Westhampton College (later part of the University of Richmond); and Martha Patteson Branch Bowie, a former Hollins College instructor. They lobbied government directly for policies advantageous to women wage-earners and tried to secure educations and jobs for white women. The bureau steered women into jobs that its counselors considered appropriate for the applicants, whose academic skills were often tested before placement. The bureau concentrated on sharing information about suitable fields of work for women and how to obtain the necessary training. In 1917, it helped establish Richmond's School of Social Work and Public Health, whose subsequent awareness campaign about the need for public health training for women resulted in the opening of the Medical College of Virginia to women. The bureau's large building in downtown Richmond housed professional women's offices, leased office space to female professionals, and rented rooms to traveling businesswomen. It also served as an education center, and between 1921 and 1923 funded 97 college loans and scholarships for women. In 1921, it became the Southern Woman's Educational Alliance, reflecting the expansion of its work beyond Virginia.[56]

The efforts of white clubwomen were primarily on behalf of other white women, and African American women became leaders in efforts to improve living conditions and access to education within their own communities. Racial segregation sometimes afforded black women more opportunities to work alongside men in establishing and directing charitable organizations. In 1909, a group of men and women formed the Negro Organization Society to advocate better educational facilities, longer school years, increased teacher salaries, and public health work. Women sat on the NOS executive committee and served as committee chairs, including Hampton activist Janie Porter Barrett, who headed the committee of charities and corrections. In 1908, she had helped organize the Virginia State Federation of Colored Women's Clubs to unite the activities of women's groups across the state and highlight the "work of the faithful women who are working so patiently and earnestly" for the betterment of their communities. These women were often teachers who established local mothers' clubs to encourage parental involvement in education and child welfare.[57]

Many of these black and white activist women focused their efforts on helping poor women and children. For this, they became known as "maternalists," partly because they called on the values of motherhood when demanding reforms for needy children and their mothers. To justify their activities in public reform movements, they capitalized on their own status as mothers or promoted a universal notion of womanhood that suggested because women could be mothers they understood what society needed. In Virginia, women worked to bring services to poor and needy women early in the twentieth century. Richmond's Young Women's Christian Association continued to expand its offerings for working-class women. By 1912, the YWCA's paid four-person staff and a host of middle-class volunteers directed activities for numerous women and girls. Among its goals was the protection of vulnerable young women from what the YWCA workers perceived as the dangers of the city. YWCA staff members and volunteers met women at train stations with information and offers of assistance, in 1913, meeting more than 1,900 women. A year later, the YWCA established a domestic science program, and a Business Women's Club with approximately 200 members in clerical and service work. Its volunteer roll boasted 75 women. Richmond's African American YWCA branch had more than 200 members by 1912 and later opened the city's first library for the black community, in addition to assisting working-class women and providing them with recreational and educational opportunities. In 1910, black women in Norfolk established a YWCA to provide space for young women traveling through the city and to help them find employment.[58]

Women's clubs became active leaders in Progressive maternalist movement. The Woman's Club of Richmond had resisted political causes in the nineteenth century, but became an organization that lobbied for many reform efforts, including conservation, separate prisons for women and juveniles, and better conditions for working women. The club hosted the national Women's Welfare Conference in 1911 and sent a representative to the state-sponsored conference on child welfare in that same year. By 1913 the club had created a welfare committee that in its first year advocated for the establishment of more playgrounds, a public library, and protection of birds. Through these decades it continued to speak out on issues affecting children, education, health, and peace. Women across the state established clubs to accomplish similar goals. In Radford, Julia W. Bullard organized the Kings Daughters in 1901 to help needy children. Later known as the Radford Woman's Club, in 1916 it funded a nurse for the city's schools. The Pulaski Civic League followed suit a few months later and in 1917 raised enough money to hire a nurse for the schools in Dublin and Pulaski.[59]

African American clubwomen often had trouble securing institutional support from outside their own neighborhoods and networks. The Children's Home Society of Virginia, in Richmond, refused to take black children on the grounds that there were no black families prosperous enough with which to place them. Facing such discrimination, it is not surprising that black women relied on themselves to help their own. For example, Amelia Perry Pride took children into her home to make up for the lack of public facilities in Lynchburg. Ora Brown Stokes, president of the Richmond Neighborhood Association, supported a day nursery for African American children, among other projects to aid poor children and women. Although white women had advocated establishing a juvenile facility for black girls, Janie Porter Barrett and the Virginia State Federation of Colored Women's Clubs made it a reality. Barrett recruited white women such as Mary-Cooke Branch Munford and Katherine Waller Barrett to serve on the board of the Industrial Home School for Colored Girls (later Virginia Industrial School for Colored Girls), which opened in Hanover County in 1915. Under Janie Porter Barrett's superintendence, the school cared for the young women with "kind treatment and the honor system" while providing an education as well as practical training in domestic service and farmwork to enable them to find employment after being released. African American women across the state helped raise funds to support the school, including teachers Lucy Addison, of Roanoke, and Rosa Dixon Bowser, of Richmond, who promoted educational reforms and served as president of the Virginia State Teachers Association from 1890 to 1892.[60]

The United Daughters of the Confederacy marshaled its forces to support less-fortunate white women. In Richmond, the Ladies' Auxiliary of the George E. Pickett Camp, Confederate Veterans, saw the need for a home for Confederate veterans' impoverished female relatives. The Home for Needy Confederate Women opened in 1900 after holding two successful fund-raising festivals and soliciting money from the General Assembly. Ten women originally moved into the home, but in 1902 finances were tight enough that the home was already in financial straits. The board asked Elizabeth Lyne Hoskins Montague, the wife of the new governor, for help. She went on home visits to raise money, not only in Virginia but also along the East Coast. Financial supporters included wives of wealthy financiers and even Alice Roosevelt, Theodore Roosevelt's daughter. The board secured food and clothing from donors across the city. Montague ultimately solicited money from forty-one UDC chapters outside the state, and her political connections enabled her to secure $5,000 of funding from the General Assembly. By 1904, the UDC had raised enough money to buy and open another home, and in 1918 Montague became president of the home's board, serving for thirty-three years. UDC members also assisted needy white women with monthly assistance on a case-by-case basis.[61]

It is clear that women's efforts on behalf of their communities affected the state legislature and local governing bodies. In 1923, the General Assembly increased public welfare funding by 26 percent, and funding for children in foster care by 45 percent. It also increased funding of the industrial homes for boys and girls by $65,000.[62] Although the Co-ordinate College League did not succeed in establishing a college for women at the University of Virginia, the General Assembly passed legislation in 1918 to allow women to attend the College of William and Mary and in 1920 to attend the University of Virginia's graduate programs. By late in the 1920s, General Assembly appropriations for the Home for Needy Confederate Women were up to $25,000 a year, and it continued to fund the home through 1982. In 1918, the General Assembly passed legislation allowing local governments to give mothers' pensions to widows. Only Richmond and Wise County provided pensions, though, and Richmond's city government funded the pensions largely because of the white clubwomen who lobbied aggressively in support of the measure.[63]

While most clubwomen focused their efforts on urban areas, rural women were not entirely left out of either leading or benefiting from reform movements. In 1910, Ella Graham Agnew became the first woman field-worker for the United States Department of Agriculture when she was hired to create tomato-canning clubs for girls in two rural Virginia counties. Born in Prince Edward County in 1871, Agnew had attended Smithdeal Business College, in Richmond, been principal of a girls' boarding school in South Africa, and worked for the YWCA in North Carolina and Ohio before returning to Virginia. She believed strongly in rural reform through club work and was a staunch advocate for woman suffrage. In her first summer, Agnew organized forty-six girls in Halifax and Nottoway Counties and lobbied county boards of supervisors and local suffrage clubs for funds to operate the program. The 1914 Smith-Lever Act enabled the establishment of an extension division at the Virginia Agricultural and Mechanical College and Polytechnic Institute (later Virginia Tech), and during the First World War white and black agents conducted educational campaigns in more than half of Virginia's counties.[64]

In 1914, a group of Augusta County women organized the Tuesday Club. These rural women hailed from upper- and middle-class families, and like their urban counterparts many had at least some college education. This club, organized and led in part by Louise Moffett, established a county nurse program, endorsed stronger childhood education programs, and called for movie censorship. By 1917, the group had started a canning program to help farm women raise and preserve more nutritious food economically and safely. The first instructor, Louise Moffett's sister Elsie Moffett, had attended Mary Baldwin Seminary, taught Sunday school, and was instrumental in establishing the county nurse program. She had taken a home demonstration summer class at Virginia Agricultural and Mechanical College and Polytechnic Institute and wanted to start a program in her hometown.[65]

Local governments needed to match state funds to receive federal money for such programs, and rural women's clubs like the Tuesday Club had to lobby for home demonstration agents in their counties. Although the Tuesday Club initially encountered resistance from Augusta County officials, the women persuaded the local agricultural agent to secure travel funding for Elsie Moffett.

The Tuesday Club then pressured the county supervisors, who agreed to provide $300, with Staunton business owners and the city government providing another $300. Moffett began work full-time in 1918. She organized eight girls' canning clubs and ran cooking and sewing clubs in schools. She also had three poultry clubs with twenty members.[66]

Home demonstration agents embodied a mix of progressive reform and rural advocacy impulses. They worked to establish middle-class urban norms for their club members through efficiency training and decorating and sewing programs meant to bring modernity to the farm. They also empowered farm women through selling their own products and gaining the power over their own finances. Participants in these programs generally found them beneficial and shaped them to help themselves and their families. Participants often formed strong bonds with home demonstration agents and remembered the programs—and the skills they learned, like canning and sewing—with pride.[67]

Given that black and white activist women were engaged with the political process in trying to reform health, education, and welfare for poor women and children, it is not surprising that many of these women were part of the woman suffrage movement in the twentieth century. The majority of Virginia women either stayed silent on the suffrage issue or opposed woman suffrage, but others believed that securing the vote was the only way to secure lasting reform in the state and nation. Journalist Orra Langhorne, of Lynchburg, attended conventions of the National American Woman Suffrage Association in the 1890s and was most likely instrumental in securing Susan B. Anthony's speaking engagement during a stopover in Culpeper County in 1895 and Carrie Chapman Catt's speaking to the suffrage committee of the state constitutional convention in 1901. The movement faltered after Langhorne died in 1904.[68]

In 1909, a group of women in Richmond, led by Woman's Club member Lila Meade Valentine, founded the Equal Suffrage League (ESL) as an affiliate branch of the NAWSA. The group fought for the vote on maternalist grounds, arguing that the vote was the best way to secure better schools, park and playground improvements, anticrime initiatives, and prison reforms. The league made clear its stance on protection of children and women. Its 1912 convention resolutions listed among its goals equal pay and an eight-hour workday for women, a living wage for women, and the abolition of child labor. The ESL published *Virginia Suffrage News* from its Richmond office and sent out more than 368,000 pieces of literature in 1915–1916. Members staffed booths at fairs, held essay contests for children, and conducted bake sales to raise money—all traditionally gendered methods of working for a political cause. By 1916 the Equal Suffrage League had 3,000 Richmond members and 115 chapters throughout the state with a total membership of more than 13,000.[69]

Many white Virginians feared that giving women the right to vote would endanger white supremacy by allowing black women to vote as well as white. A 1915 editorial in the *Richmond Evening Journal* described suffragists as "not very practical or very logical or very well informed" women who did not understand the implications of allowing black women to vote freely.[70] But the majority of prominent suffragists had been extremely successful in navigating party politics to secure reforms. Valentine had already successfully

Members of the Equal Suffrage League of Virginia, Capitol Square, ca. 1915. Members of the Equal Suffrage League demonstrated for suffrage outside the Capitol Building in 1915. These women represented the white elite of Richmond, including Adèle Clark (*far left*), Sarah Harvie Wormeley (*fourth from left*), Nora Houston, Rosalie Fontaine Jones Armistead, and Sophie Rose Meredith (*all in car*), although they varied in age. *Courtesy of the Library of Virginia.*

worked for education as a member of the Richmond Education Association, and she also was involved with the IVNA and antituberculosis campaigns, both of which received government funding as a result of lobbying by the ladies' board. Novelist Mary Johnston joined Valentine as a leader of the ESL. A well-known and widely published author, Johnston had championed various public causes, including protective legislation for women and children, compulsory education, delinquency laws, punishment for child neglecters, eugenics, and the peace movement.[71] Membership in the Equal Suffrage League certainly did not duplicate, but had many members in common with, the Woman's Club of Richmond. And many suffragists shared common backgrounds. Like Kate Seeley Tuttle, a Vassar graduate and Virginia suffragist, the leaders of ESL chapters often had attended four-year colleges. They were also more likely to work for

Woman suffrage ribbons and buttons, 1910s–1920s. These Equal Suffrage League and League of Women Voters buttons were used by women campaigning for the vote. The delegate badges belonged to Norfolk suffragist Jessie Fremont Easton Townsend. The picture of Lucy Stone in the lower button references the vanguard of feminist activists who started the formal suffrage movement in the 1840s. *Courtesy of the Library of Virginia, Equal Suffrage League of Virginia Papers, Acc. 22002.*

wages or salaries than antisuffragists, and they were more likely to work in or be involved in some way with nontraditional urban modern professions.[72]

Beyond these commonalities, however, lay a diverse state movement. In Norfolk, suffragists abounded. Jessie Fremont Easton Townsend, a partner in her husband's real estate business, and Pauline Forstall Colclough Adams, an Irish immigrant who became involved in local civic activities after moving to the city with her physician husband, were extremely outspoken proponents of the franchise. In 1910, they created an Equal Suffrage League chapter composed of homemakers, working women, and the wives of military officers that became one of the largest in the state. Townsend took a more traditional approach to advocacy, while Adams embraced militant tactics and served time in the federal workhouse at Occoquan after being arrested for picketing in front of the president during a Selective Service parade in 1917. In other areas of the state, it was a bit harder to attract women. Elizabeth Dabney Langhorne Lewis (later Otey), of Lynchburg, worked to recruit women one by one through her personal networks, and it was slow-going. Women's colleges could not always be counted on for support. Although Randolph-Macon Woman's College, in Lynchburg, had an extremely active chapter, boasting 150 members by 1914, Sweet Briar College, in nearby Amherst County, never had a chapter at all. The ESL did not reach out to African American women, although black clubwomen established their own informal prosuffrage networks. Maggie Walker and Ora Brown Stokes worked together to support suffrage in Richmond and later led registration drives for women after the Nineteenth Amendment was ratified.[73]

As the Equal Suffrage League became large and powerful enough to be noticed, a formal antisuffrage movement quickly emerged to counter its progress. Antisuffragist men and women feared that allowing women to vote would overturn the carefully crafted segregation they had worked hard to create. They also believed and argued that biblical, biological, and sociological principles prohibited women from participating in electoral politics, and they used these tenets, in conjunction with racial and states' rights arguments, to fight against the vote. The Virginia Association Opposed to Woman Suffrage was established in 1912 after an antisuffrage speech by novelist Molly Elliot Seawell, a Gloucester County native. The association's leader was Jane Meade Rutherfoord, a member of many exclusive white, ancestry-based societies such as the Daughters of the American Revolution and the United Daughters of the

Confederacy. VAOWS argued that women had heavy home responsibilities and mental and physical characteristics that prevented them from voting. Molly Seawell, one of Virginia's most-vocal antisuffragists, declared that of women in the United States only 8 percent "are on record as favoring suffrage." In her 1914 essay "Two Suffrage Mistakes," she asserted that a state's right to determine its electorate was critical when "there is a race problem involved." The Virginia Association Opposed to Woman Suffrage affiliated with the national antisuffrage movement, and in 1914 it had more than 2,000 members in nine branches throughout the state. The active Charlottesville chapter recruited women through existing social networks and had several categories of membership to enable as many women as possible to participate. Its leader was Caroline Preston Davis, who had successfully petitioned the University of Virginia in 1892 to take the mathematics examinations required for a degree (she passed and was given a certificate of proficiency).[74]

As leaders of the state Equal Suffrage League, Valentine and Johnston faced opposition from antisuffragists as well as more-radical prosuffrage activists, such as Pauline Adams. Valentine and Johnston walked a thin line between the two groups. Both women deplored the confrontational tactics of the National Woman's Party, which during the World War protested outside the gates of the White House. Both women also were extremely uncomfortable with the openly racist tone of the Southern States Woman Suffrage Conference, which echoed the racist arguments of antisuffragists with the same race-baiting language. The ESL attempted to diminish racial issues by using statistics to show that black voting would not overtake the white population as a result of woman suffrage.[75]

The Equal Suffrage League also tried not to appear too radical. Johnston was sympathetic to the socialist platform, although she refused to support the group openly. While speaking to a suffrage group in Alexandria, Johnston stated plainly that "I am not a foe of the state," before she made her point that "you cannot have a democracy until you enfranchise women." Valentine sometimes spoke to labor organizations, going to Danville in 1914 at the request of a Roanoke suffragist to speak to garment workers there. Valentine also spoke before the Central Trade and Labor Council of Richmond that same year, but later regretted that decision and told the Norfolk chapter to downplay its connections with the labor unions there. Ultimately, the Equal Suffrage League purged its members affiliated with the more radical Congressional Union and publicly denounced the actions of Alice Paul and her National Woman's Party. The ESL focused on steering a moderate course that might gain the support of legislators.[76]

In 1912, the General Assembly held its first-ever hearing on woman suffrage. More than a dozen speakers, including Valentine, Johnston, and Richmond writer Kate Lee Langley Bosher, addressed the legislative committee at the January hearing. They avoided racial politics and appearances of radicalism while arguing that since many Virginia women were already self-supporting, they did not want to remain in a subordinate place any longer. Lynchburg suffragist Elizabeth Lewis declared that "this assumption of representation of the whole community by one-half of its members is an act of flagrant and open injustice." Although no group voiced opposition to the ESL representatives, the House defeated the woman suffrage measure in February by a vote of 85 to 12, and the Senate simply refused to schedule a hearing. The House of Delegates easily defeated woman suffrage again in 1914 and in 1916.[77]

The realities of war in Europe interrupted the battle for woman suffrage and Progressive reform, particularly after the United States joined the war in April 1917. Women's groups, including suffragists, turned their energies to volunteer efforts on the home front to win the war. The Equal Suffrage League pledged to make mittens, shirts, robes, pillowcases, towels, and sweaters on its sewing and knitting machines. The Roanoke chapter joined twenty other women's groups to increase garden productivity, ultimately canning 28,000 quarts of fruits and vegetables, some of it sent to France for wounded soldiers. Fully three-quarters of Virginia's wartime volunteers came from women's groups, both white and black. Mary-Cooke Branch Munford coordinated the work of white women as the head of the Virginia Division of the Woman's Committee of the Council of National Defense while Margaret R. Johnson led the Working Force of Negro Women. Active on the home front in many capacities, women spun and knit garments for soldiers, rolled bandages, and even created munitions. Marguerite Inman Davis, the wife of the governor, headed the Women's Munitions Reserve, and worked with 2,000 other women at Seven Pines Camp, in Henrico County, where they sewed silk bags and filled them with smokeless gunpowder.[78]

Women also served as hostesses for soldiers and sailors. The YWCA worked with the Colored Work Committee of the War Work Council to aid African

American soldiers and their families at Camp Lee, near Petersburg, and war workers stationed at Camp Alexander, near Newport News. Members of the Council of Jewish Women and Congregation Beth Ahabah visited hospitals at Camp Lee and staffed the Red Cross canteens. The Young Women's Hebrew Association of Norfolk distributed flowers, cigarettes, and food to soldiers convalescing at local military hospitals, and hundreds of other women's clubs and organizations hosted similar activities across the state. Clubwomen also raised money for the war. The Virginia Federation of Women's Clubs, under the direction of Janie Gray Hagan, of Danville, organized 115 Women's Liberty Loan committees that sold more than $54,000 in bonds during the war. Such groups as the National Society of the Colonial Dames of America, Daughters of the American Revolution, and United Daughters of the Confederacy worked for the War Orphans' League, the Fatherless Children of France, and numerous other refugee relief organizations.[79]

Many Virginia women benefited from wartime employment opportunities. Sara Espley Clark was one of the 1,071 Virginia women who enlisted in the Naval Coast Defense Reserves. After graduating from high school in Amelia County, Clark moved to Norfolk to take a job as a clerk in the navy yard. Women drew equal pay for their work as clerks, translators, draftsmen, fingerprint analysts, and recruiting agents, and many relished the opportunity to move to better-paying jobs when they had the chance. Women from across the state enlisted in the armed forces as nurses and many served in France. "Ready and willing at all times" to serve, Anna Elizabeth McFadden left her job as a surgical nurse in Winchester to enlist in the United States Naval Reserves. Edna Breareley Bishop graduated from the Medical College of Virginia's training school for nurses in 1917 and was sent to France, where she was one of fifteen nurses at an 800-bed hospital. Clifton Forge resident Verna Mae Smith worked "only three miles behind the rear trenches" and "often could not sleep for the sound of guns" despite working eighteen-hour days to help organize and operate the hospital where she was stationed.[80]

The debate over woman suffrage did not disappear during World War I, and the efforts of women who volunteered at home and overseas may have contributed to the congressional passage of the Nineteenth Amendment in 1919. Southern suffragists had a difficult time convincing their own state legislatures to pass the amendment, and Virginia was no different. The Equal

Victoria Ruth Good, ca. 1917. Thousands of women volunteered for the war effort throughout the country, including in Red Cross units as bandage rollers, seamstresses, and in nursing and canteen work. Virginia Ruth Good, of Clifton Forge, is pictured here in her nursing uniform. Good was a graduate of Columbia Training School for Nurses, in Washington, D.C. She was stationed at naval hospitals in Norfolk and Brooklyn, where she died of influenza. *Courtesy of the Library of Virginia, Virginia War History Commission Records, 1915–1931, Individual Service Records, Cities. Acc. 37219.*

Suffrage League had about 30,000 members, but it was unable to overcome resistance to so significant a change in the role of women in society or to counter the claim of the Virginia Association Opposed to Woman Suffrage that the federal amendment would threaten white supremacy in the state. Despite the ESL's campaign to show that black women could be as easily excluded from voting as black men, the General Assembly rejected the amendment in February 1920. Tennessee's state legislature was the thirty-sixth to ratify the amendment, thus giving women all over the country the franchise in time for the 1920 elections.[81]

The right to vote changed the fortunes of Virginia women. While many white women exercised their newfound political power, African American women tried as best they could to use the vote to their advantage, with varying results. Although urban white women were busy enjoying the experience of having politicians ask for their support, African American women worked to gain the recognition of the Republican Party and continued to help their communities through traditional social networks and volunteer efforts. The progress that Virginia's white upper- and middle-class urbanites made in the 1920s, however, starkly contrasted with the realities of the decade for most other Virginians. As Virginia's countryside slipped into the depths of an agricultural depression, rural women struggled to take advantage of any opportunity they could find. The progressive tendencies of the early twentieth century evolved into social control policies in the 1920s, affecting race relations, reproductive rights, and personal freedom.

Many women, black and white, former pro- and antisuffragists, showed that they understood the implications of obtaining the franchise in 1920 and immediately registered to vote. For African American women, this was an opportunity they had long sought, and they had high hopes for the formal representation the vote could bring. Fifty-eight-year-old Puralee Sampson was the first black woman to register in Richmond, reportedly visiting the registrar's office as soon as she learned the Nineteenth Amendment had been ratified. Following her were thirty-year-old Blanch Wines, fifty-three-year-old nurse Katie D. Pratt, and forty-three-year-old teacher Rosa DeWitt. African American women in Virginia were more successful in securing the franchise than their counterparts in other southern states, perhaps because they had such a vigorous voting registration campaign in this period.[82]

In September 1920, Maggie Walker and Ora Brown Stokes planned massive voter registration meetings in the city, and turnout to the city registrars was so heavy that Walker demanded the city place more registrars in black neighborhoods to decrease women's wait time, and Stokes suggested the city hire deputies to assist with the registration. In Richmond, 2,410 black women registered to vote. In Phoebus and Hampton, black men helped women train for the encounters they would have with hostile registrars, drilling them on their knowledge of the state constitution. In Norfolk, civic leaders Emma Virginia Lee

First African American women registered to vote in Ettrick, 1920. In 1920, African American women took advantage of the passage of the Ninteenth Amendment and registered to vote in Virginia. Pictured here, *left to right*, are Virginia Normal and Industrial Institute (later Virginia State University) faculty members Eva Conner, Evie Carpenter, Odelle Green (*back row*), Virginia Mary Branch, Anna Lindsay, Edna Colson, Edwina Wright, Johnella Frazer, and Nannie Nichols (*front row*). *Courtesy of Virginia State University.*

Kelley, Rebecca Pride Bowling, and Bessie Morris challenged the registrar in court after he refused their applications. They won when the registrar incorrectly answered the question he had posed to them. Sometimes, black clubwomen who spearheaded the registration campaign found assistance from white allies. Adèle Goodman Clark, who later served as president of the Virginia League of Women Voters, the successor to the Equal Suffrage League, accompanied several white women to African American neighborhoods to make sure that women were not intimidated. She defended black women's right to vote because of their patriotic participation in World War I and because they had the same interests in social reform, including education.[83] African American women, however, created their own nonpartisan civic organization, the Virginia Negro Women's League of Voters, because the white League of Women Voters remained as segregated as the ESL had been during the suffrage campaign.[84]

White women, too, registered in large numbers. On the morning after the official ratification of the Nineteenth Amendment, two white women qualified as voters in Winchester, where about 60 percent of the eligible women registered to vote. By the time registration closed in October 1920, women had flooded registrars' offices across the state. More than 1,200 women registered successfully in Wythe County. The registrar in Newport News had estimated that 500 women might register, but was surprised when about 1,400 white and black women paid their poll taxes to gain the franchise. In the city of Suffolk, which had about 900 qualified male voters, 423 white women and 52 black women joined the rolls. Two members of the LWV volunteered in Richmond's overwhelmed office and between them registered more than half of the 10,645 white women added to the city's poll book. The LWV took advantage of its nonpartisan status and encouraged candidates to listen and respond to women's concerns. As Ida Mae Thompson, secretary of the League of Women Voters, pointed out to a friend in 1921, "We (the women) are the most popular people ever. The candidates all <u>think</u> they have always wanted the women to have the vote and have always worked hard to attain this end."[85]

Both political parties understood the power of white women's vote. In 1920, the secretary of the Republican Executive Committee wrote an open letter to Virginia women, offering its assistance in registering women of either party but also reminding women that it was the Democrats who defeated the Nineteenth Amendment's ratification. The chair of Richmond's Democratic committee issued a public appeal for "every woman who regards the domination of the white race as essential" to register to vote. The Democratic Party had an almost complete hold on the state, but the legislative chair of the League of Women Voters wrote to State Democratic Committee members to warn them that the Republicans had adopted almost all of the planks in the LWV platform.[86]

The Republicans also tried to appeal to new white women voters by running a "lily-white" ticket for the first time in 1921, which signaled its move away from attempting to gain votes in the black community. In response, the African American community mounted its own "lily-black" Republican ticket. Maggie Walker, a candidate for superintendent of public instruction on the "lily-black" ballot, was one of its most outspoken proponents. She spoke at churches and in club meetings, and she published proticket pieces in newsletters. Although the ticket lost overwhelmingly, Walker received almost 7,000 votes. Walker was not the only woman who ran for statewide office in 1921. The "lily-white" Republicans nominated suffrage activist Elizabeth Lewis Otey, of Lynchburg, for superintendent of public instruction, in part for her "knowledge and demonstrated executive ability...." She garnered more than 59,000 votes in the November election. In October 1921, Lillie Davis Custis, of Accomack County, announced her candidacy for governor. Running as an independent socialist with the slogan "Let the Women Do the Work," she received 251 votes.[87]

Virginia women began to participate in national party politics as well. In 1920 Mary-Cooke Branch Munford was appointed to the Democratic National Committee, and in 1924 Willie Walker Caldwell became the state's first Republican national committeewoman. In Marion, Democrats approached businesswoman Laura Lu Scherer Copenhaver to challenge the district's incumbent Republican congressman. Writing anonymously in the *Atlantic Monthly*, she expressed her desire to "be at the heart of our national life" and to know whether "a middle-aged woman" like herself could "get done the obvious things that the common people of this country want to see done," but ultimately she decided that she could not leave her family for Washington, D.C.[88]

Women enjoyed some success in local legislative races. In 1923, Sarah Lee Odend'hal Fain and Helen Timmons Henderson won election to become the first women members of the House of Delegates. Henderson was a Missouri native who had moved with her husband to Buchanan County in 1911 to run a Baptist mission school. Fain was a former teacher and secretary-treasurer

Legislative Debutantes

Mrs. Walter Colquitt Fain, left and Mrs. Robert Anderson Henderson, first women to be elected to the Virginia General Assembly.
—Photo by Staff Photographer.

First Women Elected
To General Assembly
Guests At Reception

"Legislative Debutantes," published in Norfolk *Virginian-Pilot*, 1924. In 1924, Sarah Lee Fain and Helen Timmons Henderson were the first women elected to the General Assembly, a sign that women's electoral power translated into direct political power. Fain, a Democrat, had been active in local Norfolk politics and focused mainly on maritime and educational issues that were important to her constituents. She served three terms and in 1930, was an unsuccessful candidate in the party primary for a congressional seat. Also a Democrat, Henderson represented Buchanan and Russell Counties. An advocate for better education and roads in southwestern Virginia, she was active on many committees in the assembly. When she died in 1925, the Capitol flags flew at half staff. *Courtesy of the Library of Virginia.*

of her husband's construction company in Norfolk. A member of the League of Women Voters who had campaigned for United States senator Claude A. Swanson in 1922, Fain was one of nine Democratic candidates for Norfolk's four delegate seats. Fain and Henderson attracted much attention when they took their seats in the General Assembly in January 1924, although neither of them challenged traditional assumptions about the role of women in society. Henderson died before the election in 1925, but Fain won two more terms, in 1925 and 1927. Three other women served with her during the 1920s: Sallie Cook Booker, of Henry County; Nancy Melvina "Vinnie" Caldwell, of Carroll County, and Henderson's daughter Helen Ruth Henderson, of Buchanan. Despite their individual victories, most female activists chose to remain on the lobbyist side of politics in the face of traditional gender roles and restrictions.[89]

Women's political activism secured significant reforms in the 1920s. Among its first activities, the League of Women Voters lobbied the governor to establish a commission to propose legislation beneficial to children. He appointed four women and five men to the Children's Code Commission in 1921. The Commission proposed twenty-six bills before the next assembly session, including mother's pensions, compulsory school attendance, a state welfare board, and regulation of child labor. Among the bills passed at the 1922 session were revised laws governing adoption and child labor, a new compulsory school attendance law, a law requiring fire escapes for public schools, a law requiring that some public hospitals and institutions offer occupational training, a law creating a children's bureau within the state department of public welfare, and two laws establishing the first of what became a statewide system of local juvenile and domestic relations courts. The assembly also terminated the inequality that had allowed widowers to inherit all of the property of their wives but had prohibited widows under the same circumstances from inheriting all of the property of their husbands. In the same session, women secured state matching funds for the federal Sheppard-Towner Act, which provided prenatal and child care to rural women.[90]

Organized clubwomen gave high priority to public welfare funding as part of their maternalist program to assist women and children. In 1919, the legislature appropriated $11,700 for public welfare programs, but by 1927–1928, the annual appropriation rose to $40,000 even though the state's overall budget remained largely flat. By 1931, the commonwealth spent nearly $90,000 per year on public relief programs.[91] Much of this new focus on funding health and welfare initiatives was the result of lobbying efforts of the Virginia Women's Council of Legislative Chairmen of State Organizations. Founded in 1923 by Adèle Goodman Clark and Naomi Silverman Cohn, a prominent member of Richmond's chapter of the National Council of Jewish Women, this umbrella organization represented many state women's clubs. It monitored bills of interest to women and coordinated lobbying efforts for any bill supported by three or more of its member groups. Although composed only of white women's organizations, in 1926 it protested proposed legislation that excluded black women tobacco workers from a work-hour restriction bill. The bill never made it out of committee.[92]

Increased funding enabled the State Board of Public Welfare to capitalize on the talents of one of its new employees. In 1927, the board named Emily Wayland Dinwiddie director of its Children's Bureau. A Virginia native, Dinwiddie had worked as an inspector for the New York City Tenement House Department and supervised publication of the *Handbook of Social Resources of the United States* (1921). During her seven-year tenure with the Children's Bureau, then one of the largest in the country, Dinwiddie oversaw the care of more than 3,000 children in state custody, supervised all public and private institutions for children in the state, and published and presented information on child health and welfare.[93]

While white women increased their direct involvement in political activity, African American women had less ability to influence politicians as a result of their being excluded from the polls. Black women did not lobby their legislators for reforms, but rather continued to employ their traditional organizing strategies of raising funds and awareness within their communities. They brought the attention of white reformers and politicians to community needs, and worked to prove that their calls for reform were as valid as those promoted by white women.[94]

As many white women saw their political power increase, they also began to embrace the eugenics movement during the 1920s. Defined as the science of creating a better human race through population management and control, eugenics was seen as an outgrowth of efforts to ameliorate poverty and prevent disease in Virginia. Modernization had brought unwelcome changes to Virginia's traditional social order in the eyes of its elite citizens, who viewed increased immigration and urbanization as sources of increased criminal and deviant behavior. After gaining suffrage, many white women supported the repressive policies enacted by Virginia's political leaders to control the behavior of marginalized white and black citizens whom doctors and social workers deemed feebleminded or delinquent.

Maternalist reformers had long been interested in forms of social control, and white clubwomen and former suffrage activists participated in the movement to censor movies. In 1922, Virginia became one of the first states to create a movie censorship board, ensuring that the same class of people who controlled politics at the time regulated cultural freedom of expression. In many ways, this was a logical extension of their work to outlaw liquor, as it was part of their morality-based purity programs meant to improve Virginia.[95]

The elimination of moral delinquency was at the heart of many women's reform efforts during this period. Poor white women were often regarded as a threat to society because they had more children than middle- and upper-class educated women as well as having more children outside of marriage. Lower-class white and black women were often targeted as feebleminded and the cause of a host of problems stemming from poverty, prostitution, and crime. Progressive women embraced the establishment of homes to reform and rehabilitate delinquent girls, and some of them came to see sterilization as a more efficient way to solve what were considered inheritable problems of degeneracy. Although men led the fight for a sterilization law in the state, they were supported by elite white women, some of whom had learned about the principles of eugenics in their classes at such prominent women's colleges as Hollins, Sweet Briar, Westhampton (later part of the University of Richmond), and Randolph-Macon Woman's College. Doctors at the Virginia State Colony for Epileptics and Feeble-Minded, at Lynchburg, began sterilizing patients as early as 1916. Although they kept no records of sterilization at that time, one doctor estimated that he sterilized upwards of eighty women a year. Women often found themselves the victims of sterilization as doctors and social workers colluded to stop "disorderly" women from reproducing.[96]

The General Assembly approved a sterilization law in 1924. The superintendent of the colony at Lynchburg launched a test case to secure the constitutionality of the law. The carefully selected teenage defendant, Carrie Elizabeth Buck, gave birth to a daughter in 1924 after being raped by the nephew of her foster parents. That year she was committed to the Lynchburg facility and adjudged epileptic and feebleminded. Because her mother had previously been committed to the colony, doctors and social workers argued that Buck's deficiencies were inherited and could not be helped with strong good influences. The colony's superintendent selected Buck's lawyer, who made few arguments in her favor. The Amherst County Court ruled that Buck's "welfare and that of society will be promoted by her sterilization." The Virginia Supreme Court of Appeals upheld the ruling in 1925. The case of *Buck* v. *Bell* went to the Supreme Court of the United States, which validated Virginia's sterilization law in 1927. Buck was sterilized later that year, and between 1927 and 1979 more than 8,000 Virginians, most of them women, were sterilized at state hospitals. The state issued an apology in 2002.[97]

Further strengthening social control by white Virginians, in 1924 state legislators also passed the Racial Integrity Act, which tightened definitions of race in Virginia. Previous acts had considered anyone with one-fourth, and later with one-sixteenth, African ancestry to be black, but the new law defined a person with any amount of African ancestry as black. People with no less than one-sixteenth Indian ancestry were classified as white to protect elite Virginians who claimed descent from Pocahontas. Interracial marriage remained a felony with a penitentiary sentence of up to five years, as had been enacted in 1878. Black Virginians also had to register their race with local registrars, and providing false information carried a one-year jail sentence. Many couples became unwitting victims of the law. Mary Hall, a white resident of Amherst County, married Mott Hamilton Wood, who had lived as white his entire life. Someone informed the Bureau of Vital Statistics that Wood was one-sixteenth black, and in 1928 the couple was convicted of violating the Racial Integrity Act and sentenced to two-year prison terms. In addition to these new laws restricting the freedom of Virginia citizens, the Commonwealth enabled Walter Ashby Plecker, the state's first registrar of vital statistics, to reduce the categories of race from six to two—white and colored. During his tenure from 1912 to 1946, he effectively erased the American Indian background of two generations of Virginians, and his actions have continued to frustrate the efforts of Virginia Indian nations to benefit from federal grants, because Plecker's actions made it almost impossible to prove their continuous existence since 1900.[98]

Elite women saw such legislation as necessary to preserve social order. Other white women who supported these extreme actions may have been reacting to an economic crisis that severely affected people in rural Virginia. Rural residents saw their fortunes decline from 1919 to 1921, watching gross farm income fall 55 percent as farm prices declined 65 percent. Fewer rural residents voted. In Augusta County, for example, only 20 percent of home demonstration club members had registered as late as 1940. It was clear that New South boosters had failed rural Virginians. Rural women did what they could to survive, taking advantage of opportunities that home demonstration agents and other supportive institutions provided for their families and farms.[99]

The United States Department of Agriculture extension service expanded to answer the needs of rural residents in the 1920s, and many women looked to home demonstration agents for assistance and support. Many agents were themselves from rural areas, such as Ruth Jamison, an Augusta County agent who had grown up on a Franklin County farm. Her mother encouraged all of her children to go to college, and Jamison later earned a B.S. and an M.A. in home economics from Columbia University and became the home management and house furnishings specialist for the state. Agents saw themselves as social workers, teaching nutrition and diet in canning classes and using handicraft and home improvement techniques to instill urban middle-class norms and lifestyles. They also understood the dire straits of rural residents and encouraged women to produce for consumer markets, enabling the women to gain power and self-sufficiency as they made their own money.[100]

White women who joined home demonstration clubs often used the clubs to extend their social networks, increase their recreational activities, and engage in community work, although they still took advantage of the money-saving and money-making programs of the home demonstration agents. As the rural depression deepened in the 1920s, the extension service helped women increase food production. By 1932, 515 women in Augusta County reported that they produced much of their own food, and 625 grew a share of the household vegetables. Women used what they learned from the extension service to earn money through their cultivation efforts. Some grew vegetables for sale, made butter and sold milk, or manufactured baskets, generally under the instruction of the agents. Raising poultry became a significant moneymaker for women during the 1920s. The industry was not yet commercialized and caring for poultry had traditionally been part of women's farmwork. Home demonstration agents encouraged a systematic approach to individual operations that involved breeding standardized flocks and employing artificial incubation. The extension division held annual egg-laying contests during the 1920s and women's flocks often led the competition. Women could earn significant sums through raising poultry, such as Albemarle County resident Virginia C. Beck, who reported in 1930 that she had "been able to clear from $1,000 to $2,000 a year on my chickens." These women saw their work as absolutely essential to keeping their family farms afloat.[101]

Women enjoyed and participated in home beautification and renovation projects, as well as sewing projects. Agents focused on modern technology and upgrading homes, and they also taught about refurbishing and reworking old furniture and rooms to save money. Virginia's extension service participated in the national Better Homes Week that began in 1922 to bring home improvement ideas to rural women. During its first campaign, 128 meetings attended by 12,248 people were held in twenty-seven Virginia counties. Home beautification projects might have seemed frivolous, but there was great practicality in women's learning to renovate and restore homes and furniture. While urban standards of cleanliness, electricity, and household technologies increased, farm women faced many of the same conditions they had in the nineteenth century, including a lack of electricity. The agents who taught sewing and home management projects assisted farm women in economically updating their homes. The money farm women earned helped fund home improvements ranging from new curtains and window screens to the installation of running water and electricity, although the poorest rural women often lacked the ability to participate in such programs. The extension service recognized the importance of such work in 1928, when in conjunction with *Farmers' Wife*, a national magazine, it named five Virginia women as Master Farm Homemakers.[102]

Thousands of African American women also benefited from extension service activities. Lizzie A. Jenkins, a 1902 Hampton graduate, began work under the auspices of the U.S. Department of Agriculture in 1913 to supervise a group of industrial teachers in more than thirty counties who taught sewing and cooking and organized poultry and garden clubs for black girls and women. In 1916, she joined the extension department of the Virginia

Agricultural and Mechanical College and Polytechnic Institute as the district home demonstration agent for African Americans in the state. During that year more than 1,800 women and 2,400 girls enrolled in canning, home demonstration, and other clubs. A decade later, home demonstration work was limited to only six counties, although black women in thirty-one clubs learned such skills as rug making, basketry, and furniture refinishing in addition to canning, cooking, and sewing. Like white women, black women also received lessons in home improvement, sanitation, and efficiency "to raise their standard of living," Jenkins later noted, "so that they and their children could get more enjoyment of life." Unlike the middle-class white farm women most often reached through home demonstration projects, many of the black women and their families were tenant farmers in precarious financial situations. Jenkins and her agents provided much-needed assistance through their programs to improve daily life and farm practices that resulted in increased land ownership and higher living standards for rural African Americans.[103]

Rural women were open to any measures that could help their farms and their families. In 1920, tobacco growers in Virginia, North Carolina, and South Carolina formed the Tobacco Growers' Cooperative Association (also known as the Tri-State Tobacco Growers' Association) to garner higher prices at the market by cutting out middlemen. Home demonstration agents strongly supported this measure, as did the male agriculture agents. Black and white women immediately became involved in the association, partly because many women received a share of the profits from their tobacco cultivation on family farms. Women organized meetings, acted as secretaries, and wrote pro-association poems, letters, and songs. As the growers' association faced increasing challenges in the 1920s, partly as a result of falling tobacco prices, women often came to its aid and urged men to keep their promises to sell through the association. Some women, however, joined their male relatives in fraudulent practices if they believed it would benefit their families. Some allowed their relatives to put portions of the tobacco crop directly in their name so it could be sold outside of the association in spite of signing a contract to sell only to the association. These actions suggest that rural women were willing to go to great lengths to secure futures for their families and to keep their property. Despite the efforts of thousands of Virginians, however, a 1926 study maintained that more than 500,000 rural families in Virginia still lived below the basic subsistence level.[104]

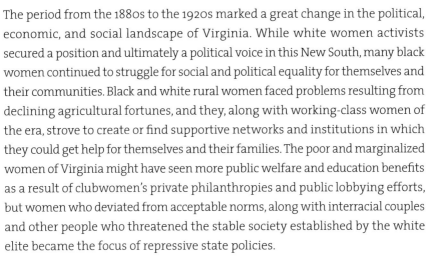

The period from the 1880s to the 1920s marked a great change in the political, economic, and social landscape of Virginia. While white women activists secured a position and ultimately a political voice in this New South, many black women continued to struggle for social and political equality for themselves and their communities. Black and white rural women faced problems resulting from declining agricultural fortunes, and they, along with working-class women of the era, strove to create or find supportive networks and institutions in which they could get help for themselves and their families. The poor and marginalized women of Virginia might have seen more public welfare and education benefits as a result of clubwomen's private philanthropies and public lobbying efforts, but women who deviated from acceptable norms, along with interracial couples and other people who threatened the stable society established by the white elite became the focus of repressive state policies.

For some women, the Progressive Era in Virginia brought tremendous vocational opportunities, an increased public presence, and a strong political voice. For other women, the Progressive Era brought low wages and long hours in factories, a growing gap between themselves and urban-dwellers, and even the loss of control over their reproductive, sexual, and marital freedom. For black women, the Progressive Era was marked by ambivalence. Those who could afford to pay the poll tax could vote, and the era marked an emergence of women as prominent leaders of their communities, but at the same time these women witnessed the emergence of Jim Crow laws and other repressive measures that defined them as second-class citizens. During these tumultuous decades, it is clear that the majority of women in the state made the most of any opportunity they could to increase their economic, political, and social capital during this era.

CHAPTER 6

"Our Future Freedom Rests in How Willing We Are to Face Realities": Women, Citizenship, and Change, 1930s–1950s

Despite state leaders' touting Virginia's "New South" status, the stranglehold Democrats held on the political system, persistent rural poverty, and active oppression of the poor and racial minorities marred this Progressive picture. The economic, social, and political change experienced in the middle decades of the twentieth century caused many to question the efficacy of the one-party, Jim Crow system. Failures or abject refusals by the commonwealth's political leaders to help impoverished citizens or provide unrestricted access to the polls radicalized many white women and provided African American women with a new language of protest, which they coupled with more militant efforts to fight for equality.

From the 1930s to early in the 1950s, Virginia women from all socioeconomic backgrounds became activists in their own right. Whether they were fighting for economic security, civil rights, or better communities, women's activism in this period moved from asking the government to support their positions to demanding action from their political leaders and effecting change in their own communities. Most important, African American women stepped forward as leaders of a civil rights movement that quickly gained support and became more militant. From the 1940s to the 1950s, African American women led some of the most radical attempts to reshape Virginia's social, economic, and political landscape. On the other hand, white women had to choose whether they would support the fight for democratization alongside black women leaders or ignore the burgeoning change in their communities.

The Great Depression exacerbated pre-existing problems in the impoverished rural countryside, and threw industrializing Virginia into an economic tailspin. It also involved the federal government in Virginia's internal affairs in a way that state lawmakers could never have anticipated. Virginia's mixed economy based on agriculture, manufacturing, and commerce helped cushion the immediate effect of the Depression. By 1931, however, urban areas had begun experiencing layoffs and closures of mills and factories and tobacco farmers' income had decreased by 50 percent.[1] In 1932, the state was in trouble. Unemployment peaked at 145,000, industrial wages were down 25 percent, and coal production was reduced by 23 percent, its lowest level since 1911. In addition, Virginia's tourist trade declined by 20 percent, the lowest level in thirty-two years. As a result of drought, the tobacco crop was the smallest since 1876.[2]

Virginia's state and federal leaders, most of whom were part of the conservative Democratic Party organization controlled by Harry F. Byrd Sr., reacted with an ambivalent attitude that surprised even some of the state's most politically involved women. The General Assembly answered the economic dislocation by having the state take over the road system in almost all the counties. Byrd recommended that Virginians lobby their local governments to pass the resulting tax savings to the citizens. The state provided a limited amount of help to poor women with a paltry increase in mothers' pensions that enabled widowed women to care for their children at home. In 1933, the mothers' pension program helped only 98 families at a cost to the state of only $13,000. In 1934, only 122 families were listed on the state welfare rolls. Welfare at this time generally consisted of limited public health initiatives and food or clothing handouts, which were provided only with the help of privately matched donations.[3] Meanwhile, Virginia's United States senators Harry F. Byrd Sr. and Carter Glass opposed much of Franklin D. Roosevelt's New Deal.

"Mrs. Dodson and one of her nine children, Shenandoah National Park, Virginia," photographed by Arthur Rothstein, October 1935. The agricultural depression in Virginia affected farmers long before the Great Depression hit nonrural areas. Poverty, a lack of education, and unsanitary health conditions plagued poor rural Virginians, both black and white. *Courtesy of the Library of Congress, Prints and Photographs Division, LC-USF33-T01-002186-M2.*

The attitudes of the state's conservative politicians belied the desperate situation of Virginians during the Depression. The records of the Virginia Writers' Project attest to the abject poverty experienced by rural and urban, black and white Virginians. Established in 1935 under the auspices of the Works Progress Administration, the VWP employed thousands of Virginians in compiling state and local guidebooks and anthologies of folklore and music, and interviewing people grappling with the effects of the Depression across the commonwealth. More than 1,300 Virginians were interviewed, including women and men of different races, occupations, and income levels. The interviews reveal that women experienced the Depression in ways that differed from men, working to hold their families together and keep their children from starvation. The life stories of women in these records suggest that poor women of Virginia, regardless of whether they were mill-town residents or lived on farms, shared several disadvantages that hindered their ability to support their families. Most of these women tended to have little education, and either came from, or had, extremely large families, which greatly restricted their ability to leave the area or even obtain better jobs.[4]

Poor African American women suffered the most from the economic crisis. In 1930, 62 percent of employed black women and girls worked as domestic servants or laundresses in Virginia, while only 5.7 percent worked in tobacco factories or textile mills.[5] Because of their segregation into low-paying domestic jobs before the Depression, these women found themselves without work, or without a living wage, as their white employers cut back. While the typical black domestic worker in the South made approximately $312 a year in 1934, white women working in Richmond's factories made $666 a year. In the worst years of the Depression, black maids, such as Elsie James, of Petersburg, earned fifty cents and two meals a day in exchange for doing all of the washing, cleaning, and cooking in her employer's household.[6] By May 1934, about 80 percent of Norfolk's public relief recipients were black. Of those, more than 40 percent listed their occupation as domestic worker. When one of the few Norfolk factories employing black women, the American Cigar Company, closed in the mid-1930s, even more African American women faced desperate circumstances. In Danville, domestics lost so many jobs that the local newspaper pleaded with city residents to stop firing their servants, as there were certainly more "humane" ways to economize.[7]

Eudora Ramsay Richardson, ca. 1935. A suffragist, prominent writer, and ardent New Deal supporter, in 1937 Richardson took over the directorship of the Virginia Writers' Project, a program of the Works Progress Administration. Under her direction, writers and researchers across the state collected more than 3,850 items related to folklore and music, more than 1,300 life histories, and more than 300 narratives from former slaves. Here she is pictured supporting the National Recovery Administration, which had charge over enforcing the codes set forth in the National Industrial Recovery Act of 1933. *Courtesy of the Valentine Richmond History Center, X47.05.188.*

Although federal New Deal programs helped many Virginians, women often received little direct assistance through WPA and other programs. Poor women had to find their own ways to survive the crisis. Women of the commonwealth dealt with their financial problems in many ways, depending on their geographic and social location. Rural women often brought in the necessary cash for a family's survival. As Beulah Handly, a Lee County resident and farmer's wife noted: "Of course a farmer eats hearty, but that's all he does have for his work. He gets mighty little money, and it takes money to live even when you're on a farm."[8] Many rural women, like Handly, produced enough on the farm to purchase commodities for the family. Handly said that "about the only cash we get year round is the little that comes from cream and eggs. The cream runs around $1.50 a week." Handly also sold fryers, eggs, and strawberry preserves.[9] A tenant farmer's wife in Franklin County told the WPA interviewer that she could "sometimes manage to sell a little butter" and kept "lots of chickens and I sell eggs to buy sugar, and thread, and things like that."[10]

Other rural women participated in federally and locally sponsored programs that helped them to create products directly for sale in the commercial market. Women produced commodities for the Old Dominion Home Industries Cooperative in Stafford County from 1938 to 1942. Jo Perry, the Stafford County home demonstration agent, supervised the store and Annie Catherine Powers oversaw daily operations. Pamunkey Indians made dolls and pocketbooks for sale at the store. Other women made jewelry, bonnets, bedspreads, brooms, and preserves. This store provided important supplemental income for talented crafts workers who could make items at home.[11] In 1932, some Pamunkey Indian women and men participated in a state-sponsored pottery school. The white teachers altered the way in which Virginia Indians had been making pottery for centuries and introduced molds, kiln firing, and southwestern motifs. The women produced this pottery for sale as extra income. After the state discontinued the program, women produced both the traditional and new styles for sale, a practice that continued into the twenty-first century on the Mattaponi and Pamunkey reservations.[12]

In Augusta County, women succeeded in setting up a curbside market with the assistance of the county's home demonstration agent, Ruth Jamison. The market officially opened in April 1930 with about two dozen sellers and 500 customers. By July, the vendors were earning between $135–$140 a week selling

A 4-H Club member storing the food canned from the vegetables grown in her garden, Rockbridge County, Va., ca. 1942. Long a program of the home demonstration agents in Virginia, canning became an increasingly important part of rural outreach programs during the Great Depression through the Farm Security Administration programs and into the 1940s. This Office of War Information picture shows a young woman stockpiling home-canned food, an important World War II home-front activity. *Courtesy of the Library of Congress, Prints and Photographs Division, FSA/OWI collection, loc.pnp/cph.3b45912.*

dairy products, baked goods, meats, vegetables, and flowers. Some women continued to sell products through the winter months. Market sales skyrocketed from almost $16,000 in 1931 to more than $56,000 in 1936. These curbside markets were extremely beneficial for the white women who participated. The average vendor earned $456 in 1934, and the highest earner made more than $2,100 in 1936.[13]

Such programs gave women direct access to and control of the money that they earned. Women used this money, which was sometimes their family's only cash, to invest in farm equipment, purchase children's clothing for school, pay for education, and modernize kitchens and homes to improve their living conditions. Husbands pitched in to take supporting roles in the process, often helping to pack and drive the trucks to market. In Augusta, some women left the market to strike out on their own as entrepreneurs, selling sandwiches and running catering businesses. Others sold directly from their farms so that they would not have to rely on their husbands for transportation to the markets.[14] While this project benefited the white home demonstration club participants in Augusta County, most rural women interviewed by the Virginia Writers' Project simply got by doing whatever labor they could to maintain themselves and their families.

Sometimes, rural women's strategies for survival involved moving away from the farms, but during the Great Depression, moving to a mill town often posed more problems than it solved. VWP interviews of women from Culpeper, Farmville, Hopewell, and Roanoke note that they moved from rural areas to take opportunities in industry.[15] As mills laid off workers and moved to half-time

Family of Russell Tombs leaving home, Caroline Co., photographed by Jack Delano, 1941. The Great Depression took its toll on rural families. Many farmers slipped further into debt as tenant farmers or sharecroppers, and landowners faced mounting debts. Thousands of Virginians left rural areas early in the 1940s to take advantage of the burgenoning war industries in Richmond, Norfolk, Roanoke, and northern Virginia. *Courtesy of the Library of Congress, FSA/OWI Collection, LC-DIG-fsa-8a-36111.*

schedules in the 1930s, this option became increasingly fraught with difficulty. Edith Blanche Brown, a 21-year-old employee at a garment factory in Culpeper, reported that she made a decent living working as a machine operator in 1939. "If I work full-time I get twelve dollars a week," she told her interviewer, "but I don't hardly ever work full time. I worked part of every week last year but not every day."[16] Mary Broyhill, of Hopewell, stated that she had worked in the silk mill in the town making $17 a week from 1923 to 1929, but quit when she got married. The Depression destroyed her husband's business, but by that time it was too late to go back to work, as hundreds were laid off from the factory.[17] Mary Garrett's experience was similar to that of many other white women employed in textile factories. She had attended school through the fifth grade and at age thirteen moved with her married sister to Salem to work in a silk mill. She married at 22, moved to Roanoke, and stopped working just before her son's birth. After her husband left the family, Garrett returned to work in the silk mill to support her three-year-old child. After being laid off, she worked at the Blue Ridge Overall factory in Roanoke. When the plant closed and moved to Christiansburg, she had to pay a co-worker 50¢ a day to drive her to the factory to work at a piecework job averaging about $2 per day.[18]

In tobacco and textile factories, poor pay and bad working conditions plagued the predominantly female workforce, and the terrible economic crisis could make trouble with supervisors more difficult than when employment was plentiful. In 1939, a white worker at a cigarette factory in Richmond described the uncertain schedules she faced at the cigarette factory where she worked. "Maybe around two o'clock the woman foreman tells you that you're going to work an hour or two overtime today," Nancy Carter told a VWP interviewer. "Or again," she went on, "perhaps you will be told not to come to work the next two days . . . and, of course, it isn't a good idea to protest." She went on to stress that "I feel like a machine, but it's a good-paying job."[19] Florence Walker, a black tobacco stemmer from Richmond, noted a much more dangerous and demeaning situation: "We had a 'straw boss' and as many women as he could get to go back in the 'hole' with him in the daytime, he got 'em." When Walker refused to have sex with him, he fired her. As she later recalled, "we had absolutely no protection . . . they fired you when they got ready . . . and treated you any kind of way, and there wasn't anything you could do about it."[20]

Even in small shops, women faced problems. Mamie E. Rohr and Bertie R. Thornhill, of Lynchburg, became famous for their Virginia Art Goods Studio, which sold high-end handbags crafted by local young women, some of whom were "society girls" who did not need to work for a living. The poor working conditions were described by employee Julia Keese Carwile, who noted that "they will employ a person one season who will work themselves to death for them and the next season they will take on some one else in their place." She went on to describe bosses who threatened to fire workers who did not work fast enough, the irregular paychecks, and the seasonal speedups and early layoffs.[21]

Despite the poor working conditions and near-constant layoffs and slowdowns, employers may have assumed that their workers were grateful for any kind of employment at a time when so many were suffering. During the 1930s, however, working-class women began to fight for their rights, possibly motivated by the movement of labor unions into the South to organize groups of workers, or simply by the fact that they were tired of low pay, erratic work schedules, and harassment. Later in the decade, it may well have been the workers' familiarity with new federal standards that dictated working conditions and maximum hours in the tobacco and textile industries. Whatever the reason, it is clear that workers organized in the state, and that women stepped in as vocal leaders for change.

Strikes stood out as the most dramatic way in which workers could call for change. Arlington County native Matilda Lindsay saw the growing ranks of female laborers as the key component for organized labor in the South. While working as the Richmond-based southern field representative for the National Women's Trade Union League, she played a leading role in forming Danville's United Textile Workers of America Local 1685 early in 1930.[22] In September, 4,000 unionized workers went on strike at the Riverside and Dan River Cotton Mills to protest cutbacks and reduced wages.[23]

The company could not blame this strike solely on outside agitators, as Virginia leaders often did. Roxy Prescott Dodson, a vocal leader during the strike, had started working in the mill as a teenager and had worked her way up to weaver. She later explained that "the Mill folks were clamoring for a leader, a woman leader, somebody extra special, and I let myself be fooled into thinking I filled the bill." After four months, the strikers, women and men who had "lived weeks and weeks without wages," were confronted by the National Guard unit sent by the governor to squelch the action and protect workers who crossed the picket lines. The strikers returned to work, and Dodson and others who stood out as leaders were not rehired. Dodson opened a successful boardinghouse, but she remained bitter toward the union, which she believed set her up as a leader but failed to support her when the strike was broken.[24] Also in 1930, sixty-eight women walked out of the Industrial Rayon Corporation plant, in Covington, to protest a new wage scale that the company assured its employees would enable the women to earn more money. Whether the women believed that or not, many had returned to work the next morning and the company expected more to follow.[25]

Strikes occurred at many textile mills and plants during the 1930s, with varying degrees of success. At S&K Knee Pants Company, in Lynchburg, 160 workers struck in 1935 to protest women's pay rates, which ranged from 8 to 11¢ an hour. S&K agreed to better pay and a forty-hour workweek, but the company moved its factory to Culpeper. The newly minted National Labor Relations Board found this a violation of the Wagner Act, which was intended to protect collective bargaining and workers who joined unions, but it did not help the women who lost their jobs.[26] In another strike at the Industrial Rayon Corporation in 1937, unionized workers were not able to achieve a wage increase or recognition of the union.[27] Perhaps one of the most successful, and stunning, strikes occurred at Richmond's Carrington and Michaux tobacco stemmery in that year. African American women comprised 60 percent of the workforce involved in tobacco rehandling and made 15 to 25¢ an hour. When Carrington and Michaux ordered a faster work pace to increase productivity, women walked off the job spontaneously to protest this new action and their low wages. About 300 black women and men struck that day and leaders soon organized their own union, the Tobacco Stemmers and Laborers Union, with the help of the Southern Negro Youth Congress. The strike lasted four days—and the organizers gained everything they wanted: a 10 to 20 percent pay increase, a forty-hour workweek, and recognition of their new union.[28] Within six months, the TSLU had expanded to several other Richmond factories and affiliated with the CIO. The union continued to organize and lead strikes against low wages and poor working hours and conditions during the remainder of the decade.[29]

Rural and industrial poor women met varying degrees of success in creating strategies for their own survival, but many relied on material assistance provided through the efforts of elite clubwomen. These clubwomen worked to fill the needs of citizens who had been ignored by Virginia's political leadership. White women's clubs across the state created dental and medical clinics for poor children. In 1934, the Virginia Federation of Women's Clubs held a school in Roanoke for sixty unemployed women, and helped some to find jobs or get into college. Most, however, simply "went away renewed in courage," which may have been sufficient to meet some participants' needs. Members of the Woman's Club of Richmond volunteered with the Red Cross, the Community Service Exchange, and other organizations providing social services to more than 17,500 people. Between 1934 and 1935, clubs affiliated with the all-white Virginia Federation of Women's Clubs spent more than $10,000 on welfare projects.[30] In 1938, local chapters of the all-white Virginia Federation of Business and Professional Women's Clubs took on a variety of projects, such as providing a day nursery school at the Salvation Army in Fredericksburg, cosponsoring a playground in Harrisonburg, and successfully lobbying for a playground and recreation centers in Hopewell.[31] A parent-teacher association in Roanoke held clothing drives for needy children, although supply often outstripped demand, and on one occasion about twenty-five children "were turned away empty-handed" when they went for assistance.[32] Augusta County's Beverley Manor Club served almost 5,000 school meals in four months in the depths of the Depression. Members of Augusta County clubs also furnished school improvements, paid for medical exams for underprivileged children, and adopted families in its community.[33]

African American women's organizations provided help to their communities in the face of growing desperation and poverty. The Farmville Council of Colored Women, for example, helped sponsor a youth recreation center, donated large sums to the black wing of the hospital, and contributed to the needy at holidays. The council also helped black students receive a decent education in a county that badly neglected black schools by raising a prodigious amount of money for scholarships, to bolster unequal teacher salaries, to extend the school year, and to construct a new school building.[34] Richmond's Council of Colored Women suffered financial setbacks in 1931 and was forced to sell its clubhouse. Its members continued to support the Virginia Industrial School for Colored Girls, in Hanover County, and in 1934 provided $100 for the annual Christmas dinner.[35] The African American YWCA branch in Roanoke supplied lodging to transients and held well-baby clinics in addition to its other outreach programs. In 1937, the branch served 175 babies a month.[36]

There was no denying that the women who provided this volunteer support greatly aided efforts to sustain the poor. While these efforts undoubtedly assisted those who benefited directly from them, they could not begin to address the crushing poverty faced by so many citizens in the state. Private charities were strained to the breaking point, attempting to fill in where the state refused to help. Richmond's Instructive Visiting Nurses' Association had to cut staff and wages while balancing increasing demands for its services, and private charity groups like Richmond's Ladies' Hebrew Benevolent Association watched donations dry up as their caseloads increased by the hundreds.[37] By 1932, the Salem Community Association had only 71¢ in its account as a result of having served 180 hot meals a week at the school lunchroom and providing medical supplies and mileage for the nurse who made 1,572 calls in the previous year as well as other expenses. It could no longer afford the salary of the nurse.[38]

State leaders continued to adhere to the policy of low taxes and few public services favored by the Democratic Party. The hostility of elected officials toward federal aid programs did not stop Virginia's citizens from taking advantage of New Deal programs. In fact, beginning with the Federal Emergency Relief funds, which theoretically required matching state funds, the legislature failed to put any money toward these projects. Still, the federal government fronted 92 percent of all relief funding, with localities pitching in the remaining 8 percent. By mid-1935, an estimated 40,000–50,000 Virginians worked on 2,500 Federal Emergency Relief Administration projects. Some 95,000 Virginians earned a combined $66 million in salary from the Works Progress Administration, which built schools, roads, and other infrastructure and ran clinics and other community-support centers.[39]

Jobs for women, however, were limited in number and scope. Ella Graham Agnew, state director of the Division of Women's and Professional Projects of the WPA, worked to increase opportunities for rural and urban women. The program's goals "to fit women to face life more efficiently as homemakers," as well as "to train women and girls in some type of home industry that may prove marketable when the finished articles are of the required standard," often reinforced traditional gender roles, however. In a 1936 report, she wrote that "since opportunities for permanent employment of women in clothing factories are limited in Virginia, and since most of the women on relief were sadly in need of instruction and experience in providing proper clothes for their families, it was decided to place the emphasis in all sewing rooms on training for better homemaking."[40]

Under Agnew's direction, the division placed women in nursing projects, home-visiting projects, recreation and school lunch programs, home demonstration projects, sewing rooms, wildlife and bird conservation programs, and slum clearance initiatives. By 1935, federally trained women grew flax and spun it into thread, created woolen clothing from the 23,000 pounds of raw wool received from the Surplus Commodity Division, and wove coats, including lumber jackets for residents of "the mountain section."[41] Between 1937 and 1939,

ARTS AND CRAFTS PROJECT IN NORTHAMPTON COUNTY
With the cooperation of the Emergency Education Program

"Arts and Crafts Project in Northampton County," 1936. The Emergency Education Division, a project of the Federal Emergency Relief Administration, employed women and men to teach a variety of classes, including vocational training courses. In this picture, instructors are teaching basket weaving and sewing to women. Generally, New Deal programs were gender and race segregated; white women tended to work on crafts and sewing projects, as well as in clerical, teaching, and child-care work. *Courtesy of the Library of Virginia.*

women across the state canned 353,000 jars of food, made 9 million lunches, cared for 5,500 children, made 1.7 million garments, and created the Norfolk Azalea Garden. The National Youth Association established sixteen homemaking centers to train young women as housewives. The Civil Works Administration sponsored a housekeeper project in Richmond, in which unemployed women cleaned the homes of sick or incapacitated patients of the Instructive Visiting Nurses' Association, although the work was part-time with low pay.[42]

Middle-class, educated women also found opportunities through federal government programs. In addition to working for the Virginia Writers' Project, working in libraries, and serving as nurses in community projects, educated women had more career options than their poorly educated counterparts.

N. Y. A. GIRLS RECEIVING TRAINING IN CHILD CARE
AT THE DANVILLE NEGRO DAY NURSERY

"N.Y.A. Girls Receiving Training in Child Care at the Danville Negro Day Nursery," 1936. This National Youth Administration photograph from 1936 illustrates the racial division and gendered assumptions of New Deal programs. Here, these African American girls are being trained to care for children, which was often a significant component in one of the few jobs historically open—indeed, practically reserved—for black women; that of domestic servant. *Courtesy of the Library of Virginia.*

Under the Emergency Education Division of the Federal Emergency Relief Administration, in 1933 and 1934, more than 600 unemployed female teachers, 30 percent of whom were black, taught home economics, agriculture, business, and industrial classes. By 1935, the program employed 1,547 teachers, most of whom were women, and had expanded to include rural schools.[43] The Medical College of Virginia received a Civil Works Administration grant in 1933 that enabled nursing director Frances Helen Ziegler to hire both skilled and unskilled women. At the time, 1,250 private duty nurses were registered in the state, with more than half them "not making enough to keep body and soul together." MCV hired as many as 78 trained black and white hospital workers before funding ran out in 1934, whereupon a WPA grant allowed the hospital to employ 93, including "eight white and seven registered colored nurses, 43 cleaners, 19 laborers, one biologist, seven seamstresses, and one timekeeper."[44] By 1936, WPA women could also be found indexing court records, real estate deeds, and marriage licenses.[45]

These programs were surely a boon to individual recipients. "I don't think you have any idea of what they have done to the women themselves," FERA investigator Lorena Hickok wrote to the agency's administrator in 1934. She reported that the women who participated "came in, sullen, dejected, half starved. Working in pleasant surroundings, having some money and food have done wonders to restore their health and their morale."[46] The programs were never enough, however, to alleviate the plight of most poor women in Virginia. The General Assembly refused to provide matching funds for federal programs, and less than 9 percent of Virginia's population received direct aid, making the state one of the lowest in the nation in aid recipients.[47] Women were also excluded from the massive Civilian Conservation Corps, Blue Ridge Parkway, and WPA construction projects that hired tens of thousands of men.

Because federal government jobs were segregated, African American women received the least desirable jobs and little financial support. For example, African American women in Norfolk were forced to take manual labor jobs on outdoor projects to keep their WPA benefits when the sewing rooms were closed; but rumors emerged that the rooms had not closed and that white women had replaced black women.[48] The problem may have stemmed from administrators' assumptions about African American women. As Ella Graham Agnew reported, the "Landscaping, Bird, and Wild Flower Sanctuary" projects provided "work to many unskilled Negro women whom we could place nowhere else." She failed to mention training these unskilled women for better jobs as a viable option.[49] Skilled black teachers also experienced discrimination. The hourly pay rate was the same for both black and white teachers, but black teachers worked fewer hours, so their monthly pay ranged from $25 to $75, while white teachers earned monthly salaries of $90 to $125. Black women often had the hardest jobs. Catherine Johnson described her work at a WPA-funded nature preserve in Petersburg, which included hauling baskets of gravel up steep hills, digging shrubs, and sawing wood in frigid weather. When she asked to take a break on a grueling day, her white supervisor noted in her record that she was a "careless worker." Johnson informed a Virginia Writers' Project interviewer that many other black women faced similar discrimination, but the all-white supervisory staff made it difficult for African American workers to change the situation.[50]

Virginia's political leaders did little to address the economic and social problems caused or exacerbated by the Depression. Women shifted their tactics

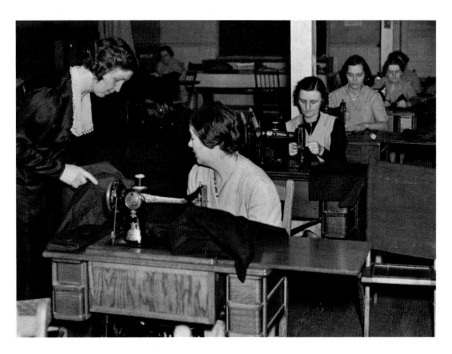

WPA Workers, Suffolk, Va., 1938. White women work in a segregated sewing room established as a Works Progress Administration women's project. *Courtesy of the Library of Virginia.*

and employed a new sense of urgency in their language. The attitude of many white women reformers suggested that they would no longer be complacent with their governmental leaders. In 1935, the Richmond League of Women Voters wrote to Senator Harry F. Byrd Sr., to express its "regret that you did not see fit to support the President's Social Legislation Program." The League deplored his reported reason for voting against federal aid programs "on the grounds that as the standard of living in Virginia was so much lower than in other states that outside help was not necessary to maintain this subsistence level."[51]

Such critiques were backed by direct action. The Virginia Women's Council of Legislative Chairmen of State Organizations, representing more than 100,000 white Virginia women, demanded that the General Assembly assist the citizens of the commonwealth. Progressive white women fought for ratification of a federal child labor amendment, a retirement fund for teachers, and an adequate appropriation to the state farm for women inmates.[52] Richmond activist Naomi Silverman Cohn, who had organized the VCLC with fellow suffrage advocate Adèle Goodman Clark in 1923, helped lead the charge for legislation to help Virginia's working women. As the executive secretary of the Virginia Consumers' League, established in 1936, Cohn sought legislation to ameliorate poor working conditions across the state. In 1938, she lobbied at the State Capitol for a new maximum workweek law for women. Working as a volunteer up to thirteen hours on some days, Cohn secured a victory of sorts for the VCLC. The General Assembly passed legislation that limited women's work week to forty-eight hours, down from a maximum of seventy. The law, however, exempted women working as bookkeepers and stenographers, as well as those engaged in agricultural work, domestic service, and such seasonal employment as tobacco stemming, peanut shelling, and oyster shucking. As a result many white women, and the majority of black women, did not benefit from the legislation.[53]

The Virginia Federation of Women's Clubs and the Virginia Federation of Business and Professional Women Clubs established legislative committees and urged their members to advocate legislation and programs beneficial to women and children. The VFBPW stressed the importance of registering to vote and regularly implored members to contact their representatives at the State Capitol and in Congress regarding particular bills. "The Virginia club women are in a position to do much to create such public sentiment," wrote one committee chair in 1939, "since our clubs are situated in every part of the state and comprised of public spirited women." During the 1930s, clubwomen favored such legislation as increased spending on education, providing suitable facilities for juvenile offenders, ratification of a child labor amendment, and jury service for women. Women's clubs also advocated birth control clinics and education and testing for venereal diseases.[54]

Many women saw testing and treatment of venereal disease as integral to improving public health, but it also served to preserve social control by elite white Virginians. Testing and treatment programs often fell hardest on the backs of the working poor and African Americans, although black supporters of the social hygiene movement had long sought to reduce rates of venereal disease within their communities. A disproportionate number of African Americans were tested—with white women often taking their domestic workers to the health department for testing. Mill owners worked with officials to test their employees. Men underwent testing, but women in general were unduly burdened with testing. After finding a high percentage of pregnant women with venereal disease in Richmond, public health officials and social workers brought in working-class and poor women for testing on a regular basis, effectively surveilling them until they gave birth. In addition, a higher percentage of women prison inmates in Richmond faced testing than men. White clubwomen supported these efforts, which culminated in the 1940 law that required venereal disease testing of all couples applying for a marriage license. Although the law did not prohibit marriage and mandated treatment instead, it made state public health agents responsible for women's sexual purity, a matter once relegated to the family. By strongly supporting these state interventions, white clubwomen tacitly enabled the government to intrude in the lives of its citizens in a way not possible before.[55]

The Virginia Federation of Women's Clubs also concentrated its efforts on young people who suffered from the state's failure to provide adequate funding for health, education, and welfare projects. "Club women can not sit complacently by and let these injustices continue," argued Lucille Churchill Burgess Alexander, former federation president. "As sympathetic, intelligent citizens they must arouse public opinion to a recognition of the exploitation and waste of youth which now exists." She urged clubwomen to "mobilize their forces during 1939 in urging that all the resources of government, religion, and education be concentrated upon this battle against inadequate economic and educational opportunities for youth, poor housing and slums, human erosion, and crime. The preservation of democracy and the promotion of peace in the United States are dependent upon the solution of these fundamental human needs."[56]

Some women went beyond aggressive lobbying for programs to ameliorate poverty and focused on assisting women in family-planning projects. The Virginia Federation of Women's Clubs sponsored two birth control clinics during the 1930s, and Richmond's YWCA began discreetly distributing condoms after one of its residents almost died from a botched abortion. The Woman's Club of Richmond risked membership revolution when it endorsed the birth control platform of the VSFW, and at least three prominent members resigned.[57]

Lucy Randolph Mason, a descendant of several of Virginia's oldest families, went further than most. Mason began working for Richmond's YWCA in 1914 and as general secretary oversaw programs to help young black and white women. Named general secretary of the National Consumers League in 1932, she worked in Virginia and South Carolina for the passage of laws in both states to improve wages and limit working hours. Having spent months lobbying in Virginia, her efforts stalled when the state senate failed to vote on a bill establishing an eight-hour workday that had been approved in the House of Delegates. Mason joined the Congress of Industrial Organizations in 1937 to negotiate on behalf of organized labor in the South. In 1938, she interceded with Virginia's governor to free three workers jailed for picketing at a factory in Covington.[58]

African American women, too, began to demand changes in new ways. The 1930s witnessed a number of African American women acting as plaintiffs in equalization lawsuits. In 1935, Virginia Union University student Alice Carlotta Jackson applied to the graduate school of the University of Virginia after studying at Smith College. Rejected because of her race, she inquired about the university's decision and the NAACP threatened legal action on her behalf. Her efforts provoked the General Assembly to provide a tuition supplement fund to cover costs for African American students to seek degrees out of state. In 1936–1937, 128 black students applied for the scholarship funds.[59]

African American women also took the lead in cases to equalize teacher salaries. Since the establishment of Virginia's public school system, black teachers had earned smaller salaries than white teachers. In 1938, Aline Elizabeth Black agreed to serve as the test case for NAACP litigation against the Norfolk board of education. Black lost her job for her efforts, although she was later reinstated, and a male teacher took her place as plaintiff. The case was reopened and in 1940, the U.S. Supreme Court upheld an appellate court ruling that the Fourteenth Amendment protected teachers' salaries.[60] The case served as a precedent for subsequent salary equalization cases, including one in Richmond with Antoinette Bowler as plaintiff, and one in Newport News, with Dorothy E. Roles. While the teacher associations sometimes settled with local school boards, Roles's case secured a federal court order for immediate equalization in 1943. The Newport News School Board dragged its feet, however, and in 1945, the federal judge issued another order to equalize salaries and also to pay interest on the teachers' back pay.[61]

The 1930s posed a series of economic and social challenges for the women of Virginia, and the Depression served to radicalize some women who began to recognize the importance of speaking out for the rights of the oppressed. As they continued to assist the poor in their communities, clubwomen took strong stands on birth control and antipoverty measures. When they could, rural and urban unemployed women took federal jobs in many different occupations. Rural women employed a myriad of strategies to survive, and many working-class women demanded fair pay and working standards with a series of strikes. The white community's new visions of social justice often ignored black women, who remained among the most impoverished people in the state, and who had to look to their own communities, or to the federal government, for support.

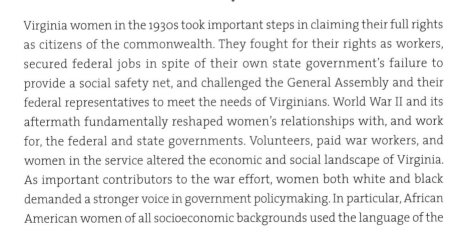

Virginia women in the 1930s took important steps in claiming their full rights as citizens of the commonwealth. They fought for their rights as workers, secured federal jobs in spite of their own state government's failure to provide a social safety net, and challenged the General Assembly and their federal representatives to meet the needs of Virginians. World War II and its aftermath fundamentally reshaped women's relationships with, and work for, the federal and state governments. Volunteers, paid war workers, and women in the service altered the economic and social landscape of Virginia. As important contributors to the war effort, women both white and black demanded a stronger voice in government policymaking. In particular, African American women of all socioeconomic backgrounds used the language of the

Roosevelt administration—that victory for the Allied forces meant a victory for democracy—to demand an end to Virginia's segregationist laws and culture in a way they never could before.

One can argue that Virginia was a model of World War II American society. Tobacco, textile, and foundry production shifted to fabrication of cigarettes for C-rations, parachutes and uniforms, and ammunition. Production was up, and by the end of the war the per capita income of the state had more than doubled to $972. Federal spending constituted 30 percent of the state's total income. Tens of thousands of soldiers trained in Virginia camps, and more than 1.7 million soldiers shipped out from the state. More than 300,000 Virginians served in the military, and 400,000 women and men volunteered for civilian defense service. The Office of Civilian Defense mobilized civilians through fifty-four programs, including rationing, Victory gardens, child-care centers, nursing, and recreation for servicemen through the United Service Organizations. Women dominated volunteer efforts on the home front. Virginia's social landscape changed dramatically during the war, but old problems remained unsolved. Jim Crow laws dominated the state, and Virginia ranked forty-third in its percentage of registered voters. Only 22 percent of the adult population voted in 1940, and between 1920 and 1946, only 12 percent on average participated in the Democratic Party's gubernatorial primaries, which often were the only contested set of elections in much of the commonwealth.[62] Against this backdrop, women of all socioeconomic backgrounds stepped forward to demand recognition of their volunteer and paid work for the war. Women's labor on the home front was critical, and they knew it. Their efforts came with new demands for respect, autonomy, and recognition.

Virginia women were among the first admitted to the armed forces. The Women's Army Auxiliary Corps was created in May 1942, and in Norfolk an influx of women requesting applications at the army's recruitment office for the officers candidate school was described in the local newspaper as resembling "the traditional feminine rush to the bargain counter."[63] Although the account describes the women with a traditional, and quite derogatory, feminine stereotype, the reality was that many of the women wanted something more out of their work life. Seventy-five women showed up for thirty-four applications. Two African American women were turned away and told to come back later for applications, foreshadowing the treatment of Virginia's

"Pitch in and Help! Join the Women's Land Army of the U.S. Crop Corps," 1940s. From 1943 to 1945, the Women's Land Army recruited millions of women from both urban and rural places to work in agricultural production. Their work was critical in producing the food necessary for the troops and citizens at home during World War II. While this work might have been new to urban dwellers, both white and African American women who grew up on farms were already involved in farm production, from planting and harvesting various crops, to canning and selling foodstuffs. *Courtesy of the Library of Virginia.*

black women throughout the war. Many of the women attempting to secure positions in the officer candidate school were employed as teachers, secretarial workers, and clerical workers. Successful candidates for officer training in both the WAAC (later Women's Army Corps) and Women's Reserve of the U.S. Navy (known as WAVES) often had a degree from an accredited university and professional work experience. Regular enlisted women also needed to have a level of education that was beyond the reach of many rural Virginians. Recruitment standards fluctuated during the war, but generally the army and navy preferred women to possess at least two years of high school education, with some professional skills. The armed services used women in many traditional roles—stenographers, typists—but as the war continued women also served as radio operators, photographers, intelligence analysts, mechanics, carpenters, and heavy equipment operators. Women could gain valuable jobs and training at good federal pay rates, and possibly work overseas. What is clear from one newspaper article is that hundreds of Virginia women looked to avoid the work traditionally thrust on women by volunteering for the service. Blacksburg resident Louise Sheabor was described as "a mighty patriotic girl," for being the only recruit in the Fifth Naval District who was earning a "U Rating," or "housekeeper status," which would enable her to supervise cleaning, laundry, and mess hall facilities.[64]

Many women volunteered for the war effort in a myriad of capacities, and while they often described a sense of patriotic duty, much of their language emphasized that they expected to get something more out of their work. In many communities, women led volunteer efforts during the war. Etta Belle Walker Northington, vice president of the Virginia Federation of Women's Clubs, wrote in 1942 that "we don't have the leisure for some of our peace time pleasures nor do we have the inclination for their pursuits." Instead, women were busy "heading Red Cross committees, war chest drives, USO recreational schemes, war savings staffs, church work and local welfare projects."[65] More than two hundred women's clubs joined forces to raise the money to purchase two ambulances for the Red Cross.[66] Members of Covington's Business and Professional Women's Club sewed surgical dressings and took classes in advanced first aid, nursing, and nutrition. Club members in Martinsville taught first aid classes and worked for the Ambulance Corps. Wytheville's club sponsored a nursery to allow mothers to work in the nearby ordnance plant.[67]

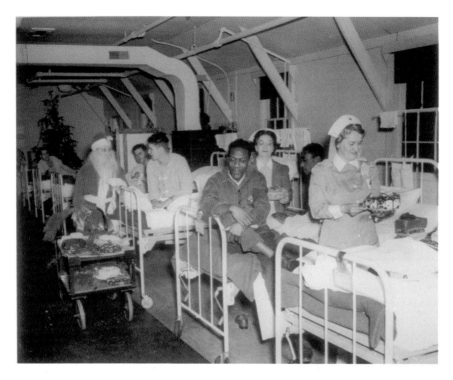

"Gifts of Cake and Ice Cream brought by the Red Cross Gray Ladies and 'Santa Claus,'" 1944. Red Cross Gray Ladies hosting a Christmas party for hospitalized troops at Camp Patrick Henry, near Newport News. What is unusual about this picture is the fact that the ward is not segregated, and that white volunteers were serving the African American soldiers pictured here. *Courtesy of the Library of Virginia.*

Women sold millions of dollars in war bonds and stamps. During the national Women at War Week, in November 1942, Virginia women set a goal of raising more than $5 million to finance the war. The Virginia Federation of Women's Clubs sold war stamps as admission to tea and card parties, and the Junior League, Business and Professional Women's Clubs, African American clubwomen, and industrial workers all sponsored events to encourage the purchase of stamps and bonds. The Democratic Women's Organization sold bonds at football games. Such organizations as the Virginia Daughters of the American Revolution and the Society of the Colonial Dames of America in the State of Virginia held roller-skating events and carnivals on "Stamp Yourself Day," and the Girl Scouts and local parent-teacher associations rounded out the

War Bonds Drive, Richmond, 1942. Women volunteers sold war bonds and stamps, as in this photograph, as one of their many home-front activities to support the troops during World War II. *Courtesy of the Library of Virginia.*

week with activities for children. Women of the Fauquier County War Savings Staff put on a vaudeville show that raised $40,000.[68]

Clubwomen recognized the importance of their war work for the community, and believed that it would provide them with more respect, and more responsibility for leading the country into the postwar future. In 1941, Suffolk resident Dorothy Morrison Eley informed members of the Virginia Federation of Women's Clubs that they must help all women see themselves "as a very vital link in the defense chain," and embrace new responsibilities that will provide "a wonderful opportunity to make our communities realize, as perhaps never before, that our woman's club is an absolute necessity for the best interest of our towns and cities."[69] The VFWC established a postwar planning department, and in February 1945 its chair, Judith B. Dickenson, of Hampton, wrote that "unpreparedness and lack of vision" after the First World

War had led to the Second. She warned club members that "we cannot afford to make this mistake a second time. Our future freedom rests in how willing we are to face realities and give of our best that the foundations for a permanent peace may be laid." She urged women to accept the "challenge before us" and to "assume our responsibility for the building of tomorrow's world."[70] To that end the Virginia Federation of Women's Clubs laid out a plan for peacetime Virginia that entailed campaigning for improved educational opportunities, slum clearance, reducing juvenile delinquency, and actively participating in the political process. Dickenson asserted that "citizenship is a privilege and it is necessary for us to exercise our right as free people or we may find that through indifference we have lost this precious heritage."[71]

As elite white volunteers took the opportunity to flex their muscles building political capital for the future, the stakes were much higher for African American women. They saw the war as an opportunity to demand from Virginia and the federal government rights previously denied to them. As the United States fought a war to save democracy abroad, African American women volunteered their services as part of their overall program of "responsible patriotism." The Women's Army Auxiliary Corps was open to black women at the time of its creation and Virginia women quickly signed up, such as Staunton native Frances B. Howard, who joined out of a sense of "duty to serve in this war in any capacity that I could," but also because she believed that being a WAAC "will prove beneficial to me later in civilian life." Numerous women volunteered for civilian duty, including a group in Roanoke that in 1942 established the Maggie Walker Ambulance Corps, which became a unit of the Women's Ambulance and Defense Corps of America.[72] As they donated their time and effort to help win the war, black women called on the government to provide them with the equality they had so long been denied.

African American clubwomen faced segregation in every aspect of volunteer war work, and they called out white Virginians for their hypocrisy in supporting democracy abroad and not at home. Antoinette Bowler, president of the Richmond chapter of the National Council of Negro Women, wrote to the national headquarters in 1941 to voice her concern that although women were urged to assist the war effort, black women were not being called on to do their part. Bowler went on to serve as chaperone of the city's black USO unit in 1942.[73] African American clubwomen, in particular, registered for Red Cross sewing and knitting units, canteen service, and other activities. Often ignored by the white community, they provided much of the funding and logistical planning themselves. The York County USO for African Americans did not exist until 1943, when the black community began organizing a center, which opened the following year. To provide enough volunteers for the facility, senior hostesses called on young women from all over the area, including Hampton, Newport News, Williamsburg, and sometimes from as far as Richmond to secure enough help for the only recreational facility available to African Americans in the area.[74]

African American women also raised thousands of dollars for the war effort. Richmond's Alpha Kappa Alpha sorority chapter held an incredibly successful war loan drive in 1943 that included several weeks of fun-filled events for the

Helen Alston, Red Cross canteen worker, Newport News, 1 February 1944. During World War II, recreational and relief facilities for soldiers were segregated, as were the units in which they served. Here, an African American woman volunteers as a canteen worker, serving coffee to black GIs. *Courtesy of the Library of Virginia.*

black community. From a jamboree kickoff, to a series of picnics, and an event at a roller rink that included servicemen performing skits and music by the Ninth Regiment Band, AKAs made sure that the people buying bonds at these events were well entertained. They exceeded even their own expectations, selling more than $10,000 worth in war stamps and bonds in just two weeks.[75]

Black women used their volunteer efforts to point out their treatment as second-class citizens. Sometimes, women challenged organizations directly for their refusal to work with black women. In a memorandum, Ada Burroughs, director of the USO's Colored Division in Richmond, criticized local white Red Cross officials who "refused to convey Negro hostesses to McGuire [General Hospital] although taking white hostesses. After many conferences between Special Services and them, the Henrico County Red Cross consented to transport once a week, eight hostesses to McGuire in a small station wagon.... Red Cross needs Christianity."[76]

Challenging segregation in volunteer efforts was just the beginning of middle-class black women's efforts to reorder society. At the same time that they worked for the Office of Civilian Defense, Red Cross, and USO, they also engaged directly in civil rights activism. Richmond's chapter of the National Council of Negro Women carried out programs in July 1943 as part of a national "We Serve America Week" that were meant to challenge white America. Held shortly after riots in Detroit and Harlem that were caused by overcrowded and segregated living conditions, rampant underemployment of African Americans in high-paying wartime industries, and white fear of the black community's literal and political encroachment on its traditional space in these urban areas, the NCNW intended to "enlighten" whites about the daily humiliations blacks endured as a result of discrimination and segregation. Members of Richmond's NCNW chapter held a parade in their volunteer uniforms and sponsored interracial programs. Although it is unknown whether whites actually attended these events, they could not have missed African American women marching through the streets in their USO, Red Cross, and Office of Civilian Defense uniforms.[77]

Many of these same women joined dozens of other clubwomen in fund-raising for the NAACP. In Richmond, an active member of the Virginia State Federation of Colored Women's Clubs, Senora Lawson, chaired the NAACP membership committee. Beginning in 1940, a cadre of women volunteers under her direction signed up members to raise money for NAACP court battles. By 1942, dozens of women had signed up 1,790 new members. Within two years, canvassing efforts netted 3,452 new members, most of them women. These women were intrinsic to the NAACP's national effort, as were women in other communities across the country. During the war, national NAACP membership skyrocketed from 50,000 in 1940 to more than 450,000 six years later. The money raised by these women funded local and national legal efforts, which included teacher salary equalization battles in Richmond from 1940 to 1942, the fight to desegregate Prince Edward County schools (ultimately part of the 1954 *Brown* v. *Board of Education* decision), and continued lawsuits against Virginia's program of Massive Resistance designed to maintain school segregation after 1954.[78]

Through their service-oriented volunteer efforts, African American clubwomen upheld traditional gender roles of women as comforters and caretakers. While they reinforced already-established gender conventions, their activities could be quite subversive. Taken in context with demands to desegregate, or at least equalize volunteer facilities and their fund-raising efforts for the NAACP, and the teachers' salary equalization case in Richmond, these activities provided black women legitimacy as volunteers for the government as they sought first-class citizenship from segregationist leaders.

Women in factories also faced new realities that prompted a change in their attitudes toward work and their rights. As a result of wartime production and the loss of many male workers, industrial opportunities for white women expanded dramatically. In 1939, manufacturing firms in Virginia employed 49,137 women (28 percent of manufacturing employees), who made an average of $19.13 per week in tobacco factories and $13.67 per week in textile mills. Women's employment in manufacturing firms reached its height in 1944, when 71,083 black and white women comprised 35.7 percent of the state's total industrial population. In 1945, weekly wages in the tobacco industry had increased to $31.83 and in textile mills to $26.56.[79] These increases resulted from stepped-up production and hours, as well as federal standards mandated to essential war industries.

White women continued to dominate the tobacco, textile, and needlework industries, but they also sought new industrial employment. In 1942, training schools across the state welcomed white women. In Washington County and in the cities of Danville, Winchester, and Norfolk, women took courses in sheet metal work, welding, machine shop work, and inspection to prepare for jobs

Ruth Hooker, Newport News, 8 January 1944. Ruth Hooker works on the generator of a Chevrolet in the final processing line of a facility that prepared vehicles for shipment overseas. Hooker secured the position in 1943. War work opened up heavy industrial jobs that had been previously closed to women, and Hooker was one of fifty women employed in this position. *Courtesy of the Library of Virginia.*

previously held only by men. Riverside and Dan River Cotton Mills started a "Ladies Loom–Fixing School" to teach them work formerly restricted to "brawny men with mighty muscles."[80] Women gained footholds in other industries formerly dominated by men. In Covington, women worked as truck drivers, furniture saleswomen, storeroom keepers, and paper machine operatives.[81] In Roanoke, the personnel manager of the Johnson-Carper Furniture Company praised its women workers: "Don't say a woman can never drive a nail straight; for they are doing it and hitting the nail on the head every time."[82] Other women took new jobs created by the war industry. The Radford Ordnance Works and the New River Ordnance Plant were among the earliest to employ women in producing smokeless powder explosives, and women made up the majority of its large workforce, about 90 percent in 1943. Women sought and gained employment at the Norfolk Navy Yard in 1942 as welders, mechanics, chauffeurs, painters, and machine operators. By 1944, the navy yard employed 6,425 women.[83]

Black women, however, faced continued discrimination in industrial employment. During the early months of the war, there were no training centers for black women in Norfolk. In March 1942, Norfolk resident Alice Knight answered the navy yard's call for two thousand women to learn the bench and lathe trade. She inquired about the training course at the United States Employment Service office, where she learned the center did not take on black women. Told to go to a training center for African Americans, she discovered that the center did not have places for black women trainees. After her story appeared in the Norfolk *Journal and Guide*, local activists successfully advocated mechanical training for African American women. Alice Knight's experience was matched by millions of other black women across the country. Hoping that the shortage of male workers would finally allow them new opportunities, African American women learned that they would be the last hired in defense industries. Like other black women around the country, Virginia women attempting to secure jobs in these lucrative positions turned to the Fair Employment Practices Commission, the NAACP and Urban League, and the community at large for support as they attempted to break down long-established racial and gender barriers.[84]

Like African American clubwomen, the women attempting to gain defense-related employment equated the segregation they experienced to hypocrisy. They began to define themselves as patriotic workers helping their country, despite the barriers they encountered in the form of racist hiring officers. Many young black women who passed the civil service exam could not gain employment at the Bellwood Quartermaster Depot, just outside of Richmond. Elizabeth Smith and Ora Cogbill Branch took on the discrimination there. Employed at the depot as a janitor, Smith wrote the FEPC, the NAACP, and the Civil Service Commission about one employment officer who seemed to turn away every black applicant who wanted more than a service job. Noting that "I understand that many complaints have been filed with your office about the conditions here," Smith did not mince words as she explained that "it seems as if the patrolman #7 think that the Four Freedoms consist of serving the White Lords first and then come out and ask the 'Negro Slaves' what in the hell do they want; and then inform them that no maids were being hired at present. . . ." She expressed the hope "that you would see that Negroes are not barred from opportunity to participate in the war work at the RQM Depot other then that of common labor; for we have persons who are qualified for such jobs as typist, stenographers, checkers, clerks, formans, guards and timekeepers."[85]

Having received an appointment as a junior clerk at the depot and later at the patent office in Richmond, Ora Branch wrote directly to the United States president after personnel directors refused to employ her. She pointed out that "several whites have been put in at both plants but they refuse to take me." She implored the president for help, declaring that "I'm a true American, whole heartedly and I'm exceedingly anxious to do my share in this great war."[86] The FEPC investigated Branch's case and determined that she lacked familiarity with the engineering supplies she would have to catalog and considered the case closed. Branch, however, questioned whether white women were expected to know about all the supplies before being hired.[87]

African American women heard many excuses when searching for jobs outside of domestic and similar types of service work during the war. In September 1942, the Norfolk Navy Yard called in nineteen-year-old Philadelphia native Corona M. Browner as a welder. When she reported for duty, she was informed that there were no restroom facilities for black women and told that she could work only as a janitor. She protested her treatment to the rear admiral in command of the navy yard and told a Norfolk *Journal and Guide* reporter that "I seem to recall that President Roosevelt ordered some time ago that there must be no discrimination shown in federal government plants."[88] The admiral ordered that Browner be admitted to her post, but she was fired nine days later "because she failed to qualify and had little aptitude for welding" according to the official reason provided by the navy. Browner countered that although her training had been in a different welding method, she was learning the new technique. An investigator for the FEPC ruled that no discrimination was present and closed the case. In April 1943, the Norfolk Navy Yard began employing African American women in welding and machinists positions.[89]

The excuses used against hiring and retaining Browner were sounded again and again by industrial managers in Virginia. In 1942, a Richmond paper company that produced cotton duck material during the war claimed that it did not advertise for African American women because they did not have the requisite experience with weaving looms, although its advertisements for white women employees did not require prior textile experience. Two years later, when questioned by an FEPC investigator about the lack of black women employed at the factory, the company maintained that it lacked the space for segregated bathrooms. As Browner had learned, getting a foot in the door did not ensure that an African American woman would necessarily remain employed. In 1944, the Riverside and Dan River Cotton Mills hired twenty black spinners, and about 400 spinners and spoolers walked out in protest. The union "recognized no color lines," but the company fired the black workers.[90]

In the face of numerous roadblocks, African American women in Virginia made limited progress on the job front. A look at the numbers is revealing.

Bus Drivers, Richmond, photographed by Tom Bie, 1940s. World War II opened up a variety of occupations previously closed to women, and thousands of Virginia women took advantage of new opportunities. White women, like these bus drivers, found it easier to secure higher-paying jobs than African American women did. *Courtesy of the Valentine Richmond History Center, V89.133.11.*

Between 1939 and 1944, the percentage of black women employed in manufacturing firms declined from 28.6 percent to 21.6 percent of the total number of women in industrial work. African American women were able to secure jobs in nondomestic service work as white women vacated positions for better-paying war-related factory jobs. African American women took jobs as waitresses, elevator operators, and stockroom workers in department stores. In short, they worked anywhere they could find new employment to avoid domestic service. The Richmond Urban League reported problems in filling housekeeping jobs listed in its registry. By 1944, black women's refusal to work as domestics could no longer escape the notice of white women, as one news writer noted: "Few problems have been more discussed in recent months than that of domestic help. The PT-A meetings, the Red Cross production rooms have become merely the places where Mrs. Brown bemoans the fact that Susie has left the kitchen to take up welding or Mrs. Smith discussed the high wages she is forced to pay Clara."[91]

The World War II economy of Virginia did not last. After the war ended, white clubwomen went back to volunteering in their communities, and working women struggled to hold on to their gains. By October 1945, the number of women in manufacturing dropped by more than 8,000 as men returned from service and reclaimed their jobs and as wartime contracts were cancelled. Between 1945 and 1946, 18,700 women left production jobs and women's employment declined 26.5 percent. By 1946, the Norfolk Navy Yard no longer had a female labor force.[92] Most women in the armed services returned home, although beginning in 1948 women were granted permanent status in the four branches of the military.

But something was different at home. Just before the war ended, at an interracial meeting of the Richmond YWCA to observe the annual National Industrial Progress Day, Lucille Harris, a black elevator operator at the telephone company, addressed the audience. She told the black and white women in attendance that she obtained her $25 a week job after "a white boy . . . was called to the armed services." She did not like her pay, but it was better than the $7 a week she had made in her previous job as a "nurse maid." Connecting her job, her status as a citizen, and her future political activism, she declared that "the war has caused me to think and act more soberly. I feel that we as a minority group need not fear as to the future because we are citizens, who do our jobs well on the home fronts. . . . I pay my poll taxes and vote in every election. . . . I am preparing myself for a better job now, as in the post-war world."[93] Sarah Jackson also spoke that day. Employed before the war as a seasonal stemmer at a local tobacco factory, she had advanced to the position of timekeeper as a result of the shortage of workers. She held little hope of maintaining her job in the postwar world, in part because she was black. Whatever happened, she warned her white listeners that she would not stop fighting for equality: "Three years ago I paid my poll taxes and met all other voting requirements. I voted in the presidential election. . . . I have tried to influence others to become first-class American citizens. I believe that legislation, coupled with education and determination, will make our today's racial problem a thing of the past."[94]

In 1944, Irene Amos Morgan, of Gloucester County, backed the rhetoric of racial justice with direct action. Her action toppled decades of segregation in interstate bus transportation. A twenty-seven-year-old mother of two, Morgan was traveling to Maryland to visit her physician after having recently suffered a miscarriage. When more passengers boarded the bus in Middlesex County, the driver ordered her to give up her seat to a white couple. She refused, resisted arrest, and was jailed until her mother provided a $500 bond. The local circuit court found Morgan guilty of violating the state's segregation statute, but with the help of NAACP lawyers, she appealed her case. The Virginia Supreme Court of Appeals upheld the conviction, but in 1946, the U.S. Supreme Court decided in her favor—and overturned state segregation laws in interstate transportation— in *Irene Morgan* v. *Commonwealth of Virginia*.[95] This landmark case signaled the beginning of a change in how the nation would deal with segregation.

Some white women began to recognize that Virginia's society could not continue on its same path. In her 1945 address to the Virginia Federation of Women's Clubs, President Etta Belle Walker Northington admitted that "we must cultivate a rational approach to problems of racial and minority groups." She pointed out "that racial cleavages in this country have grown deeper, that racial feeling is more charged with emotion," and she stressed that "the hope for opposing this dangerous trend lies first of all in a practical application of Christianity, in the observance of that precept by which we profess to live." She went on to urge citizens to cultivate "the attitude of objectivity along with a thoughtful analysis of the implications of democracy to racial problems."[96]

Irene Morgan, 1946. More than a decade before the Montgomery Bus Boycott, Irene Morgan challenged segregation on buses and won. Arrested in 1944, Morgan was convicted of violating Virginia's 1930 law requiring separation of black and white passengers. She appealed her case to the Supreme Court of the United States, which ruled segregation in interstate travel illegal in 1946. *Courtesy of the Virginia Historical Society with permission of the Washington* Afro-American.

Virginia had changed, but at this time the extent of that change remained uncertain. From the tobacco stemmer-turned-timekeeper to the president of an elite group of women in the state, women recognized a need for their leadership on race issues, among other problems. Where this would take them was unclear in 1945, but what is apparent is that women stood at the vanguard of an important shift in Virginia's political, social, and economic landscape.

In the period immediately following World War II, women continued to provide much of the leadership for change in Virginia. Not only did they participate directly in the political process in an attempt to challenge the powerful Byrd organization, they also focused their efforts on working interracially in community efforts. Moreover, African American women again took the lead in many civil rights actions, focusing attention on desegregating public transportation and facilities and fighting police brutality. Change would come late in the 1940s and early in the 1950s, and those efforts formed the groundwork for the later school desegregation efforts after 1954.

Middle-class women continued to step up efforts to increase participation in the electoral process in Virginia, and their work affected many levels of government. In 1947, Dorothy Morrison Eley, president of the Virginia Federation of Women's Clubs, stressed to members that "it is the God-given privilege of every citizen to participate in our government, and we must work toward that end." In the pages of the *Virginia Club Woman*, she urged the 16,000 members to vote in November elections. Clubwomen, she maintained, were a powerful force and could "strengthen our democracy" significantly.[97] Virginia's white clubwomen stepped up their lobbying efforts in the General Assembly. Cornelia Storrs Adair, a former president of the National Education Association and the legislative chair of the VFWC, laid out the organization's goals for 1947. They included reducing the severe teacher shortage by raising state minimum salary standards; funding for tuberculosis and cancer control, as well as for rural health initiatives and welfare disbursements; raising the work age to sixteen; serving on juries (but with an exemption for mothers who could not leave children); and continuing their 1946 initiative to end the oppressive poll tax that disfranchised much of the potential Virginia electorate. In this effort, the Virginia Federation of Women's Clubs stood firm with the all-white League of Women Voters and with African American organizations that were engaged in similar lobbying efforts.[98]

Poll tax battles continued throughout the 1940s and 1950s. In May 1944, Roanoke resident Dorothy Bentley Jones, the wife of a soldier stationed overseas, filed suit against the city's registrar, Hazeltine Settle, after she refused to register Jones for nonpayment of the poll tax. Jones argued that she could not pay a poll tax for that year because she did not turn twenty-one until May of that year and that "the right to register . . . is a right and privilege arising out of the Constitution of the United States and is not subject to state taxation in any form. . . ." The United States district court ruled in Jones's favor, but she was not allowed to register in subsequent elections. Other women filed similar suits challenging the constitutionality of Virginia's poll tax, including Roanoke resident Eileen S. Evans in 1945 and Arlington resident Jessie Butler in 1950.[99] Although these suits did not succeed in their immediate aims, the strategy of these women to employ the judicial system in attempting to reverse Virginia's restrictive political system marked a change in the way African Americans responded to the oppression they faced from the Byrd organization.

Many African American women worked to register voters in broad-based community efforts. Mary C. Stowrs, of Newport News, organized the Senior Women's Civic League in 1936 and a Junior Women's Civic League in 1942. During the war her groups led poll tax drives to register voters, and for decades she exhorted African Americans to register and urged women to go to the polls. She brought together a committee that successfully lobbied the city council to hire its the first juvenile police officer and welfare caseworkers. An active member of the National Association of Colored Women, the National Council of Negro Women, and the NAACP, Stowrs was credited with increasing the number of registered black voters in Newport News from 64 to 3,000 by 1950. She was the only African American woman sent as a delegate to the state's Democratic convention in 1948 and she served as an alternate delegate to the National Democratic convention.[100] Other women also worked hard to involve African Americans in the electoral process, both statewide and locally. Julia E. Spaulding Tucker, the wife of one of the state's influential civil rights attorneys, directed poll tax registration and voting drives for the NAACP. Working on an NAACP suffrage project with Brownie Lee Jones in 1951, she helped bring cases against registrars in Sussex County that resulted in African Americans' being allowed to register in one local precinct for the first time in almost fifty years.

At the 1953 NAACP state convention, she addressed the topic "Strengthening Our Democracy Through the Effective Use of the Ballot."[101]

Many organizations also used their networks to encourage voter registration. In Norfolk, for example, the Daughter Elks Civil Liberties Department organized a "Get Out the Vote" campaign in conjunction with local women's groups and the National Council of Negro Women. Focusing on voter registration, club members from local civic and social groups, sororities, and parent-teacher associations supported the effort to provide instructions about voting requirements and to encourage greater voter participation. The Virginia Voters League sponsored certificates of honor for all clubs in the state that reported 100 percent membership of qualified voters.[102] Given the extremely low voting rate in the commonwealth, casting a ballot was a simple way for African Americans to show that they would not be denied their political rights, as much as the state government tried to do so.

Some women directly challenged the white male establishment that dominated Virginia politics at that time. In Arlington, Esther Georgia Irving Cooper, president of the local NAACP chapter, joined several other women who attempted to be placed on the ballot as candidates for the Arlington Democratic Executive Committee in 1947. They were among a group of "Progressive Democratic candidates" who opposed the local party's control by supporters of Harry F. Byrd. Cooper, Beatrice B. Smythe, Josephine Y. Barber, Elizabeth W. White, Virginia Thatcher, and Martha P. Wildhack joined eleven men in a boycott of a "party inquiry" meant to look into their "Party background and loyalty," which caused the local party to purge them from the ballot. Cooper challenged the action, noting that she had run for the party's executive committee the previous year and had been vetted at that time. She pointed out to a reporter that she had lived in Arlington thirty-two years and in that time "nobody has ever challenged my qualifications as a Democrat." Cooper's statement challenged the back-room political maneuverings of the Byrd organization. Despite her fight for reinstatement, she was one of six who were not reinstated on the roster by the Democratic Committee of the Eighth Congressional District, for the stated reason of not having voted a straight party ticket in the previous general election.[103]

Although few women successfully campaigned for elected positions in state government at this time—indeed, there were no female delegates in the

General Assembly for two decades after Emma Lee Smith White represented Gloucester and Mathews Counties in 1930–1933—white women did secure positions on local councils. Clintwood, an Appalachian mining town of 2,500, made international news when an all-female slate of candidates swept the local elections in 1948. Minnie "Sis" Miller became mayor of the small town, and her slate of compatriots, Ferne Skeen, Beuna Smith, Kate Friend, Marion Shortt, and Ida Cunningham, took all of the town's elected positions by a 2-1 majority. All but one were members of the Woman's Club of Clintwood, and according to the *Virginia Club Woman*, most had been employed by the Dickenson County school system, while Miller was described as a "businesswoman" who had served as a gas ration clerk during World War II. According to the *Virginia Club Woman*, the six women ran because "the men who had been elected to the municipal offices in the past year had not given a great deal of attention to the town, and were not particularly interested in its cleanliness, orderliness, and beauty." The women campaigned door-to-door in the small town, running on a platform of beautification and progressive town policies, including street and sewer improvements, playground construction, and vacant-lot cleanup. Once elected, the women immediately filled the town clerk position with fellow club member Betty Sutherland, but since they could not get women to fill the police positions, they retained the two men who already employed. In 1950, voters in the Rappahannock County town of Washington elected a woman mayor and six women to fill all the seats on the town council, which remained dominated by women throughout the decade. Women won council seats in other communities across the state, suggesting that some members of the voting population were unwilling to continue with the status quo, and that women were both constituents and actors in reshaping the political climate.[104]

The Virginia Federation of Women's Clubs made it clear that the organization supported its members who ran for elective office in Clintwood. In 1952, it took an even stronger stand for women politicians and its president stressed that "a major Federation objective is the promotion of women in public affairs." In her November message to VFWC members, Odessa Pittard Bailey, a former judge of Roanoke's Juvenile and Domestic Relations Court who managed the work of Virginia women on behalf of the Democratic presidential candidate that year, argued that women's recent experiences in politics would allow them "to exert greater influence than ever before in the affairs of the Commonwealth." Bailey pointed out that "in the past several years a good many women have been elected to local office," but not to the General Assembly, despite the fact that many women "have wide knowledge of the governmental affairs of Virginia." She hoped that throughout the state "when women's groups come together you will feel it advisable to get behind some capable woman. Here I urge you to induce the best informed, the ablest public spirited woman to be found to become a candidate," and to offer her much-needed support.[105]

This direct critique of women's lack of visibility in the political landscape of Virginia was notable for its candor. As a representative of thousands of white middle- and upper-class women in Virginia, Bailey used her clout to call for women to support female candidates—because of their gender. Perhaps their efforts paid off. The following year, Kathryn Haeseler Meyers Stone won election to the House of Delegates as one of three members representing Arlington County. Still, the VFWC was a relatively staid group, not looking for anyone to question their respectability. Bailey asked her readers to find "women of competency, of character" to run for office while reminding women of their duties as "homemakers, Christians, and citizens."[106]

As relatively privileged white women fought for a political foothold in a state known for its oligarchic machine system, African American women continued to work for equal footing in the segregated commonwealth. In the years following World War II, black women from different socioeconomic strata came together in an effort to fight against racism in general and the brutality of city police forces in particular. These fights moved into direct demands for the end to Jim Crow laws at the start of the 1950s, signaling another turning point for civil rights in the commonwealth.

One of the many concerns shared by black women in Virginia was their treatment by white police officers, and in the years after World War II many secured surprising victories when challenging the brutality they faced. The year 1946 was a bad one for black women dealing with the police in Richmond, and women responded by attempting to file lawsuits against the aggressors. Geraldine Polite became a victim as she attempted to intercede in a police beating of a black woman who allegedly shoplifted from a local store. Polite, the mother of a ten-month-old child, resisted arrest, and became the target of the officers. Witnesses saw her kicked and beaten with nightsticks before she was hauled off to the police station. Although Polite sought criminal charges against the officers, the police department refused to release the officers' names, so she could not secure either criminal or civil suits against them. Later that year, Norfolk resident Louella Tazewell fought back against an officer who tried to arrest her at the Greyhound bus station in Richmond for using vulgar language. The officer carried her to a private room, sat on her chest, and repeatedly hit her in the mouth. Although a witness told a local reporter that Tazewell was, in fact, "cursing a blue streak," Tazewell received assistance from a local civil rights attorney and filed a complaint against the officer with the deputy of public safety and police chief.[107]

Although most of the women who filed suits against the police in Richmond did not succeed in gaining a judgment in their favor, one case stood out as a victory for black women in the community. Thirty-two-year-old wife and mother Nannie Strayhorne was picked up by two officers in October 1946 as she attempted to return home from a party. The officers raped her in their patrol car. Strayhorne reported the incident, and the city's commonwealth's attorney prosecuted it. In the course of the trial, defense attorneys employed numerous negative stereotypes of black women. They claimed that Strayhorne was obviously a prostitute because "no respectable woman would be leaving a drinking party at 2 o'clock in the morning," and because she had been in a car with a man she did not know. They also cited a lack of defensive injuries as evidence that she was not raped. Despite these scurrilous attacks on her character, and the fact that many southerners considered the sexual exploitation of black women within the bounds of expected, if not acceptable, male behavior, an all-white, all-male jury convicted the two officers. The verdict shook the base of race and gender relations in the commonwealth, as evidenced by the fact that the assistant to the commonwealth's attorney received death threats for agreeing to take on the case and that the defense attempted to appeal the verdict in part because white men could not be guilty of a criminal attack on a nonwhite woman. The judge denied the appeal and one of the officers began his seven-year sentence while the other escaped and remained a fugitive from the law.[108]

The case opened the way for other women to challenge brutal treatment at the hands of police. In Richmond, two women successfully prosecuted civil and criminal suits against white officers in the next seven years. In Norfolk, the case of Viola Casel helped convince the local NAACP to launch a formal investigation into local police practices in 1950. In February, Casel was taken to the hospital on a stretcher after being assaulted by a police officer who thought she was concealing a numbers ticket rather than her sewing thread in her mouth.[109] As local agents of state power, police represented the very oppression African Americans had faced for centuries in the commonwealth. By fighting back against their aggression, these African American women demonstrated that they were no longer willing to submit to practices that endangered their lives, destroyed their psyches, and trampled on their basic civil and human rights.

African American women began to enter the ranks of law enforcement at the close of the 1940s. Although Petersburg had hired a black policewoman, Lizzie B. Forbes, in 1921,[110] it was almost three decades before other localities across Virginia began employing African American women in law enforcement. In 1949, only seven African American women were members of police forces in southern cities.[111] That year, Virginia Union University graduate Ruth Brown Blair joined Richmond's police force and in 1952 Margaret Cornick Barfield and Virginia Drew Randolph took their oaths as Norfolk policewomen. Like most early female police officers, they were assigned primarily to juvenile departments, which was deemed the type of police work most suitable for women. When Newport News hired its first female officers, both white and black, they served as crossing guards.[112] It was not until the 1970s that policewomen were given less gender-specific duties and were allowed to go on patrol duty, although African American policewomen continued to face both racial and gender discrimination through the remainder of the twentieth century.[113]

During the period after World War II, African American women helped lead their communities into direct challenges to segregation. In 1947, some black women challenged segregation on public transportation, possibly in attempts to apply locally the Supreme Court's 1946 ban on segregated interstate transportation. Late in the 1940s, veteran schoolteacher Lavalette Allen and nurse Willa Johnson were arrested in separate instances for refusing to abide by streetcar segregation in Richmond. They each faced the same judge, who fined Allen for disorderly conduct and Johnson for violation of the segregation law. With the help of the NAACP, each appealed her case to the city's hustings court, which promptly threw out their cases on technicalities rather than deal with engaging the segregation law head on.[114]

Attempts to challenge transportation segregation laws coalesced in 1950, when Alexandria delegate Armistead L. Boothe introduced a bill in the General Assembly to end segregation on all forms of transportation in Virginia and another bill to create a civil rights commission to study race relations. African American women's organizations took a prominent role in supporting this bill. The Virginia State Federation of Colored Women's Clubs led a massive petition drive in support of the bill. Chaired by Bernice Nelson Sampson, of Richmond, the organization's local clubs sent petitions to churches, movie theaters, and stores, as well as to other women's clubs and organizations. Norfolk's chapter collected 6,000 signatures on one petition alone. Sampson also went to the governor along with NAACP lawyers Oliver Hill and Spottswood Robinson and other African American community leaders to lobby for the bill.[115]

Vivian Carter Mason, of the National Council of Negro Women, spoke in favor of the bill during a public meeting held by members of Norfolk's delegation to the General Assembly. The only African American to speak during the six and a half hour meeting, she took the opportunity to call out segregation as undemocratic, telling the legislators that "the laws of segregation are based on the theory that here are inferior beings and they brand the people being segregated as inferior." She went on to stress that segregation conflicted with "our religious and national teachings" and that African American voters would like "one of our representatives put into motion the legislation that would remove these laws from our statutes." For good measure, she also demanded an end to the poll tax and a plan to address the problems of segregated schools. Not mincing words, Mason argued that opponents of America used segregation laws to promote "hostile propaganda" against the country.[116]

Mason followed the cues of many national black leaders who suggested that the segregationist American society helped to advance the cause of communism and that Jim Crow laws made American democratic ideals ring hollow. Neither Mason nor other black leaders could move the General Assembly, however. The bills were stopped through parliamentary trickery. The Committee for Courts of Justice in the House of Delegates met in executive session to consider the bills, switched to its regular meeting by unlocking the door quietly, and while waiting reporters sat uninformed about what was happening, the committee defeated the transportation measure by a 9-7 vote and the civil rights commission by a 10-6 vote.[117]

Although black women leaders did not succeed in overturning the Jim Crow laws in public transportation, their demand to end segregation in this arena highlighted an important growing movement across Virginia—that of interracial efforts by clubwomen to better their communities and fight for justice. The Boothe Bill won not only the support of the Virginia State Federation of Colored Women's Clubs and the NCNW, but also of the Virginia League of Women Voters and Norfolk's Women's Council for Interracial Cooperation, which had been established in 1945. The Women's Council also endorsed a repeal of the poll tax and held its integrated meetings at the Central YWCA, which supported the mission of interracial cooperation.[118]

In the immediate postwar period, the black press took note of the many emerging interracial efforts. Some of these efforts were more political than others, but each suggested that substantial change had occurred at some level, among some socioeconomic classes, in the commonwealth. Many of these organizing efforts came from progressive women leaders, such as labor activist Brownie Lee Jones, who had relocated the Southern School for Workers to Richmond in 1944. Jones, a white woman, trained working- and middle-class women and men to become leaders and provided educational programs to union members. Jones believed strongly in interracial cooperation and the school held only integrated conferences and discussion groups, and also provided material and financial support to voter registration and poll tax payment drives. Jones's integrated, female staff supported the interracial Virginia Civil Rights Organization, which was formed in 1947 to call for an end to all segregation in Virginia. While Jones's stand on civil rights made her a target of anticommunist attacks, she continued to sponsor voter registration drives, and in 1950, sent former staff member Helen Estes Baker, an African American, and Polly Hayden to register voters in counties with a large black populations in a campaign funded by the political action committee of the CIO. When the School for Southern Workers closed late in 1950, Jones worked for the NAACP in voter registration drives in Nansemond County, Sussex County, and other areas.[119]

Jones was not the only white woman leading civil rights efforts in the state. Virginia Foster Durr, a transplanted Alabamian who made her home in Alexandria, co-chaired the Committee for Virginia, established in 1946 as an affiliate of the Southern Conference for Human Welfare. With Virginia State College (later University) professor and civil rights activist Luther Porter

Jackson as co-chair and Vivian Carter Mason as secretary, the organization challenged the Byrd organization's hold on the state and strove to end the poll tax and gain full civil rights for all Virginia citizens. At a speech given by Henry Wallace in Norfolk just prior to his 1947 announcement of his candidacy for president on the Progressive Party ticket, police attempted to keep Durr from the platform because the organizers refused to segregate the seating according to law. Durr asked a local minister to pray and audience members sang the national anthem to hold off police from making arrests and the integrated event took place. Like Jones, Durr was red-baited and was under federal surveillance as a potential communist for her support of the Progressive Party and her opposition to segregation.[120]

Only a few extraordinary women risked their reputations to stand publicly alongside African Americans in the fight against inequality in Virginia. Most white women supported Virginia's segregated society, although some participated in less-radical interracial activities. The Norfolk Baptist Interracial Missionary Group, for example, held integrated meetings and special services and supported mission projects of white and African American churches.[121] The white Hampton Woman's Club created an interracial department by 1950 to exchange information among all clubwomen in the area and invited Audrey J. Walker, a prominent black clubwoman, to speak on "The Unfinished Task." While Walker focused on community building as the main theme of her lecture, possibly to avoid offending the more conservative in the crowd, she drew commonalities between the groups when she said people everywhere "are looking to us to lead them and guide them in the building of that 'better world.' They are looking to us; they are depending on us, and that is the task before us."[122] A variety of women's groups held interracial meetings and events, such as YWCA dinners in Danville and Norfolk and the Women's Council for Interracial Cooperation's Christmas parties for children. And early in the 1950s, Roanoke area women's clubs teamed with the local chapter of the National Council of Negro Women to exchange children's "weird and lurid comic books" for "good books and magazines."[123]

These clubwomen's activities suggest that many Virginia women emerged from World War II with different political and social outlooks. In 1946, Harry F. Byrd Sr. for the first time faced opposition in the Democratic Party primary

Packing Lucky Strikes, Richmond, 1952. Young white women who worked in Richmond's cigarette factories secured jobs primarily as packers and in other positions that enabled them to enjoy far better working conditions than African American women, whose work was more often seasonal in nature, low paid, physically demanding, and dirty. *Courtesy of the Library of Virginia.*

for his seat in the U.S. Senate, in part as a result of the organizing strategies of African Americans and unions. The era saw the first in a series of litigation efforts against segregation in the state.[124] The vast changes that occurred from the 1930s to early in 1950s did not fundamentally alter the political, social, or economic landscape of the commonwealth. Women failed to obtain long-term gains in industrial employment, and African American women continued to be concentrated in low-paying domestic, tobacco stemmery, and laundry work. Legal segregation remained in place despite these forays into the judicial system, and for the most part, racial structures were unaffected by the dramatic citizenship and civil rights campaigns of the 1940s and 1950s. White women, however, did feel the change and became agents of change in the state by taking stands against the restrictive poll tax and reaching across the color barrier to work with black women in their own social class. Their efforts formed the groundwork for the ultimately successful civil rights campaigns of the mid-1950s and 1960s, and the feminist movement of the 1970s and 1980s.

CHAPTER 7

"The Real Issue … Is One of Power": Women, Civil Rights, and Feminism in the 1950s and Beyond

In the second half of the twentieth century, "change" was the catchword of the day. African Americans successfully challenged the Commonwealth for political and social equality. The political control of the Byrd organization finally toppled, as did impediments to the franchise. Statewide elections became competitive. The state looked different politically and demographically. The farm population made up only one-fourth of Virginia's population in 1945, but dropped to only 5 percent in 1970. This population shift occurred because of significant growth in northern and eastern Virginia.[1] Much of the growth came from migrants to the state, who brought a different set of values, and held no ties with the old-style politics or racial and gender hierarchies. The feminist movement took hold first in Northern Virginia and then erupted throughout the state. Between the 1960s and 1980s, feminists coalesced around state support of equal opportunities for women and for passage of the Equal Rights Amendment. In this period, educated middle-class women fought for, and often succeeded in gaining, positions in state politics and the judiciary, as well as in private enterprise. Working-class women fought to ameliorate conditions in factories and for welfare rights. Virginia Indian women helped to lead recognition movements across the commonwealth. The late twentieth century saw the patriarchal traditions of male-only public education come to an end as well. Not all Virginians welcomed the new era, however. State politicians often succeeded in stemming the tide of federal litigation and legislation against Jim Crow, while ERA and other feminist initiatives often went down to defeat in the 1970s and 1980s. In all of these social changes, women stood at the front lines as activists, no matter whether they were supporting the changes or were attempting to stem the tide.

One of the most significant changes in post-1940s Virginia occurred as African Americans moved from litigating for equal facilities to demanding first-class citizenship through lawsuits and mass demonstrations. Virginia's civil rights activists joined with other protesters throughout the country to end discriminatory employment practices, segregated educational institutions, and Jim Crow accommodations. Many white Virginians, like many other whites throughout the country, fought to maintain the racial status quo, but they did not succeed in holding back civil rights efforts.

The change demanded by the black community ultimately came through federal channels, but it could not have happened without the efforts of local activists and supporters, black and white, to restructure race relations. Many federal cases involved Virginia litigants, particularly because Virginia legislators created a strategy of Massive Resistance. In avoiding full compliance with federal judicial decisions and blocking the advancement of civil rights, Virginia's local and state public officials provided a model to other white communities across the country that wanted to maintain strict racial divides. The governor and local officials circumvented federal desegregation mandates by shutting down schools that attempted to follow the federal guidelines. White women lined up on both sides of Massive Resistance and fought to advance their goals. The ultimate gains of the civil rights movement in the commonwealth could not have been made without the support and leadership of both black and white women.

For more than a decade, Virginia's black community had been litigating for equal teacher salaries and equal school facilities. The best-known and most high-profile civil rights issues in the state centered on school desegregation. In many cases, young black women stood as the plaintiffs in the lawsuits. While some white women took a stand in fighting the forced closure of integrated public schools, other white women assisted in the Massive Resistance movement against desegregation. The fight for desegregation began early in the 1950s in Prince Edward County, when Barbara Johns, a student at Robert Russa Moton High School, mobilized a walkout in 1951 to protest the blatant inequalities in her school. Tar-paper shacks in the back of the school served as makeshift classrooms; one sewing machine served its 130 students, while the white high school had a home economics wing complete with kitchens. Black students also had inadequate bus transportation. When the Prince Edward County school board finally provided some secondhand buses for the students, one was involved in an accident that killed five students when it most likely stalled on train tracks.[2]

Originally, Johns organized a protest for equal facilities. When the students contacted NAACP lawyers, who then asked if they might be willing to fight to desegregate the educational system, Johns stood up as a community leader to support the idea and became an important part of American civil rights history. Johns called out local male black leaders for their unwillingness to fight for total desegregation. When she spoke and asked for the support of parents and older community leaders, she galvanized the community, and a majority of parents backed the lawsuit filed as *Dorothy Davis* v. *County School Board of Prince Edward County*. The battle did not end until 1965 and claimed the careers of several teachers and principals, as well as the education of hundreds of black Prince Edward County students.[3] Ultimately, the Prince Edward lawsuit was subsumed under the *Brown v. Board of Education of Topeka* desegregation case, in which the U.S. Supreme Court overturned segregation in public education in 1954.

Most Virginia legislators, still strongly affiliated with the three-decades-old Byrd organization, attempted to stop the court's desegregation mandate by any means possible other than violence, and the women of the commonwealth reacted to their efforts in several ways. In a special session in August 1956, the General Assembly passed a series of laws designed to halt any integration efforts, including closing any school that enrolled black children in white schools. It also passed legislation meant to harass the NAACP, in an attempt to hamstring the organization's ability to file lawsuits against individual school districts.[4] Other organizations emerged, such as the Farmville-based Defenders of State Sovereignty and Individual Liberties, which had a membership of nearly

12,000 in 1956. Capitalizing on the fears and suspicions of the Cold War Era, the Defenders claimed that the civil rights movement was a communist plot designed to attack parental rights and create a government dictatorship.[5]

White women across the state supported these efforts and many of the hundreds of letters received by the governor in support of segregation at any cost came from women. These women repeated an old southern fear in their correspondence, one mirrored by the male-dominated segregationist organizations: that of racial mixing. Segregationist women believed that school desegregation was the first step in miscegenation, which many of the letter writers claimed was against God's will and a sure step down the path of eternal damnation. While some writers of these letters claimed to support equal education for African Americans, they feared that desegregation was dangerous.[6]

Other white women, however, feared that state legislators were taking actions one step too far in their threats to shut down the public education of the state, and they took strong stands against the entrenched machine. The only woman delegate in the General Assembly, Kathryn Stone opposed not only the bill to shut down integrated public schools, but also all seven of the anti-NAACP bills that eventually passed. Described by journalist and former state senator Benjamin Muse as "a gracious and indomitable lady member," Stone stood among a small minority of legislators in the session.[7] Along with state senator Armistead L. Boothe, the sponsor of the failed transportation desegregation bill, Stone led the Virginia Society for the Preservation of Public Schools.[8] Stone was not the only woman in Virginia who questioned the thinking of the General Assembly during those contentious years. The board of directors of Virginia's chapter of the American Association of University Women sent a telegram to Governor J. Lindsay Almond demanding that he call a session of the General Assembly to "enact realistic laws that will reopen closed schools and that will keep open the public schools now in operation."[9] Virginia's League of Women Voters stood by the AAUW, calling on all Virginians to protest the legislation "openly and firmly by letter, telegram, and word-of-mouth to city or county officials, to state legislators and to the governor" to end Massive Resistance.[10] At least one white girl—Catherine Drew Gilpin of Boyce, Virginia, voiced her opinion on the matter. In 1957, she wrote to President Dwight D. Eisenhower, asking him to "try and have schools and other things accept colored people."[11] In May 1958, Roanoke resident Helen W. Kavanaugh, president of the Virginia Congress of Parents and Teachers (PTA), admitted that the issue was causing controversy among parents, but urged all PTAs to support keeping the schools open.[12] These women never made clear their position on black and white children attending the same schools, making public their stand only on supporting free education for the children of Virginia.

One group, however, clearly stated its view on civil rights. In September 1956, the program chair of the Norfolk Women's Council for Interracial Cooperation (NWCIC) testified before the General Assembly in a failed attempt to stop the creation of the Pupil Placement Board, a measure that forced all black students to apply for admission to their local schools through a state-appointed body that sat in Richmond. Betty B. Brewer presented the NWCIC's statement, which concluded by declaring that "we, the Women's Council for Interracial Cooperation, do not set fire or burn crosses but we are typical of thousands and thousands of Virginia citizens who value the security of the public schools over and above racial prejudice."[13]

Other women worked valiantly at the local level to fight Massive Resistance. White and black women were involved in varying ways in trying to end the legislature's chokehold on local school boards. Some black women and girls, such as fourteen-year-old Olivia Ferguson, of Charlottesville, elementary school student Jane Cooper, of Richmond (with the help of her mother Elizabeth Cooper), and Leola Pearl Beckett, a mother in Norfolk, led groups of other plaintiffs in filing separate suits demanding integration of their local schools between 1955 and 1958, hoping to end Massive Resistance through individual rulings.[14] Some women's organizations in urban areas spoke out against the actions of the General Assembly. In 1955, the NWCIC analyzed more than 100 letters to the editor of the Norfolk *Virginian-Pilot* written after the *Brown* v. *Board* decision and concluded that "there exists in this area of the South a body of moderate, informed, thoughtful, educated and earnest public opinion which would accept desegregation easily."[15] That summer the group sponsored an integrated kindergarten and spoke out against proposed tuition grants from public funding, claiming that the Gray Commission of thirty-two white male legislators did not represent Virginia and could not speak for all of its residents.[16] The NWCIC was joined by several chapters of the National Council of Jewish

Women and the League of Women Voters, which was particularly active on this issue in Northern Virginia.[17]

In response to directed desegregation rulings against the cities of Norfolk and Charlottesville and the county of Warren, the governor shut down public schools there in 1958. In Charlottesville, ten mothers started the Parents' Committee for Emergency Schooling. They drew on traditional understandings of motherhood, including their responsibility to educate their children, to shift the focus of school closings away from race and toward a statement on support of public education. The ten women—Ruth Caplin, Margaret Garnett, Emily Male, Nancy Manson, Peggy McLean, Dorothy Owen, Mary Moon, Evelyn Rathburn, Margaret Via, and Lillian Wilson—were friends before the school crisis, and many were married to University of Virginia faculty members. They were not career women, and they viewed their central role in life as mothers, which hearkened back to the traditional Progressive Era reform-oriented women of Virginia's past. When the governor shut down two schools in Charlottesville, the women revealed their plan that had been put in place months before. They had visited teachers personally and convinced them to teach in classroom space that the group had secured from private organizations. All parents who enrolled their children in the emergency schools had to pledge to return their children to the two public schools, which reopened in 1959 with limited desegregation. The women successfully challenged the segregationists who wanted to put all whites into private schools, and they deflected criticism by calling on their role as mothers and by claiming only to support public education. Their approach failed to address the systemic problem of racism in Virginia and the women refused to discuss civil rights issues at all. Their efforts garnered more support than either the resistance of the segregationists or the staunch integrationist position of civil rights activists, and they experienced some success.[18]

Members of the Parents' Committee undoubtedly noticed the reaction to the integrationist stand taken by Charlottesville resident Sarah Lindsay Patton Boyle. Early in the 1950s, she advocated immediate integration through letters, columns, and articles published in local, state, and national newspapers and periodicals. She promoted interracial dialogue across the state as the only field-worker for the Virginia Council on Human Relations from 1955 to 1958. The National Council of Negro Women named Boyle its "Woman of the Year" in 1956, but her work was not similarly recognized by the white community.

Shunned in white society in Charlottesville, she found that longtime friends and acquaintances refused to speak with her. Opponents of her stance burned a cross on her lawn and harassed her children. This treatment of one white woman who spoke in favor of equality for African Americans may well have dissuaded other white women from working for integration.[19]

Public opposition to the school closings, combined with rulings of the Virginia Supreme Court of Appeals and U.S. district court declaring the action unconstitutional, effectively ended Massive Resistance in 1959, except in Prince Edward County. The county board of supervisors kept the schools shut down until 1964. Black and white women provided most of the only locally available options for African American children to attend school. Approximately 1,700 black

Farmville marchers, photographed by Carl Lynn, 25 July 1963. African American civil rights activists demonstrated against segregation and the four-year closure of public schools in Prince Edward County. Their actions did not sway the county school board, however, and only a court intervention compelled the board to reopen the schools. *Courtesy of the Richmond Times-Dispatch.*

children lost their access to an education during this period, while the local school board funneled tax money into tuition grants for white children to attend the newly established and nominally private Prince Edward Academy (later Fuqua School). Many white women supported the academy. The Farmville Woman's Club offered space for classrooms in its clubhouse, and the Virginia Division of the United Daughters of the Confederacy used its Richmond headquarters as a collection station for all state donations to the segregated academy.[20] Few local white women challenged the closings. Notable exceptions were Annie V. Putney and her daughter-in-law, who in 1959 opposed the county's elimination of funds for public schools from its budget. Speaking before the county board of supervisors to reiterate her point, Annie Putney stated that "we're not doing right by either race. The action is unchristian in so far as we have failed to work together." Grace Putney declared that she "wouldn't care to live in a community where any sizeable segment of the population goes uneducated."[21] While Mildred Dickinson Davis, a Longwood College (later University) professor and Prince Edward County native, did not blast the county's actions, she defended a few college professors who criticized the school closings by stating that they lived in the community and had a right to speak.[22]

But most white women in Prince Edward County, like most other white women across the commonwealth, stayed silent about this drastic step. African American women were left to deal with the situation. Almost immediately, the African American community organized grassroots schools and centers for children to learn fundamentals. These centers were staffed almost entirely by African American women, most of whom were parents, and all of whom were local. Women held their classes in churches, homes, and anywhere else there was space. Flossie Scott White, a Moton graduate and local hairdresser who had been secretary of the local NAACP, hosted approximately fifty children in her home, where classes met Monday through Friday from September to June. During the four years she operated her school, she taught reading, math, and other academic subjects as well as providing recreational activities.[23]

Other centers operated under the sponsorship of the Prince Edward County Christian Association, some of which employed a curriculum developed by Carlene Brumbrey Wooden, a member of the state NAACP, that included health and nutrition, hygiene, parliamentary procedure, reading, writing, science, math, and black history. Many of the teachers and supervisors of the centers had taught in the public schools prior to their closing, such as Alease Baker, who had been a substitute teacher and had taken two years of classes at Virginia State College (later University), and Lucretia Fears, who had taken two years of coursework at Saint Paul's College and had taught before becoming an egg farmer and businesswoman.[24] The National Council of Negro Women and the American Friends Service Committee provided some money to the centers, but much of the work was done on a volunteer basis. The centers served more than 600 children and the curricula suggest that the women taught on their own terms. The mostly male ministers' action group claimed publicly that the centers should not focus on a rigorous education, partly to make the point that students were being denied the education they deserved. The women who taught in these schools refused to do that, and instead they attempted to prepare children for the future, securing help with this educational plan from their church groups and other local networks in which they were involved.[25]

Most of these centers closed after the second year of the crisis, but women continued to take part in other actions to salvage an education as another desegregation case against the school board continued to make its way through the court system. Under the auspices of the American Friends Service Committee, its national representative for Southern Programs, Jean Fairfax, created a placement program for junior high and high-school students to attend schools outside of the county with varying levels of success. As resident director of the AFSC's program in Prince Edward, Helen Estes Baker created a Leadership Institute for the training center teachers in 1960, worked with Edward Peeples to establish a baseball league for black boys and a recreation center with social programs and craft opportunities, and sponsored a Teenage Club to provide activities and dances for students. Nancy Adams, the white AFSC Community Relations Director, went to Farmville in 1964 to build interracial ties. She assembled groups and planned events to draw out white moderates, including some Longwood College students who became activists themselves, organizing and participating in interracial workshops and conferences. The students persevered despite opposition from Longwood's president, who even contacted parents of students who planned to visit students on the campus of historically black North Carolina College (later North Carolina Central University).[26] Ultimately, the lawsuit on behalf of the Prince Edward County students (*Griffin* v. *County School Board of Prince Edward County*) succeeded. Officials reopened the public schools with little funding in 1964, and thus the official chapter on school desegregation closed in the commonwealth.

In Norfolk, Vivian Carter Mason, a prominent clubwoman and national executive director of the NCNW, became the spokesperson for the integration effort in an attempt to deflect problems from the seventeen African Americans who qualified for admittance into Norfolk City's all-white schools in 1959. In an interview with a reporter from a Roanoke television station about the desegregation process, Mason appeared every inch the respectable matron she was, from her modest blouse closed with a large jeweled brooch to her hair smoothed back into a bun. In the interview, which took place in her home in front of a bookcase, Mason drew on the language of citizenship employed by African Americans during World War II when she said the admission of black students to formerly segregated schools "demonstrates conclusively that integrated schools are a real possibility, not only in Virginia but in other states in the South," and that the response of all Norfolk citizens to desegregation showed "an acknowledgement of citizenship responsibility in this regard." She also noted that the students "feel that they are now on the road to first-class citizenship." Community leaders limited the amount of contact students had with the press so as to not appear attention-seeking and because media attention would distract from their studies, which could very much be construed as a typical middle-class response from the black community—it achieved what it wanted without the hoopla and problems associated with the issue in other places.[27]

The story, however, was far from over. It was left to pupils to sort out the racial situation that decades of negative stereotypes, coupled with years of Massive Resistance hostility, brought to the classrooms. In many cases, young women again took the lead in attempting to navigate the treacherous waters of desegregation. Joyce Russell integrated Gar-Field High School in Woodbridge, in 1961. "I walked through those doors alone and into the face of hell," she remembered. "I persevered, endured, sacrificed, and made it through. . . . A film crew came into my biology class which resulted in me looking like a sad lost child in [the 1987 documentary] *Eyes on the Prize*." Her negative experience prompted her to write a memoir that exposed the "truth about the integration experience and does not sugar coat anything."[28]

Twelve-year-old Jane Cooper entered a previously all-white Richmond junior high school in 1961. Accompanied by her mother and the dean of Virginia

Union University students, she later described the scene she encountered: "I don't remember seeing anyone except those traveling to and fro in their cars." The school's principal made it clear that he would not tolerate any outbursts against Cooper, but she described the climate there as "polite but unfriendly." When she chose to go to Thomas Jefferson High School instead of the all-black Maggie Walker, her experience was completely different. She recalled that "I received a lot of name-calling, being picked on, just harassment, not hurt physically, but a lot of emotional trauma." Every day during her first year, a group of white boys blocked her path to a classroom, spitting at her and calling her names, but the principal told Cooper that he could not take action without a "definitive description" of the boys. She "learned the value of vigilance" because she made enough mental notes to describe them in detail to the principal, and eventually they stopped. Other students harassed her by cutting her off in lunch lines and throwing food at her in the cafeteria, and her eleventh grade history teacher used the term "nigra" in class and accused her of plagiarism. Elizabeth Cooper later praised her daughter, saying that "she seemed to be more and more courageous." Jane Cooper Johnson made the situation a life lesson: "My experiences have taught me not to allow obstacles or barriers to keep me from striving toward accomplishing my goals."[29]

Stories like these illustrate that neat endings did not occur in school desegregation. Although many black and white women stood as leaders in the fight to comply with federal laws, their results were mixed. In 1960, only 170 of 204,000 black students were enrolled in formerly white schools. In Richmond in 1963, only 312 of 26,000 black students were enrolled in twelve formerly white schools. The freedom of choice plan concocted by the General Assembly did exactly what legislators had hoped—it kept many African Americans from applying to the Pupil Placement Board to attend white schools. After the stories students heard about what happened to black students there, it was not surprising that many black students remained at their former schools for fear of intimidation. A 1968 Virginia court case overturned the legality of the "freedom of choice" plans, but white academies, white flight from cities, and busing controversies continued to make many question just whether Virginia's school system would ever become truly integrated, and many believe this question remains unanswered.[30] It is important to note, though, that the racial hierarchy cracked, and change would continue to come to the commonwealth.

The women who fought against educational inequality and their supporters shifted the racial climate of the state, and were a large part of fomenting even more protest against other inequalities during the same period.

Virginia was not immune from the sit-in movement of the 1960s. This movement coalesced early in the 1960s with a number of sit-ins, pickets, and marches, but it clearly came out of the earlier protests of the 1940s and 1950s. As in the school desegregation process, women were prominent as leaders and participants, and although it took federal court orders and legislation ultimately to end Jim Crow, their efforts, combined with those of thousands of other civil rights activists throughout the South, had an important effect on Americans' racial attitudes and assumptions.

As in other southern states in the 1960s, Virginia had seen little social progress in terms of equal facilities, accommodations, and employment. It is difficult for many people today to envision a world so divided along racial lines. Edwilda Allen Isaac, a resident of Farmville, remembered, "if I wanted to get a hamburger, I had to go to a window and they would hand it out to me. I could never go inside a place and ask for it. If I wanted to ride on the train, I knew that there were two doors." And she also understood the ways in which Virginia and other Jim Crow states barely skimmed the legalities of federal integration laws. When she left for college, she noticed that the integrated railcars that went out of state were few and far between: "You rode on an integrated car but that car was always like on the end of the train. So there was just that one coach that is integrated. The rest of the train was still segregated."[31] Many jobs remained closed to African Americans. This posed a continued problem for African American women, who found limited success in fields traditionally designated for white women. Early in the 1960s, Dan River Mills employed about 10,000 workers, only about 1,100 of whom were black. Even those jobs designated for African American women were not secure. Lawrence M. Clark remembered his mother and other women in Danville attempting to obtain seasonal tobacco stemming jobs. He recalled, "This white fellow would stand on a platform—he would hire certain people in the crowd.... This fellow would hire maybe three or four people every hour." He also recalled that women would stand waiting for six hours just to get a job, and that "my mom would go every night trying to get this job."[32]

The year 1960 signaled a turning point in Virginia, and in the nation, as African Americans and sympathetic whites took stands against the unjust racial codes. Protests took on an added dimension of danger after the General Assembly altered a trespass code that year in order to provide stiffer punishments for civil rights activists. In Richmond, hundreds of students from Virginia Union University led planned sit-ins downtown to desegregate lunch counters. Among the thirty-four arrested at the tea room and lunch counter at Thalhimers department store were ten women, including Elizabeth Johnson, a nineteen-year-old student, who explained to the press that she and the other students had been inspired by the sit-ins held in Greensboro, North Carolina. She and the other arrested students were convicted and received fines, which were upheld in 1961 by the Virginia Supreme Court of Appeals. The group took its case to the U.S. Supreme Court, but by the time it ruled on the case in 1963, the dining facilities at Thalhimers had been desegregated for two years. Nevertheless, the court did overturn all of the sit-in convictions it received.[33]

The day after the arrests in February 1960, thousands of African Americans met at the Fifth Street Baptist Church to demonstrate in support, where they were advised to boycott the store rather than hold sit-ins. The previous day, a prominent black matron of Richmond became one of the symbols of upper-South racism for the country. Ruth E. Tinsley, the wife of a national NAACP board member and herself an advisor to the NAACP's youth group, was arrested for loitering outside of Thalhimers. A black photographer snapped a picture of the middle-aged Tinsley in her fur-trimmed coat and pillbox hat being dragged away by two uniformed policemen accompanied by a police dog. *Life* magazine published the compelling photograph, the ultimate imagery of the "respectability" of those who were trying to effect change.[34]

Similar events occurred throughout Virginia early in the 1960s, with women playing prominent roles each time. In Lynchburg, an interracial group of six students from Randolph-Macon Woman's College, Virginia Theological Seminary and College (later Virginia University of Lynchburg), and Lynchburg College were arrested for sitting in at Patterson's Drug Store. Three of the students were women, including African American seminar student Barbara Thomas. Her sister Miriam Gaines, an eighteen-year-old high school student, participated in another demonstration at People's Drug Store the next day, along with four Randolph-Macon students. The white women placed orders and then slid a drink over to Gaines, which prompted the manager to close the counter and turn out the lights, although the women were allowed to finish their drinks without incident. The original six sit-in activists received 30-day jail sentences.[35] Similar activities occurred in Fredericksburg, Petersburg, Farmville, and Danville.[36]

Years later, Rebecca M. Owen, a Middlesex County native and Randolph-Macon Woman's College student, remembered how her ingrained racial attitudes made her feel as she sat at the counter with her black colleagues, looking at the group in the mirror behind the counter: "It was in that moment in that drugstore I saw in their faces the mirror of something incredibly … obscene

Mrs. Ruth E. Tinsley, being dragged from a Richmond, Va. department store by two policemen, after she refused to move on during picketing, 23 February 1960. Ruth E. Tinsley was dragged from in front of Thalhimers department store by uniformed police. This picture shows the stark realities of civil disobedience in Virginia—despite her personification of respectability in her clothing and her mannerisms, Mrs. Tinsley and other civil rights activists received rough treatment. This picture was broadcast to the nation in *Life* magazine. *Courtesy of the Library of Congress, New York World-Telegram and Sun Newspaper Photograph Collection, LC-USZ62-119523.*

is the word that comes to mind. Something dirty. The spectacle of white and black students sitting at a lunch counter together." Although the incident made her uncomfortable, she recalled: "To be seen in that way, to see myself in that mirror, was a strange experience. . . . I was not ashamed of what I was doing. I knew it was what I wanted to do. But I felt shame."[37] Her comment reflects just how influential were many white Virginians' racial attitudes. Although Owen stood up for what she believed was the right course of action, she could not divorce herself from her own sensibilities about racial mixing.

In 1963, brutal incidents in Danville compelled Martin Luther King Jr. to come to the state to boost the spirits of protesters, including many African American women. Danville's struggle began at the end of May when two clergymen led African Americans on daily marches to city hall to protest inequality in municipal employment and to advocate desegregation in all public places and the creation of an interracial committee. During a sit-in at city hall on 5 June, police rushed the crowd and a "young Negro girl, who, not properly schooled in non-violence" hit a policeman with her pocketbook when he tried to choke her. The action precipitated a wave of protests and violence during the summer, and hundreds were arrested for violating a local injunction the local judge issued to prohibit the protests. Leaders of the demonstration were indicted for violating an antebellum statute commonly referred to as "John Brown's law," but which had been revised in 1960 to punish people who "conspire with another to incite the colored population of the state in acts of violence and war against the white population."[38]

On the afternoon of 10 June, police used fire hoses to disperse demonstrators at city hall. That evening a group composed primarily of black women sang hymns and held a prayer vigil. Police and deputized garbage workers attacked the group with fire hoses and clubs, sending almost all of the demonstrators to a local hospital. In his account of the events in Danville, civil rights attorney Len Holt, of Norfolk, described a scene where "women had been beaten between their thighs, on their buttocks and breasts; men and boys had their bodies clubbed into numbness."[39] The inescapable sexual imagery inherent in his comment highlighted the fact that this incident was one bound by the traditions of sexually stereotyping and victimizing black women in the South. The *Richmond Afro-American* ran stories on the violence, one quoting funeral home owner Mabel Cunningham Hughes, who drove dozens of people to the hospital that night and described it as looking "like a slaughterhouse." The paper also focused on the fact that women had been brutally beaten when editors published a photograph of Dorothy Miller, a white field-worker with the Student Nonviolent Coordinating Committee, with a large, ugly bruise on her forehead and accompanied by a caption that read, "Cops even beat her."[40]

During a hearing later in June to move the trials to federal court, some of the injured women testified to the violence perpetrated on them by the police chief and his force. Several women stood up in court and faced their attackers in the unsuccessful attempt to persuade the U.S. district court judge that a local trial could not be unbiased. Gloria Campbell, the wife of one of the main organizers of the civil rights actions, was injured in the protest, and she testified that she "saw the fire hoses being unwound out in the street. It was

Danville Civil Rights protest, 1963. Danville police taking demonstrators to jail in handcuffs. The 1963 atrocities in Danville proved that, in fact, violent reactions to civil rights activities "did happen in Virginia," and drew Martin Luther King Jr. to the city in support of the activists. *Courtesy of the Library of Virginia.*

a most horrible moment to wait for the water to hit us. All of a sudden a great force of water hit me from my back and I was thrown to the pavement. . . . I was lying on the pavement with my dress over my head. As I tried to get up I was beaten on my back by a policeman." Assisted to a car by another woman, she was rushed to the Bibleway Church, where she saw that "someone with a pickup truck had picked up a truckload of people who looked like butchered cattle with bloody, torn clothes." Marie Carey testified in court that Danville's chief of police had been the one beating Gloria Campbell.[41] Responding to the police chief's protests that he had not seen or heard of injuries sustained by protestors in the incident, twenty-four-year-old mother Mary Thomas testified that he had smashed her face and beaten her leg.[42]

The events in Danville and the brutal attack gained the national spotlight. The fact that numerous people were badly injured, that they had been trapped in an alley by policemen and municipal workers acting on their behalf, and the belief held by many white Virginians that such violence did not happen in Virginia led SNCC to publish a lengthy pamphlet on the problems in Danville and for the national news to focus attention on the incidents. News coverage moved several civil rights attorneys from around the country to come to Danville to help the legal team. Angered by the "desperate" state of affairs, Los Angeles attorney Leo Branton declared that "my stomach is still sick from the sight of those women and girls whose heads were gashed and bloody. That hospital was a sight that every American should see."[43] After seeing news reports, fifty-three-year-old mother Anne Karro left her home in Maryland to travel to Danville to see the situation for herself and spent more than a week protesting and serving time in jail with the hundreds of other activists who fought for civil rights in Danville between June and August 1963. Later that year, Karro organized a group to drive down to Danville and provide support to the movement.[44]

Local African American women played important roles in the Danville movement to support those injured and arrested. Ruth LaCountess Harvey, long known for her civil rights activism in Virginia, was one of the five black Danville lawyers who provided the bulk of the labor in the cases, both defending those charged and attempting to move the trial to federal courts. Dorothy O. Harris, a Danville teacher, worked as an informal recording secretary, keeping records of marchers, numbers arrested, and those who needed bail. She and her husband, a bank teller, allowed the lawyers to use their basement for a makeshift office. Mabel Cunningham Hughes posted her successful funeral home, worth $40,000, as a surety bond for forty-four of the arrested protesters, nineteen of whom were high school students. Women from High Street Baptist Church and other "ladies from the community" brought sandwiches and drinks to protestors who stood for upwards of nine hours trying to see the community leaders who allowed these atrocities to happen.[45] During one all-night vigil at city hall, Len Holt remembered "a sweet and determined lady in the sunset of her life, whose name must be withheld. She quickly badgered her neighbors and secured a car to carry the blankets hustled from other neighbors to take to the people on city hall steps."[46] These women used their prominence and their pre-existing social networks to assist in any way they could, even if they were not among those marching in the streets. Few local white women were involved, although the sisters of the Catholic Society of Christ Our King housed demonstrators who came from elsewhere at their convent just outside of town.[47]

In August, the U.S. Court of Appeals temporarily banned further trials of protestors charged with violating the city's injunction against protests, although federal courts later ruled that the injunction was constitutional.[48] Trials later continued in the city's corporation court, and fines and jail sentences were appealed to the Virginia Supreme Court of Appeals, which ten years later suspended the jail sentences of the hundreds of protesters arrested. Nothing happened to the police.[49] It took the federal Civil Rights Act of 1964 to end discriminatory practices in hiring and public accommodations, and much of the pressure on national politicians to pass the act came as a direct result of national coverage of civil rights protests that occurred in Virginia and throughout the rest of the South.

African American women in Virginia continued their fight for the equal franchise through the eradication of the poll tax. The same year that Danville African Americans witnessed an eruption of violence unlike anything else witnessed in Virginia, Norfolk civil rights activist Evelyn Thomas Butts filed suit in federal court to challenge the state's poll tax as placing an undue constitutional burden on her right to vote and as violating the equal protection clause of the Fourteenth Amendment. A few months later, four African Americans in Northern Virginia, domestic worker Annie E. Harper, unemployed mother Gladys A. Berry, Curtis Burr, and Myrtle Burr, turned to

American Civil Liberties Union lawyers to file a similar suit against the state's board of elections. The two cases were later consolidated in the U.S. district court and heard under the style *Harper* v. *Virginia State Board of Elections*. In a brief to the court Butts's lawyer declared that Butts had "voted in the past and paid the poll tax in the past," but pointed out that "the poll tax created an economic hardship for her and had been a hardship for many years, and solely because of this hardship, although she wants to vote, she has not paid her current poll tax." Like many other civil rights activists, Butts understood the equation of civic duty with citizenship—her lawyer noted that "her sole support is her disabled husband, whose sole income is his veteran's pension."[50] Federal judges upheld the constitutionality of the poll tax in November 1964. The cases continued through the appeals process, and in March 1966, the U.S. Supreme Court struck down Virginia's poll tax. Speaking to a journalist before a dinner held in her honor the following year, an elated Butts said, "I felt like it was just one more step ahead for civil rights. It was an accomplishment for poor Negroes like myself, but also a victory for the poor white man, too. There were a number of poor whites who couldn't afford to pay the tax."[51]

By 1966, federal court decisions and laws had eradicated many of Virginia's racial inequalities. One of the last legal bastions came tumbling down in 1967, when the U.S. Supreme Court overturned state bans on interracial marriage in *Loving* v. *Virginia*. On first glance, Mildred Jeter Loving and Richard Loving were unlikely civil rights heroes. Mildred Loving, by all accounts, was the bolder of the two. Jeter, who claimed African American and Virginia Indian heritage, met Richard Loving, who was white, when she was eleven. In their rural Caroline County community of Central Point, whites and blacks mixed socially and residents were more often identified by their socioeconomic status than by their race. As a result, the isolated community did not conform to the traditional racial codes of the commonwealth. Loving was six years older than Jeter, but they became friends. Friendship turned into courtship, and when Mildred Jeter was eighteen and pregnant with Richard Loving's child, the couple went to Washington, D.C., in June 1958 to marry. They returned home and a month later they were awakened at two in the morning by local police acting on the authority of the local commonwealth's attorney, and both were taken from their home and arrested for violating Virginia's ban on interracial marriage. They received suspended sentences once they agreed not to live together in Virginia for twenty-five years. They moved to Washington, but flouted the sentence by returning to Central Point in separate cars and meeting at the homes of family members. Neither of them could bear the situation, and Mildred Loving wrote to U.S. attorney general Robert F. Kennedy asking for assistance in moving back to Virginia permanently and living with her husband. Kennedy referred her to the ACLU, which took the case.[52]

The Lovings never claimed to be civil rights activists or leaders, but their success suggested just how much power Virginia's elected officials had lost in the face of great national change. It was symbolic of the tumbling of the old regime that had put one of the country's strictest antimiscegenation laws into place during the 1920s. Indeed, just two years later, the steadily growing anti-Byrd forces achieved a powerful breakthrough when A. Linwood Holton, a Republican lawyer, was elected governor. That the new governor personally accompanied his children to their new desegregated, and predominately black, Richmond public schools is testament to how much Virginia had changed.[53]

Ultimately, the lawsuits, sit-ins, marches, strikes, and protests did not prompt the commonwealth's legislators to overturn Jim Crow laws—it took federal intervention to end the legal inequalities that oppressed thousands of African Americans. However little state legislators did to address the numerous civil rights protests across the state, the protestors made a difference. The young women who were willing to file as plaintiffs to demand integrated schooling finally secured that right, albeit in a limited way, as a result of their hard-fought actions. The women involved in the civil rights actions in Danville may have been described as helpless victims by those who told the story for them, but in standing up to the violence they faced, these women helped to reshape society. The determination of Evelyn Butts and the other plaintiffs to take their cases to the Supreme Court opened the franchise to poor white and black residents of the commonwealth. Mildred Jeter Loving may not have wanted to do anything but live with the man she loved in the community she cared for—but her letter to Kennedy sparked the litigation that allowed interracial couples to marry not only in Virginia, but also in the rest of the country as well.

Women played an important role in Virginia's civil rights movement. Familial, community, and professional ties had brought these women together before mass protest movements and these connections helped sustain momentum through the era. Local activists were critically important to the success of the civil rights movement and certainly those in club and educational networks were well aware of the groundwork being laid by national women leaders to promote equal citizenship.

The civil rights movement in Virginia helped to launch a feminist movement in the state in the second half of the twentieth century. In 1964, women in Virginia received an unexpected boon from Alexandria congressman Howard W. Smith, who vigorously opposed the Civil Rights Act. In an attempt to derail its support, Smith introduced an amendment to the act making discrimination based on gender illegal, because he believed men in Congress would never agree to the equal treatment of women. While the amendment was met with mockery in the House, it became an important component of the Civil Rights Act.[54] Women now had a federal legislative initiative to back their fight for equality.

The second-wave feminist movement radically altered the status of women in the United States as it swept through the nation in the 1960s and 1970s. Activist women and men across the country filed lawsuits and staged protests, sit-ins, marches, and other political actions to demand equality. Feminists campaigned to open avenues of power to women in a variety of ways, including providing equal employment opportunities and access to educational institutions, reproductive freedom with access to birth control and abortion, laws to protect women from domestic violence, and stronger laws to prosecute rapists. They also demanded that advertising agencies, magazines, television shows, and other popular culture forums stop portraying women in traditional or sexist ways.[55]

From 1964 to early in the 1980s, Virginia feminists formed an important part of the overall national movement. Their goals included establishing a statewide Women's Commission, passing the Equal Rights Amendment, increasing educational and political opportunities for women, establishing and maintaining abortion rights, and protecting the rights of the poor and victims of violence. Self-described feminists created statewide and grassroots networks, and they forever changed the face of Virginia. As powerful as feminists were, because they were predominantly white and middle class, they failed to connect strongly with black, working-class, or Virginia Indian activists. Moreover, not all women agreed with the feminist platforms, and some challenged feminist initiatives. As a result, women who more strongly identified either against the feminist movement or as members of racial or ethnic community networks than as feminists created their own strategies to fight for causes important to them. The combined efforts of these diverse groups of women helped further reshape Virginia society.

Eager to establish a Women's Commission, on 27 June 1964, more than 130 women representing more than thirty organizations attended a meeting sponsored by the Virginia Federation of Business and Professional Women's Clubs to discuss the issue in response to the 1963 report of the Presidential Commission on the Status of Women. Arlington delegate Kathryn Stone, joined by Delegates Dorothy McDiarmid and Marian Galland, both from the same region, spoke at the meeting. Stone noted that the commonwealth was one of only eighteen states without a commission. In the previous assembly session, she had introduced a bill to establish a state commission, but it was killed in committee. McDiarmid acknowledged that times had changed from the days when men considered a woman's measurements her most significant qualifications, but she sought to reassure "some of our Virginia gentlemen" who feared the commission "was an effort to 'elect a woman Governor tomorrow.'"[56] The women in attendance agreed that a large-scale study group would help women achieve full citizenship in Virginia.[57]

Progressive in its demand for the commission, the group's outlook was relatively conservative. The male representative from the Virginia Employment Commission asserted that technology opened up more jobs for women and that more women needed to go to college, especially to prevent a shortage of teachers. Janet Cameron, of the Virginia Polytechnic Institute and State University extension service, thought that more instruction of women was necessary, as they were the primary educators of young people in teaching better nutrition, health, and other home-initiatives. Denying that they were militant feminists, the steering committee behind the call for a commission sounded more like a Progressive Era organization than one meant to restructure society radically.[58] Ultimately, the group decided to focus on studying opportunities for women in the workforce and education and to make recommendations for changes to the governor. The group also decided to look at how better to support "women as heads of families" and women who wanted to be mothers and take jobs in the workforce at the same time.[59]

The governor established a Virginia Commission on the Status of Women in 1965 and appointed Martha Bell Conway, the secretary of the commonwealth, as its chair. The commission made numerous recommendations to the assembly, including the establishment of a permanent commission, which was finally created in 1970. Composed of a nineteen-member council, it was authorized to conduct studies and issue reports on women's economic, legal, and social status. It received meager appropriations from the legislature, and members were barred from actively lobbying for legislative action on its reports, thus hampering its effectiveness. Later called the Virginia Council on the Status of Women, it was subsumed into the Department of Social Services when its funding was cut in 1990.[60] It served mainly in an advisory capacity and issued important reports on everything from laws affecting women to violence against women.

Women engaged directly with the legislature during debate about ratification of the Equal Rights Amendment. In 1972, Congress passed the ERA and three years later, thirty-four states had ratified it. Virginia, like most other southern states, remained a holdout. Although many organizations in Virginia supported the ERA, including the AFL-CIO of Virginia, the American Business Women's Association, local YWCA branches, the Virginia State Federation of Colored Women's Clubs, and the state division of the AAUW, legislators continually held up ratification in committee.[61]

Feminists fought to bring the amendment up for a vote in the General Assembly. In 1978, Jean D. Hellmuth, chair of the ad hoc committee for Virginia ERA Ratification Council (VERARC), helped to plan pro-ERA marches at the State Capitol. In one event, sponsored by Labor for Equal Rights Now, 3,000 people marched to a rally and heard speakers from Virginia's United Mine Workers, AFL-CIO of Virginia, and Teamsters. Eleanor Smeal, president of the National Organization for Women, also spoke at the event. Kathryn Brooks of the ERA Ratification Council led a letter-writing campaign to all of the state's newspapers and legislators; two nursing homes participated by sending photocopied letters, as their residents could not write their own. Local chapters of the League of Women voters lobbied for a release of the amendment, and to stop passage of a bill calling for a statewide referendum on ERA. Many activists, including members of the Richmond League of Women Voters, and VERARC, participated in silent vigils to support ratification.[62] The councils for ratification also took out pro-ERA ads in newspapers throughout the state, paid for by the

Women stand vigil on the U.S. Capitol steps, 7 October 1970. Flora Crater, a longtime women's rights activist, editor of the *Woman Activist* newsletter, and the first president of Virginia NOW, stands between two younger women activists (Frances Kolb and Dana Kline) as they demonstrate for passage of the ERA on the steps of the U.S. Capitol. *Image by © Bettmann/CORBIS.*

AAUW and other organizations. Lynda Johnson Robb, the wife of the pro-ERA lieutenant governor Charles S. Robb, spoke personally with legislators to urge release of the amendment and to garner more support for the cause. A local newspaper intimated that she did not persuade senior members of the House of Delegates who laughed during her visit and called her "sweetie."[63]

Sometimes, lobbyists adopted tongue-in-cheek protest strategies. Once, pro-ERA forces delivered apple pies to legislators with a note that read "ERA's as American as apple pie—we want a slice."[64] When the amendment first went down to defeat in a committee meeting, NOW members and other activists delivered red and white carnations and a red impatiens plant in a white chamber pot to the attorney general and to Delegate James M. Thomson, chair of the Committee of Privileges and Elections, whom they held personally

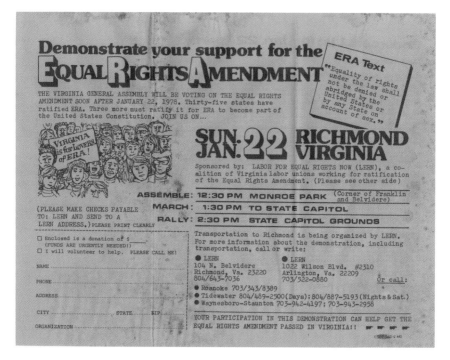

ERA Demonstration Flyer, 1978. This pro-ERA demonstration saw thousands of people rally outside Virginia's Capitol in support of the amendment and was sponsored by Labor for Equal Rights Now, a coalition of labor unions working for ERA ratification. *Courtesy of the Library of Virginia.*

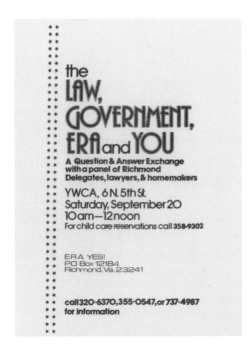

the
LAW,
GOVERNMENT,
ERA and YOU

A Question & Answer Exchange
with a panel of Richmond
Delegates, lawyers, & homemakers

YWCA, 6 N. 5th St.
Saturday, September 20
10 am—12 noon
For child care reservations call 358-9302

ERA YES!
PO Box 12184
Richmond, Va. 23241

call 320-6370, 355-0547, or 737-4987
for information

"The Law, Government, ERA and You" Flyer, 1980. ERA activists organized in such groups as Virginia-NOW, Virginia ERA Ratification Council, and League of Women Voters to co-sponsor educational events such as this one. Organizers reached out to broad constituencies to garner support for ERA's passage. *Courtesy of the Library of Virginia.*

responsible for the amendment's fate. Thomson seemed particularly nonplussed by the move, which, according to a newspaper reporter "showed the caliber of the people . . . and the methods and conduct they have stooped to."[65] Toward the end of the ERA ratification campaign, volunteers for the VERARC passed out pro-ERA cookies at a press breakfast in 1982 as the Virginia Women Attorneys Association formally endorsed the ERA.[66]

Conversely, many Virginia women fought against the ERA, using many of the same tactics as their opponents. Some of the opposition was homegrown. Taking a stand in opposition to the General Federation of Women's Clubs, the Virginia Federation of Women's Clubs spoke out against ERA. For example, Elvira B. Shaw, legislative chair of the organization, testified against the amendment before the Committee of Privileges and Elections in 1973.[67] Perhaps the most ironic grassroots effort in opposing ERA was led by Adèle Goodman Clark, the Progressive reformer who had not only advocated woman suffrage early in the twentieth century, but also kept the state's only functioning League of Women Voters chapter alive in Richmond through the 1930s and 1940s. She lobbied against ERA, claiming in a letter to the editor that among other indignities, ERA would "eradicate laws on marriage, divorce, the responsibilities of fatherhood and motherhood. It would confuse laws on the relationship of the sexes, such as age of consent, seduction and rape."[68]

One anti-ERA group was the outgrowth of a national movement. Virginia's STOP-ERA (Stop Taking Our Privileges) was led by Alyse O'Neill, who was personally picked by Phyllis Schlafly, an Illinois native who began the Eagle Forum to oppose ERA. O'Neill was assisted by General Assembly delegates James M. Thomson and Eva Fleming Scott, who in 1979 became the first woman elected to the Senate of Virginia, representing Amelia, Powhatan, and other rural Southside counties. The women and men who opposed ERA employed the arguments promulgated by the Eagle Forum. They claimed that ERA would end enforcement of spousal support, force mothers to work for wages, force women to be drafted, and create unisex dorms and bathrooms. Some also believed that ERA would fundamentally alter the Christian patriarchal household that provided women privileges based on their inherent need to be protected, and would undermine society by allowing for "homosexual 'marriage.'" ERA opponents regularly dubbed pro-ERA activists "women's libbers," and posited that they threatened the very foundations of Virginia society. Some argued that ERA would take away even more states' rights, just as federal civil rights mandates did.[69]

STOP-ERA often blamed the pro-ERA activities on feminists from outside the state. In 1980, chairwoman Geline Bowman Williams, later the mayor of Richmond, explained that her anti-ERA protest was much smaller than the 7,500 person pro-ERA march the previous day because her activists were homegrown, whereas ERA advocates had bused in people from outside Virginia. This argument rang particularly false, as STOP-ERA was an appendage of the Midwestern Schlafly's anti-ERA efforts (and indeed, Schlafly came to Virginia to testify against ERA on several occasions), but newspapers such as the *Richmond Times-Dispatch*, *Richmond News Leader*, and *Roanoke Times* took an uncritical view of these activists and strongly opposed ERA in editorials. The newspaper coverage was so misleading in some markets that Roanoke Valley Women's Coalition urged members to write pro-ERA editorials to counter the negative press.[70]

Although opponents to ERA were strong and vocal, a 1977 poll revealed that 59 percent of Virginians favored passage of the bill, and that the numbers were evenly distributed throughout the state. Perhaps because of this simple fact, or perhaps because they were tired of the constant lobbying, the Senate of Virginia finally allowed ERA to go to a floor vote in 1982. VERARC set up a toll-free telephone number, provided babysitting for mothers who wanted to lobby their legislators, and sent out information packets to legislators. Newly elected governor Charles S. Robb came out in support of ERA in his inaugural address. ERA proponents could afford to be optimistic—nine long years of lobbying, strategizing, and organizing had yielded what looked like a tie vote, which would be broken by the twenty-first vote in the Senate, that of the pro-ERA lieutenant governor Richard Davis. Because ERA had to pass with twenty-one votes, anti-ERA forces pulled a political maneuver that killed the amendment for good. Bridgewater senator Nathan Miller, an opponent of ERA,

"*Yes Virginia, there is an ERA,*" 1970s. ERA proponents fought for a decade in support of the amendment, but it languished in committee in the House of Delegates and failed to pass a floor vote in the all-male state senate. *Courtesy of the Library of Virginia.*

took a business trip the day of the vote to prevent a tie, thus allowing ERA to receive only twenty votes.[71]

ERA activists and NOW members Marianne Fowler and Patricia Winton Goodman, along with several other lobbyists, went to the Richmond airport at 7:00 AM to confront Miller in the lobby. Fowler told the Associated Press that "we asked him to stay and do what he was elected to do. He said, 'I can't do it.' . . . He looked very sheepish. He finally ducked into the men's room."[72]

The failed attempt to adopt the ERA, however, created a strong political network throughout the state. Virginia NOW used paid and volunteer workers to staff phone banks, which mobilized voters and brought in donations for future feminist projects. VERA activists established a political action committee and targeted delegate James M. Thomson as the primary obstacle to ratification of ERA. Canvassing by telephone, mail, and door-to-door in his Alexandria district, the VERA PAC helped defeat the twelve-term veteran in 1977. Supporters were jubilant and one PAC member boasted that "if we can do it to Jim Thomson, the most powerful legislator in the state, we can do it to anyone." NOW started a Political Action Committee in 1978 specifically to fund pro-ERA candidates. Aided by a $10,000 matching gift challenge from Emily McCoy and Fred McCoy of Fairfax County, NOW campaigned all over the state for more financial support. Members sent out press releases supporting pro-ERA legislators and denouncing those, such as state senator Virgil Goode who, NOW informed his constituents, planned to oppose ERA despite the fact that a survey showed that 42 percent of his constituents supported ERA while only 35 percent opposed it. Prior to the 1979 election, the NOW PAC spent more than $13,000 to support specific candidates for seats in the General Assembly, and $10,000 for lobbying expenses. Candidates from districts including Ferrum, Dumfries, Grottoes, Roanoke, Vienna, Wytheville, Norfolk, and Newport News received $200 to $500 contributions. The geographical spread of NOW's money suggests that it wanted a strong statewide presence.[73] PAC actions and Thomson's defeat upset some legislators and infuriated others but revealed that these organizing women had a level of power unanticipated by the General Assembly.[74]

NOW and VERARC were joined by the Virginia Business and Professional Women's Club PAC, which raised $5,000 in a matter of minutes to support candidates. In 1981–1982, it gave $4,000 to twenty candidates, and the following fiscal year it gave $4,400 to twenty-three candidates, all to support women's issues.[75] This kind of financial support reflected women activists' commitment to win on issues they valued. Not only willing to go after candidates they considered "bad" for women, they put their money where their sentiments lay. In 1981, Blacksburg native Joan Hardie Munford, an administrator for a chain of nursing homes and a pro-ERA candidate, won a surprising victory to the House of Delegates as the only Democrat in the race. Munford herself was shocked at her victory—she thought that the "mathematics were against me," as three male Republicans also vied for the three seats in a district that had not elected a Democrat since 1965. Munford secured the support of hundreds of pro-ERA volunteers from NOW and the Virginia Women's Political Caucus, who Munford admitted "may have had a great deal to do with the fact that I won the election." ERA supporters helped elect more legislators who were sympathetic to the amendment, but they did not succeed in getting the ERA passed.[76] Virginia NOW PAC continued to support candidates who focused on health, reproductive rights, and workplace and educational equality, and had some important victories late in the 1980s through the 1990s.[77]

Another salient issue for feminists in the 1960s and 1970s was to secure reproductive rights. Feminists may not have achieved ratification of ERA in Virginia, but throughout the 1970s and 1980s they succeeded in protecting abortion rights as decided in the 1973 Supreme Court case *Roe* v. *Wade*. Even before then, many feminists recognized the importance of securing reproductive freedom for women. In 1969, the Women's Alliance of the First Unitarian Church, for example, sponsored a statewide organizational meeting for abortion

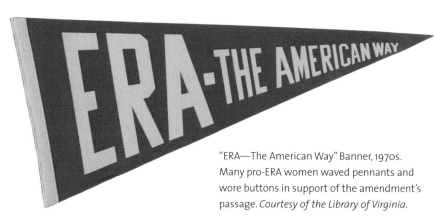

"ERA—The American Way" Banner, 1970s. Many pro-ERA women waved pennants and wore buttons in support of the amendment's passage. *Courtesy of the Library of Virginia.*

reform. Eighty people attended the Richmond meeting and formed a steering committee chaired by Betty G. Kenley. The committee adopted a resolution calling for an end to abortions "performed by non-licensed persons in non-accredited places," which often happened as a result of the illegality of abortion. The alliance resolved to lobby the General Assembly for abortion reform.[78] NOW activists in Virginia also published newsletters and advocated access to safe, legal abortions.

Following the U.S. Supreme Court's ruling that declared abortion a constitutionally protected medical procedure, antiabortion women became more vocal and active. Some members of the General Assembly tried to stall the rewriting of Virginia's laws to comply with the decision; others, such as Eva Fleming Scott, a vocal opponent of ERA, wanted to ignore the court's decision and retain Virginia's law, which allowed abortion only in the cases of rape, deformity of the fetus, or to save the life of the mother. Ultimately, the assembly complied with the ruling, but wrote in serious restrictions for abortion after the first trimester of pregnancy.[79]

Others were not content to leave the issue to the courts and legislators. Jerry Falwell, pastor of Thomas Road Baptist Church, in Lynchburg, rose to prominence nationally because of his stand on abortion, crystallized when he helped to launch the "Moral Majority" movement. While male ministers often took vocal leadership positions in the antiabortion debate, women participated at the grassroots level in attempting to stop abortions. In 1967, antiabortion activists, including Geline Bowman Williams, organized the country's first statewide organization advocating the right to life, and several years later members of the Virginia Society for Human Life helped establish the National Right to Life Committee. During the mid-1970s, activists began to block the path to clinics that provided reproductive health services, including abortion. In Fairfax County, dozens of women and men regularly picketed in front of the Northern Virginia Women's Medical Center, which performed first trimester abortions. Contending that all children have a right to life, protesters carried graphic signs, passed out leaflets, and confronted clinic clients, for which many protestors were arrested and faced fines and jail time. Jean Marshall Clarke, state coordinator for NOW, acknowledged in 1977 that antiabortion forces were "getting stronger and more sophisticated" and that the organization was "definitely worried about it" as a threat to women's autonomy.[80]

Women lobbied the General Assembly and the Virginia State Board of Health to restrict funding for abortions for those who received Medicaid. Geline Williams, a board member of the National Right to Life Committee, argued in 1977 that elimination of the funding would not automatically reduce poor women to back-alley abortions.[81] Others showed up in force to attend a 1980 hearing by the State Board of Health when it considered liberalizing Medicaid restrictions on abortion. These women were united in the belief that abortion violated the sanctity of life. Maureen Whalen, a housewife from Chesapeake, called abortion "abhorrent" and an act that could bring on "God's wrath." Lois S. Hurdle, who had traveled from Virginia Beach, equated abortion with the genocide committed by the Nazis. For these women, and thousands like them, abortion was a moral issue on which there was no middle ground. Their efforts paid off, and the State Health Board recommended facilitation of Medicaid-assisted abortions, but only in the case of rape or incest. The governor rejected even those recommendations.[82] Late in the 1980s, when abortion rights came under assault, feminists again fought to retain their rights to make their own reproductive choices in the face of fierce opposition.

During the 1960s and 1970s, women strove to gain access to education and jobs. As with black civil rights in Virginia, many of the gains came through legal action, although grassroots activist strategies galvanized the public and revealed the willingness of women to go to great lengths for change. Perhaps one of the greatest signifiers of change came in 1970, when the University of Virginia opened its doors to the regular enrollment of women as undergraduates in the College of Arts and Sciences, though not without a battle. Since 1920 white women had been able to attend certain graduate and professional programs at the university, but during the 1960s pressure to admit women on an equal basis gained strength. In 1967, the board of visitors authorized a committee to explore the admission of women, which upset many male students who protested and threatened to refuse financial support as alumni if the university went coeducational. Some students feared that the school "would lose the traditions it values most highly" and that women "would undermine the honor system," one of the campus's most treasured institutions. On 15 February 1969, the board voted "that the restrictions heretofore placed on the admission of women . . . are hereby removed" and that women should be admitted for the 1970–1971 academic year. Four women did not want to wait an additional year, and in 1969, Virginia

Anne Scott, Nancy L. Anderson, Nancy Jaffe, and Jo Ann Kirstein approached the American Civil Liberties Union about filing lawsuits after being denied admission to the University of Virginia on account of their gender. The federal judge in the case ordered that they be admitted immediately and in February 1970, the district court upheld the constitutionality of the university's timeline for full enrollment of women. In 1970, 450 women entered the university, and in 1974, women comprised 42 percent of that year's entering class.[83]

In 1970, the Women's Rights Organization of Richmond, cofounded by feminist Zelda Kingoff Nordlinger, challenged the sex-segregated Soup Bar at Thalhimers department store and sex-segregated want ads in the city's newspapers. Although these two institutions seem disparate, they reflected the persistence of gendered spaces and so became targets of the group. A newspaper reported the sit-in at the Soup Bar on "male-only day," as five women sat down and placed their orders. A photograph of the event reflected the shock on one man's face as Beverly Pitts prepared to take a bite of her hamburger, while another man "threw down a menu, and walking out, shouted 'There goes the last place to eat in town!'"[84] Nordlinger took no chances that her group's action would be ignored. She had contacted the local ACLU chapter, which stood ready to help her file a lawsuit if necessary. In a followup to the action, Nordlinger said that she was requesting Thalhimers' management to remove the "Men Only" sign from the window, and that she would inform the ACLU if the sign remained. "In the meantime," she wrote, "I plan to have lunch again at the Soup Bar in the near future."[85]

The Thalhimers action highlighted persistent discrimination in facilities, but the protest against want ads reflected a serious economic problem for women. Late in 1970, the Women's Rights Organization planned a demonstration outside of the Richmond Newspaper offices. After contacting the ACLU and press outlets, as well as the police (to assure the force that women would be protesting peacefully), Nordlinger and another protester showed up outside of the offices. Determined to "desexigrate" the want ads, Nordlinger and other women began filing lawsuits through the Equal Employment Opportunity Commission. By 1974, Nordlinger had filed twenty-six suits charging discrimination, most of which were settled through arbitration.[86] A ruling by the U.S. Supreme Court in 1973 upheld the elimination of sex-specific want ads, so once again it took federal action to change social practices in Virginia.

Women Take Last Fort

IT'S ALL GONE----The last all-male sanctuary in Richmond fell last week before the onslaught of the Women's Liberation Movement. Beverly Pitts takes the first bite ever by a woman on a "male-only-day" in Thalhimers' Soup Bar, as Zelda Nordlinger prepares to join her. An oldtime male raises his napkin in shock. Five of ladies cited the Civil Rights Act and were served. When asked if this marked a change in policy, manager Saiad Ameen said: "I can't answer that, but it probably will be. I think the ladies, however, will be more comfortable in our facilities on the fourth floor." Another male customer threw down a menu, and walking out shouted, "There goes the last place to eat in town!"

"Women Take Last Fort," 1970. Women in Richmond fought gender discrimination at Thalhimers department store, when Zelda Nordlinger, Beverly Pitts, and three others sat down to dine at the Soup Bar on a "male-only-day." Some of the male customers were dismayed when the staff served the women. *Courtesy of the Library of Virginia.*

Women in Virginia also fought for equality in the workforce. In 1971, for example, the Women's Rights Organization complained about job and pay discrimination in municipal jobs to Richmond's Human Relations Commission. A year later, twenty speakers from a variety of organizations including the League of Women Voters and the Jaycees spoke before the city council in favor of an equal employment opportunity provision for the city's charter, which the council agreed to consider.[87] Other women filed lawsuits to end discriminatory practices. With the help of the ACLU, Alice C. Cook, of Virginia Beach, sued the U.S. Navy for discrimination. A married lieutenant commander in the Navy Nurse Corps, she became pregnant in 1966. She had been in service since the 1950s and had excellent ratings. When she learned she was pregnant, she was told to resign her commission immediately and was not advised of the waivers that allowed pregnant women to remain on duty, or of the severance pay owed to her. Cook resigned, but in 1968 appealed to the U.S. comptroller general to correct her pay status and severance pay. Cook later recalled that "civil rights was a big thing, especially for women. . . . I knew when I got out of the Navy that they were wrong to dismiss me." When her appeal was denied, she filed a lawsuit in 1973 with the U.S. district court, and in 1978 reached a settlement with the Navy to receive her retirement. Cook's lawsuit, as well as others filed during this period, led the Navy to stop discharging pregnant women and begin providing maternity care by 1975.[88]

Zelda Nordlinger turned to the EEOC in her case against Southwest General Life Insurance Company, which refused her a job as an agent because she was a woman. In the settlement brokered by the EEOC, Southwest General refused to admit violating Title VII of the Civil Rights Act, which prohibited employment discrimination, but did pay her $425.38, the wages plus interest she claimed she lost the day she was refused an interview. The company agreed to work through the Virginia State Employment Services to hire women.[89] Thus, some Virginia women were willing to use any available resource to gain equal access to vocational opportunities.

Although feminist organizations fought for equality for all Virginia women and made some gains during the 1960s and 1970s, their efforts often did not include many women beyond middle-class, educated white women. Many perceived feminist groups to be irrelevant in the larger scheme of economic dislocation and lack of advancement faced by the poor in Virginia, black and white. This fact did not go unnoticed and some feminists believed that white women's focus on reproductive rights alienated black women and contributed to the divide between them. For example, Zelda Nordlinger asked a journalist to write about the "controversy" over abortion, noting that "for many years, the Black women have been accused of being immoral as regards illicit sex." She wrote that "they are having to live down that reputation. And here we are . . . middle-class White women talking about sexual freedom!" She acknowledged that "furthermore, the Black woman has some idea that abortion-on-demand will somehow bring about 'genocide' of the Black race because doctors will willingly perform sterilization at the same time they give an abortion."[90] Perhaps one of the problems was with the way in which NOW addressed what it perceived as issues important to women of color, making assumptions without directly engaging with black women.

No matter what the issue, the problem remained constant in organizations like NOW. In 1973, the NOW chapter of Richmond admitted that it had no black members, although Willie Dell, the first black woman city council member, attended a meeting to discuss women's "tokenism" on appointed boards.[91] This issue with NOW's predominantly white membership continued through the 1980s, and leaders seemed stymied in their attempts to reach out to black women. In Arlington NOW's 1990 annual report, for example, Marian Patey wrote, "The diversity of participation in the chapter is sadly lacking." She noted that when she tried to discuss specific issues she thought "women of color" faced, she felt "an undercurrent of apathy." She ended her missive to national headquarters with a plea: "We need help!"[92]

Historians have long noted the disconnect between women's activist organizations in the 1970s.[93] As a representative from the all-black Women for Political Action explained in 1971 at a statewide meeting in Norfolk: "Black women have problems that are different from yours."[94] Representing the organization at the Virginia Commission on the Status of Women meeting that same year, Norfolk civil rights activist Vivian Carter Mason highlighted specific problems faced by African American women—persistent racism and sexism in hiring practices in both public and private industry.[95]

More research is necessary to uncover the activities of black activist women in the 1970s and early in the 1980s, but preliminary exploration suggests that African American women focused many of their efforts on organizing against social injustice, including poverty and political dislocation. LaVerne Byrd Smith, a professor at Virginia Union University, served as vice president of the Virginia Council on Human Relations and as president of the Richmond Council on Human Relations late in the 1960s. During her tenure with the Richmond council, she oversaw committees that focused on legal, urban planning, and housing issues. Action teams were led by women like Hilda Warden, one of Richmond's first black social workers. Warden headed the civil concerns team, which often met five to six times per week and focused on fixing problems in the city jail. Ruby Walker headed the law and justice team, which focused its efforts on police brutality. Peace activist Marii K. Hasegawa ran the housing team, which created the Housing Opportunities Made Equal (HOME) program. Smith believed that the council's work was primarily responsible for averting any major civil rights unrest in the city during that time, and she credits the group with helping to implement programs that continued into the twenty-first century, including HOME and the Offender Aid and Restoration program.[96]

Norfolk resident Evelyn Butts, whose lawsuit led to the invalidation of Virginia's poll tax, became a neighborhood organizer. A leader in the Citizens Advisory Commission, she was appointed to the Norfolk Redevelopment and Housing Authority. Butts herself was a resident of a redevelopment district, and her proponents on the city council believed she could best relate the needs of the residents in those districts. As a member of the board, she accused the director of not making an effort to hire women and African Americans. She also used her clout to relocate a Department of Motor Vehicles office away from an area that residents wanted to reserve for low-income housing by reminding the region's legislators of the support given to them by the residents at the previous election. Long considered a political powerhouse who could command black votes through her group, Concerned Citizens for Political Education, she unsuccessfully ran for city council three times. In 1982, the governor appointed her to the State Board of Housing and Community Development.[97] Butts's experience highlights how black women remained politically active in the 1970s and 1980s, helping their own communities and fighting for equal opportunities for all.

Other black and white women continued the path taken by such earlier activists as Lucy Randolph Mason and Brownie Lee Jones, focusing their efforts on helping the poor and working class of the commonwealth. Women worked for change through Virginia Action, a social justice organization that advocated tenant, welfare, and blue-collar worker rights. Alma Barlow co-chaired its sponsoring committee as a representative from the Richmond Tenants Organization. In 1981, she worked with residents of nine housing projects to fight budget cuts that came from the federal government. She helped to create Virginia Action, she said, because "the real issue, even more important than the particular problems of tenants, or neighborhood groups, or the budget cuts, is one of power. The rich white men that run our state have no time to listen to poor people or working people, but instead believe that their money and power can make all the decisions that affect *our* lives."[98] Yvonne Myles, representative from the Norfolk Tenants Council, joined Barlow in organizing Virginia Action. Darlene Weaver became involved after having worked with an organization in southwestern Virginia that aimed to open up school board meetings to the public, so that board members could be held accountable for their decisions.[99]

In 1980, women were at the forefront in establishing a Virginia chapter of the Brown Lung Association, which had emerged during the 1970s from advocacy efforts in North Carolina for textile mill workers who had contracted the disease byssinosis. At a 1981 hearing before the House of Delegates' Committee on Labor and Commerce, mill workers and association members testified about the effects of brown lung disease and the difficulties they faced in filing worker compensation claims. According to staff organizer Elizabeth Scott, many mill-town doctors refused to diagnose the disease and mill owners often forced workers to sign away their rights to compensation. Alice Adkins, a relative of Dan River Mills workers, told the committee that many employees signed waivers because they did not understand what they were doing as a result of their hearing loss from working in the weaving rooms. She also claimed that people did not know what the papers were, but were told they had to sign in order to keep their jobs. Adkins pointed out that "there are plenty of people who are so desperate for a job that they'll sign almost anything." The General Assembly established a joint subcommittee to study the compensation law related to brown lung disease, which pleased seventy-five-year-old vice president Annie Allen, who noted, "We are not asking to be babied, because we are men and women, but we do want justice." In 1982, the assembly increased the amount of time in which textile employees could file a claim from five years to seven.[100]

It was not just Virginia's African American and working-class women activists who organized politically to answer the needs of their communities. Late in the 1960s, American Indians across the country began to challenge lack of tribal autonomy on reservation lands, racism in society, poverty, and high unemployment rates. The American Indian Movement (AIM) also attempted to foster relations between all tribes and nations in North America and South America in order to promote solidarity and gain strength to negotiate with governments in the region. In 1972, activists marched on Washington and took over the Bureau of Indian Affairs. They demanded restoration of land taken by the federal government, the power to make treaties with the government, the abolishment of state government intrusion in reservation affairs, and the abolishment of the BIA in favor of a new Office of Federal Indian Relations and Community Reconstruction.[101] As a result of AIM, many local tribes and nations began fighting for autonomy and recognition in their own states.

Virginia Indians organized politically to gain official tribal recognition early in the 1980s, successfully gaining autonomy and rights, as well as cultural authority. Women were intrinsic to all of these efforts, which continue into the twenty-first century. Women gained increased prominence in the Monacan nation because they spearheaded the movement for state recognition that ended successfully in 1989. In fact, because of their role in the effort, women continue to take an important role in the tribal government. In 1996, Monacan women formed a "Women's Circle" to bring together the community through a formal network of organizations.[102] Women's efforts did not go unrecognized in other tribes, either. In 1996, the Nansemond elected five women to the seven-member tribal council, and in 1997, Nokomis Fortune Lemons became chief of a faction of the Rappahannock. The following year, the state-recognized Rappahannock tribe elected G. Anne Nelson Richardson its chief. Her work on a study of the historical predecessors of modern tribes in Virginia had helped the Rappahannock achieve state recognition in 1983. One researcher noted that some Virginia Indian women believed that the growing prominence of women in tribal affairs reflected a growing recognition of tribal traditions and history.[103]

Virginia Indian women continued to work for rights beyond simple recognition, too. In 1997, Mary "Laughing Dove" Belvin Wade, Monacan representative on the Virginia Council on Indians, successfully lobbied for a law providing free corrections of twentieth-century birth certificates listing Indians as Negroes. Women of other tribes worked to create educational programs, claiming their heritage at the same time they shared it proudly with others. In 1995, Phyllis Hicks became the director of the Monacan Museum, which is housed in the three buildings of the Indian Schools that she and her mother attended. She helped to oversee the conversion to a museum that houses historical artifacts and a cultural center to tell the story of the Monacan people. Marie D. Fortune taught children tribal history and crafts at the Rappahannock Tribal Center.[104] Shirley "Little Dove" Custalow-McGowan, a Mattaponi, created a living history program that she took to schools and organizations in the 1990s. She wore traditional clothing and taught the history, cooking methods, and traditions of her people to "teach the importance of honoring and respecting yourself, other people, and the natural environment; values that have been passed down from her ancestors."[105] These women did not call themselves feminists, but they employed women's networks and took on roles as storytellers and community advocates, which promoted not only the history of their tribes and nation, but also their own stature as experts in cultural and historic knowledge of their people.

Beginning in the 1970s, Virginia witnessed new levels of activism on the part of women who wanted to further equality in the state, from grassroots actions to lobbying and running for office. So how much had actually changed? Women early in the 1980s could view the commonwealth with ambivalence. Want ads were no longer segregated, and more women had appointments on state boards and committees than in the past. The University of Virginia was now open to women, but Virginia Military Institute, another publicly funded university, was not. A survey by the Committee on the Status of Women identified major unresolved issues in 1984: equal pay, affordable and available child care, equal educational opportunities, freedom of reproductive choice, an end to the glass ceiling, and an increase in the number of women in government.[106] Some women had achieved high levels of success, particularly in the legal profession; in 1982, for example, George Washington University graduate Barbara Keenan was appointed the first female judge of Virginia's Circuit Court, having previously served as assistant commonwealth's attorney and then as a judge of the General District Court in Fairfax County. In 1985, Elizabeth Bermingham Lacy became the first woman judge on the three-member State Corporation Commission, and in 1989 became the first female justice on the Supreme Court of Virginia. That same year, Rebecca Beach Smith became the first female judge on the federal bench in the commonwealth. Throughout the decade, increasing numbers of women attended law schools, and during the mid-1980s women had begun to compose more than one-third of law school classes at the University of Virginia.[107]

Active as lobbyists, women formed political action committees to elect politicians aligned with their concerns, although a 1981 *Washington Post* article highlighted that the General Assembly remained a bastion of male privilege. Of 140 members, only nine were women, and they and about two dozen other women who worked or lobbied there described numerous obstacles to their ability to work effectively. The article reported that "most of the women agreed there is a heavy sexual undercurrent in their dealings with the male-dominated political and bureaucratic establishment here." This affected not only their own work, but often the legislative agenda. Delegate Elise Brookfield Heinz, representing Arlington County and Alexandria City, informed reporters that the previous week one legislator pinched her cheek and addressed her in a subcommittee meeting as "you little devil." The problem was not just one of personal inconvenience, argued Heinz, since male legislators considering important legislation on such issues as marital property rights, divorce, sexual assault, and sterilization often "snicker, giggle, and poke fun at it like a bunch of adolescents." Confronted with accounts of his behavior that included kissing lobbyist Barbara Pratt on the cheek and making lewd comments to her about getting turned on in elevators, the majority leader of the House of Delegates admitted to the reporters that there was a certain group of men who did not view women as equals, but claimed that he was not one of them and that perhaps his attempts at humor were misunderstood. Jean Marshall Clarke, former state coordinator for NOW, described the scene at the Capitol as being like "one big fraternity party or locker room."[108]

The *Washington Post* reported on an event in 1984, in which about 400 male General Assembly members, lobbyists, and government officials participated in a "stag luncheon" to roast the speaker of the House of Delegates. Entertainment included dancers in pasties and G-strings. The event attracted attention after one of its participants used crude descriptions of female anatomy that were repeated in news outlets. Picketers showed up at the luncheon, but a Richmond organizer saw nothing wrong with the event itself or with failing to invite women legislators to the event.[109] Perhaps the legislators were reacting to the fact that times were, in fact, changing. This may have been their proverbial shot across the bow—while they knew women were gaining more of a voice in politics the men still controlled the legislature.

It would take more than the lobbying and grassroots efforts of women to change Virginia society in the 1970s and 1980s. Many women activists continued to fight to protect reproductive rights and secure equal legal, educational, and employment opportunities late in the 1980s and beyond. While women had tried to change legislation to help victims of sexual assault in domestic violence beginning in the 1970s, they did not make significant gains until late in the 1980s and in the 1990s. Some women focused their efforts on securing equal rights for the gay community, more political representation, and equality in education throughout the late 1980s and beyond. They were successful in several of these efforts, but at the end of the twentieth century many issues were still unaddressed or unresolved.

Although feminists secured a national victory with *Roe* v. *Wade*, the grassroots strategies and lobbying efforts of antiabortion advocates stirred women to action late in the 1980s and in the 1990s. Virginia's NOW chapter used its PAC money to support pro-choice candidates.[110] Throughout the decade, Virginia NOW also joined other pro-choice groups to protect abortion rights. For many years, its efforts helped prevent passage of a parental notification law that would have affected underage girls seeking an abortion. Locally, many chapters held training sessions and joined forces to provide escort protection for women entering clinics that performed abortions, as one of the strategies of antiabortion activists was to block entry to the clinics and intimidate those attempting to enter. Many chapters held pro-choice rallies and vigils, marched in Washington, and participated in phone banks and lobby days to protect women's right to choose.[111]

Pro-choice activists lost the fight in the General Assembly against a parental notification, or in their words, "teen endangerment" law in 1997, but they continued to battle for reproductive rights. In the twenty-first century, NOW organizers and other supporters of choice fought against bans on partial-birth and second-trimester abortions, as well as other laws designed to restrict access to late-term abortions. As a 2003 press release noted, "Virginia NOW is proud to continue to work for women's rights to legal and safe abortion. . . . More anti-choice bills than ever have been introduced in the Virginia legislature. So our struggle is important—NOW more than ever."[112]

Women continued to fight for equal educational and employment in the commonwealth in this period. Elizabeth Howze filed a lawsuit in 1992 against Virginia Polytechnic Institute and State University after being denied tenure based on her lack of "collegiality." The lack of collegiality charge stemmed from her filing a lawsuit the previous year against the university for multiple counts of sex discrimination. The university ultimately granted Howze tenure and a salary commensurate with her rank while the case was pending, but she left the university shortly thereafter.[113] In another significant settlement, fifty-two women received almost $604,000 in back pay from Fairfax Hospital, which had paid women in management positions lower salaries than men. This case was settled by the U.S. Labor Department in 1993, and it had a direct impact on the forty-four women still employed at the hospital in those positions.[114]

Women made significant gains in the workforce in the last decade of the twentieth century, but those gains belied some uncomfortable truths. In 2000, 60 percent of women in Virginia were employed and made up 52 percent of the state's workforce. A 2003 study, however, showed that of 199 directors on the boards of the Fortune 500 companies headquartered in Virginia, only 25 (12.6 percent) were women. Four of the eighteen companies, Capital One, General Dynamics Corporation, NVR Incorporated, and Performance Food Group Company, did not have any women on their boards. Circuit City Stores boasted the highest number, with four women sitting on its ten-member board of directors.[115]

Virginia women also made progress securing formal positions of leadership in their churches during second half of the twentieth century. Although Virginia women, like other women across the country, had always been active in their religious institutions to promote charitable and mission causes, it was not until the 1960s and 1970s that women could secure ordination in many denominations. Previously, women's religious work was couched in traditional concepts of appropriate behavior. Mary Elizabeth "Toddy" Collins, for example, was a native of England who in 1906 arrived as a missionary in Wise County, where she spent the next forty years evangelizing and providing for the needs of the coal mining community of Roda. In 1910, Elizabeth James Morris Downes became superintendent of the Eastern Shore chapters of the Woman's Missionary Union of the Southern Baptist Convention, and successfully steered the WMU of Virginia through the Great Depression as its president. Elizabeth Coles Bouey worked as a missionary with her husband in Liberia during the 1920s, and after returning home to Richmond founded the National Association of Ministers' Wives, of which she served as president from 1939 to 1957.[116]

In the mid-1960s, however, two women in Virginia made national history by becoming the first to be ordained in their denominations. Addie Davis, a native of Covington, was the first woman ordained into the Southern Baptist Convention in 1964. Throughout her long career she served Baptist churches in Vermont and Rhode Island, but in Virginia she could not find a Baptist church that would accept her and she pastored an ecumenical church instead. In 1965, the Presbyterian Church in the U.S. ordained Rachel Henderlite, a professor at the Presbyterian School of Christian Education (later Union Presbyterian Seminary), at All Souls Presbyterian Church, in Richmond, before an integrated audience.[117]

These women paved the way for hundreds more who sought careers in the ministry, and women in Virginia continue to stand at the forefront of religious change. In 1984, Richmond resident and minister Leontine Turpeau Current Kelly became the first African American woman elected a bishop by the United Methodist Church. In 1987, Isabel Wood Rogers, a professor at the Presbyterian School of Christian Education, in Richmond, became the moderator of the Presbyterian Church (U.S.A.), the highest-elected office in the denomination. Rabbi Amy M. Schwartzman became the senior rabbi in 1998 at Temple Rodef Shalom, in Falls Church. With a congregation of 1,400 at the time, she claimed the title of serving the largest congregation with a senior female rabbi in the country. Several years later, Carol Joy Gallagher became one of only nine female Episcopal bishops—and the first American Indian woman bishop—in the country when she accepted a call from the Diocese of Southern Virginia in 2002.[118]

Women gained more access to political power in the commonwealth during this period. Joining the few women already serving in the General Assembly, in 1983 Norfolk Democrat Yvonne Bond Miller became the first African American woman elected to the House of Delegates, and then in 1987 became the first elected to the Senate. By the second half of the twentieth century, women began to set their sights on statewide and national offices. Louise Oftedal Wenzel ran as

Inauguration of L. Douglas Wilder, Donald Beyer, and Mary Sue Terry, 13 January 1990. Mary Sue Terry on the day she was sworn in as Virginia's attorney general. Terry represented Henry, Patrick, and Pittsylvania Counties and Martinsville in the House of Delegates from 1978 to 1985. In 1985, when she was elected attorney general, she became the first woman in Virginia and only the second in the country to serve in this position. She ran successfully for reelection in 1989, garnering more than one million votes. In 1993, she resigned from her position and ran unsuccessfully for governor. *Courtesy of the Library of Virginia.*

an Independent against the indomitable Harry F. Byrd Sr., albeit unsuccessfully, for his United States Senate seat in 1958. Although also unsuccessful, in 1961 Republican Hazel Kathleen Doss Barger was the first woman in forty years to be nominated by one of the two large parties for a major state office, that of lieutenant governor. These women foreshadowed the success of others who succeeded in gaining statewide or national office. Having served in the House of Delegates for nearly a decade, Martinsville native Mary Sue Terry became the first woman to win statewide office when she was elected Virginia's attorney general in 1985. Reelected in 1989, she resigned in 1993 to run for governor, although she lost following a lackluster campaign. Democrat Leslie Larkin Byrne was the first congresswoman elected from Virginia and represented the Eleventh District in Northern Virginia from 1993 to 1995. Republican Jo Ann Davis represented eastern Virginia's First Congressional District from 2001 to 2007 and Republican Thelma Drake represented the Norfolk area's Second Congressional District from 2005 to 2009.[119] These individual successes were impressive, but women continued to be underrepresented in local, statewide, and national offices.

One of the last educational barriers for women fell in Virginia during this era, ending Virginia Military Institute's status as the last publicly funded single-sex university in the country. When the Peninsula Chapter of the New University Conference addressed the fledgling Virginia Commission on the Status of Women in 1971, proposing to make the Virginia Military Institute a coeducational liberal arts college, reporter Betty Parker Ashton called the comments "startling."[120] By 1990, Virginia NOW had a VMI Committee in support of opening up the university.[121] It took an investigation by the U.S. Department of Justice and a subsequent federal lawsuit against the Commonwealth to end gender discrimination at VMI. In *United States* v. *Virginia*, the U.S. Supreme Court decided against the state in 1996, although subsequent legal maneuverings and stalling delayed the first official mixed-gender class matriculation until 1997.[122]

Following a long struggle, domestic violence and sexual assault laws were transformed to protect more victims. Late in the 1970s, Virginia NOW reported that Virginia was fifteenth in the country and third in the South for reported rapes. Because of the archaic laws in the state, however, some local commonwealth's attorneys treated the victims as willing participants in a sexual act. Women's organizations, including the League of Women Voters, NOW, and the Virginia Women's Political Caucus lobbied for a more-defined sexual assault bill that would protect the victim, which included broader definitions of sexual assault and marital rape. They fought together with other women's activists to include provisions in a sexual assault reform bill that would also allow for the protection of a woman's identity and prosecution without evidence of resistance.[123] Women won some early victories, as in 1981 when the General Assembly passed provisions that prohibited the sexual history of the victim from being introduced as evidence in a rape trial, and added sexual battery

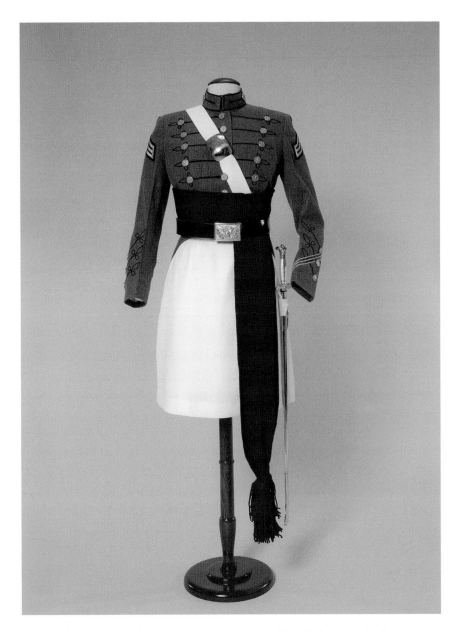

Cadet uniform, Virginia Military Institute, ca. 2004. In 1996 the U.S. Supreme Court determined that VMI must admit women if it continued to accept public funding. The first female students matriculated the following year. *Courtesy of the Virginia Military Institute; photograph courtesy of the Library of Virginia.*

when the perpetrator used a weapon, as well as aggravated sexual battery for a child. The law also allowed for charges to be filed without physical evidence of assault. The law still allowed a victim's sexual history to be admissible to show prior sexual acts with the defendant, however, and it did not deal with the issue of marital rape.[124]

As late as 2003, marital rape could be prosecuted only if the couple were separated or if physical violence had occurred during the act. The problem with this limited definition of marital rape was highlighted in a tragic event that occurred in Manassas in 1993. After suffering years of physical abuse, including rape, twenty-four-year-old Lorena Bobbitt cut off her husband's penis as he slept. This became the subject of late-night talk show jokes and fodder for the tabloids nationwide, but it was no laughing matter. A neighbor describing the situation to a reporter recalled that Bobbitt had moved out, but returned because her husband promised to stop hitting her, a situation familiar to many abused partners. Ultimately, his actions precipitated her violent reaction that night, and she was charged with malicious wounding, a felony. Not originally charged with a crime, her husband was later tried for marital sexual assault and acquitted by a jury concerned about the lack of physical evidence. Following the verdict, women's organizations feared that it would discourage other women in similar situations from seeking justice.[125]

Lorena Bobbitt's trial took place in January 1994, six months after a law had taken effect in Virginia that allowed evidence of abuse to be admissible in court proceedings, although the psychological effects of the abuse were not. After hearing testimony from colleagues and neighbors about the violence Bobbitt experienced at the hands of her husband and from a psychiatrist who testified to her mental state, a jury declared Lorena Bobbitt not guilty by reason of insanity. An anonymous juror told *the Washington Post* that "we felt she'd been really abused, a victim. . . . Unfortunately, over a period of time, most of us would be able to react [differently]. . . . We didn't feel she was strong enough. She had been stripped of everything at that point."[126]

In Virginia there remained a great need for domestic violence shelters and awareness campaigns about sexual assault and relational violence. Throughout the last quarter of the twentieth century, local YWCAs provided and staffed battered women's shelters, NOW sponsored seminars on how to prevent and deal with sexual harassment and domestic violence, and Virginia sororities, clubs, and universities sponsored the Clothesline Project, which began as a program to help victims cope with sexual assault and domestic violence, and in the twenty-first century continues to be a fixture on college campuses to raise awareness about the issue.[127] In 1991, Northern Virginia NOW joined with the Dulles Area NOW and other women's organizations to save the Women's Shelter and Victim Assistance Network when Fairfax County tried to save money by drastically cutting space and staff. The organizations leafleted their communities, held petition drives, sent letters to and visited county supervisors, and attended budget meetings wearing support stickers. These efforts restored 100 percent of the funding.[128]

College groups, women's clubs, and church organizations sponsored shelters throughout the state, holding clothing and toy drives for residents, and university students produced *The Vagina Monologues*, a play written by Eve Ensler to address issues of rape, empowerment, and engagement in women's issues and designed to assist localities in fund-raising for domestic violence and rape assistance shelters and networks.[129] In 2003, Longwood University's Women Involved in Learning and Leadership (WILL) produced and directed the play. During intermission the students sold chocolate vagina-shaped lollipops, and their efforts netted thousands of dollars for Madeline's House, the only domestic violence shelter that served several large rural Southside counties.[130] University student organizations, Women's Studies departments, and Health Centers throughout the state continue to sponsor Take Back the Night events to promote awareness of sexual assault and relational violence on their campuses.[131]

Women's efforts on behalf of victim's rights often resulted in legislation protecting women, but others who historically have been victimized by society and the government have only become visible in the last quarter century as they fight for equality and build their own networks of support. Virginia NOW members discussed the issue of lesbianism, but as tangential to larger problems with ERA, reproductive rights, and violence against women. For lesbians living in the conservative commonwealth, however, the problems they faced were neither trivial nor easily solvable.

In the 1970s and 1980s, much of lesbians' activist strategies focused on creating community. For example, Babe's, in Richmond's Carytown neighborhood, not only began providing a gathering place for lesbians in the

1970s, but also sponsored Iris, the first women's rugby team in the area. The Richmond Lesbian Feminist organization began in 1975, and members marched alongside NOW and the League of Women Voters for ERA ratification, held women's music and book festivals, and early in the 1980s, sponsored weekend events with music, workshops, contests, and even a prom.[132] In Charlottesville, lesbians were welcomed at the Downtown Ladies Club, whose founder, Joan Schatzman, called herself the "contact dyke" in the rolodex at the University of Virginia's Women's Center. A successful businesswoman, Schatzman owned a Charlottesville restaurant during the 1980s and JCS Construction, an all-women construction firm in the 1990s.[133] These efforts by women were important, not just to build community, but also to claim space in a society where many people considered homosexuality deviant behavior.[134]

In the last decade of the twentieth century, lesbian activists began to fight for their rights as mothers and citizens in the face of a hostile state government. Virginia's designation of lesbian mothers as deviant was particularly evident in 1993, when Sharon Lynne Bottoms lost custody of her son to her own mother, who filed for sole custody to take the child away from Sharon Bottoms and her live-in partner April Wade, with whom she had a committed relationship. A Henrico County juvenile court judge deemed Sharon Bottoms an "unfit parent" because of her sexuality, and propelled Bottoms into a role as a gay rights activist, something she did reluctantly. In an interview with *Time* magazine, she challenged the decision: "I'm a good mother. I'm a good person. I don't understand why, if you're gay or lesbian, you don't have the same rights as anyone else."[135] Lesbian Women of Color co-sponsored a fund-raiser with other lesbian organizations for Bottoms's appeal, which had a decidedly ambivalent ending.[136] The Virginia Court of Appeals ruled in 1994 that custody should be returned to Sharon Bottoms because her sexuality did not determine her fitness as a parent. Virginia's Supreme Court overturned the ruling in 1995, and in 1996, the juvenile court judge again denied custody to Sharon Bottoms, in part because she cooperated with producers of a television movie about the case, and because of her spotty job history. Bottoms lost custody of her son, but was allowed visitation on the condition that her partner not be present during visits.[137]

Five years later, Arlington resident Linda Kaufman learned of her unequal citizenship when she was approved to adopt a child through Washington, D.C., welfare services, but was held up by Virginia's Department of Social Services for two years. An Episcopal priest, Kaufman and her partner had already adopted one son. She filed a suit with the assistance of the Lambda Legal Defense Fund because she claimed that state officials called her home an "inappropriate placement," citing a more-than-200-year-old sodomy law that had not been removed from the books. In a 2003 column in the *Washington Post*, Kaufman referred to the pending case in the U.S. Supreme Court that later overturned Texas's sodomy law. As she said, "looking back, I now vaguely recall hearing about efforts to strike down Virginia's sodomy law a few years ago. I didn't pay attention and forgot all about it because it didn't have anything to do with me. . . . Now I know this is about basic freedoms, privacy and fairness. It's about me and my family."[138] Ultimately, Kaufman won her case, and she resided with her partner Liane Rozzell and her two adopted sons in Arlington.[139]

While some lesbian couples have navigated the prejudice of Virginia society to make families and gain recognition of their status as couples in their communities, the fight is far from over in the lesbian, gay, bisexual, and transgender community's search for equality. In 2006, Virginia voters approved by a 57 percent to 43 percent margin a state constitutional amendment that not only defined marriage as between one man and one woman, but also prohibited any county or city from allowing gay or lesbians couples to enter into legalized civil unions.[140]

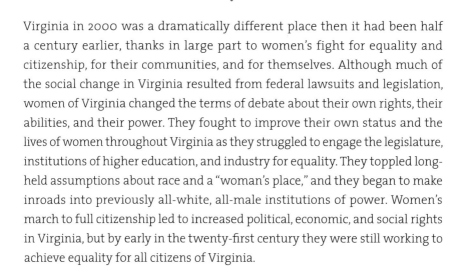

Virginia in 2000 was a dramatically different place then it had been half a century earlier, thanks in large part to women's fight for equality and citizenship, for their communities, and for themselves. Although much of the social change in Virginia resulted from federal lawsuits and legislation, women of Virginia changed the terms of debate about their own rights, their abilities, and their power. They fought to improve their own status and the lives of women throughout Virginia as they struggled to engage the legislature, institutions of higher education, and industry for equality. They toppled long-held assumptions about race and a "woman's place," and they began to make inroads into previously all-white, all-male institutions of power. Women's march to full citizenship led to increased political, economic, and social rights in Virginia, but by early in the twenty-first century they were still working to achieve equality for all citizens of Virginia.

Epilogue

In February 2009, the student body at one of Virginia's largest universities elected senior Ryan Allen's alter ego Reann Ballslee homecoming queen. Allen, who hails from Goochland County, had experienced discrimination in this rural community after coming out as gay in ninth grade. But after moving to Northern Virginia, he found acceptance, began performing in drag shows, and ultimately defeated two female candidates to win George Mason University's homecoming title. Allen joined Ricky Malebranche, a male African American student from Woodbridge, on the basketball court at halftime to receive the crowd's applause as the newly chosen Ms. Mason and Mr. Mason, respectively.[1]

This episode raises fascinating questions about gender and sexuality in twenty-first century Virginia. By choosing a man as their homecoming queen, were those student voters challenging the longstanding tradition of pageants that celebrate women for their physical beauty, a practice that seems anachronistic and antithetical to the ideals and principles of a coeducational public university? Or was the selection of a gay, cross-dressing man to represent their school as its "queen" rather an expression of tolerance and inclusiveness on the part of students who attended an unusually diverse institution of higher learning located in the most liberal region of the commonwealth? Significantly, not only many of the students but also the university's administration supported the selection of Allen/Ballslee, as did many readers who contributed online comments about the story as reported in the *Washington Post*. At the same time, other readers were less accepting and an outraged minority expressed disgust at what one reader called the corruption of "tradition" by "sexual folly fueled by gender disorientation."[2]

The election of a transgender homecoming queen, Jessee Vasold, at the venerable College of William and Mary eight months later raised similar issues and elicited opinions that seem to have varied along generational lines. A column in the *Richmond Times-Dispatch* quoted three students, each of whom praised the election's outcome, which two explicitly attributed to young people's more tolerant and inclusive stance on issues involving gender and sexuality. By contrast, the five *Times-Dispatch* readers who contributed online comments—most of whom appear to have been adults—to different degrees criticized what they interpreted as a harbinger of the decline of "traditional" families and values. "Diversity is just liberal code for dilution . . . of traditional values and morals," wrote one reader, who saw Vasold's election as part of the same misguided agenda that included removing the Wren Cross from the college chapel and phasing out the school's Indian mascot, which offended Native Americans. "First you take away the cross, then the feather [from the college's athletic logo], now this," he fumed. The most supportive comment came from a reader who compared William and Mary's homecoming election to recent violence at Virginia Tech. "Comparatively speaking," he wrote, damning with faint (and tasteless) praise, "I suppose William & Mary has nothing to be ashamed of."[3]

In the twenty-first century, Virginia remains a commonwealth of contradictions on many levels. Lesbians and other members of the lesbian, gay, bisexual, and transgender community have fought for open acceptance since the 1970s, and what happened at George Mason can be interpreted as a sign of progress. In much the same vein, we have presented a story of Virginia women whose rights have expanded over time: enslaved women became free; wives became property owners; women of all races attained greater access to education, suffrage, and other basic civil rights. But though our story may be one of overall improvement, women's gains have not always been steady over time, and they have varied by class, race, and region. And progress, though laudable, is not full equality.

Moreover, women themselves have divided historically over what agendas to pursue and what values to embrace. In the colonial period, Virginia women were slaves and servants, but they were also ladies who owned (and sometimes abused) their servants and slaves. In the nineteenth century, female Virginians worked in factories, wrote novels, escaped or otherwise undermined slavery, honored Confederate defenders of slavery and white supremacy, and strove to improve the lives of freed African Americans. Generations later, some sought to preserve time-honored gender and racial boundaries, while others fought tirelessly for ERA and civil rights. So, too, in the twenty-first century, there is no consensus among Virginia women about many important and timely issues. Future research must probe the many still-unexamined questions surrounding the economic, political, and social histories of women in what some have dubbed the "New Dominion."[4]

Virginia women, like those elsewhere, continue to face economic challenges, many of which stem from their still fundamentally unequal position in society. In the first decade of the new millennium, full-time women workers in the state earned only 77 percent of what men made in similar positions, which was slightly below the national average. This income inequality existed in all occupational fields. The salaries of women in managerial positions were only 69 percent of those of men; women in sales were paid only 70 percent of what men received for comparable work. Wage inequality was even more severe for women of color: African American women received 59 percent of what white men earned for equivalent jobs, and Latinas earned only 53 percent of white men's wages.[5]

These disparities became painfully evident for many Virginia families during the first major recession of the twenty-first century. With a statewide unemployment rate of 7.3 percent in 2010, the highest in almost twenty-seven years, women and their families faced even greater challenges as a result of a weak job market, stagnant wages, and the continually increasing costs of health care and other necessities. The vast majority of workers who lost their jobs were men. As a result, women's inadequate salaries became the sole support of many families, some of whom lost between 55 and 80 percent of their total income when their male breadwinner became unemployed. At the same time,

Salvador Dali's conception of a monument to Sally Tompkins, drawn by Bill Wynne, 1966. In 1966, several prominent Richmond residents proposed erecting a statue on the city's Monument Avenue to Sally Louisa Tompkins, who had been commissioned a Confederate captain in order to operate her hospital during the Civil War. The committee approached Salvador Dali for a design, which portrayed Tompkins as a modern Saint George slaying a dragon representing a microbe. The design was widely panned, and the statue honoring a Virginia woman was never built. More than forty years later, the General Assembly created a commission in 2010 to honor the achievements of Virginia women with a monument on the grounds of Capitol Square. *Photo: Reproduced courtesy of the Estate of Bill Wynne. Image provided by the Virginia Historical Society.*

unemployed women were less likely than their male counterparts to find new jobs as the economy slowly improved after 2010. One study suggests that women were hit harder by the elimination of government jobs and also by a decrease in the numbers of positions in traditionally female-dominated fields. Meanwhile, some jobless men regained employment by moving into those fields, such as health care and retail, and others may have benefited from what one study called employers' "discrimination against women or increased bias in favor of men."[6]

As the historical experiences of Virginia's working women show, gender discrimination and unequal compensation are nothing new. Women have long performed unpaid (and often unacknowledged) domestic work in their own homes, and generations of female wage laborers have toiled alongside more highly paid males. In the past, women were paid less because they had few occupational choices and comparatively little access to education or job training. But why has this historical trend persisted in an era when females constitute a majority of college students in the state and in the nation?[7] How have recent structural changes in the economy affected women's employment and earning opportunities in the commonwealth? Historians need to investigate how the relocation of textile mills and clothing factories overseas affected their largely female workforces in Virginia. New research should also examine the impact of the emergence of technology industries and the expansion of institutions of higher education on women's employment possibilities late in the twentieth and early in the twenty-first centuries. The effect of recent immigration trends on women's participation in the labor market is another increasingly salient topic. What skills did Latina and Asian immigrants bring with them, and to which occupational fields did they gravitate? How did their arrival and employment in Virginia affect the occupational options of other women in the state? How, if at all, did occupational choices differ for second-generation immigrant women?

At the same time, historians must acknowledge, document, and explain the enormous gains made by Virginia's business and professional women, especially during the twentieth century. In 1920, the first year that women were admitted to the graduate and professional schools at the University of Virginia, Innis Steinmetz became the first female graduate of the Medical College of Virginia in Richmond; in 1923, Elizabeth Nelson Tompkins became the first woman to graduate from the University of Virginia's School of Law. Since then, and especially since the 1970s, women have become increasingly prominent in both the legal and medical professions, in Virginia and nationally. So, too, have they become religious leaders, not only as influential laypersons, but also as formally sanctioned members of the clergy in most denominations.[8]

In 2007, women owned nearly one-third of all businesses in the commonwealth. The entrepreneurial success of some women, such as Lillie Pearl Fearnow of Hanover County, who became famous after developing her locally known brunswick stew into an eponymous canned product in 1946, brought them iconic status. Other female business leaders, such as Betty Sams Christian, the Staunton native who became the first female CEO of Central Coca-Cola Company, Sheila Crump Johnson, cofounder of Black Entertainment Television and reputedly the nation's first black billionaire, and Sukhbans K. Dhillon, the Indian-American cofounder of a multimillion-dollar Falls Church computer programming and consulting firm known for hiring the physically disabled, all became important philanthropists in Virginia and beyond. Elizabeth Musgrave Merrill Furness, who established Fauquier County's Piedmont Vineyards and Winery, Virginia's first commercial vinifera vineyard, was a pioneer in what has become a significant industry in the state. While the overwhelming majority of Virginia's businesswomen are less well known and less successful, their overall numbers suggest the pervasiveness of female entrepreneurship in the commonwealth.[9]

Politically, Virginia women also have made tangible progress, attaining high office in gradually increasing numbers. Two women—Mary Sue Terry (1986–1993) and Judith Williams Jagdmann (2005–2006)—have served as the commonwealth's attorney general; one of three women appointed to the Supreme Court of Virginia since 1997, Cynthia D. Kinser was elevated to the rank of chief justice in 2011. In the first decade of the twenty-first century, women typically occupied slightly less than one-fifth of the seats in the General Assembly. Although the commonwealth's lawmakers therefore have remained disproportionately male, the number of women legislators has increased, and their ranks have included some long-tenured members holding leadership positions or important committee appointments. NOW-PAC counted the election of Charniele Herring, an African American woman, as a representative from Alexandria among its victories in 2009, and Democrats chose Herring as their party's minority whip in the House of Delegates in December 2011. The presence and influence of women in the General Assembly have contributed decisively to the success of legislative efforts benefiting women, including domestic violence and health care initiatives.[10]

Still, the electoral achievements of Virginia women are below the national average, with the state ranking fortieth in the nation in 2012 for the number of women holding political office.[11] NOW-PAC and Mary Sue Terry's program to raise money for Democratic women candidates at all levels of government seek to change that statistic, although there is no comparable effort underway among Republicans. Do sizeable numbers of Virginia women see politics as a viable means to pursue and attain their policy objectives? More research needs to be done to assess the extent to which women are trying to win access to political office and how they are pursuing their political goals.

Inside and outside the formal political process, some Virginia women continue to press for social change, with varying results. Eradicating sexual and domestic violence remains an important priority for many Virginia feminists. Established in 1984, the Virginia Sexual and Domestic Violence Action Alliance (VSDVAA) continues to lobby the General Assembly for stronger rape and abuse laws, as well as for better funding for shelters and abuse prevention programs. In the first decade of the twenty-first century, the number of women and children seeking shelter from abusers doubled, but state funding remained at 1990s levels. In 2007, shelters provided the equivalent of 314,480 safe nights for 6,436 clients, but 1,759 families were turned away for lack of space. Recent VSDVAA efforts also include lobbying for legislation to address the growing incidence of abuse between young sexual partners in high school and college, as well as efforts to promote public awareness of domestic violence and legal options available to its targets.[12]

Abortion and reproductive rights generally continue to be crucial issues for Virginia women, as well as important battlegrounds for feminists and their adversaries. Virginia NOW and other feminist groups sponsor pro-choice vigils yearly at the State Capitol in Richmond to support the preservation of women's existing abortion rights. But advocates for women's right to choose suffered a notable setback in 2009 when the governor approved "Choose Life" license plates, whose profits go to fund forty pro-life (and anti-choice) pregnancy centers. While Victoria Cobb, head of the conservative Family Foundation of

Virginia, cheered the governor's action, pro-choice women mourned it. "Is there a pro-choice license plate?" queried one self-described female pro-choice reader of the *Richmond Times-Dispatch*, who got her wish the following year with the introduction of a new "Trust Women, Defend Choice" license plate. Nevertheless, the proceeds from the "Trust Women" plates fund "women's health services in Virginia" provided by Planned Parenthood affiliates, "but shall not be used to provide abortion services."[13]

Historians need to do more research on women's efforts to safeguard hard-won reproductive rights, while acknowledging persistent differences and divisions among feminists and, even more so, between feminists and other women who oppose them politically. In 2012, Virginia legislators debated whether an egg became a rights-bearing person at the moment of fertilization. The "personhood" bill, which ultimately failed, nonetheless raised the specter of grave limitations on women's right to employ certain types of contraception, besides effectively ending access to abortion under any circumstances. Another bill, which became law in 2012, requires a woman to have an ultrasound before having an abortion. Although that law mandates the performance of an abdominal ultrasound—a comparatively routine process—the original bill required a more invasive procedure that involved inserting a probe into the woman's vagina. Feminists and others decried the vaginal ultrasound as state-mandated medical rape. The debate was a galvanizing moment, which resulted in protests in Richmond and the formation of Women's Strike Force, a nonpartisan political action committee to oppose the re-election of legislators who voted for the transvaginal ultrasound and personhood bills. Yet some Virginia women fought hard for both initiatives.[14]

Historians also need to learn more about the goals and strategies of lesbian activists and their allies. Currently, Virginia has no law banning workplace discrimination against LGBT workers, despite the fact that polls show that more than 85 percent of Virginians believe that LGBT people should be protected against such discrimination. Equality Virginia lobbies continually for protection in the workforce, for domestic partner insurance benefits, and to overturn the recent constitutional amendment that legally defines marriage as the union between a man and a woman. The group and its supporters also actively oppose the "conscience clause," which allows even publicly funded child placement agencies to discriminate against gays and lesbians who wish to provide foster care or to adopt. Early in 2012, Virginia's Board of Social Services implemented a regulation that enabled any state-licensed private agency to deny adoption to same-sex couples.[15] Like Virginians generally, women disagree on these issues and others concerning the LGBT community.

Finally, one of the most important topics in the recent history of Virginia is how immigrants are changing the commonwealth in ways that go far beyond the labor market and the economy. Between 1990 and 2010, the Latino population nearly quadrupled in Virginia to reach 631,825. The Asian population, concentrated in Northern Virginia, rose to 439,890, almost three times what it was in 1990. Together, these two groups make up more than 13 percent of the total population of the state, with a majority being either naturalized or native-born U.S. citizens.[16]

Virginia's immigrant women have been involved in community support efforts, and they have also enriched the cultural life of many localities. In 1997, Ana Ines King, a native of Colombia, founded the Latin Ballet of Virginia in Richmond, which holds more than 100 classes each week in Latin dancing throughout the Richmond region and supports a dance troupe that performs in Virginia, North Carolina, and Washington, D.C. Laura Brown, from the Virginia Migrant Education Program and Albemarle County's English for Speakers of Other Languages, founded a Latina discussion group at a local middle school, which, though originally conceived as a temporary program to foster girls' self-esteem and embrace cultural diversity, was so well-received that it became an ongoing program for young Latinas. Asian-American women have undertaken significant cultural and community work in Northern Virginia, especially in Fairfax County, which contains the state's largest Asian population. Heisung Lee, who emigrated from South Korea to the United States in 1971, was honored for her work as director of the nonprofit Korean Senior Center, which serves more than 400 senior citizens. A native of the Philippines, Corazón Sandoval Foley has been praised for her achievements as co-founder and co-chair of the Fairfax County Asian American History Project, which created oral histories and a website to document and preserve the stories of local Asian immigrants and their families.[17]

Some immigrant women also have emerged as political leaders in their communities. Women have held leadership posts in the Democratic Latino Organization of Virginia and in the Republican National Association of

Virginia, both of which seek to mobilize partisan political support among the state's Latino voters. Beginning in 2002, three women—Maribel Ramos, Sindy Benavides, and Luisa Soaterna—served successively as Latino Liaison to the governor's office, the first appointees to hold that newly established post. Soaterna had been active in the Latino community in Richmond and was a founding member of the local chapter of the League of United Latin American Citizens. Women have also been prominent among the leadership of the Northern Virginia chapter of the Organization of Chinese Americans, a nonpartisan civic group. Asian women of diverse nationalities have served on the governor's Virginia Asian Advisory Board, which, since its inception in 2001, has represented the Asian community across the commonwealth.[18]

As these women, and so many who came before them, have sought their places in Virginia, they have irrevocably reshaped the Old Dominion. We believe that their stories deserve to be known. Virginia women changed history, and looking at the past from their varied perspectives offers a potentially changed view of Virginia's four centuries. We encourage our readers to reflect on these women, their stories, and their achievements as they think about the future of the New Dominion.

Short Titles and Abbreviations

Acc.	Accession number
APS	American Philosophical Society, Philadelphia, Pa.
Co.	County
CWF	John D. Rockefeller Jr. Library, Colonial Williamsburg Foundation, Williamsburg, Va.
Duke	David M. Rubenstein Rare Book and Manuscript Library, Duke University, Durham, N.C.
DVB	*Dictionary of Virginia Biography*, 3 vols. (Richmond, 1998–2006)
JSH	*Journal of Southern History*
LC	Library of Congress, Washington, D.C.
LVA	Library of Virginia, Richmond, Va.
M/Ms/Mss	Manuscript(s) Collection
NARA	National Archives and Records Administration, Washington, D.C.
PRO CO	Public Record Office, Colonial Office, National Archives of Great Britain, Kew, Eng.
RG	Record Group

UNC	Southern Historical Collection, Wilson Library, University of North Carolina at Chapel Hill, N.C.
UVA	Albert and Shirley Small Special Collections Library, University of Virginia, Charlottesville
VCU	James Branch Cabell Library, Virginia Commonwealth University, Richmond, Va.
VHS	Virginia Historical Society, Richmond, Va.
VMHB	*Virginia Magazine of History and Biography*
W&M	Earl Gregg Swem Library, College of William and Mary, Williamsburg, Va.
WMQ	*William and Mary Quarterly*

Notes

CHAPTER 1

1. Keith Egloff and Deborah Woodward, *First People: The Early Indians of Virginia*, 2d ed. (Charlottesville, 2006), 5, 9–10, 31–45.

2. Helen C. Rountree, *The Powhatan Indians of Virginia: Their Traditional Culture* (Norman, Okla., 1989), 15; Rountree, *Pocahontas's People: The Powhatan Indians of Virginia through Four Centuries* (Norman, Okla., 1990), 5–7, 15.

3. Rountree, *Powhatan Indians of Virginia*, 88–89.

4. "Observations gathered out of a Discourse of . . . Virginia . . . , 1606, Written by . . . George Percy," in *Hakluytus Posthumus or Purchas His Pilgrimes* . . . , ed. Samuel Purchas (Glasgow, 1906), 18:415–416 (quotations); Kathleen M. Brown, *Good Wives, Nasty Wenches, and Anxious Patriarchs: Gender, Race, and Power in Colonia Virginia* (Chapel Hill, 1996), 55–58.

5. Rountree, *Powhatan Indians of Virginia*, 89–90; Brown, *Good Wives, Nasty Wenches, and Anxious Patriarchs*, 46.

6. Helen C. Rountree, *Pocahontas, Powhatan, Opechancanough: Three Indian Lives Changed by Jamestown* (Charlottesville, 2005), 23–24, 34; Rountree, *Powhatan Indians of Virginia*, 93–94; Brown, *Good Wives, Nasty Wenches, and Anxious Patriarchs*, 129.

7. Brown, *Good Wives, Nasty Wenches, and Anxious Patriarchs*, 51–53, 72; Rountree, *Pocahontas, Powhatan, Opechancanough*, 158–167; Camilla Townsend, *Pocahontas and the Powhatan Dilemma: An American Portrait* (New York, 2004), 114–123; Rountree, *Pocahontas's People*, 84; David D. Smits, "'Abominable Mixture': Toward the Repudiation of Anglo-Indian Intermarriage in Seventeenth-Century Virginia," *VMHB* 95 (1987): 157–192.

8. Gabriel Archer, "A relatyon of the discovery of our River, from James Forte into the Maine," 21 May–21 June 1607, PRO CO 1/1, fol. 49v (quotations), with modernized version in Edward Wright Haile, ed., *Jamestown Narratives: Eyewitness Accounts of the Virginia Colony, The First Decade, 1607–1617* (Champlain, Va., 1998), 101–118; Opossunoquonuske biography at Virginia Women in History, 2007, LVA, http://www.lva.virginia.gov/public/vawomen/2007/ opossunoquonuske.htm (accessed 15 June 2012).

9. Brown, *Good Wives, Nasty Wenches, and Anxious Patriarchs*, 55–64.

10. Rountree, *Pocahontas's People*, 73–88, 96; Warren M. Billings, ed., *The Papers of Sir William Berkeley, 1605–1677* (Richmond, 2007), 395.

11. Edmund S. Morgan, *American Slavery, American Freedom: The Ordeal of Colonial Virginia* (New York, 1975), 407.

12. Ibid., 407; William M. Kelso, *Jamestown: The Buried Truth* (Charlottesville, 2006), 39–40; David R. Ransome, "Wives for Virginia, 1621," *WMQ*, 3d ser., 48 (1991): 3–4, 6, 11–15; "The names of the maydes sent in the Marmaduke bounde for Virginia Ano. 1621 Augt.," Ferrar Papers (1590–1637), Magdalene College, University of Cambridge (quotations).

13. Gervase Markham, *The English Housewife . . .* , ed. Michael R. Best (Montreal, 1994), 5. The book's full subtitle appears on the title page of this modern edition.

14. Lawrence Stone, *The Family, Sex, and Marriage in England, 1500–1800* (New York, 1977), 195–202, 356–358, 501–507; Roger Thompson, *Women in Stuart England and America: A Comparative Study* (London, 1974), 8–11, 162–163; Susan Dwyer Amussen, *An Ordered Society: Gender and Class in Early Modern England* (London, 1988), 35–47, 95–104; William Blackstone, *Commentaries on the Laws of England: In Four Books*, ed. George Sharswood, 2 vols. (1765; Philadelphia, 1875), 1:441 (quotation).

15. Morgan, *American Slavery, American Freedom*, 408–410; James Horn, "Servant Emigration to the Chesapeake in the Seventeenth Century," in *The Chesapeake in the Seventeenth Century: Essays on Anglo-American Society*, ed. Thad W. Tate and David L. Ammerman (Chapel Hill, 1979), 51–65.

16. Lois Green Carr and Lorena S. Walsh, "The Planter's Wife: The Experience of White Women in Seventeenth-Century Maryland," *WMQ*, 3d ser., 34 (1977): 547; Brown, *Good Wives, Nasty Wenches, and Anxious Patriarchs*, 83–88.

17. Lorena S. Walsh, "'Till Death Us Do Part': Marriage and Family in Seventeenth-Century Maryland," in Tate and Ammerman, *Chesapeake in the Seventeenth Century*, 126–152; Darrett B. Rutman and Anita H. Rutman, "'Now-Wives and Sons-in-Law': Parental Death in Early Virginia," ibid., 153–182.

18. Morgan, *American Slavery, American Freedom*, 126–127; Mary Beth Norton, *Founding Fathers and Mothers: Gendered Power and the Formation of American Society* (New York, 1996), 124–125; Irmina Wawrzyczek, "The Women of Accomack Versus Henry Smith: Gender, Legal Recourse, and the Social Order in Seventeenth-Century Virginia," *VMHB* 105 (1997): 5, 10–11; Henry R. McIlwaine, ed., *Minutes of the Council and General Court of Colonial Virginia, 1622–1632, 1670–1676*, 2d ed. (Richmond, 1979), 23 (first quotation); Accomack Co. Orders (1666–1670), 73 (second quotation), LVA; Lower Norfolk Co. Court, 31 July 1649, Lower Norfolk Co. Wills and Deeds B (1646–1651), fol. 120 (third, fourth, and fifth quotations), LVA.

19. Brown, *Good Wives, Nasty Wenches, and Anxious Patriarchs*, 207–209; Norton, *Founding Fathers and Mothers*, 122–123; Terri L. Snyder, *Brabbling Women: Disorderly Speech and the Law in Early Virginia* (Ithaca, N.Y., 2003), 42–49.

20. Brown, *Good Wives, Nasty Wenches, and Anxious Patriarchs*, 192–194; John Ruston Pagan, *Anne Orthwood's Bastard: Sex and Law in Early Virginia* (New York, 2003), 121–129.

21. Pagan, *Anne Orthwood's Bastard*, esp. 3–10, 131–136.

22. Wawrzyczek, "Women of Accomack," 5–26; McIlwaine, *Minutes of the Council and General Court*, 212 (quotations); Accomack Co. Orders (1666–1670), 74, LVA.

23. Carr and Walsh, "The Planter's Wife," 542–543, 550–551; Morgan, *American Slavery, American Freedom*, 166–167, 170; Suzanne Lebsock, *Virginia Women, 1600–1945: "A Share of Honour"* (Richmond, 1987), 21; *DVB*, 1:540; "Papers Relating to the Administration of Governor Nicholson and to the Founding of William and Mary College," *VMHB* 7 (1899–1900): 278 (quotation).

24. Darrett B. Rutman and Anita H. Rutman, *A Place in Time: Middlesex County, Virginia, 1650–1750* (New York, 1984), 103–113; Linda E. Speth, "More than her 'Thirds': Wives and Widows in Colonial Virginia," in Linda E. Speth and Alison Duncan Hirsch, *Women, Family, and Community in Colonial America: Two Perspectives* (New York, 1983), 6, 17–20; Walsh, "'Till Death Us Do Part,'" 136–137; Morgan, *American Slavery, American Freedom*, 164–170.

25. Snyder, *Brabbling Women*, 67–71, 81–86, 92–108.

26. Engel Sluiter, "New Light on the '20. and Odd Negroes' Arriving in Virginia, August 1619," *WMQ*, 3d ser., 54 (1997): 395–398; *Historical Statistics of the United States, Colonial Times to 1970*, 2 vols. (Washington, D.C., 1975), 2:1168; Susan Myra Kingsbury, ed., *The Records of the Virginia Company of London*, 4 vols. (Washington, D.C., 1933), 3:243 (quotation).

27. In general, see the discussion in T. H. Breen and Stephen Innes, *"Myne Owne Ground": Race and Freedom on Virginia's Eastern Shore, 1640–1676* (New York, 1980), 4–5, 19–32.

28. Brown, *Good Wives, Nasty Wenches, and Anxious Patriarchs*, 107–116; Breen and Innes, *"Myne Owne Ground,"* 8–17; Musters of Inhabitants in Virginia, 1625, PRO CO 1/3, fol. 153 (quotation).

29. Warren M. Billings, "The Cases of Fernando and Elizabeth Key: A Note on the Status of Blacks in Seventeenth-Century Virginia," *WMQ*, 3d ser., 30 (1973): 467–474; Anthony S. Parent, Jr., *Foul Means: The Formation of a Slave Society in Virginia, 1660–1740* (Chapel Hill, 2003), 107–123; William Waller Hening, ed., *The Statutes at Large; Being a Collection of All the Laws of Virginia . . .* 13 vols. (1823; reprint, Charlottesville, 1969), 2:260 (quotation).

30. Hening, *Statutes at Large*, 1:242 (quotation); Brown, *Good Wives, Nasty Wenches, and Anxious Patriarchs*, 108, 118–128. On demeaning images of black women, see Jennifer L. Morgan, *Laboring Women: Reproduction and Labor in New World Slavery* (Philadelphia, 2004), chap. 1.

31. Morgan, *American Slavery, American Freedom*, chaps. 12–13; Brent Tarter, "Bacon's Rebellion, the Grievances of the People, and the Political Culture of Seventeenth-Century Virginia," *VMHB* 119 (2011): 3–41.

32. Snyder, *Brabbling Women*, 34–37; Brown, *Good Wives, Nasty Wenches, and Anxious Patriarchs*, 162–166; *DVB*, 3:193–194; Herbert R. Paschal, ed., "George Bancroft's 'Lost Notes' on the General Court Records of Seventeenth-Century Virginia," *VMHB* 91 (1983): 356 (first quotation); Sir William Berkeley, proclamation, 10 Feb. 1677, PRO CO 1/39, fol. 64 (second quotation); John Cotton, "[The History of Bacon's and Ingram's Rebellion, 1675–1676]" (n.d.), 24 (fourth quotation), 38 (third quotation), Mss 2C8295a1, VHS.

33. Snyder, *Brabbling Women*, 19–32; *DVB*, 1:450–451.

34. Martha W. McCartney, "Cockacoeske, Queen of the Pamunkey: Diplomat and Suzeraine," in *Powhatan's Mantle: Indians in the Colonial Southeast*, ed. Peter H. Wood, Gregory A. Waselkov, and M. Thomas Hatley (Lincoln, Nebr., 1989), 173–195; *DVB*, 3:321–322.

35. Snyder, *Brabbling Women*, 24–27, 150; William Hand Browne, ed., *Archives of Maryland: Proceedings of the Council of Maryland, 1667–1687/8* (Baltimore, 1887), 134 (first quotation); Herbert Jeffreys to Henry Coventry, 4 July 1678, Coventry Papers, Longleat House, Wiltshire, Eng, fol. 269 (second quotation). See also Mary Beth Norton, *Separated by Their Sex: Women in Public and Private in the Colonial Atlantic World* (Ithaca, N.Y., 2011), chap. 1.

36. Snyder, *Brabbling Women*, 37–38, Brown, *Good Wives, Nasty Wenches, and Anxious Patriarchs*, chap. 6; Morgan, *American Slavery, American Freedom*, chap. 15; Hening, *Statutes at Large*, 2:385 (quotation).

37. Morgan, *American Slavery, American Freedom*, 162–166, 180–184, 297–307; Brown, *Good Wives, Nasty Wenches, and Anxious Patriarchs*, chap. 5; Parent, *Foul Means*, 67–79.

38. Snyder, *Brabbling Women*, 136–139; Henry Louis Gates, Jr., and Evelyn Brooks Higginbotham, eds., *African American National Biography*, 8 vols. (New York, 2008), 8:186–187.

39. *DVB*, 1:178–179, 3:321–322; Rountree, *Pocahontas's People*, 154–155.

40. Billings, *Papers of Sir William Berkeley*, 395; Emily J. Salmon and Edward D. C. Campbell, Jr., eds., *The Hornbook of Virginia History: A Ready-Reference Guide to the Old Dominion's People, Places, and Past*, 4th ed. (Richmond, 1994), 92; Philip D. Morgan, *Slave Counterpoint: Black Culture in the Eighteenth-Century Chesapeake and Lowcountry* (Chapel Hill, 1998), 58–61, 81.

41. Salmon and Campbell, *Hornbook*, 159–171; Ronald L. Heinemann, John G. Kolp, Anthony S. Parent, Jr., and William G. Shade, *Old Dominion, New Commonwealth: A History of Virginia, 1607–2007* (Charlottesville, 2007), 85–86, 92–93; John K. Nelson, *A Blessed Company: Parishes, Parsons, and Parishioners in Anglican Virginia, 1690–1776* (Chapel Hill, 2001), 18, 26.

42. Allan Kulikoff, *Tobacco and Slaves: The Development of Southern Cultures in the Chesapeake, 1680–1800* (Chapel Hill, 1986), 168–174; Daniel Blake Smith, *Inside the Great House: Planter Family Life in Eighteenth-Century Chesapeake Society* (Ithaca, N.Y., 1980), 26–27, 32, 44–45, 80.

43. Smith, *Inside the Great House*, 130–133; Brown, *Good Wives, Nasty Wenches, and Anxious Patriarchs*, 187–194, 253–260, 342–350.

44. Rhys Isaac, *Landon Carter's Uneasy Kingdom: Revolution and Rebellion on a Virginia Plantation* (New York, 2004), 37–39, 50–54; Jack P. Greene, ed., *The Diary of Colonel Landon Carter of Sabine Hall, 1752–1778*, 2 vols. (Charlottesville, 1965), 2:680 (quotation).

45. Speth, "More than her 'Thirds,'" 17–20; Kulikoff, *Tobacco and Slaves*, 188–193; Marylynn Salmon, *Women and the Law of Property in Early America* (Chapel Hill, 1986), 147–160, 168–175; Lois Green Carr, "Inheritance in the Colonial Chesapeake," in *Women in the Age of the American Revolution*, ed. Ronald Hoffman and Peter J. Albert (Charlottesville, 1989), 163–166, 171–181; Joan R. Gundersen and Gwen Victor Gampel, "Married Women's Legal Status in Eighteenth-Century New York and Virginia," *WMQ*, 3d ser., 39 (1982): 133–134. A study that emphasizes women's continuing economic power, while acknowledging that women who engaged in business activities were neither average nor typical, is Linda L. Sturtz, *Within Her Power: Propertied Women in Colonial Virginia* (New York, 2002), esp. chaps. 1–3.

46. Sturtz, *Within Her Power*, 158–160; Joseph E. Fields, comp., *"Worthy Partner": The Papers of Martha Washington* (Westport, Conn., 1994), xx, 3–61, 103–104; List of rents owed to Robert Carter, 1770, Carter Family Papers (1651–1861), Mss1 C2468a, VHS; Petition of Mary Dandridge Spotswood Campbell to John Murray, earl of Dunmore, [ca. 1772], and Mary Dandridge Spotswood Campbell to [John Spotswood], [ca. 1790], 29 Nov. 1794, 23 Dec. 1794, Spotswood Family Papers (1760–1953), Mss1 Sp687b, VHS.

47. Carole Shammas, "Black Women's Work and the Evolution of Plantation Society in Virginia," *Labor History* 26 (1985): 12–13; Joan R. Gundersen, *To Be Useful to the World*, rev. ed. (Chapel Hill, 2006), 4; Hunter Dickinson Farish, ed., *Journal and Letters of Philip Vickers Fithian, 1773–1774: A Plantation Tutor of the Old Dominion* (Williamsburg, 1943), 90 (second quotation), 105 (first quotation). See also Julia Cherry Spruill, *Women's Life and Work in the Southern Colonies* (Chapel Hill, 1938), 66–70.

48. E[liza] Smith, *The Compleat Housewife or, Accomplish'd Gentlewoman's Companion* . . . (Williamsburg, 1742) (first quotation); Jane Carson, *Colonial Virginia Cookery: Procedures, Equipment, and Ingredients in Colonial Cooking* (Williamsburg, 1968); Sally Cary Fairfax diary (26 Dec. 1771–8 Jan. 1772), Mss5:1 F1616:1, VHS (second quotation).

49. Markham, *The English Housewife*, 146 (first quotation); *Oxford English Dictionary*, ed. J. A. Simpson and E. S. C. Weiner, 2d ed., 20 vols. (Oxford, 1989), 7:447; Williamsburg *Virginia Gazette* (Purdie and Dixon), 6 Oct. 1768, 13 Apr. 1769; Williamsburg *Virginia Gazette* (Rind), 6 Oct. 1768 (second quotation), 13 Apr. 1769.

50. Maria Taylor Byrd to William Byrd III, 15 Aug. 1760, in *The Correspondence of the Three William Byrds of Westover, Virginia, 1684–1776*, ed. Marion Tinling, 2 vols. (Charlottesville, 1977), 2:701; Judith Carter Banks to Landon Carter, June 1765, Papers of Carter and Wellford Family of Sabine Hall, Acc. 1959, UVA; Greene, *Diary of Landon Carter*, 2:1067; Farish, *Journal and Letters of Philip Vickers Fithian*, 51; Sarah Fouace Nourse diary, 1781–1783, Nourse and Morris Family Papers, Acc. 3490b, UVA.

51. Joan Rezner Gundersen, "The Double Bonds of Race and Sex: Black and White Women in a Colonial Virginia Parish," *JSH* 52 (1986): 369; Gundersen, *To Be Useful to the World*, 74; Shammas, "Black Women's Work," 23–24.

52. Sturtz, *Within Her Power*, 115–117; Sarah Hand Meacham, "'They Will Be Adjudged by their Drink, What Kinde of Housewives They Are': Gender, Technology, and Household Cidering in England and the Chesapeake, 1690–1760," *VMHB* 111 (2003): 117–150.

53. Morgan, *Slave Counterpoint*, 45–54, 196, 211, 245.

54. Ibid., 41–42, 244–247; Shammas, "Black Women's Work," 13–19.

55. Isaac, *Landon Carter's Uneasy Kingdom*, 28, 30n, 347; Morgan, *Slave Counterpoint*, 354–358.

56. Kulikoff, *Tobacco and Slaves*, chap. 9; Jean Butenhoff Lee, "The Problem of Slave Community in the Eighteenth-Century Chesapeake," *WMQ*, 3d ser., 43 (1986): 333–361; Morgan, *Slave Counterpoint*, chap. 9; Williamsburg *Virginia Gazette* (Rind), 8 Nov. 1770 (quotation); Gerald W. Mullin, *Flight and Rebellion: Slave Resistance in Eighteenth-Century Virginia* (New York, 1972), 103–108. On motherhood as a deterrent to running away, see also Stephanie M. H. Camp, *Closer to Freedom: Enslaved Women and Everyday Resistance in the Plantation South* (Chapel Hill, 2004), 36–38.

57. Morgan, *Slave Counterpoint*, 348–353, 518, 526–530; Williamsburg *Virginia Gazette* (Purdie and Dixon), 26 Mar. 1767 (first quotation), 28 Jan. 1768 (second quotation); Williamsburg *Virginia Gazette* (Rind), 25 Aug. 1774 (third quotation); Williamsburg *Virginia Gazette* (Purdie), 27 Sept. 1776.

58. Morgan, *Slave Counterpoint*, 140, 193–194; Shammas, "Black Women's Work," 16; Farish, *Journal and Letters of Philip Vickers Fithian*, 128 (quotation).

59. William Byrd to Charles Boyle, earl of Orrery, 5 July 1726, in Tinling, *Byrd Correspondence*, 1:355 (first quotation); Louis B. Wright and Marion Tinling, eds., *The Secret Diary of William Byrd of Westover, 1709–1712* (Richmond, 1941), 113 (second quotation); Kenneth A. Lockridge,

The Diary, and Life, of William Byrd II of Virginia, 1674–1744 (Chapel Hill, 1987), 66–70; Paula A. Treckel, "'The Empire of My Heart': The Marriage of William Byrd II and Lucy Parke Byrd," *VMHB* 105 (1997): 125–156.

60. *DVB*, 1:534–535; Williamsburg *Virginia Gazette* (Purdie and Dixon), 24 Oct. 1771 (quotation); Spruill, *Women's Life and Work in the Southern Colonies*, 272–275. See also Laurel Thatcher Ulrich, *A Midwife's Tale: The Life of Martha Ballard, Based on Her Diary, 1785–1812* (New York, 1990), 199–200.

61. Sarah Hand Meacham, "Keeping the Trade: The Persistence of Tavernkeeping among Middling Women in Colonial Virginia," *Early American Studies* 3 (2005): 140–163; Sturtz, *Within Her Power*, 92–100.

62. Meacham, "Keeping the Trade," 140, 150, 153, 154, 163; *DVB*, 2:558–559; Spruill, *Women's Life and Work in the Southern Colonies*, 298–299; "Journal of a French Traveller in the Colonies, 1765," *American Historical Review* 26 (1921): 741 (first quotation); Williamsburg *Virginia Gazette* (Purdie and Dixon), 3 Oct. 1771 (second and third quotations).

63. Meacham, "Keeping the Trade," 144–147; Sturtz, *Within Her Power*, 102–105; Petition of Jane Vobe, 24 Nov. 1784, Legislative Petitions, Williamsburg, RG 78, LVA. Few legislative petitions are dated. Unless otherwise noted, petitions are filed by the date on which they were presented to the General Assembly.

64. Sturtz, *Within Her Power*, chap. 6; Eleanor Kelley Cabell, "Women Merchants and Milliners in Eighteenth Century Williamsburg" (1988 typescript report; 1989 microfiche ed.), 95–114, 147–153, CWF.

65. Cabell, "Women Merchants and Milliners," 50–89; Sturtz, *Within Her Power*, 172–174; Williamsburg *Virginia Gazette* (Purdie and Dixon), 10 Oct. 1771 (quotations).

66. Leona M. Hudak, *Early American Women Printers and Publishers, 1639–1820* (Metuchen, N.J., 1978), 300–309; Williamsburg *Virginia Gazette* (Rind), 2 Sept. 1773 (first and second quotations); Williamsburg *Virginia Gazette* (Purdie and Dixon), 29 Sept. 1774 (third quotation); Edward T. James et al., eds., *Notable American Women, 1607–1950: A Biographical Dictionary*, 3 vols. (Cambridge, Mass., 1971), 3:161–162; John A. Garraty and Mark C. Carnes, eds., *American National Biography*, 24 vols. (New York, 1999), 18:522–523.

67. Williamsburg *Virginia Gazette*, 14 Apr. 1738; Williamsburg *Virginia Gazette* (Purdie and Dixon), 4 Mar. 1773.

68. Cynthia A. Kierner, *Beyond the Household: Women's Place in the Early South, 1700–1835* (Ithaca, N.Y., 1998), 59–67; Catherine Kerrison, *Claiming the Pen: Women and Intellectual Life in the Early American South* (Ithaca, N.Y., 2006), 11–17; Farish, *Journal and Letters of Philip Vickers Fithian*, 6, 20–22, 26, 28, 90; Charles Avison, *An Essay on Musical Expression* (London, 1753), 4 (quotation).

69. James Fordyce, *Sermons to Young Women: in Two Volumes*, 6th ed. (London, 1766), 209–212 (first quotation); Betty Pratt to Keith William Pratt, 10 Aug. 1732, in "Jones Papers," *VMHB* 26 (1918): 288 (second quotation); William D. Hoyt, Jr., ed., "Self-Portrait: Eliza Custis, 1808," ibid., 53 (1945): 97–98 (third quotation); Kerrison, *Claiming the Pen*, chap. 2.

70. Cynthia A. Kierner, "Genteel Balls and Republican Parades: Gender and Early Southern Civic Rituals, 1677–1826," *VMHB* 104 (1996): 185–193; Hugh Jones, *Present State of Virginia* (London, 1724), 31; Williamsburg *Virginia Gazette*, 5 Nov. 1736 (quotations); Williamsburg *Virginia Gazette* (Purdie and Dixon), 13 June 1766, 7 June 1770.

71. Jane Carson, *Colonial Virginians at Play* (Williamsburg, 1965), 118–129; Nancy L. Struna, "The Formalizing of Sport and the Formation of an Elite: The Chesapeake Gentry, 1650–1720s,"

Journal of Sport History 13 (1986): 228; Linda L. Sturtz, "The Ladies and the Lottery: Elite Women's Gambling in Eighteenth-Century Virginia," *VMHB* 104 (1996): 165–184; Edward Miles Riley, ed., *The Journal of John Harrower: An Indentured Servant in the Colony of Virginia, 1773–1776* (Williamsburg, 1963), 65; Donald Jackson et al., eds., *The Diaries of George Washington*, 6 vols. (Charlottesville, 1976–1979), 2:113–114; Nicholas Cresswell, *The Journal of Nicholas Cresswell, 1774–1777* (Port Washington, N.Y., 1968), 28 (quotations); Charles S. Sydnor, *Gentlemen Freeholders: Political Practices in Washington's Virginia* (Chapel Hill, 1952), 27, 53–54.

72. John Gregory, *A Father's Legacy to His Daughters* (1774; Philadelphia, 1787), 7 (quotations); Joan R. Gundersen, "The Non-Institutional Church: The Religious Role of Women in Eighteenth-Century Virginia," *Historical Magazine of the Protestant Episcopal Church* 51 (1982): 347–357; Gundersen, *To Be Useful to the World*, 110–111; Spruill, *Women's Life and Work in the Southern Colonies*, 304–351; Nelson, *Blessed Company*, 59.

73. "Journal of Col. James Gordon, of Lancaster County, Va.," *WMQ*, 1st ser., 11 (1902–1903): 101, 196, 227; Ralph Emmett Fall, ed., *The Diary of Robert Rose: A View of Virginia by a Scottish Colonial Parson, 1746–1751* (Verona, Va., 1977), 28, 49, 53–54, 60, 63, 76, 86, 90, 93, 96; "Free Schools in Isle of Wight County," *WMQ*, 1st ser., 5 (1896–1897): 113–117; Nelson, *Blessed Company*, 76–77, 255–256.

74. Brown, *Good Wives, Nasty Wenches, and Anxious Patriarchs*, 140–144; Jay Worrall, Jr., *The Friendly Virginians: America's First Quakers* (Athens, Ga., 1994), 85–86, chap. 6; Polly Grose, *Hannah: The Story of Hannah Ingledew Janney, 1725–1818* (York, Eng., 1997), 44–68.

75. Rhys Isaac, *The Transformation of Virginia, 1740–1790* (Chapel Hill, 1982), 161–177; Gundersen, *To Be Useful to the World*, 114–116; Catherine A. Brekus, *Strangers and Pilgrims: Female Preaching in America, 1740–1845* (Chapel Hill, 1998), 61–65; Monica Najar, *Evangelizing the South: A Social History of Church and State in Early America* (New York, 2008), 53–61, 80–84. For a more skeptical—but not necessarily conflicting—interpretation, see Jewel L. Spangler, *Virginians Reborn: Anglican Monopoly, Evangelical Dissent, and the Rise of the Baptists in the Late Eighteenth Century* (Charlottesville, 2008), esp. 135–137, 151–157.

76. William L. Lumpkin, "The Role of Women in 18th Century Virginia Baptist Life," *Baptist History and Heritage* 8 (1973): 164–165; Brekus, *Strangers and Pilgrims*, 62–63.

77. *DVB*, 3:463–465; Kerrison, *Claiming the Pen*, 77–79.

CHAPTER 2

1. *Journal of the House of Burgesses of Virginia, 1761–1765* (Richmond, 1907), 360 (quotation).

2. Williamsburg *Virginia Gazette* (Purdie and Dixon), 6, 20 June 1766 (first quotation), 14 Dec. 1769 (second quotation); Donald Jackson and Dorothy Twohig, eds., *The Diaries of George Washington*, 6 vols. (Charlottesville, 1976–1979), 2:201; Hunter Dickinson Farish, ed., *Journal and Letters of Philip Vickers Fithian, 1773–1774: A Plantation Tutor in the Old Dominion* (Williamsburg, 1943), 76 (third and fourth quotations); Nicholas Cresswell, *The Journal of Nicholas Cresswell, 1774–1777* (1924; New York, 1968), 53.

3. Williamsburg *Virginia Gazette* (Purdie and Dixon), 24 Dec. 1767.

4. Joan Rezner Gundersen, "The Double Bonds of Race and Sex: Black and White Women in a Colonial Virginia Parish," *JSH* 52 (1986): 369; Gundersen, *To Be Useful to the World: Women in Revolutionary America, 1740–1790*, rev. ed. (Chapel Hill, 2006), 74; Carole Shammas, "Black Women's Work and the Evolution of Plantation Society in Virginia," *Labor History* 26 (1985): 23–24; Thomas Anburey, *Travels through the Interior Parts of America . . .*, 2 vols. (Boston, 1823), 2:246–247 (quotation).

5. Carole Shammas, "How Self-Sufficient Was Early America?," *Journal of Interdisciplinary History* 13 (1982): 267; Shammas, "The Domestic Environment in Early Modern England and America," *Journal of Social History* 14 (1980): 12, 14–15; T. H. Breen, *The Marketplace of Revolution: How Consumer Politics Shaped American Independence* (New York, 2004), 176–180, 288–289.

6. Williamsburg *Virginia Gazette* (Purdie and Dixon), 20 Jan. 1774, 16 June 1774.

7. Williamsburg *Virginia Gazette* (Rind), 15 Sept. 1774.

8. Ibid.

9. Williamsburg *Virginia Gazette* (Purdie and Dixon), 9 June 1774.

10. *Virginia Gazette or, Norfolk Intelligencer*, 11 Aug. 1774. The author thanks Jon Kukla for this reference.

11. Michael A. McDonnell, "Popular Mobilization and Political Culture in Revolutionary Virginia: The Failure of the Minutemen and the Revolution from Below," *Journal of American History* 85 (1998): 961; Cynthia A. Kierner, *Beyond the Household: Women's Place in the Early South, 1700–1835* (Ithaca, N.Y., 1998), 82, 84–85.

12. Williamsburg *Virginia Gazette* (Pinkney), 4 Nov. 1774; Williamsburg *Virginia Gazette* (Purdie and Dixon), 18 Apr. 1766; Williamsburg *Virginia Gazette* (Purdie), 6 Oct. 1775 (quotation), 24 Nov. 1775, 26 Nov. 1775, 16 Feb. 1776; Williamsburg *Virginia Gazette* (Dixon and Hunter), 29 Apr. 1775, 26 Nov. 1775, 17 Feb. 1776.

13. Elizabeth Feilde to Maria Carter Armistead, 8 Feb., 3 June (first quotation), 13 June 1776 (second quotation), Armistead-Cocke Family Papers, Mss. 65 Ar6, W&M; Martha Washington to Elizabeth Ramsay, 30 Dec. 1775, in *"Worthy Partner": The Papers of Martha Washington*, comp. Joseph E. Fields (Westport, Conn., 1994), 164–165 (third and fourth quotations).

14. Williamsburg *Virginia Gazette* (Dixon and Hunter), 21 Sept. 1776 (quotations); Woody Holton, *Forced Founders: Indians, Debtors, Slaves, and the Making of the American Revolution in Virginia* (Chapel Hill, 1999), 6–28; John Dabney Terrell, Sr., to John Davis Terrell, n.d. [transcription], Acc. 41738, Personal Papers Collection, LVA.

15. Williamsburg *Virginia Gazette* (Dixon and Hunter), 21 Sept. 1776.

16. Theda Perdue, *Cherokee Women: Gender and Culture Change, 1700–1835* (Lincoln, Nebr., 1998), 106–108; Colin G. Calloway, *The American Revolution in Indian Country: Crisis and Diversity in Native American Communities* (Cambridge, Eng., 1995), chap. 7; Gary B. Nash, *The Unknown American Revolution: The Unruly Birth of Democracy and the Struggle to Create America* (New York, 2005), 166–167; Declaration of William Robinson, printed in Thomas Jefferson, *Notes on the State of Virginia*, ed. William Peden (Williamsburg, 1955), appendix 4, "Relative to the Murder of Logan's Family," 243 (quotation).

17. John E. Selby, *The Revolution in Virginia, 1775–1783* (Williamsburg, 1988), chap. 4; Williamsburg *Virginia Gazette* (Purdie), 24 Nov. 1775 (quotation); Brent Tarter, "'An Infant Borough entirely supported by Commerce': The Great Fire of 1776 and the Rebuilding of Norfolk," *Virginia Cavalcade* 28 (1978–1979): 53–57.

18. Petition of Mary Webley, 11 Oct. 1776, Legislative Petitions, Norfolk City, RG 78, LVA; Petition of Sarah Hutchings, 26 Oct. 1786 (reported 1787), Legislative Petitions, Norfolk County, RG 78, LVA; Tarter, "'An Infant Borough,'" 55–58; Joan R. Gundersen, "'We Bear the Yoke with a Reluctant Impatience': The War for Independence and Virginia's Displaced Women," in *War and Society in the American Revolution: Mobilization and Home Fronts*, ed. John Resch and Walter Sargent (DeKalb, Ill., 2007), 270–274.

19. Petition of Margaret Rawlings, 1 Dec. 1777, Legislative Petitions, Miscellaneous Petitions, RG 78, LVA (first quotation); Elizabeth Feilde to Maria Carter Armistead, 8 Feb. 1776, Armistead-

Cocke Family Papers, Mss. 65 Ar6, W&M; Williamsburg *Virginia Gazette* (Purdie), 26 July 1776 (second quotation); Holly A. Mayer, *Belonging to the Army: Camp Followers and Community during the American Revolution* (Columbia, S.C., 1996), 221–223; Linda K. Kerber, *Women of the Republic: Intellect and Ideology in Revolutionary America* (Chapel Hill, 1980), 58–61.

20. Cassandra Pybus, *Epic Journeys of Freedom: Runaway Slaves of the American Revolution and Their Global Quest for Liberty* (Boston, 2006), 14–15, 215; Gundersen, "'We Bear the Yoke,'" 274–276.

21. Gundersen, "'We Bear the Yoke,'" 271–274; Tarter, "'An Infant Borough,'" 57–58; Jenny Steuart to Charles Steuart, Nov. 1779, in "Letters from Virginia, 1774–1781," *The Magazine of History* 3 (1906): 215 (quotations).

22. Selby, *Revolution in Virginia*, 149–150, 155–156; Adele Hast, *Loyalism in Revolutionary Virginia: The Norfolk Area and the Eastern Shore* (Ann Arbor, Mich., 1982), 128, 208 n. 29.

23. Gundersen, "'We Bear the Yoke,'" 265, 271–273; Hast, *Loyalism in Revolutionary Virginia*, 127–134, 165–170.

24. Mayer, *Belonging to the Army*, chaps. 4–6; Carol Berkin, *Revolutionary Mothers: Women in the Struggle for America's Independence* (New York, 2005), chaps. 4–5; Patricia Brady, *Martha Washington: An American Life* (New York, 2005), chap. 7; Easton (Md.) *Republican Star, and General Advertiser*, 19 Aug. 1828 (quotation).

25. Alfred F. Young, *Masquerade: The Life and Times of Deborah Sampson, Continental Soldier* (New York, 2004); Sandra Gioia Treadway, "Anna Maria Lane: An Uncommon Soldier of the American Revolution," *Virginia Cavalcade* 37 (1987–1988): 134–143; Samuel Shepherd, *Statutes at Large of Virginia, from . . . 1792, to . . . 1806 . . .* , 3 vols. (Richmond, 1836), 3:432 (quotation).

26. This figure is based on estimates in Gundersen, "'We Bear the Yoke,'" 284.

27. Williamsburg *Virginia Gazette* (Purdie), 6 Sept. 1776.

28. Gundersen, "'We Bear the Yoke,'" 271–272; James A. Bear, Jr., and Lucia C. Stanton, eds., *Jefferson's Memorandum Books: Accounts, with Legal Records and Miscellany, 1767–1826*, 2 vols. (Princeton, 1997), 1:391 n; Margaret Parker to Charles Steuart, 3 Jan. 1779, in "Letters from Virginia, 1774–1781," *The Magazine of History* 3 (1906): 214–215 (quotation); Sarah Fouace Nourse diary, 1781–1783, esp. 27 Feb., 27 July, and 19 Nov. 1781, Nourse and Morris Family Papers, Acc. 3490b, UVA. See also Mary Beth Norton, *Liberty's Daughters: The Revolutionary Experience of American Women, 1750–1800* (Boston, 1980), chap. 7.

29. *DVB*, 2:64–65; Catherine Park to Thomas Jefferson, 30 Mar. 1781, in *The Papers of Thomas Jefferson*, ed. Julian P. Boyd et al. (Princeton, 1950–), 5:296.

30. Petition of Margaret Irvine, 10 Nov. 1777, Legislative Petitions, York County, RG 78, LVA; Sarah Fouace Nourse diary, 1781–1783, Nourse and Morris Family Papers, Acc. 3490b, UVA, Brady, *Martha Washington*, 97; Norton, *Liberty's Daughters*, 216–218, 222; Berkin, *Revolutionary Mothers*, 29–31.

31. Petition of Martha Hodges, 8 Nov. 1777, Legislative Petitions, York County, RG 78, LVA. The author thanks Brent Tarter for this reference.

32. Petition of Frances Seayers, 23 Oct. 1779, Legislative Petitions, Miscellaneous Petitions, RG 78, LVA.

33. Petition of Elizabeth Crowley, 23 Nov. 1780, Legislative Petitions, Henry County, RG 78, LVA; Petition of Sundry Inhabitants of the County of Brunswick, 11 Nov. 1780, Legislative Petitions, Brunswick County, RG 78, LVA.

34. Richmond *Virginia Gazette, or, the American Advertiser*, 10 May 1783.

35. *DVB*, 3:463–465. Hannah Lee Corbin's original letter has not survived; her sentiments are known through her brother's reply, Richard Henry Lee to Hannah Corbin, 17 Mar. 1778, printed in *The Letters of Richard Henry Lee*, ed. James Curtis Ballagh, 2 vols. (New York, 1911–1914), 1:392–394 (quotation).

36. *DVB*, 2:457–459; Mildred H. Arthur, "The Widow of Westover and Women's Rights," *Colonial Williamsburg* 12 (summer 1990): 28–34; Mary Willing Byrd to Thomas Jefferson, 23 Feb. 1781, in Boyd et al., *Jefferson Papers*, 4:691 (first quotation); Byrd to [Thomas Nelson?], 10 Aug. 1781, in ibid., 5:703–704 (second, third, and fourth quotations).

37. Selby, *Revolution in Virginia*, 204–207; Williamsburg *Virginia Gazette* (Dixon and Nicolson), 15 May 1779.

38. Berkin, *Revolutionary Mothers*, 39–41; Sharon Block, "Rape without Women: Print Culture and the Politicization of Rape, 1765–1815," *Journal of American History* 89 (2002): 849–868.

39. "The able Doctor, or America Swallowing the Bitter Draught," originally printed in *London Magazine*, 1 May 1774, reprinted in Joan D. Dolmetsch, *Rebellion and Reconciliation: Satirical Prints on the Revolution at Williamsburg* (Williamsburg, 1976), 7. A digital copy is in the Prints and Photographs Collection at the Library of Congress American Memory website, http://www.loc.gov/pictures/item/97514782/ (accessed 18 June 2012).

40. Catherine Kerrison, "By the Book: Eliza Ambler Brent Carrington and Conduct Literature in Eighteenth-Century Virginia," *VMHB* 105 (1997): 27–52.

41. *DVB*, 1:283–284; Curtis Carroll Davis, "Helping to Hold the Fort, Elizabeth Zane at Wheeling, 1782: A Case Study in Renown," *West Virginia History* 44 (1983): 212–225.

42. Selby, *Revolution in Virginia*, 216–224; Mary Willing Byrd to Thomas Jefferson, 23 Feb. 1781, in Boyd et al., *Jefferson Papers*, 4:692 (quotation); Appendix 1, "'The Affair of Westover,'" in ibid., 5:671–705; *DVB*, 2:64–65.

43. Elizabeth Ambler to Mildred Smith, 1781, Elizabeth Jaquelin Ambler Papers, 1780–1832, CWF.

44. Selby, *Revolution in Virginia*, 223–224, 273–277; Dumas Malone, *Jefferson and His Time*, vol. 1: *Jefferson the Virginian* (Boston, 1948), 336–341, 349–350; "Diary of Arnold's Invasion and Notes on Subsequent Events in 1781: The 1796? Version," in Boyd et al., *Jefferson Papers*, 4:259–261.

45. Isaac, as dictated to Charles Campbell, "Memoirs of a Monticello Slave," in *Jefferson at Monticello*, ed. James A. Bear, Jr. (Charlottesville, 1967), 7–8 (first quotation), 10–11 (second quotation); Sylvia R. Frey, "Between Slavery and Freedom: Virginia Blacks in the American Revolution," *JSH* 49 (1983): 381–384; Lucia Stanton, *Free Some Day: The African-American Families of Monticello* (Charlottesville, 2000), 33; Pybus, *Epic Journeys of Freedom*, 45–47, 53–55, 71; Gundersen, "'We Bear the Yoke,'" 277, 279; Henry Wiencek, *An Imperfect God: George Washington, His Slaves, and the Creation of America* (New York, 2003), 251–259.

46. Mildred Smith to Elizabeth Ambler, [1782], Elizabeth Jaquelin Ambler Papers, 1780–1832, CWF.

47. Cassandra Pybus, "Jefferson's Faulty Math: The Question of Slave Defections in the American Revolution," *WMQ*, 3d ser., 62 (2005): 258-61; Gundersen, "'We Bear the Yoke,'" 284, 288 n; Hast, *Loyalism in Revolutionary Virginia*, 127–134.

48. Petition of Elizabeth Flood, 18 May 1782, Legislative Petitions, Essex County, RG 78, LVA (quotations); Joseph S. Ewing, ed., "The Correspondence of Archibald McCall and George McCall, 1777–1783," *VMHB* 73 (1965): 312–353, 425–454.

49. Hast, *Loyalism in Revolutionary Virginia*, 49–50, 74–76, 128–130, 165–170; Gundersen, *To Be Useful to the World*, 203–204; *The Proceedings of the Convention of Delegates, Held at the Capitol . . . [May–July 1776]* (Williamsburg, 1776), 80 (presentation of petition of Margaret Goodrich, 5 June 1776); Petition of Margaret Goodrich, 23 Oct. 1778, Legislative Petitions, Nansemond County, RG 78, LVA.

50. Mary Blair Braxton Burwell to Betsey Whiting, 30 Dec. 1781, Blair, Banister, Braxton, Horner, and Whiting Papers, Mss 39.1B58, W&M; Sarah Fouace Nourse diary, 1781–1783, entries for May–Aug. 1782, Nourse and Morris Family Papers, Acc. 3490b, UVA.

51. Johann David Schoepf, *Travels in the Confederation [1783–1784]*, trans. and ed. Alfred J. Morrison (1911; reprint, New York, 1968), 63–64; Richmond *Virginia Gazette, or, the American Advertiser*, 17 May 1783 (quotations).

52. Martha Wayles Skelton Jefferson to Eleanor Conway Madison, 8 Aug. 1780, in Boyd et al., *Jefferson Papers*, 3:532–533; Norton, *Liberty's Daughters*, 177–288, Kerber, *Women of the Republic*, 99–103.

53. See generally Cynthia A. Kierner, *Southern Women in Revolution, 1776–1800: Personal and Political Narratives* (Columbia. S.C., 1998), xix–xxvi, 231–232; Randolph W. Church, comp., *Virginia Legislative Petitions: Bibliography, Calendar, and Abstracts from Original Sources, 6 May 1776–21 June 1782* (Richmond, 1984). On the Pamunkey and Mattaponi, see Helen C. Rountree, *Pocahontas's People: The Powhatan Indians of Virginia through Four Centuries* (Norman, Okla., 1990), 165. List of payments by the King William County Court to Betty Edwards and others, 23 June 1779, Legislative Petitions, King William County, RG 78, LVA; Petition of John Quarles, 6 Nov. 1779, ibid.

54. Petition of Rachel and her infant child Rachel, 3 June 1777, Legislative Petitions, Northumberland County, RG 78, LVA; Petition of Ann Rose and Margaret Rose, 5 Dec. 1783, Legislative Petitions, Halifax County, RG 78, LVA; Hening, *Statutes at Large*, 9:320–321, 11:362–363.

55. Joan R. Gundersen, "Independence, Citizenship, and the American Revolution," *Signs* 13 (1987): 59–77. For women's place in the political thought of the Founding Fathers, see Jan Lewis, "'Of Every Age Sex & Condition': The Representation of Women in the Constitution," *Journal of the Early Republic* 15 (1995): 359–387.

56. Eleanor Parke Custis to Elizabeth Bordley, 14 May 1798, in *George Washington's Beautiful Nelly: The Letters of Eleanor Parke Custis Lewis to Elizabeth Bordley Gibson, 1794–1851*, ed. Patricia Brady (Columbia, S.C., 1991), 52 (first quotation); Eleanor Parke Custis Lewis to Mary Stead Pinckney, 9 May 1801, Pinckney Family Papers, 1708–1878, Call No. 37/38, South Carolina Historical Society; Elizabeth Washington Gamble to Thomas Bayly, 11–12 Mar. 1801, Elizabeth Washington Gamble Wirt Letter, VHS (second quotation); Ann Cary Randolph to St. George Tucker, 29 Oct. 1797, Tucker-Coleman Papers, W&M; Judith Randolph to St. George Tucker, 5 Nov. 1797, ibid.; Cynthia A. Kierner, *Scandal at Bizarre: Rumor and Reputation in Jefferson's America* (New York, 2004), 141–143. See also Rosemarie Zagarri, *Revolutionary Backlash: Women and Politics in the Early American Republic* (Philadelphia, 2007), esp. chap. 2.

57. Elizabeth House Trist to Thomas Jefferson, 1 Mar. [1801], in Boyd et al., *Jefferson Papers*, 33:115–116.

58. Martha Dandridge Custis Washington to Fanny Bassett Washington, 25 Feb. 1788, in Fields, *"Worthy Partner,"* 205; Elizabeth Preston Madison to John Preston, 9 Dec. 1798 (first quotation), 8 Jan. 1799, Preston Family Papers, 1727–1896, Mss1 P9267f FA2, VHS; Dolley Payne Todd Madison to James Madison, 1 Nov. [1805], in *The Selected Letters of Dolley Payne Madison*, ed. David B. Mattern and Holly C. Shulman (Charlottesville, 2003), 70 (second quotation). See

also Catherine Allgor, *A Perfect Union: Dolley Madison and the Creation of the American Nation* (New York, 2006).

59. Catherine Allgor, *Parlor Politics: In Which the Ladies of Washington Help Build a City and a Government* (Charlottesville, 2000), chap. 2; Zagarri, *Revolutionary Backlash*, esp. 68–81, 134–136.

60. Hening, *Statutes at Large*, 4:477 (quotation); Selby, *Revolution in Virginia*, 36–38; Len Travers, *Celebrating the Fourth: Independence Day and the Rites of Nationalism in the Early Republic* (Amherst, Mass., 1997), 55, 135–141; Cynthia A. Kierner, "Genteel Balls and Republican Parades: Gender and Early Southern Civic Rituals, 1677–1826," *VMHB* 104 (1996): 185–210.

61. Richmond *Enquirer*, 8 July 1808, 11 Jan. 1814.

62. Eva Sheppard Wolf, *Race and Liberty in the New Nation: Emancipation in Virginia from the Revolution to Nat Turner's Rebellion* (Baton Rouge, 2006), 28–38; Douglas R. Egerton, *Gabriel's Rebellion: The Virginia Slave Conspiracies of 1800 and 1802* (Chapel Hill, 1993), 6–13. Virginians' antislavery commitment should not be exaggerated. See Fredrika Teute Schmidt and Barbara Ripel Wilhelm, "Early Proslavery Petitions in Virginia," *WMQ*, 3d ser. (1973): 133–146; Wolf, *Race and Liberty*, chap. 2.

63. Kerber, *Women of the Republic*, chap. 5; Holly Brewer, "Entailing Aristocracy in Colonial Virginia: 'Ancient Feudal Restraints' and Revolutionary Reform," *WMQ*, 3d ser., 54 (1997): 340–346; Suzanne D. Lebsock, "Radical Reconstruction and the Property Rights of Southern Women," *JSH* 43 (1977): 195–216.

64. Linda L. Sturtz, *Within Her Power: Propertied Women in Colonial Virginia* (New York, 2002), 58–59, 62–70; *DVB*, 3:448–449.

65. Frank L. Dewey, "Thomas Jefferson's Notes on Divorce," *WMQ*, 3d ser., 39 (1982): 212–223 (quotation on 216); Kierner, *Southern Women in Revolution*, 195–198; Thomas E. Buckley, S.J., *The Great Catastrophe of My Life: Divorce in the Old Dominion* (Chapel Hill, 2002), 22–23.

66. Petition of Susanah Wersley, 20 Nov. 1786, Legislative Petitions, Hanover County, RG 78, LVA; Kierner, *Southern Women in Revolution*, 199–200; Buckley, *Great Catastrophe of My Life*, 1.

67. Kierner, *Southern Women in Revolution*, 196; Buckley, *Great Catastrophe of My Life*, esp. 4, 9, 36; Suzanne Lebsock, *The Free Women of Petersburg: Status and Culture in a Southern Town, 1784–1860* (New York, 1984), 68–70.

68. Lebsock, *Free Women of Petersburg*, 69 (quotation); Buckley, *Great Catastrophe of My Life*, 22–23; Tatiana Van Riemsdijk, "His Slaves or Hers?: Customary Claims, a Planter Marriage, and a Community Verdict in Lancaster County, 1793," *VMHB* 113 (2005): 47–79.

69. Thomas Jefferson to Martha Jefferson Randolph, 4 Apr. 1790, in *The Family Letters of Thomas Jefferson*, ed. Edwin Morris Betts and James Adam Bear, Jr. (Columbia, Mo., 1966), 51; diary of Elizabeth Foote Washington, 1784–1789, in *Weathering the Storm: Women of the American Revolution*, ed. Elizabeth Evans (New York, 1975), 344–345, 350–351.

70. Catherine Kerrison, *Claiming the Pen: Women and Intellectual Life in the Early American South* (Ithaca, N.Y., 2006), 79–84; Zagarri, *Revolutionary Backlash*, 120–136; Donald G. Mathews, *Religion in the Old South* (Chicago, 1977), 110–124.

71. Ruth H. Bloch, "The Gendered Meanings of Virtue in Revolutionary America," *Signs* 13 (1987): 37–58.

72. Anne Cary Randolph to Thomas Jefferson, 18 Mar. 1808, in Betts and Bear, *Family Letters of Thomas Jefferson*, 334; Jane Blair Cary Smith, "The Carysbrook Memoir," 83, Acc. 1378, UVA; Richmond *Enquirer*, 5 July 1808, 8 July 1808, 12 July 1808, 5 Jan. 1811 (quotations).

CHAPTER 3

1. Thomas Jefferson, *Notes on the State of Virginia*, ed. William Peden (Williamsburg, 1955), 92–97.

2. Helen C. Rountree, "The Termination and Dispersal of the Nottoway Indians of Virginia," *VMHB* 95 (1987): 200–203, 206–207; Edith Turner biography at Virginia Women in History, 2008, LVA http://www.lva.virginia.gov/public/vawomen/2008/honorees.asp?bio=2 (accessed 15 June 2012).

3. Joseph C. G. Kennedy, comp., *Population of the United States in 1860; Compiled from the Original Returns of the Eighth Census* . . . (Washington, D.C., 1864), 515; Francis A. Walker, comp., *A Compendium of the Ninth Census (June 1, 1870)* . . . (Washington, D.C., 1872), 101; Rountree, "Termination and Dispersal of the Nottoway," 209–213; Samuel R. Cook, *Monacans and Miners: Native American and Coal Mining Communities in Appalachia* (Lincoln, Neb., 2000), 58–60; Peter W. Houck and Mintcy D. Maxham, *Indian Island in Amherst County* (Lynchburg, 1993), 58–61.

4. Helen C. Rountree, *Pocahontas's People: The Powhatan Indians of Virginia through Four Centuries* (Norman, Okla., 1990), 168–177; Theda Perdue, *Cherokee Women: Gender and Culture Change, 1700–1835* (Lincoln, Neb., 1998), 150–158, 170–182.

5. See, for example, the conflicting but in some ways nonetheless complementary arguments in William W. Freehling, "The Founding Fathers and Slavery," *American Historical Review* 77 (1972): 81–83, and Gary B. Nash, *The Unknown American Revolution: The Unruly Birth of Democracy and the Struggle to Create America* (New York, 2005), 407–417. On interracial sex, see Jeff Forret, *Race Relations at the Margins: Slaves and Poor Whites in the Antebellum Southern Countryside* (Baton Rouge, 2006), chap. 5, and on Virginia specifically, Joshua D. Rothman, *Notorious in the Neighborhood: Sex and Families across the Color Line in Virginia, 1787–1861* (Chapel Hill, 2003).

6. Richard S. Dunn, "Black Society in the Chesapeake, 1776–1810," in *Slavery and Freedom in the Age of the American Revolution*, ed. Ira Berlin and Ronald Hoffman (Charlottesville, 1983), 49–82; Douglas R. Egerton, *Gabriel's Rebellion: The Virginia Slave Conspiracies of 1800 and 1802* (Chapel Hill, 1993), 6–13; Eva Sheppard Wolf, *Race and Liberty in the New Nation: Emancipation in Virginia from the Revolution to Nat Turner's Rebellion* (Baton Rouge, 2006), esp. chap. 3; J. D. B. DeBow, comp., *Seventh Census of the United States: 1850* . . . (Washington, D.C., 1853), 5, 258.

7. DeBow, *Seventh Census: 1850*, 256–258; Loren Schweninger, "Property-Owning Free African-American Women in the South, 1800–1870," *Journal of Women's History* 1 (1990): 20, 22, 25.

8. Brenda E. Stevenson, *Life in Black and White: Family and Community in the Slave South* (New York, 1996), 294–295; Suzanne Lebsock, *The Free Women of Petersburg: Status and Culture in a Southern Town, 1784–1860* (New York, 1984), 91, 99–100, 182–185; Stephanie Cole, "A White Woman, of Middle Age, Would be Preferred: Children's Nurses in the Old South," in *Neither Lady nor Slave: Working Women of the Old South*, ed. Susanna Delfino and Michele Gillespie (Chapel Hill, 2002), esp. 84; Tommy L. Bogger, *Free Blacks in Norfolk, Virginia, 1790–1860* (Charlottesville, 1997), 55, 73–74; Schweninger, "Property-Owning Free African-American Women," 20, 22; *Alexandria Gazette*, 24 Apr. 1852 (quotation).

9. Samuel Mordecai, *Richmond in By-Gone Days* (2d ed., 1860; reprint, Richmond, 1946), 58 (fourth, fifth, and sixth quotations), 172 (first, second, and third quotations); Schweninger, "Property-Owning Free African-American Women," 15–22; Bogger, *Free Blacks in Norfolk*, 72–73.

10. Stevenson, *Life in Black and White*, 297–298, 306–310; Lebsock, *Free Women of Petersburg*, 88–89, 103–110; Bogger, *Free Blacks in Norfolk*, 108–109; Robert Saunders,

"Modernization and the Free Peoples of Richmond: The 1780s and 1850s," *Southern Studies* 24 (1985): 265; Schweninger, "Property-Owning Free African-American Women," 23–24; Rothman, *Notorious in the Neighborhood*, chap. 2. In 1850, females accounted for 52.1 percent of Virginia's free black population.

11. Bogger, *Free Blacks in Norfolk*, 110–111; Saunders, "Modernization and the Free Peoples of Richmond," 265–266.

12. Suzanne Lebsock, *Virginia Women, 1600–1945: "A Share of Honour"* (Richmond, 1987), 59–60; Lebsock, *Free Women of Petersburg*, 94–97; Luther Porter Jackson, *Free Negro Labor and Property Holding in Virginia, 1830–1860* (New York, 1942), 191; Petersburg Hustings Court Deed Book 7 (1821–1826), 267, LVA (quotation); Stevenson, *Life in Black and White*, 262–263.

13. Petitions of Judith Hope, 21 Dec. 1819, 11 Dec. 1820 (quotations), Legislative Petitions, Richmond City, RG 78, LVA; Petition of Judith Hope, 14 Dec. 1821, Legislative Petitions, Williamsburg, RG 78, LVA; Petition of Judith Hope Judah, 23 July 1831, Richmond City Hustings Court Minute Book 11 (1831–1835), 42, LVA.

14. Stevenson, *Life in Black and White*, 260, 271–272, 286; Petition of Elvira Jones, 5 Dec. 1823, Legislative Petitions, Richmond City, RG 78, LVA; Petition of Harriet Cook, 25 Jan. 1850, Legislative Petitions, Loudoun County, RG 78, LVA. See also Gregg D. Kimball, *American City, Southern Place: A Cultural History of Antebellum Richmond* (Athens, Ga., 2000), 127–135.

15. Philip J. Schwarz, *Migrants against Slavery: Virginians and the Nation* (Charlottesville, 2001), 13; Kimball, *American City, Southern Place*, 135–138; William C. Scott and Lucy P. Scott to "My Dear Children," 29 Oct. 1854, Norvell Winsboro Wilson Papers, Collection 2957, UNC (quotations).

16. Allan Kulikoff, "Uprooted Peoples: Black Migrants in the Age of the American Revolution, 1790–1820," in Berlin and Hoffman, *Slavery and Freedom*, 148, 149, 151; Peter Wallenstein, *Cradle of America: Four Centuries of Virginia History* (Lawrence, Kans., 2007), 122–123, 155; Schwarz, *Migrants against Slavery*, esp. 1–17.

17. Gail S. Terry, "Sustaining the Bonds of Kinship in a Trans-Appalachian Migration, 1790–1811: The Cabell-Breckinridge Slaves Move West," *VMHB* 102 (1994): 455–476, esp. 465–467.

18. Anya Jabour, "'It Will Never Do for Me to Be Married': The Life of Laura Wirt Randall, 1803–1833," *Journal of the Early Republic* 17 (1997): 228–235; Laura Wirt to Louisa Cabell Carrington, 8 Oct. 1826, Laura Henrietta Wirt Randall Papers, Mss2 R1516b, VHS (first and second quotations); Cynthia A. Kierner, "'The Dark and Dense Cloud Perpetually Lowering Over Us': Gender and the Decline of the Gentry in Postrevolutionary Virginia," *Journal of the Early Republic* 20 (2000): 193, 195–196, 207, 212; Mary Elizabeth Randolph Eppes to Jane Hollins Nicholas Randolph, 20 Apr. 1828 (typescript), Randolph Family Papers, Acc. M75-86, Florida State Archives, Tallahassee; Harriet Randolph to Thomas Eston Randolph, 20 Sept. 1829, ibid.; Petition of Polly B. Glover, 10 Dec. 1818, Legislative Petitions, Buckingham County, RG 78, LVA (third quotation). See also Joan E. Cashin, *A Family Venture: Men and Women on the Southern Frontier* (New York, 1991), chap. 2.

19. Mary Elizabeth Randolph Eppes to Jane Hollins Nicholas Randolph, 1 Apr. 1827 (first and second quotations), 20 Apr. 1828 (third quotation), 9 July 1828 (typescripts), Randolph Family Papers, Acc. M75-86, Florida State Archives; Harriet Randolph to Jane Cary Randolph, 23 May 1829, 19 June 1829, ibid.; Harriet Randolph to Lucy Randolph Beverly, 8 Sept. 1829, ibid.; Harriet Randolph to Thomas Eston Randolph, 20 Sept. 1829, ibid.

20. On white women's paid employment in rural areas, see Forret, *Race Relations on the Margins*, 40–41; Cynthia A. Kierner, *Beyond the Household: Women's Place in the Early South*,

1700–1835 (Ithaca, N.Y., 1998), 173–174. On cities, see generally, Ellen Hartigan-O'Connor, *The Ties That Buy: Women and Commerce in Revolutionary America* (Philadelphia, 2009).

21. Kennedy, *Population of the United States in 1860*, 518–522; Kimball, *American City, Southern Place*, 32, 39; David T. Gleeson, *The Irish in the South, 1815–1877* (Chapel Hill, 2001), 26–27, 35–36, 42–43, 46; Randall M. Miller, "The Enemy Within: Some Effects of Foreign Immigrants on Antebellum Southern Cities," *Southern Studies* 24 (1985): 33, 36; Werner H. Steger, "German Immigrants, the Revolution of 1848, and the Politics of Liberalism in Antebellum Richmond," *Yearbook of German-American Studies* 34 (1999): 21; Herrmann Schuricht, *History of the German Element in Virginia*, 2 vols. (1898–1900; reprint, Baltimore, 1999), 2:29, 51, 53; Bogger, *Free Blacks in Norfolk*, 73, 75.

22. Kierner, "'The Dark and Dense Cloud Perpetually Lowering Over Us,'" 209–212; Saunders, "Modernization and the Free Peoples of Richmond," 264.

23. Lebsock, *Free Women of Petersburg*, 169–183; E. Susan Barber, "Depraved and Abandoned Women: Prostitution in Richmond, Virginia, across the Civil War," in Delfino and Gillespie, *Neither Lady nor Slave*, 157; Barbara J. Howe, "Patient Laborers: Women at Work in the Formal Economy of West(ern) Virginia," in ibid., 126, 128–131.

24. Frederick Law Olmsted, *A Journey in the Seaboard Slave States, with Remarks on Their Economy* (New York, 1856), 87; Anne H. Nicholas to Judith C. Applewhaite, 5 Oct. 1807, Cocke Family Papers, Acc. 640, etc., UVA (first quotation); Martha Jefferson Randolph to Ann Cary Randolph Morris, 8 Feb. 1833, Smith Family Papers, APS (second and third quotations). On working-class women's neighborhood-based approach to domestic work and childrearing in a contemporary urban context, see Christine M. Stansell, *City of Women: Sex and Class in New York, 1789–1860* (New York, 1986), 41–52. On urban visiting, see, for instance, Catherine Allgor, *Parlor Politics: In Which the Ladies of Washington Help Build a City and a Government* (Charlottesville, 2000), 117–124.

25. Kierner, *Beyond the Household*, 146–147; Sheila R. Phipps, *Genteel Rebel: The Life of Mary Greenhow Lee* (Baton Rouge, 2004), 46–50, 59–62; Norma Taylor Mitchell, "'With Humbled and Painfully Blited Feelings': A Southwest Virginia Woman in 'the Great Wourld' of Richmond, 1837–1840," in *Searching for Their Places: Women in the South across Four Centuries*, ed. Thomas H. Appleton, Jr., and Angela Boswell (Columbia, Mo., 2003), 80, 84–86, 91; Anya Jabour, *Scarlett's Sisters: Young Women in the Old South* (Chapel Hill, 2007), 114–124; Harriet Randolph to Jane Hollins Randolph, 10 Jan. [1822], Edgehill-Randolph Papers, 1749–1886, Acc. 1397, UVA (quotation). For Ellen Randolph's letters, see Ellen Wayles Randolph to Martha Jefferson Randolph, 30 Mar. [1814], 24 Apr. 1814, 31 Jan.–2 Feb. 1816, [7–17 Feb. 1816], Ellen Wayles Coolidge Correspondence, 1810–1861, Acc. 38-584, 9090, UVA.

26. Eleanor Parke Custis Lewis to Elizabeth Bordley Gibson, 1 Mar. 1815, 4 July 1817 (first quotation), 19 Mar. 1832 (second and third quotations), in *George Washington's Beautiful Nelly: The Letters of Eleanor Parke Custis Lewis to Elizabeth Bordley Gibson, 1794–1851*, ed. Patricia Brady (Columbia, S.C., 1991), 78, 82, 200.

27. On single women in southern cities, see Christine Jacobson Carter, *Southern Single Blessedness: Unmarried Women in the Urban South, 1800–1865* (Urbana, Ill., 2006), 4–9, 13–40.

28. Peter W. Bardaglio, *Reconstructing the Household: Families, Sex, and the Law in the Nineteenth-Century South* (Chapel Hill, 1995), chaps. 1–2; Bertram Wyatt-Brown, *Southern Honor: Ethics and Behavior in the Old South* (New York, 1982). On divorce specifically, see Thomas E. Buckley, S.J., *The Great Catastrophe of My Life: Divorce in the Old Dominion* (Chapel Hill, 2002), esp. 4–9, 32–33.

29. Deborah Gray White, *Ar'n't I a Woman?: Female Slaves in the Plantation South* (New York, 1985), 46–61, 110–117, 120; Olmsted, *Journey in the Seaboard Slave States*, 19 (first quotation), Fredrika Bremer, *The Homes of the New World; Impressions of America*, trans. Mary Howitt, 2 vols. (New York, 1853), 2:519 (second quotation).

30. Bardaglio, *Reconstructing the Household*, 64–68; White, *Ar'n't I a Woman?*, 34–43, 78; Rothman, *Notorious in the Neighborhood*, 14–26. See also the discussion in Annette Gordon-Reed, *The Hemingses of Monticello: An American Family* (New York, 2008), 312–325.

31. Herbert G. Gutman, *The Black Family in Slavery and Freedom, 1750–1925* (New York, 1976), 80–86; White, *Ar'n't I a Woman?*, 67–69; Olmsted, *Journey in the Seaboard Slave States*, 55–56 (quotations).

32. White, *Ar'n't I a Woman?*, 110–114; Eugene D. Genovese, *Roll, Jordan, Roll: The World the Slaves Made* (New York, 1974), 494–501; Sally G. McMillen, *Motherhood in the Old South: Pregnancy, Childbirth, and Infant Rearing* (Baton Rouge, 1990), 79–85, 106; Marie Jenkins Schwartz, *Birthing a Slave: Motherhood and Medicine in the Antebellum South* (Cambridge, Mass., 2006), esp. chaps. 4 and 6; Charles L. Perdue, Jr., Thomas E. Barden, and Robert K. Phillips, eds., *Weevils in the Wheat: Interviews with Virginia Ex-Slaves* (Charlottesville, 1976), 150 (quotation).

33. Petition of Lucinda, 27 Nov. 1815, Legislative Petitions, King George County, RG 78, LVA (first and second quotations); Maria Perkins to Richard Perkins, 8 Oct. 1852 (third quotation), facsimile, Acc. 14358, UVA, original in Ulrich Bonnell Phillips Papers, Yale University Library, New Haven, Conn., digital scan and transcription at The Valley of the Shadow: Two Communities in the American Civil War, University of Virginia, http://valley.lib.virginia.edu/papers/A8020 (accessed 15 June 2012).

34. Gutman, *Black Family*, 123–135.

35. Elizabeth Keckley, *Behind the Scenes, or, Thirty Years a Slave, and Four Years in the White House* (New York, 1868), 29.

36. Keckley, *Behind the Scenes*, 19–39 (quotations on 38–39), 43–44; Jennifer Fleischner, *Mrs. Lincoln and Mrs. Keckly: The Remarkable Story of the Friendship between a First Lady and a Former Slave* (New York, 2003), chap. 4.

37. Stephanie M. H. Camp, *Closer to Freedom: Enslaved Women and Everyday Resistance in the Plantation South* (Chapel Hill, 2004), 2–4, 50–52; White, *Ar'n't I a Woman?*, 76–84; Keckley, *Behind the Scenes*, 34–39; Sharla M. Fett, *Working Cures: Healing, Health, and Power on Southern Slave Plantations* (Chapel Hill, 2002), 130; Perdue et al., *Weevils in the Wheat*, 120 (first quotation); Brenda E. Stevenson, "'Marsa Never Sot Aunt Rebecca Down': Enslaved Women, Religion, and Social Power in the Antebellum South," *Journal of African American History* 90 (2005): 345–376; Olmsted, *Journey in the Seaboard Slave States*, 116–117 (second quotation).

38. Egerton, *Gabriel's Rebellion*, 53, 69; James Sidbury, *Ploughshares into Swords: Race, Rebellion, and Identity in Gabriel's Virginia, 1730–1810* (Cambridge, Eng., 1997), 90–92, 221 n; Michael L. Nicholls, *Whispers of Rebellion: Narrating Gabriel's Conspiracy* (Charlottesville, 2012), 117; Mary Kemp Davis, "'What Happened in This Place?': In Search of the Female Slave in the Nat Turner Slave Insurrection," in *Nat Turner: A Slave Rebellion in History and Memory*, ed. Kenneth S. Greenberg (New York, 2003), 162–176; Henry Irving Tragle, ed., *The Southampton Slave Revolt of 1831: A Compilation of Source Material* (Amherst, Mass., 1971), 229–245; Philip J. Schwarz, *Twice Condemned: Slaves and the Criminal Laws of Virginia, 1705–1865* (Baton Rouge, 1988), 323–334.

39. *Richmond Enquirer*, 30 Aug. 1831 (first, second, and third quotations); Richmond *Constitutional Whig*, 29 Aug. 1831 (fifth quotation); *American Beacon, and Norfolk and Portsmouth Daily Advertiser*, 3 Sept. 1831 (fourth quotation); Tragle, *The Southampton Slave Revolt of 1831*, 44, 53, 56, 78.

40. Virginia Randolph Cary, *Letters on Female Character, Addressed to a Young Lady, on the Death of Her Mother* (Richmond, 1828), v–vi (third quotation), 45 (fourth quotation), 49–50 (first and second quotations). See also Kierner, *Beyond the Household*, 207–211, and, more generally, Elizabeth Fox-Genovese, *Within the Plantation Household: Black and White Women of the Old South* (Chapel Hill, 1988), esp. 37–48.

41. Lucy Hopkins Johnston Ambler to Sarah Tate Steptoe Massie, 3 Aug. 1822, 18 Apr. 1823, in "Letters and Other Papers, 1735–1829," *VMHB* 23 (1915): 188–191; Stella Pickett Hardy, *Colonial Families of the Southern States of America . . .* (New York, 1911), 19–20; Catherine Clinton, *The Plantation Mistress: Woman's World in the Old South* (New York, 1982), chap. 2; D. Harland Hagler, "The Ideal Woman in the Antebellum South: Lady or Farmwife?," *JSH* 46 (1980): 405–418; Jan Lewis and Kenneth A. Lockridge, "'Sally Has Been Sick': Pregnancy and Family Limitation among Virginia Gentry Women, 1780–1830," *Journal of Social History* 22 (1988): 9–12.

42. Henry Glassie, *Folk Housing in Middle Virginia: A Structural Analysis of Historic Artifacts* (Knoxville, Tenn., 1975), 65; Frances Trollope, *Domestic Manners of the Americans*, ed. Donald Smalley (1949; reprint, Gloucester, Mass., 1974), 117 (third, fourth, and fifth quotations), 242–243 (first quotation); Olmsted, *Journey in the Seaboard Slave States*, 17 (second quotation); Anne Newport Royall, *Sketches of History, Life, and Manners, in the United States: By a Traveler* (New Haven, 1826), 30; Stephanie McCurry, "Producing Dependence: Women, Work, and Yeoman Households in Low-Country South Carolina," in Gillespie and Delfino, *Neither Lady nor Slave*, esp. 60–61.

43. Thomas Jefferson to Martha Jefferson Randolph, 4 Apr. 1790, 5 Jan. 1808, in *The Family Letters of Thomas Jefferson*, ed. Edwin Morris Betts and James Adam Bear, Jr. (Columbia, Mo., 1966), 51 (first quotation), 319–320 (second quotation); John Holt Rice, *A Sermon to Young Women . . .* (Richmond, 1819), 10 (fourth quotation), 12, 14 (third quotation), 16; Hagler, "Ideal Woman," 412–416; *Farmer and Planter* 3 (1852): 60 (fifth and sixth quotations).

44. Richmond *Daily Dispatch*, 17 Nov. 1860.

45. Christie Anne Farnham, *The Education of the Southern Belle: Higher Education and Student Socialization in the Antebellum South* (New York, 1994), 33–37; Egerton, *Gabriel's Rebellion*, 165; Wolf, *Race and Liberty*, 120–121, 196–197, 233; Chap. 39, "An Act to amend the act concerning slaves, free negros and mulattoes," enacted 7 Apr. 1831, *Acts Passed at a General Assembly of the Commonwealth of Virginia . . .* (Richmond, 1831), 107–108; Chap. 120, "An Act to reduce into one the several acts concerning crimes and punishments, and proceedings in criminal cases," enacted 14 Mar. 1848, *Acts of the General Assembly of Virginia, Passed at the Session Commencing December 6, 1847 . . .* (Richmond, 1848), 120. On schools, see generally L. Minerva Turnbull, "Private Schools in Norfolk, 1800–1860," *WMQ*, 2d ser., 11 (1931): 277–301; Margaret Meagher, *History of Education in Richmond* (Richmond, 1939), 36–78; Edgar W. Knight, *The Academy Movement in the South* (Chapel Hill, 1919), 23–24.

46. Jean E. Friedman, *The Enclosed Garden: Women and Community in the Evangelical South, 1830–1900* (Chapel Hill, 1985), 6–20; Monica Najar, *Evangelizing the South: A Social History of Church and State in Early America* (New York, 2008), 166–167; Kierner, *Beyond the Household*, 181, 188–198; Cynthia Lynn Lyerly, *Methodism and the Southern Mind, 1770–1810* (New York, 1998), 111–112; Douglas Summers Brown, "Elizabeth Henry Campbell Russell: Patroness of Early

Methodism in the Highlands of Virginia," *Virginia Cavalcade* 30 (1981): 110–117; *DVB*, 2:109–111, 3:640–642; "Lydia Mary Fay," *Encyclopedia Virginia*, http://www.encyclopediavirginia.org/ Fay_Lydia_Mary_ca_1804-1878.

47. Petition of inhabitants of Fredericksburg, [21 Dec. 1803], Legislative Petitions, Fredericksburg, RG 78, LVA (first quotation); Mary Carroll Johansen, "All Useful, Plain Branches of Education: Educating Non-Elite Women in Antebellum Virginia," *Virginia Cavalcade* 49 (2000): 76–79; Elizabeth R. Varon, *We Mean to Be Counted: White Women and Politics in Antebellum Virginia* (Chapel Hill, 1998), 29; Mary Blackford to Ralph R. Gurley, 23 Feb. 1835, American Colonization Society Records, Mss 10660, Reel 22B, LC (second quotation); Margaret Douglass, *Educational Laws of Virginia: The Personal Narrative of Mrs. Margaret Douglass, a Southern Woman, Who Was Imprisoned for One Month in the Common Jail of Norfolk, under the Laws of Virginia, for the Crime of Teaching Free Colored Children to Read* (Boston, 1854).

48. Varon, *We Mean to Be Counted*, 27–30; Kimball, *American City, Southern Place*, 68; Cynthia A. Kierner, "Woman's Piety within Patriarchy: The Religious Life of Martha Hancock Wheat of Bedford County," *VMHB* 100 (1992): 96–97; Diary of Martha Ann Hancock Wheat, p. 95 (quotation), Miscellaneous Papers, Collection 517, UNC.

49. Johansen, "All Useful, Plain Branches of Education," 76–78; School commissioners of Augusta County, account with Jane Bumgardner for session ending 30 Sept. 1850, filed 11 Feb. 1851, Legislative Petitions, Augusta County, RG 78, LVA; Petition of Martha A. Walker, 8 Feb. 1850, Legislative Petitions, Brunswick County, RG 78, LVA (quotation).

50. Richmond *Virginia Argus*, 19 Feb. 1808; Rules of the Roanoke Female Seminary, [1839], Edward William Johnston Letter, 20 Sept. 1839, Acc. 24916, Personal Papers Collection, LVA; Farnham, *Education of the Southern Belle*, chap. 3.

51. James Mercer Garnett, *Lectures on Female Education, Comprising the First and Second Series of a Course Delivered to Mrs. Garnett's Pupils, at Elm-wood, Essex County, Virginia* (Richmond, 1825), 79–80 (first, second, and third quotations), 94, 218 (fourth quotation); Jabour, *Scarlett's Sisters*, 54–55; William Wirt to "My dear Children," 23 May 1829, William Wirt Papers, 1784–1864, Ms 1011, Maryland Historical Society (fifth and sixth quotations); Henry W. Wood to Julia Wood, [1855], quoted in Sue Roberson West, *Buckingham Female Collegiate Institute, First Chartered College for Women in Virginia, 1837–1843, 1844–1863: A Documentary History* (Charlotte, N.C., 1990), 35 (seventh and eighth quotations).

52. Richmond *Enquirer*, 17 Sept. 1805 (second quotation), 5 Sept. 1809 (first quotation); Kierner, *Beyond the Household*, 155–157; Steven M. Stowe, "The Not-So-Cloistered Academy: Elite Women's Education and Family Feeling in the Old South," in *The Web of Southern Social Relations: Women, Family, and Education*, ed. Walter J. Fraser, Jr., R. Franklin Saunders, Jr., and Jon L. Wakelyn (Athens, Ga., 1985), 92–94.

53. Kierner, *Beyond the Household*, 159; Jabour, *Scarlett's Sisters*, esp. 64–82, 89–96; Kathleen Johnson, "Nineteenth-Century Reflections on Life, Love, and Loss in the Diary of Clay Dillard," *North Carolina Historical Review* 81 (2004): 168–175; *Godey's Lady's Book* 56 (May 1858): 468 (quotation).

54. Thomas Jefferson to François Barbé-Marbois, 5 Dec. 1783, in *The Papers of Thomas Jefferson*, ed. Julian P. Boyd et al. (Princeton, 1950–), 6:374 (first quotation); Rice, *Sermon to Young Women*, 6–8 (second quotation); Cary, *Letters on Female Character*, v–vii (third and fourth quotations), 22, 149 (fifth quotation).

55. Petition of the trustees of the Southern Female Institute, 9 Dec. 1850, Legislative Petitions, Spotsylvania County, RG 78, LVA.

56. West, *Buckingham Female Collegiate Institute*, 17–22, 25, 29–30, 44–46; Petition of the Young Ladies of the Female Collegiate Institute, 28 Mar. 1843, Legislative Petitions, Buckingham County, RG 78, LVA; Wallenstein, *Cradle of America*, 135–136. Augusta Female Seminary in Staunton became Mary Baldwin College, and Valley Union Seminary, in Roanoke County, became Hollins University; both remain single-sex schools, at least in terms of their undergraduate programs. Farmville Female Seminary became the State Female Normal School and later coeducational Longwood University. Baptist Female Seminary, of Danville, evolved into the coeducational Averett University.

57. Kierner, *Beyond the Household*, 203–210; Mary Randolph, *The Virginia House-Wife* (Washington, 1824), x (quotation). On southern women novelists generally, see Elizabeth Moss, *Domestic Novelists in the Old South: Defenders of Southern Culture* (Baton Rouge, 1992).

58. *DVB*, 3:139–140.

59. John Randolph to Elizabeth Coalter, 25 Dec. 1828, in William Cabell Bruce, *John Randolph of Roanoke, 1773–1833*, 2 vols. (New York, 1922), 2:363 (first quotation); Rice, *Sermon to Young Women*, 14 (second quotation). In general, see Kierner, *Beyond the Household*, 188–199; Timothy James Lockley, *Welfare and Charity in the Antebellum South* (Gainesville, Fla., 2007), chap. 2.

60. Kierner, *Beyond the Household*, 190; *DVB*, 3:35–37; *Richmond Enquirer*, 17 Feb. 1842 (quotations).

61. *Constitution and By-Laws of the Female Humane Association of the City of Richmond* ... (1898), n.p. (quotation); *Historical Sketch of Richmond's Oldest Chartered Charity: Memorial Home for Girls, Formerly Female Humane Association, 1805–1925* (Richmond, [1925]), 7–8, 27; Lockley, *Welfare and Charity*, 60, 69, 74, 76, 106–108; Varon, *We Mean to Be Counted*, 11.

62. Lebsock, *Free Women of Petersburg*, 215–229; Lockley, *Welfare and Charity*, 73, 137–138, 143, 148; Varon, *We Mean to Be Counted*, 21–23.

63. Kierner, *Beyond the Household*, 193–197; Lebsock, *Free Women of Petersburg*, 12–13, 215–220; Lockley, *Welfare and Charity*, 112–113, 141–142; Varon, *We Mean to Be Counted*, 23–25; Myron Berman, *Richmond's Jewry, 1769–1976: Shabbat in Shockoe* (Charlottesville, 1979), 56, 145; Gerald P. Fogarty, S.J., *Commonwealth Catholicism: A History of the Catholic Church in Virginia* (Notre Dame, Ind., 2001), 67, 72–73, 78; James Henry Bailey II, *A History of the Diocese of Richmond: The Formative Years* (Richmond, 1956), 128; Kimball, *American City, Southern Place*, 259; Ruth Coder Fitzgerald, *A Different Story: A Black History of Fredericksburg, Stafford, and Spotsylvania, Virginia* (Fredericksburg, 1979), 86.

64. "Female Benevolent Society: Bonds of Association," 11 Jan. 1859 (broadside 1859 F32 FF), Special Collections, LVA.

65. Cynthia A. Kierner, "Genteel Balls and Republican Parades: Gender and Early Southern Civic Rituals, 1677–1826," *VMHB* 104 (1996): 199–204; Kimball, *American City, Southern Place*, 194–196; Schuricht, *History of the German Element*, 2:31–32; Richmond *Daily Dispatch*, 15 Sept. 1857.

66. *Richmond Enquirer*, 20 Oct. 1829. The author thanks Sara B. Bearss and Marianne E. Julienne for this reference.

67. Marie Tyler-McGraw, *An African Republic: Black and White Virginians in the Making of Liberia* (Chapel Hill, 2007), 97; Susan Loushing to John Q. Adams, 31 Jan. 1837, Adams Family Papers, Reel 505, Massachusetts Historical Society, Boston (first, second, and third quotations); *Congressional Globe*, 24th Congress, 2d session, 164–165 (fourth, fifth, and sixth quotations); Susan Zaeske, *Signatures of Citizenship: Petitioning, Antislavery, and Women's Political Identity* (Chapel Hill, 2003), esp. 76–81, 133–140.

68. *Columbian Star, and Christian Index* 1 (1829): 179 (quotation)–180; Kierner, *Beyond the Household*, 199–202; Varon, *We Mean to Be Counted*, 30–36; Patricia C. Click, *The Spirit of the Times: Amusements in Nineteenth-Century Baltimore, Norfolk, and Richmond* (Charlottesville, 1989), 77–81; Ian R. Tyrrell, "Women and Temperance in Antebellum America, 1830–1860," *Civil War History* 28 (1982): 131; Tyrrell, "Drink and Temperance in the Antebellum South: An Overview and Interpretation," *JSH* 48 (1982): 495–510.

69. Petition of 26 Ladies of the County of Cabell, 19 Feb. 1849, Legislative Petitions, Cabell County, RG 78, LVA (quotations); Petition of the Citizens of Hancock County, 21 Dec. 1853, Legislative Petitions, Hancock County, RG 78, LVA; Petition of the Ladies of Hancock County, 21 Dec. 1853, Legislative Petitions, Hancock County, RG 78, LVA; Varon, *We Mean to Be Counted*, 36–37.

70. Jefferson, *Notes on the State of Virginia*, 162–163; Cary, *Letters on Female Character*, 134–135 (second and third quotations), 174 (first quotation); Patrick H. Breen, ed., "The Female Antislavery Petition Campaign of 1831–32," *VMHB* 110 (2002): 378–379; Tyler-McGraw, *An African Republic*, esp. 3–4; Douglas R. Egerton, "'Its Origin Is Not a Little Curious': A New Look at the American Colonization Society," *Journal of the Early Republic* 5 (1985): 463–480.

71. Tyler-McGraw, *An African Republic*, 83–101; Varon, *We Mean to Be Counted*, 42–45; Louis B. Gimelli, "Louisa Maxwell Cocke: An Evangelical Plantation Mistress in the Antebellum South," *Journal of the Early Republic* 9 (1989): 59–64; Charles W. Andrews, *Memoir of Mrs. Anne R. Page* (Philadelphia, 1844), 16, 23, 27 (quotation), 46–47, 55–58.

72. Varon, *We Mean to Be Counted*, 48–52. These petitions are reprinted in Breen, "Female Antislavery Petition Campaign," 384–386 (fourth, fifth, and sixth quotations), 389–391, 394–395 (first, second, and third quotations).

73. Tyler-McGraw, *An African Republic*, 89–92, 119–120; William W. Freehling, *The Road to Disunion*, vol. 1: *Secessionists at Bay, 1776–1854* (New York, 1990), 183, 188–189; Varon, *We Mean to Be Counted*, 45–56, 110; *DVB*, 1:523–524, 3:640–642.

74. Tyler-McGraw, *An African Republic*, 128–129, 142–143, 155, 169.

75. Varon, *We Mean to Be Counted*, 71–89; M. D. Clayton to her aunt, 8 May 1840 (transcription), in The Valley of the Shadow: Two Communities in the American Civil War, University of Virginia, http://etext.lib.virginia.edu/etcbin/civwarlett-browse?id=A8021 (accessed 15 June 2012) (quotations).

76. Varon, *We Mean to Be Counted*, 88–93.

77. Ibid., 103 (first quotation)–114; *DVB*, 2:443–444; Martha Haines Butt, *Antifanaticism: A Tale of the South* (Philadelphia, 1853), vii (second quotation).

78. Steven Conn, "Rescuing the Homestead of the Nation: The Mount Vernon Ladies' Association and the Preservation of Mount Vernon," *Nineteenth-Century Studies* 11 (1997): 71–93; *Charleston Mercury*, 2 Dec. 1853 (first quotation); Beverley R. Wellford, Jr., "Address Delivered Before the Ladies' Mount Vernon Association, July 4, 1855," *Southern Literary Messenger* 21 (Sept. 1855): 563, 565 (second quotation); Varon, *We Mean to Be Counted*, 124–136.

79. Thomas Nelson Page, *Mount Vernon and Its Preservation, 1858–1910* (New York, 1910), 32–34, 55; Edward Everett, *Orations and Speeches on Various Occasions*, 3 vols. (Boston, 1870), 3:622–623 (first and second quotations); Petersburg *Daily Express*, 17 May 1856 (third quotation).

80. Wellford, "Address," 563–566.

81. Evelyn L. Pugh, "Women and Slavery: Julia Gardiner Tyler and the Duchess of Sutherland," *VMHB* 88 (1980): 186–202; Robert Seager II, *And Tyler Too: A Biography of John and Julia Gardiner Tyler* (New York, 1963), 243–246, 257–265, 402–406; Varon, *We Mean to Be*

Counted, 112–114; Julia Gardiner Tyler, "To the Duchess of Sutherland and Ladies of England," *Southern Literary Messenger* 19 (Feb. 1853): 120 (first quotation)–126; F. W. Thomas to Julia Gardiner Tyler, 22 Feb. 1845, Tyler Family Papers, Mss 65 T97, Group A, W&M (second quotation).

CHAPTER 4

1. Percentage of white men in Confederate forces in Aaron Sheehan-Dean, *Why Confederates Fought: Family and Nation in Civil War Virginia* (Chapel Hill, 2007), 13.

2. See Sally Lyons Taliaferro Diary (1859–1864), 19 Nov. 1859, Acc. 24311, Personal Papers Collection, LVA; Sallie [surname unknown] to Callie Anthony, Dec. 1859, Anthony Family Papers (1785–1952), Acc. 35647, 35648, Personal Papers Collection, LVA.

3. Nancy Chappelear Baird, ed., *Journals of Amanda Virginia Edmonds: Lass of the Mosby Confederacy, 1859–1867* (Stephens City, Va., 1984), xii, 31–33 (quotation, entry for 11 Nov. 1859).

4. Sallie [surname unknown] to Callie Anthony, December 1859, Anthony Family Papers, Acc. 35647, 35648, LVA (first quotation); *Rockingham Register and Advertiser*, 2 Dec. 1859 (second, third, and fourth quotations); New Orleans *Courier*, 31 Dec. 1859 (fifth quotation); Elizabeth R. Varon, *We Mean to Be Counted: White Women and Politics in Antebellum Virginia* (Chapel Hill, 1998), 142–143.

5. For white women's antebellum political participation, see Varon, *We Mean to Be Counted*.

6. Varon, *We Mean to Be Counted*, 144–148; *New York Herald*, 1 Nov. 1860 (quotation).

7. Wheeling *Daily Intelligencer*, 4 Sept., 9, 10 Oct. 1860. See also Varon, *We Mean to Be Counted*, 148–149.

8. Cornelia Peake McDonald, *A Woman's Civil War: A Diary, with Reminiscences of the War, from March 1862*, ed. Minrose C. Gwin (Madison, Wis., 1992), 247 (first quotation); Sue Ragsdale to Callie Anthony, 21 Jan. 1861, Anthony Family Papers, Acc. 35647, 35648, LVA (second quotation); *Fredericksburg News*, 21 Dec. 1860 (third quotation). For the pervasiveness of secession as a conversation topic, see *Lynchburg Daily Virginian*, 30 Nov. 1860; *Alexandria Gazette*, 18 Jan. 1861; Sheila R. Phipps, *Genteel Rebel: The Life of Mary Greenhow Lee* (Baton Rouge, 2004), 89. On sacrificing luxuries, see *Lynchburg Daily Virginian*, 20 Dec. 1860.

9. William A. Link, *Roots of Secession: Slavery and Politics in Antebellum Virginia* (Chapel Hill, 2003), 226–227; George W. Berlin to Susan Miranda Holt Berlin, 14 Feb. 1861, Berlin-Martz Family Papers (1800–1895), Acc. 36271, Personal Papers Collection, LVA; Varon, *We Mean to Be Counted*, 155.

10. Sarah Ann Brock, *Richmond during the War: Four Years of Personal Observation, by a Richmond Lady* (New York, 1867), 17.

11. Varon, *We Mean to Be Counted*, 155; Eppa Hunton, *Autobiography of Eppa Hunton* (Richmond, 1933), 13; *Lynchburg Daily Virginian*, 27 Mar. 1861; *Staunton Vindicator*, 29 Mar. 1861.

12. Varon, *We Mean to Be Counted*, 143, 159.

13. John B. Minor to Mary B. Blackford, 16 Apr. 1861, Correspondence 1861–1865, Blackford Family Papers, Collection 1912, UNC.

14. *Richmond Semi-Weekly Examiner*, 22 Mar. 1861; *Staunton Vindicator*, 5 Apr. 1861; *Alexandria Gazette*, 26 Mar. 1861. See also Link, *Roots of Secession*, 246.

15. *Daily Richmond Examiner*, 18 Mar. 1861.

16. Ibid., 21 Mar. 1861.

17. Ibid., 16 Apr. 1861.

18. *Staunton Vindicator*, 18 Jan., 5 Apr. 1861; *Alexandria Gazette*, 22 Apr. 1861; *Rockingham Register and Advertiser*, 29 Mar. 1861.

19. Mary Berkeley Minor Blackford to John B. Minor, 18 Jan. 1861, Minor and Wilson Family Papers, Acc. 3750a, UVA; Varon, *We Mean to Be Counted*, 150–151.

20. *Alexandria Gazette*, 26 Mar., 13 Apr. 1861; Varon, *We Mean to Be Counted*, 150.

21. McDonald, *A Woman's Civil War*, 249; Judith W. McGuire, *Diary of a Southern Refugee during the War* (Lincoln, Neb., 1995), 17; Mary L. Mackall, Stevan F. Meserve, and Anne Mackall Sasscer, eds., *In the Shadow of the Enemy: The Civil War Journal of Ida Powell Dulany* (Knoxville, Tenn., 2009), 112.

22. McDonald, *A Woman's Civil War*, 250.

23. Sally Lyons Taliaferro Diary, 4 Mar., 17 (first quotation), 28 (second quotation) Apr. 1861, Acc. 24311, LVA; Varon, *We Mean to Be Counted*, 168.

24. Emmert F. Bittinger, ed., *Unionists and the Civil War Experience in the Shenandoah Valley*, 5 vols. to date (Dayton, Va., 2003–), 3:214–215, 217 (quotation).

25. Ibid., 2:69–70.

26. Varon, *We Mean to Be Counted*, 163–165.

27. *Alexandria Gazette*, 22 Apr. 1861; *Lynchburg Daily Virginian*, 2 May 1861.

28. *Staunton Vindicator*, 10 May 1861.

29. On justice of cause, see Elizabeth R. Baer, ed., *Shadows on My Heart: The Civil War Diary of Lucy Rebecca Buck of Virginia* (Athens, Ga., 1997), xxii, and McGuire, *Diary of a Southern Refugee*, 12. On disdain for Northerners, see Pattie B. Cowles to George S. Bernard, 27 May 1861, George S. Bernard Papers, Acc. 31760, Personal Papers Collection, LVA.

30. Lucy Buck to "My own dear brother-cousin," [Apr. 1861], Correspondence of Richard Bayly Buck, 1861-1865, Acc. 3064, UVA (quotation); Sheehan-Dean, *Why Confederates Fought*, 23.

31. Sarah A. Logan to John Letcher, 20 Apr. 1861, John Letcher Executive Papers (1859–1863), Acc. 36787, LVA; *Rockingham Register and Advertiser*, 12 July 1861.

32. Sheehan-Dean, *Why Confederates Fought*, 23; Myrta Lockett Avary, ed., *A Virginia Girl in the Civil War: Being a Record of the Actual Experiences of the Wife of a Confederate Officer* (1903; reprint, Santa Barbara, Calif., 2004), 20.

33. Pattie B. Cowles to George S. Bernard, 5 June 1861, George S. Bernard Papers, Acc. 31760, LVA (quotation); *Rockingham Register and Advertiser*, 5 July 1861. See also Julia Chase Diary in *Winchester Divided: The Civil War Diaries of Julia Chase and Laura Lee*, ed. Michael G. Mahon (Mechanicsburg, Pa., 2002), 59, and Mary Watkins to Richard Watkins, 8 July 1861, in *Send Me a Pair of Old Boots and Kiss My Little Girls: The Civil War Letters of Richard and Mary Watkins, 1861–1865*, ed. Jeff Toalson (New York, 2009), 13.

34. Richmond *Daily Dispatch*, 29 Apr. 1861.

35. Mackall et al., *In the Shadow of the Enemy*, 6 (second quotation), 8 (first quotation).

36. Isabella Woods to Samuel Woods, n.d., in Ruth Woods Dayton, *Samuel Woods and His Family* ([Charleston, W.Va.], 1939), 30.

37. Jacqueline Glass Campbell, *When Sherman Marched North from the Sea: Resistance on the Confederate Home Front* (Chapel Hill, 2003), 71; Caroline E. Janney, *Burying the Dead but Not the Past: Ladies' Memorial Associations and the Lost Cause* (Chapel Hill, 2008), 30.

38. McGuire, *Diary of a Southern Refugee*, 12.

39. *Fredericksburg News*, 4 June 1861.

40. Avary, *A Virginia Girl in the Civil War*, 18–19; McDonald, *A Woman's Civil War*, 252.

41. Sally Lyons Taliaferro Diary, 6 July 1861, Acc. 24311, LVA; McGuire, *Diary of a Southern Refugee*, 107; Bessie Callender, "Personal Recollections of the Civil War," quoted in Janney, *Burying the Dead but Not the Past*, 18. See also *Fredericksburg News*, 3 May 1861.

42. *Alexandria Gazette*, 20 May 1861; McDonald, *A Woman's Civil War*, 254; quotation in Pattie B. Cowles to George S. Bernard, 27 May 1861, George S. Bernard Papers, Acc. 31760, LVA (quotation).

43. *Fredericksburg News*, 28 June 1861; *Lynchburg Daily Virginian*, 21 May (quotation), 25, 30 July 1861.

44. Anne Sarah Rubin, *A Shattered Nation: The Rise and Fall of the Confederacy, 1861–1868* (Chapel Hill, 2005), 55; Eloise C. Strader, ed., *The Civil War Journal of Mary Greenhow Lee (Mrs. Hugh Holmes Lee) of Winchester, Virginia* (Winchester, 2011), 338 (quotation).

45. Maggie H. Berry to Thomas Smiley, 12 July 1861, Smiley Family Papers, 1750–1959, Acc. 1807, UVA, digital scan and transcription at The Valley of the Shadow: Two Communities in the American Civil War, University of Virginia, http://valley.lib.virginia.edu/papers/A6060 (accessed 1 June 2012).

46. Pattie B. Cowles to George S. Bernard, 27 May, 5 June (quotation) 1861, George S. Bernard Papers, Acc. 31760, LVA.

47. Wheeling *Daily Intelligencer*, 23 May 1861; *Wellsburg Herald*, 31 May 1861.

48. Wheeling *Daily Intelligencer*, 23 May 1861.

49. *Wellsburg Herald*, 31 May 1861.

50. Wheeling *Daily Intelligencer*, 30 May 1861.

51. Laura Lee Diary in Mahon, *Winchester Divided*, 66.

52. Mackall et al., *In the Shadow of the Enemy*, 7 (first quotation), 69, 78 (second quotation), 90 (third quotation).

53. Isabella Woods to Samuel Woods, 8 Oct. 1861, in Dayton, *Samuel Woods and His Family*, 47; McDonald, *A Woman's Civil War*, 142.

54. See Mahon, *Winchester Divided*; Mackall et al., *In the Shadow of the Enemy*; Baer, *Shadows on My Heart*; McDonald, *A Woman's Civil War*; McGuire, *Diary of a Southern Refugee*. See also Janney, *Burying the Dead but Not the Past*, 16, 23.

55. For example, Mackall et al., *In the Shadow of the Enemy*, 16.

56. Maggie H. Berry to Thomas M. Smiley, 12 July 1861, Smiley Family Papers, Acc. 1807, University of Virginia, digital scan and transcription on The Valley of the Shadow website, UVA, http://valley.lib.virginia.edu/papers/A6060 (accessed 1 June 2012).

57. Baer, *Shadows on My Heart*, 25.

58. Robert Kenzer, "The Uncertainty of Life: A Profile of Virginia's Civil War Widows," in *The War Was You and Me: Civilians in the American Civil War*, ed. Joan E. Cashin (Princeton, 2002), 113; Database of Virginia Military Dead, LVA, http://www.lva.virginia.gov/public/guides/vmd/vmd_Search.asp (accessed 27 June 2012).

59. Mackall et al., *In the Shadow of the Enemy*, 95 (first quotation), 99 (second quotation).

60. Emily J. Salmon, "*The Burial of Latané*: Symbol of the Lost Cause," *Virginia Cavalcade* 28 (1979): 118–129; Janney, *Burying the Dead but Not the Past*, 33–34; Drew Gilpin Faust, *Southern Stories: Slaveholders in Peace and War* (Columbia, Mo., 1992), 148–159.

61. Joan E. Cashin, "Into the Trackless Wilderness: The Refugee Experience in the Civil War," in *A Woman's War: Southern Women, Civil War, and the Confederate Legacy* in Edward D. C. Campbell, Jr., and Kym S. Rice (Richmond and Charlottesville, 1996), 43; James I. Robertson, Jr., *Civil War Virginia: Battleground for a Nation* (Charlottesville, 1991), 89; James Archer Evans,

"War Experiences of Mrs. S. G. Tinsley" (typescript dated 21–22 Sept. 1937), p. 7 (quotation), Works Progress Administration Virginia Historical Inventory, LVA; McDonald, *A Woman's Civil War*, 73.

62. Robertson, *Civil War Virginia*, 88; Drew Gilpin Faust, *Mothers of Invention: Women of the Slaveholding South in the American Civil War* (Chapel Hill, 1996), 109–111.

63. Amy R. Minton, "Defining Confederate Respectability: Morality, Patriotism, and Confederate Identity in Richmond's Civil War Public Press," in *Crucible of the Civil War: Virginia from Secession to Commemoration*, ed. Edward L. Ayers, Gary W. Gallagher, and Andrew J. Torget (Charlottesville, 2006), 92–93.

64. Drew Gilpin Faust, "'Ours as Well as That of the Men': Women and Gender in the Civil War," in *Writing the Civil War: The Quest to Understand*, ed. James M. McPherson and William J. Cooper, Jr. (Columbia, S.C., 1998), 233–234; Steven Elliott Tripp, *Yankee Town, Southern City: Race and Class Relations in Civil War Lynchburg* (New York, 1997), 123; Jane E. Schultz, *Women at the Front: Hospital Workers in Civil War America* (Chapel Hill, 2004); Wilma A. Dunaway, *The African-American Family in Slavery and Emancipation* (Cambridge, 2003), 187–188.

65. Rubin, *A Shattered Nation*, 56; McGuire, *Diary of a Southern Refugee*, 169, 178; McDonald, *A Woman's Civil War*, 38–39.

66. Drew Gilpin Faust, Thavolia Glymph, and George C. Rable, "A Woman's War: Southern Women in the Civil War," in Campbell and Rice, *A Woman's War*, 5.

67. See Bell Irvin Wiley, ed., *A Southern Woman's Story: Life in Confederate Richmond* (Jackson, Tenn., 1959).

68. Tripp, *Yankee Town, Southern City*, 122–123; Janney, *Burying the Dead but Not the Past*, 25–26.

69. Robertson, *Civil War Virginia*, 93; Janney, *Burying the Dead but Not the Past*, 26; biographical material in finding aid for Sally Louisa Tompkins and Robertson Hospital Collection, Museum of the Confederacy, Richmond, Va..

70. Mackall et al., *In the Shadow of the Enemy*, 23, 25; McGuire, *Diary of a Southern Refugee*, 163.

71. McGuire, *Diary of a Southern Refugee*, 97, 207, 218 (quotation); Laura Lee Diary, entry for 24 Dec. 1864, in Mahon, *Winchester Divided*, 177.

72. Cashin, "Into the Trackless Wilderness," in Campbell and Rice, *A Woman's War*, 43; Faust, "Ours as Well as That of the Men," in McPherson and Cooper, *Writing the Civil War*, 239.

73. Isabella N. Woods to Samuel Woods, 1 Feb. 1863, in Dayton, *Samuel Woods and His Family*, 81.

74. McDonald, *A Woman's Civil War*, 204–205; McGuire, *Diary of a Southern Refugee*, 195, 169; Mackall et al., *In the Shadow of the Enemy*, 145; Mary Watkins to Richard Watkins, 5 Sept. 1862, in Toalson, *Send Me a Pair of Old Boots and Kiss My Little Girls*, 130.

75. William Blair, *Virginia's Private War: Feeding Body and Soul in the Confederacy, 1861–1865* (New York, 1998), 79, 93; Sheehan-Dean, *Why Confederates Fought*, 88, 100.

76. McDonald, *A Woman's Civil War*, 222, 230.

77. McGuire, *Diary of a Southern Refugee*, 324–325; Avary, *A Virginia Girl in the Civil War*, 200–201.

78. Tripp, *Yankee Town, Southern City*, 125.

79. Catherine Clinton, "'Public Women' and Sexual Politics during the American Civil War," in *Battle Scars: Gender and Sexuality in the American Civil War*, ed. Catherine Clinton and Nina Silber (Oxford, 2006), 67; Michael B. Chesson, "Harlots or Heroines?: A New Look at

the Richmond Bread Riot," *VMHB* 92 (Apr. 1984): 135; Richard Watkins to Mary Watkins, 20 July 1862, in Toalson, *Send Me a Pair of Old Boots and Kiss My Little Girls*, 113 (quotation).

80. Chesson, "Harlots or Heroines?," 139–169; Clinton, "'Public Women,'" in Clinton and Silber, *Battle Scars*, 68–70, 74.

81. Janney, *Burying the Dead but Not the Past*, 18; Tripp, *Yankee Town, Southern City*, 142–144; Melvin I. Urofsky, *Commonwealth and Community: The Jewish Experience in Virginia* (Richmond, 1997), 84.

82. William Frank Zornow, "Aid for the Indigent Families of Soldiers in Virginia, 1861–1865," *VMHB* 66 (Oct. 1958): 454–458; Tripp, *Yankee Town, Southern City*, 141; Campbell, *When Sherman Marched North from the Sea*, 84; Laura F. Edwards, *Scarlett Doesn't Live Here Anymore: Southern Women in the Civil War Era* (Urbana, Ill., 2000), 81.

83. Zornow, "Aid for the Indigent Families of Soldiers"; quotation in Westmoreland County, Reports of Indigent Soldiers' Families (1861–1865), box 1, Westmoreland County Court Records, Local Government Records Collection, LVA; Kenzer, "The Uncertainty of Life," in Cashin, *The War Was You and Me*, 122–125.

84. Brock, *Richmond during the War*, 272–274.

85. David L. Burton, "Richmond's Great Homefront Disaster: Friday the 13th," *Civil War Times Illustrated* 21 (Oct. 1982): 36–40; Clinton, "'Public Women,'" in Clinton and Silber, *Battle Scars*, 68.

86. Brock, *Richmond during the War*, 272–274; *DVB*, 1:280.

87. McGuire, *Diary of a Southern Refugee*, 174, 196, 244 (first quotation), 251 (second quotation). See also, for example, Sue J. Marchant (18 Feb. 1863), Applications of Ladies for Clerkships on Virginia Treasury Notes (1861–1864), Auditor of Public Accounts, Box 1177, RG 48, LVA.

88. Faust et al., "A Woman's War," in Campbell and Rice, *A Woman's War*, 11; LeeAnn Whites, *The Civil War as a Crisis in Gender: Augusta, Georgia, 1860–1890* (Athens, Ga., 1995), 66, 72; Faust, *Mothers of Invention*, 32.

89. Isabella N. Woods to Samuel Woods, 16 Sept. 1861, in Dayton, *Samuel Woods and His Family*, 37.

90. Mackall et al., *In the Shadow of the Enemy*, xxiv, 31 (quotation), 68–69.

91. Lynda J. Morgan, *Emancipation in Virginia's Tobacco Belt, 1850–1870* (Athens, Ga., 1992), 97–98, 123; Tripp, *Yankee Town, Southern City*, 146–147.

92. Edwards, *Scarlett Doesn't Live Here Anymore*, 78; Faust et al., "A Woman's War," in Campbell and Rice, *A Woman's War*, 2–3, 20.

93. Tripp, *Yankee Town, Southern City*, 148; Faust et al., "A Woman's War," in Campbell and Rice, *A Woman's War*, 86; Mackall et al., *In the Shadow of the Enemy*, 105.

94. Mackall et al., *In the Shadow of the Enemy*, 90 (quotation); Morgan, *Emancipation in Virginia's Tobacco Belt*, 105.

95. Faust et al., "A Woman's War," in Campbell and Rice, *A Woman's War*, 16; Edwards, *Scarlett Doesn't Live Here Anymore*, 102.

96. Suzanne Lebsock, *The Free Women of Petersburg: Status and Culture in a Southern Town, 1784–1860* (New York, 1984), 245; Thavolia Glymph, "'This Species of Property': Female Slave Contrabands in the Civil War," in Campbell and Rice, *A Woman's War*, 60; Jaime Amanda Martinez, "The Slave Market in Civil War Virginia," in Ayers, Gallagher, and Torget, *Crucible of the Civil War*, 107, 124.

97. Martinez, "The Slave Market in Civil War Virginia," in Ayers, Gallagher, and Torget, *Crucible of the Civil War*, 124–125, 128, 130–131.

98. McDonald, *A Woman's Civil War*, 82–84.

99. Michelle Ann Krowl, "Dixie's Other Daughters: African-American Women in Virginia, 1861–1868" (Ph.D. diss., University of California, Berkeley, 1998), 68.

100. McGuire, *Diary of a Southern Refugee*, 128, 145; Tripp, *Yankee Town, Southern City*, 144; Julia Chase Diary, entry for 28 Jan. 1863, in Mahon, *Winchester Divided*, 79.

101. McDonald, *A Woman's Civil War*, 65; Krowl, "Dixie's Other Daughters," 292.

102. Michelle A. Krowl, "African American Women and the United States Military in Civil War Virginia," in *Afro-Virginian History and Culture*, ed. John Saillant (New York, 1999), 176–177; Krowl, "Dixie's Other Daughters," 17–20; Glymph, "'This Species of Property,'" in Campbell and Rice, *A Woman's War*, 58–59; Robert Francis Engs, *Freedom's First Generation: Black Hampton, Virginia, 1861–1890* (New York, 2004), 17–20, 31.

103. Krowl, "African American Women and the United States Military," in Saillant, *Afro-Virginian History and Culture*, 181–184; Engs, *Freedom's First Generation*, 27; Antoinette G. van Zelm, "On the Front Lines of Freedom: Black and White Women Shape Emancipation in Virginia, 1861–1890" (Ph.D. diss., College of William and Mary, 1998), 103–108.

104. van Zelm, "On the Front Lines of Freedom," 102; Krowl, "Dixie's Other Daughters," 108–113.

105. Joseph P. Reidy, "'Coming from the Shadow of the Past': The Transition from Slavery to Freedom at Freedmen's Village, 1863–1900," *VMHB* 95 (1987): 403–428.

106. Glymph, "'This Species of Property,'" in Campbell and Rice, *A Woman's War*, 58–59; Faust et al., "A Woman's War," in Campbell and Rice, *A Woman's War*, 23; Edwards, *Scarlett Doesn't Live Here Anymore*, 106, 109; Krowl, "Dixie's Other Daughters," 73; Tripp, *Yankee Town, Southern City*, 145.

107. Mackall et al., *In the Shadow of the Enemy*, 93–94; Baer, *Shadows on My Heart*, 209 (quotation).

108. McGuire, *Diary of a Southern Refugee*, 279 (quotations). See also Laura Lee Diary in Rice and Campbell, "Voices From the Tempest," in Campbell and Rice, *A Woman's War*, 83; and Baer, *Shadows on My Heart*, 209, 211.

109. Baer, *Shadows on My Heart*, 214.

110. Faust, *Mothers of Invention*, 36, 45–51; Whites, *The Civil War as a Crisis in Gender*, 33; Avary, *A Virginia Girl in the Civil War*, 25; Mary Watkins to Richard Watkins, 8 July 1861, in Toalson, *Send Me a Pair of Old Boots and Kiss My Little Girls*, 12.

111. McGuire, *Diary of a Southern Refugee*, 27 (quotation); Cashin, "Into the Trackless Wilderness," in Campbell and Rice, *A Woman's War*, 32–33.

112. Isabella N. Woods to Samuel Woods, 16 Sept. 1861, in Dayton, *Samuel Woods and His Family*, 38–39; McDonald, *A Woman's Civil War*, 236; McGuire, *Diary of a Southern Refugee*, 159–160, 358.

113. Joan Cashin, "Into the Trackless Wilderness," in Campbell and Rice, *A Woman's War*, 32–33, 36.

114. McDonald, *A Woman's Civil War*, 168–169 (quotation); McGuire, *Diary of a Southern Refugee*, 87–88, 293.

115. Krowl, "Dixie's Other Daughters," 127–130, 274; Campbell, *When Sherman Marched North from the Sea*, 47–48; Krowl, "African American Women and the United States Military,"

in Saillant, *Afro-Virginian History and Culture*, 193, 195; Ervin L. Jordan, Jr., *Black Confederates and Afro-Yankees in Civil War Virginia* (Charlottesville, 1995), 133, 284.

116. Julia Chase Diary, entry for 9 Mar. 1862, in Mahon, *Winchester Divided*, 21.

117. Mackall et al., *In the Shadow of the Enemy*, 69; Baer, *Shadows on My Heart*, 63; Isabella N. Woods to Samuel Woods, 5 Sept. 1861, in Dayton, *Samuel Woods and His Family*, 35.

118. Laura Lee Diary in Rice and Campbell, "Voices From the Tempest," in Campbell and Rice, *A Woman's War*, 83; Laura Lee Diary, entry for 28 Feb. 1865, in Mahon, *Winchester Divided*, 182–184.

119. Baer, *Shadows on My Heart*, 69–71, 99; McGuire, *Diary of a Southern Refugee*, 283, 293–396; Bittinger, *Unionists and the Civil War Experience in the Shenandoah Valley*, 1:12.

120. Annie Samuels and others to Confederate Secretary of War, 2 Dec. 1864, Records of the Office of the Secretary of War, War Department Collection of Confederate Records, RG 109, NARA.

121. Isabella N. Woods to Samuel Woods, 18 July 1861, in Dayton, *Samuel Woods and His Family*, 29.

122. Laura Lee Diary, entry for 14 Dec. 1864, in Mahon, *Winchester Divided*, 176.

123. McGuire, *Diary of a Southern Refugee*, 279–280; Lisa Tendrich Frank, "War Comes Home: Confederate Women and Union Soldiers," in *Virginia's Civil War*, ed. Peter Wallenstein and Bertram Wyatt-Brown (Charlottesville, 2005), 131.

124. Mackall et al., *In the Shadow of the Enemy*, 190.

125. McDonald, *A Woman's Civil War*, 141; Mackall et al., *In the Shadow of the Enemy*, 74–75.

126. Morgan, *Emancipation in Virginia's Tobacco Belt*, 121; McGuire, *Diary of a Southern Refugee*, 289; Mary Cary Ambler Stribling Diary, 1862 (photostatic copy), Acc. 25390, Personal Papers Collection, LVA; Mackall et al., *In the Shadow of the Enemy*, 190–191; Frank, "War Comes Home," in Wallenstein and Wyatt-Brown, *Virginia's Civil War*, 124, 128; van Zelm, "On the Front Lines of Freedom," 86.

127. Mackall et al., *In the Shadow of the Enemy*, 80.

128. Mary Watkins to Richard Watkins, 1 July 1864, in Toalson, *Send Me a Pair of Old Boots and Kiss My Little Girls*, 298; Laura Lee Diary in Rice and Campbell, "Voices From the Tempest," in Campbell and Rice, *A Woman's War*, 82; Mackall et al., *In the Shadow of the Enemy*, 69.

129. Phipps, *Genteel Rebel*, 180; McDonald, *A Woman's Civil War*, 58–59.

130. Mackall et al., *In the Shadow of the Enemy*, 72, 84 (quotation), 100–101; Campbell, *When Sherman Marched North from the Sea*, 74.

131. Laura Lee Diary in Rice and Campbell, "Voices From the Tempest," in Campbell and Rice, *A Woman's War* 83 (quotation); Baer, *Shadows on My Heart*, 55; Rubin, *A Shattered Nation*, 209; Phipps, *Genteel Rebel*, 179, 192.

132. McGuire, *Diary of a Southern Refugee*, 219.

133. *DVB*, 2:170–172.

134. "Antonia Ford (1838–1871)," *Encyclopedia Virginia*, http://www.encyclopediavirginia. org/Ford_Antonia_1838-1871 (accessed 17 Jan. 2012); Louise Leslie, *Tazewell County* (Radford, Va., 1982), 717–723.

135. Elizabeth R. Varon, *Southern Lady, Yankee Spy: The True Story of Elizabeth Van Lew, A Union Agent in the Heart of the Confederacy* (Oxford, 2003).

136. Julia Chase Diary, entry for 26 May 1862, in Mahon, *Winchester Divided*, 39–40; Delila Day application to Southern Claims Commission, in Rice and Campbell, "Voices From the

Tempest," in Campbell and Rice, *A Woman's War*, 87, 89; Bittinger, *Unionists and the Civil War Experience in the Shenandoah Valley*, 3:696–697, 704; Varon, *Southern Lady, Yankee Spy*, 69.

137. Bittinger, *Unionists and the Civil War Experience in the Shenandoah Valley*, 3:692–694.

138. Testimony of Caroline Cook, Administratrix of Major Cook, to Agent Isaac P. Baldwin, 24 July 1877 (quotation), Southern Claims Commission, Approved Claims (1871–1880), Virginia, RG 217, NARA; Bittinger, *Unionists and the Civil War Experience in the Shenandoah Valley*, 1:14.

139. Julia Chase Diary, entry for 25 May 1862, in Mahon, *Winchester Divided*, 39 (first quotation), 152; McGuire, *Diary of a Southern Refugee*, 20; Isabella N. Woods to Samuel Woods, 6 Oct. 1861, and Margaret McKendrie Neeson to Isabella N. Woods, 18 May 1862, in Dayton, *Samuel Woods and His Family*, 44 (second quotation), 73 (third quotation).

140. Rubin, *A Shattered Nation*, 79; Faust, *Mothers of Invention*, 238, 241, 243; Edwards, *Scarlett Doesn't Live Here Anymore*, 83.

141. Blair, *Virginia's Private War*, 4, 141; Sheehan-Dean, *Why Confederates Fought*, 10; Peter S. Carmichael, *The Last Generation: Young Virginians in Peace, War, and Reunion* (Chapel Hill, 2005), 173.

142. McDonald, *A Woman's Civil War*, 117.

143. Carmichael, *The Last Generation*, 173; Sheehan-Dean, *Why Confederates Fought*, 5, 191; Gallagher, *The Confederate War*, 78; Jane Woods Holt to Isabella N. Woods, 6 Apr. 1863, in Dayton, *Samuel Woods and His Family*, 98 (quotation).

144. Carmichael, *The Last Generation*, 295 n. 30; Daniel E. Sutherland, "The Absence of Violence: Confederates and Unionists in Culpeper County, Virginia," in *Guerillas, Unionists, and Violence on the Confederate Home Front*, ed. Daniel E. Sutherland (Fayetteville, Ark., 1999), 79; McDonald, *A Woman's Civil War*, 223; Campbell, *When Sherman Marched North from the Sea*, 85.

145. Avary, *A Virginia Girl in the Civil War*, 207.

146. Mary Washington Cabell Early Diary, 9–15 Apr. 1865, Early Family Papers (1764–1956), Mss1 Ea765b, VHS.

147. Mary B. Goodwin Diary (entry for 7 May 1865), Mary B. Goodwin Papers (1860–1890), Acc. 27846, Personal Papers Collection, LVA.

148. Avary, *A Virginia Girl in the Civil War*, 208.

149. Charles L. Perdue, Jr., Thomas E. Barden, and Robert K. Phillips, eds., *Weevils in the Wheat: Interviews with Virginia Ex-Slaves* (Charlottesville, 1976), 58–59.

150. Mary Farmer-Kaiser, *Freedwomen and the Freedmen's Bureau: Race, Gender, and Public Policy in the Age of Emancipation* (New York, 2010), 23, 59, 64, 67–68, 71, 77–78.

151. Krowl, "Dixie's Other Daughters," 138–142; van Zelm, "On the Front Lines of Freedom," 124–126; Mary J. Farmer, "'Because They Are Women': Gender and the Virginia Freedmen's Bureau's 'War on Dependency,'" in *The Freedmen's Bureau and Reconstruction: Reconsiderations*, ed. Paul A. Cimbala and Randall M. Miller (New York, 1999), 163–164.

152. Morgan, *Emancipation in Virginia's Tobacco Belt*, 135–138; van Zelm, "On the Front Lines of Freedom," 135 n. 28.

153. Morgan, *Emancipation in Virginia's Tobacco Belt*, 133; Krowl, "Dixie's Other Daughters," 333, 336; van Zelm, "On the Front Lines of Freedom," 179, 186, 200; Farmer-Kaiser, *Freedwomen and the Freedmen's Bureau*, 68, 71–73, 77–78.

154. See Farmer, "'Because They Are Women,'" in Cimbala and Miller, *The Freedmen's Bureau and Reconstruction*, 161–192.

155. Morgan, *Emancipation in Virginia's Tobacco Belt*, 139–140; Farmer-Kaiser, *Freedwomen and the Freedmen's Bureau*, 58–59, 61, 96–140, 167; Krowl, "Dixie's Other Daughters," 331–332.

156. Farmer-Kaiser, *Freedwomen and the Freedmen's Bureau*, 141–166, 171; van Zelm, "On the Front Lines of Freedom," 134; Krowl, "Dixie's Other Daughters," 387.

157. van Zelm, "On the Front Lines of Freedom," 140–141.

158. Farmer-Kaiser, *Freedwomen and the Freedmen's Bureau*, 110.

159. Catherine Jones, "Ties That Bind, Bonds That Break: Children in the Reorganization of Households in Postemancipation Virginia," *JSH* 76 (2010): 81–83.

160. Statement of Margaret Wesendonck, 2 Aug. 1866, Letters and Orders Received, Records of the Field Offices for the State of Virginia, Bureau of Refugees, Freedmen, and Abandoned Lands, 1865–1875, RG 105, M1913, NARA.

161. J. Tivis Wicker, "Virginia's Legitimization Act of 1866," *VMHB* 86 (1978): 339–344.

162. Dorothy Sterling, ed., *We Are Your Sisters: Black Women in the Nineteenth Century* (New York, 1984), 317–318.

163. *John Burbridge (cold.)* v. *Mary Winder (cold.)*, 19 June 1867, Subordinate Field Offices (Yorktown), Proceedings of the Freedmen's Court, Records of the Field Offices for the State of Virginia, Bureau of Refugees, Freedmen, and Abandoned Lands, 1865–1875, RG 105, M1913, NARA.

164. Krowl, "Dixie's Other Daughters," 462, 465–468; Farmer-Kaiser, *Freedwomen and the Freedmen's Bureau*, 28–29, 44, 50–52; Farmer, "'Because They Are Women,'" in Cimbala and Miller, *The Freedmen's Bureau and Reconstruction*, 161; van Zelm, "On the Front Lines of Freedom," 132–133.

165. Farmer-Kaiser, *Freedwomen and the Freedmen's Bureau*, 85, 150–151; Thavolia Glymph, *Out of the House of Bondage: The Transformation of the Plantation Household* (Cambridge, Eng., 2008), 168–169.

166. Morgan, *Emancipation in Virginia's Tobacco Belt*, 193; Farmer-Kaiser, *Freedwomen and the Freedmen's Bureau*, 69–72, 93–94; Glymph, *Out of the House of Bondage*, 150–157; van Zelm, "On the Front Lines of Freedom," 216–219.

167. Farmer-Kaiser, *Freedwomen and the Freedmen's Bureau*, 64, 74, 83.

168. Farmer-Kaiser, *Freedwomen and the Freedmen's Bureau*, 77–78, 141–166; Krowl, "Dixie's Other Daughters," 371, 383, 387, 457, 505, 552; van Zelm, "On the Front Lines of Freedom," 134, 138, 140, 145.

169. Morgan, *Emancipation in Virginia's Tobacco Belt*, 187–191; Amy Feely Morsman, *The Big House after Slavery: Virginia Plantation Families and Their Postbellum Domestic Experiment* (Charlottesville, 2010), 22–23; Jane Turner Censer, *The Reconstruction of White Southern Womanhood, 1865–1895* (Baton Rouge, 2003), 135.

170. Michael Naragon, "From Chattel to Citizen: The Transition from Slavery to Freedom in Richmond, Virginia," *Slavery and Abolition* 21 (Aug. 2000): 96–97.

171. Naragon, "From Chattel to Citizen," 103–104.

172. van Zelm, "On the Front Lines of Freedom," 165–166; Peter Rachleff, *Black Labor in the South: Richmond, Virginia, 1865–1890* (Philadelphia, 1984), 46.

173. Edwards, *Scarlett Doesn't Live Here Anymore*, 141; van Zelm, "On the Front Lines of Freedom," 172, 266.

174. van Zelm, "On the Front Lines of Freedom," 163, 284, 286; Rachleff, *Black Labor in the South*, 39, 63; Naragon, "From Chattel to Citizen," 98–99.

175. van Zelm, "On the Front Lines of Freedom," 169, 268–270; Krowl, "Dixie's Other Daughters," 367.

176. Rachleff, *Black Labor in the South*, 24–26.

177. *DVB*, 2:272–273.

178. Rachleff, *Black Labor in the South*, 16, 18, 25–28; van Zelm, "On the Front Lines of Freedom," 132, 262.

179. Rachleff, *Black Labor in the South*, 23, 24; Morgan, *Emancipation in Virginia's Tobacco Belt*, 171, 183–184.

180. J. B. Clinton to J. R. Stone, 30 Apr. 1867, Reports of Operations and Conditions in Virginia, Monthly Reports, Records of the Assistant Commissioner for the State of Virginia, Bureau of Refugees, Freedmen, and Abandoned Lands, 1865–1869, RG 105, M1048, NARA.

181. Rachleff, *Black Labor in the South*, 38; Morgan, *Emancipation in Virginia's Tobacco Belt*, 177–182; van Zelm, "On the Front Lines of Freedom," 257–259.

182. Morgan, *Emancipation in Virginia's Tobacco Belt*, 181–182; van Zelm, "On the Front Lines of Freedom," 257–258.

183. Kenzer, "The Uncertainty of Life," in Cashin, *The War Was You and Me*, 124–125.

184. Tripp, *Yankee Town, Southern City*, 191–192; Edwards, *Scarlett Doesn't Live Here Anymore*, 164; Jeffrey W. McClurken, *Take Care of the Living: Reconstructing Confederate Veteran Families in Virginia* (Charlottesville, 2009), 58.

185. Kenzer, "The Uncertainty of Life," in Cashin, *The War Was You and Me*, 114; Tripp, *Yankee Town, Southern City*, 193, 212; McClurken, *Take Care of the Living*, 83.

186. Tripp, *Yankee Town, Southern City*, 212–213, 216.

187. McClurken, *Take Care of the Living*, 103, 105; Edwards, *Scarlett Doesn't Live Here Anymore*, 159.

188. Rubin, *A Shattered Nation*, 209; Janney, *Burying the Dead but Not the Past*, 40–42; Antoinette van Zelm, "A Soldier of the Cross in Norfolk, 1865–1876: Chloe Taylor Whittle and Evangelical Womanhood," *Virginia Cavalcade* 49 (2000): 53–63; Chloe Tyler Whittle Diary (22 Mar.–30 June 1865), entry for 29 May 1865, Whittle-Green Papers, Mss. 65 W61, W&M (quotation).

189. Janney, *Burying the Dead but Not the Past*, chaps. 2–4; W. Fitzhugh Brundage, *The Southern Past: A Clash of Race and Memory* (Cambridge, Mass., 2005), 26.

190. Janney, *Burying the Dead but Not the Past*, chaps. 2–4.

191. van Zelm, "On the Front Lines of Freedom," 126; Maria Louisa Wacker Fleet to David Wacker Fleet, 9 Nov. 1870 in *Green Mount after the War: The Correspondence of Maria Louisa Wacker Fleet and Her Family, 1865–1900*, ed. Betsy Fleet (Charlottesville, 1978), 55 (quotation).

192. Jones, "Ties That Bind, Bonds That Break," 85, 90, 93–94; McClurken, *Take Care of the Living*, 53, 56; Censer, *The Reconstruction of White Southern Womanhood*, 54.

193. Censer, *The Reconstruction of White Southern Womanhood*, 15–18; Morsman, *The Big House after Slavery*, 76–78; Mary Louisa Wacker Fleet to Alexander Frederick Fleet and David Wacker Fleet, 23 July 1875, in Fleet, *Green Mount after the War*, 140 (quotation). For the school, see Fleet, *Green Mount after the War*, 110–111.

194. Elizabeth Munford to George Munford, 14 Oct. 1875, Munford-Ellis Family Papers, Duke (quotation); Censer, *The Reconstruction of White Southern Womanhood*, 122–125.

195. Censer, *The Reconstruction of White Southern Womanhood*, 59–60; van Zelm, "On the Front Lines of Freedom," 179, 186–187.

196. Censer, *The Reconstruction of White Southern Womanhood*, 69–70, 145–146; Morsman, *The Big House after Slavery*, 27–28.

197. Amy Feely Morsman, "Gender Relations in Planter Families: A Postwar Experiment and Its Lost Legacy," in Wallenstein and Wyatt-Brown, *Virginia's Civil War*, 246.

198. Sallie C. Turner to brother, June 1867, George Wilmer Turner Papers, 1846–1896, Duke (quotation); Censer, *The Reconstruction of White Southern Womanhood*, 65, 82; Mary Louisa Wacker Fleet to Alexander Frederick Fleet, 24 Feb. 1867, in Fleet, *Green Mount after the War*, 24.

199. Censer, *The Reconstruction of White Southern Womanhood*, 60, 82; Morsman, *The Big House after Slavery*, 38–40.

200. Morsman, *The Big House after Slavery*, chap. 2, pp. 100, 110; Morsman, "Gender Relations in Planter Families," in Wallenstein and Wyatt-Brown, *Virginia's Civil War*, 243–244, 247.

201. Morsman, *The Big House after Slavery*, 175–176; Censer, *The Reconstruction of White Southern Womanhood*, 128, 154–155; Mrs. E. T. Michard to Gilbert C. Walker, 11 Jan. 1871, Gilbert Carlton Walker Executive Papers (1869–1874), Acc. 40233, LVA (quotation).

202. Robyn Lynn Mundy, "A Profile of Virginia Businesswomen during the Civil War Era" (M.A. thesis, University of Richmond, 1999).

203. Maria Louisa Fleet to Maria Louisa Wacker Fleet, 11 Feb. 1873, in Fleet, *Green Mount after the War*, 93 (quotation); see also Maria Louisa Wacker Fleet to Alexander Frederick Fleet, 16 Nov. 1869, and Betsy Pollard Fleet to David Wacker Fleet, 7 Nov. 1871, in ibid., 42, 70; Morsman, *The Big House after Slavery*, 171–173; Censer, *The Reconstruction of White Southern Womanhood*, 153–183.

204. Censer, *The Reconstruction of White Southern Womanhood*, 118–119, 126.

205. Suzanne D. Lebsock, "Radical Reconstruction and the Property Rights of Southern Women," *JSH* 43 (1977): 204; Censer, *The Reconstruction of White Southern Womanhood*, 99, 107–111.

206. Brent Tarter, "When 'Kind and Thrifty Husbands' Are Not Enough: Some Thoughts on the Legal Status of Women in Virginia," *Magazine of Virginia Genealogy* 33 (May 1995): 90.

207. *Property-Rights of Married Women: Speech of Senator C. T. Smith, (of Nelson,) in the Senate of Virginia, on Securing to Married Women, on Conditions, Property Acquired by Them Before or After Marriage, March 6, 1877* (Richmond, 1877), 4.

208. Morsman, *The Big House after Slavery*, 144–145; Lebsock, "Radical Reconstruction and the Property Rights of Southern Women," 204.

209. Smith, *Property-Rights of Married Women*, 5.

210. *The Debates and Proceedings of the Constitutional Convention of the State of Virginia, Assembled at the City of Richmond, Tuesday, December 3, 1867 . . .* (Richmond, 1868), 467 (quotation); Lebsock, "Radical Reconstruction and the Property Rights of Southern Women," 206.

211. Varon, *We Mean to Be Counted*, 173–174.

212. *DVB*, 2:46–48; Sandra Gioia Treadway, "A Most Brilliant Woman: Anna Whitehead Bodeker and the First Woman Suffrage Association in Virginia," *Virginia Cavalcade* 43 (1994): 166–177; *Richmond Enquirer*, 18 Mar. 1870 (quotation). Bodeker became deeply involved in spiritualism, and her earnestly expressed belief that she was a powerful medium led her family to commit her to the Western Lunatic Asylum, from which she was released in 1874 after a thirteen-month stay.

213. Varon, *We Mean to be Counted*, 175–176.

214. Morsman, *The Big House after Slavery*, 128–129.

215. Ibid., chap. 4.

216. Censer, *The Reconstruction of White Southern Womanhood*, 189; Varon, *We Mean to Be Counted*, 175.

217. Janney, *Burying the Dead but Not the Past*, 129; *Winchester News*, 5 July 1878 (quotation).

218. Lavalette Dupuy to Mary Purnell Dupuy Watkins, 14 Nov. 1871, Emily Howe Dupuy Papers (1834–1883), Mss1 D9295b, VHS.

219. Maria Louisa Fleet to David Wacker Fleet, 9 Dec. 1879, in Fleet, *Green Mount after the War*, 189 (first quotation); "Public Free Schools! Let every Mother read, and by the facts which these figures below establish, determine for herself who are the friends to the Children" (broadside 1882 P97 FF), [1882?], LVA (second quotation).

CHAPTER 5

1. Jane Dailey, *Before Jim Crow: The Politics of Race in Postemancipation Virginia* (Chapel Hill, 2000), 32, 152; Peter Wallenstein, *Cradle of America: Four Centuries of Virginia History* (Lawrence, Kan., 2007), 231.

2. Ronald L. Heinemann, John G. Kolp, Anthony S. Parent, Jr., and William G. Shade, *Old Dominion, New Commonwealth: A History of Virginia, 1607–2007* (Charlottesville, 2007), 261–264.

3. Rand Dotson, *Roanoke, Virginia, 1882–1912: Magic City of the New South* (Knoxville, 2007), 67–69; Michael Spar, "100 Years of Immigration to Virginia," presentation, annual meeting of Virginia Local Government Managers Association, Staunton, 21 Feb. 2008), http://www.coopercenter.org/demographics/publications/100-years-immigration-virginia (accessed 25 Apr. 2012); *Abstract of the Twelfth Census of the United States, 1900* (Washington, D.C., 1902), 42; U.S. Census Office, *Census Reports*, Vol. 1, *Twelfth Census of the United States, Taken in the Year 1900, Population*, part 1 (Washington, D.C., 1901), clxxiii, 605.

4. Melvin I. Urofsky, *Commonwealth and Community: The Jewish Experience in Virginia* (Richmond, 1997), 127–128.

5. Lori Barfield, "The Fenwick Mine Complex: The Lack of Physical and Cultural Impact," *Tennessee Anthropologist* 16 (Spring 1991), 40–42; Jack M. Jones, *Early Coal Mining in Pocahontas, Virginia* (Lynchburg, 1983), 17; Margaret Ripley Wolfe, "Catholicism and Community: Mountain Missions and 'New' Immigrants in Appalachia," *Border States: Journal of the Kentucky-Tennessee American Studies Association* 10 (1995): 18–19.

6. Heinemann et al., *Old Dominion, New Commonwealth*, 264–267.

7. For more general information about the Progressive Era, see Robert Wiebe, *The Search for Order, 1877–1920* (New York, 1968); Glenda Elizabeth Gilmore, ed., *Who Were the Progressives?* (New York, 2002); Noralee Frankel and Nancy S. Dye, eds., *Gender, Class, Race, and Reform in the Progressive Era* (Lexington, 1994); Dorothy Schneider and Carl J. Schneider, *American Women in the Progressive Era, 1900–1920* (New York, 1993).

8. Jane Turner Censer, *The Reconstruction of White Southern Womanhood, 1865–1895* (Baton Rouge, 2003), 6, 25, 34–41. Suzanne Lebsock writes in *"A Share of Honour": Virginia Women, 1600–1945* (Richmond, 1984), 141, that in 1936 only one-fifth of school boards would even consider hiring a married woman, and half fired women after marriage.

9. Censer, *The Reconstruction of White Southern Womanhood*, 124–125.

10. Ibid., 135–136, 157.

11. Wallenstein, *Cradle of America*, 240, 329.

12. Censer, *The Reconstruction of White Southern Womanhood*, 157–158, 170–172, 175.

13. Lebsock, *"A Share of Honour,"* 99, 102; Wallenstein, *Cradle of America*, 234–236; for Jennie Serepta Dean, see Stephen Johnson Lewis, *Undaunted Faith: The Life Story of Jennie Dean: Missionary, Teacher, Crusader, Builder, Founder of the Manassas Industrial School* (Manassas, 1994 ed.) and "Jennie Serepta Dean (1848–1913)," *Encyclopedia Virginia*, http://www.encyclopediavirginia.org/Dean_Jennie_Serepta_1848-1913.

14. Linda B. Pincham, "A League of Willing Workers: The Impact of Northern Philanthropy, Virginia Estelle Randolph and the Jeanes Teachers in Early Twentieth-Century Virginia, *Journal of Negro Education* 74 (2005): 112–123; Lance G. El Jones, *The Jeanes Teacher in the United States, 1908–1933: An Account of Twenty-Five Years' Experience in the Supervision of Negro Schools* (Chapel Hill, 1937), esp. 22–38, 127 (quotation)–132; for Matilda Moseley Booker, see *DVB*, 2:85–86.

15. Otto Wilson, "Life of Dr. Kate Waller Barrett," reprinted with *Some Practical Suggestions on the Conduct of a Rescue Home* by Kate Waller Barrett (New York, 1974), 144–145, 150–153, 156–164, 178; *DVB*, 1:360–362.

16. For Ethel Bailey Furman, see Vincent Brooks, "Records of Pioneering Architect Donated to Library of Virginia," Library of Virginia *Official Newsletter* (Mar./Apr. 2004), 5, and Dreck Spurlock Wilson, ed., *African American Architects: A Biographical Dictionary, 1865–1945* (New York, 2004), 162–163. For Mary B. Channel, see Norfolk *Virginian-Pilot*, 27 Jan. 2006, and Donna Dunay, "Mary Brown Channel, A Pioneer Architect," International Archive of Women in Architecture *Center News* (fall 2008): 4.

17. Peter Wallenstein, *Blue Laws and Black Codes: Conflict, Courts, and Change in Twentieth-Century Virginia* (Charlottesville, 2004), 69–72; Urofsky, *Commonwealth and Community*, 128.

18. "Pauline Adelaide Haislip Duncan (1888–1973)," *Encyclopedia Virginia*, http://www.encyclopediavirginia.org/Duncan_Pauline_Adelaide_Haislip_1888-1973 (accessed 25 Oct. 2012).

19. Censer, *The Reconstruction of White Southern Womanhood*, 214–225, 225, 236–239; Lebsock, *"A Share of Honour,"* 134; Mary Johnston, *Hagar* (Boston, 1913), 261 (quotation).

20. Barbara J. Howe, "Women in the Nineteenth-Century Preservation Movement," in *Restoring Women's History Through Historic Preservation*, ed., Gail Lee Dubrow and Jennifer B. Goodwin (Baltimore, 2003), 24–28; James M. Lindgren, *Preserving the Old Dominion: Historic Preservation and Virginia Traditionalism* (Charlottesville, 1993), esp. chap. 2.

21. Mary H. Mitchell, *Hollywood Cemetery: The History of a Southern Shrine* (Richmond, 1985), 64, 122; John Coski and Amy R. Feely, "A Monument to Southern Womanhood: The Founding Generation of the Confederate Museum," in *A Woman's War: Southern Women, Civil War, and the Confederate Legacy*, ed. Edward D. C. Campbell, Jr., and Kym S. Rice (Richmond and Charlottesville, 1996), 139–150.

22. Karen L. Cox, *Dixie's Daughters: The United Daughters of the Confederacy and the Preservation of Confederate Culture* (Gainesville, Fla., 2003), 52–53, 59, 61–62, 74; John M. Coski, "The Life & Career of Mrs. Norman V. Randolph Challenge the Stereotype of a 'Confederate Woman,'" Museum of the Confederacy *Magazine* (summer 2007): 10–14.

23. Cox, *Dixie's Daughters*, 126, 130, 134–135; William Henry Elson, *History of the United States of America* (New York, 1904), 745 (quotation); *DVB*, 3:121–122.

24. For a discussion of the backgrounds of UDC women, see Cox, *Dixie's Daughters; DVB*, 2:347–349.

25. Quotation in "Negro Women's Club Work," *Club Woman* 10 (1903): 296.

26. Stephanie J. Shaw, *What a Woman Ought to Be and to Do: Black Professional Woman Workers in the Jim Crow Era* (Chicago, 1996), 69, 76; L. B. Tefft, "Hartshorn Memorial College," *Baptist Home Mission Monthly* 20 (1898): 58 (quotation).

27. "Carrie Victoria Dyer (1839–1921)," *Encyclopedia Virginia*, http://www.encyclopediavirginia.org/Dyer_Carrie_Victoria_1839-1921 (accessed 25 Oct. 2012).

28. Shaw, *What a Woman Ought to Be and to Do*, 76, 85–86, 95; *Twenty-Two Years' Work of the Hampton Normal and Agricultural Institute at Hampton, Virginia* (Hampton, 1893), 104 (quotation).

29. Shaw, *What a Woman Ought to Be and to Do*, 132–133, 185, 164; *DVB*, 1:357–359.

30. Suzanne Lebsock, *A Murder in Virginia: Southern Justice on Trial* (New York, 2003), 106–108, 147–151, 164–165, 186, 264, 310–311.

31. Elna C. Green, *This Business of Relief: Confronting Poverty in a Southern City* (Athens, Ga., 2003), 106, 109–111, 113–117; Samuel C. Shepherd Jr., *Avenues of Faith: Shaping the Urban Religious Culture of Richmond, Virginia, 1900–1929* (Tuscaloosa, 2001), 180; Richmond *Daily Dispatch*, 11 Dec. 1881 (quotation).

32. Urofsky, *Commonwealth and Community*, 143.

33. Elizabeth Stevens Brinson, "'Helping Others to Help Themselves': Social Advocacy and Wage-Earning Women in Richmond, Virginia, 1910–1932" (Ph.D. diss., The Union for Experimenting Colleges and Universities, 1984), 53–54; Lebsock, *"Share of Honour,"* 104.

34. *DVB*, 3:458–459; *Commonwealth* 4 (Feb. 1937): 12–13 (quotation).

35. Brinson, "'Helping Others to Help Themselves,'" 84–86; Lebsock, *"Share of Honour,"* 127–128; Mrs. R. R. Chappell and Mrs. J. W. S. Gilchrist, "A History of the Y.W.C.A.," in *Virginia Capital Bicentennial Commission, Sketches of Societies and Institutions, together with Descriptions of Phases of Social, Political and Economic Development in Richmond, Virginia* (Richmond, 1937).

36. Elizabeth Hogg Ironmonger and Pauline Landrum Phillips, *History of the Woman's Christian Temperance Union of Virginia and a Glimpse of Seventy-Five Years, 1883–1958* (Richmond, 1958), 26–31, 211–212, 228–231, 245–246; *Twenty-Two Years' Work of the Hampton Normal and Agricultural Institute*, 29 (quotation), 99, 101, 116.

37. Heinemann et al., *Old Dominion, New Commonwealth*, 284–285; *Anti-Saloon League Year Book, 1920* (Westerville, Ohio, 1920), 209–210; Brinson, "'Helping Others to Help Themselves,'" 26; Ironmonger and Phillips, *History of the Woman's Christian Temperance Union of Virginia*, 72–73.

38. Lebsock, *"Share of Honour,"* 105, 107; Gertrude Woodruff Marlowe, *A Right Worthy Grand Mission: Maggie Lena Walker and the Quest for Black Economic Empowerment* (Washington, D.C., 2003), 87–88; Brinson, "'Helping Others to Help Themselves,'" 52.

39. Lebsock, *"Share of Honour,"* 104; Heinemann et al., *Old Dominion, New Commonwealth*, 266–267; Brinson, "'Helping Others to Help Themselves,'" 52.

40. Beth English, "'I Have . . . a Lot of Work to Do': Cotton Mill Work and Women's Culture in Matoaca, Virginia, 1888–95" *VMHB* 114 (2006): 356–383.

41. Green, *This Business of Relief*, 164–169. Green's statistics bear out the fact that black women had to rely on the almshouse to give birth if they had nowhere else to go.

42. Lebsock, *A Murder in Virginia*, 87.

43. Evan Bennett, "'A Responsibility on Women That Cannot Be Delegated to Father, Husband, or Son': Farm Women and Cooperation in the Tobacco South," in *Work, Faith, and Family: Rural Southern Women in the Twentieth Century*, ed. Rebecca Sharpless and Melissa Walker (Columbia, Mo., 2006), 69–73.

44. Shaw, *What a Woman Ought to Be and to Do*, 179.

45. Dailey, *Before Jim Crow*, 163; Lebsock, *"A Share of Honour,"* 103; Heinemann et al., *Old Dominion, New Commonwealth*, 277.

46. Wallenstein, *Cradle of America*, 263, 285–287.

47. Lisa Lindquist Dorr, *White Women, Rape, and the Power of Race in Virginia, 1900–1960* (Chapel Hill, 2004), 17–28, 31.

48. Heinemann et al., *Old Dominion, New Commonwealth*, 279; Lebsock, *Share of Honour*, 128–129; Green, *This Business of Relief*, 136; Brinson, "'Helping Others to Help Themselves,'"

21; Anne Firor Scott, *Natural Allies: Women's Associations in American History* (Urbana, Ill., 1991), 2–3.

49. Sandra Gioia Treadway, *Women of Mark: A History of the Woman's Club of Richmond, Virginia, 1894–1994* (Richmond, 1995), 44–45; Elna C. Green, "Gendering the City, Gendering the Welfare State: The Nurses' Settlement of Richmond, 1900–1930," *VMHB* 113 (2005): 277–311.

50. Treadway, *Women of Mark*, 44–45; Lebsock, "A Share of Honour," 128; *DVB* 3:347; Green, "Gendering the City, Gendering the Welfare State," 276–311.

51. Brinson, "'Helping Others to Help Themselves,'" 23–24. For more information about the life and activities of Maggie Lena Walker, see Marlowe, *A Right Worthy Grand Mission*; Elsa Barkley Brown, "Womanist Consciousness: Maggie Lena Walker and the Independent Order of St. Luke," *Signs* 14 (spring 1989): 610–633; and Muriel Miller Branch and Dorothy Marie Rice, *Pennies to Dollars: The Story of Maggie Lena Walker* (North Haven, Conn., 1997).

52. Dotson, *Roanoke*, 10, 35, 218–220, 241; U.S. Census Office, *Census Reports*, Vol. 1, *Twelfth Census of the United States, Taken in the Year 1900, Population*, part 1 (Washington, D.C., 1901), 478; *DVB*, 3:338–339.

53. Dotson, *Roanoke*, 221–237; *DVB*, 2:506–507; *Roanoke Times*, 17 May 1908, p. 3 (quotation).

54. Brinson, "'Helping Others to Help Themselves,'" 33–36; Treadway, *Women of Mark*, 43; Walter Russell Bowie, *Sunrise in the South: The Life of Mary-Cooke Branch Munford* (Richmond, 1942), 70–76; Heinemann et al., *Old Dominion, New Commonwealth*, 281; *Richmond News Leader*, 31 July 1931, p. 1.

55. Wallenstein, *Cradle of America*, 259; Brinson, "'Helping Others to Help Themselves,'" 34–35; Lebsock, "A Share of Honour," 129–131; Anne Hobson Freeman, "Mary Munford's Fight for a College for Women Co-Ordinate with the University of Virginia," *VMHB* 78 (1970): 481–491; Mary C. B. Munford and Virginia S. McKenney, "A Plea for Co-Ordination," University of Virginia *Alumni Bulletin*, 3d ser., 7 (Jan. 1914): 4–11 (quotation); *Richmond Times-Dispatch*, 8 Mar. 1916, pp. 1, 5.

56. Brinson, "'Helping Others to Help Themselves,'" 117–118, 121–129; Orie Latham Hatcher, *The Virginia Bureau of Vocations for Women* (Richmond, [1919]); *Report of the Southern Woman's Educational Alliance* (Richmond, 1921), 3–4.

57. *Fifteenth Annual Report of Hampton Negro Conference* (Hampton, 1911), 47–52; *Sixteenth Annual Report of Hampton Negro Conference* (Hampton, 1912), 8–9; Janie Porter Barrett, "Negro Women's Clubs and the Community," *Southern Workman* 39 (1910): 33–34 (quotation).

58. Brinson, "'Helping Others to Help Themselves,'" 85–92; *Fifteenth Annual Report of Hampton Negro Conference*, 54–59.

59. Treadway, *Women of Mark*, 47; Radford *News Journal*, 19 Apr. 1983, p. 3; Pulaski *Southwest Times and News-Review*, 29 Jan. 1917, pp. 1, 3, 19 Mar. 1917, p. 2.

60. Green, *This Business of Relief*, 137–138; Brinson, "'Helping Others to Help Themselves,'" 23; Lebsock, "A Share of Honour," 125–127; Shaw, *What a Woman Ought to Be and to Do*, 165; *DVB*, 1:357–359, 2:160–162, 3:261–262; *First Annual Report of the Industrial Home School for Colored Girls* (1916), quotation on 7.

61. Susan Hamburger, "We Take Care of Our Womenfolk: The Home for Needy Confederate Women in Richmond, Virginia, 1898–1990," in *Before the New Deal: Social Welfare in the South, 1830–1930*, ed. Elna C. Green (Athens, Ga., 1999), 62–68; Cox, *Dixie's Daughters*, 76–78.

62. Lorraine Gates Schuyler, *The Weight of Their Votes: Southern Women and Political Leverage in the 1920s* (Chapel Hill, 2006), 180–181.

63. Brinson, "'Helping Others to Help Themselves,'" 34–35; Lebsock, "A Share of Honour," 129–131; Green, *This Business of Relief*, 134, 137–138; Hamburger, "We Take Care of Our Womenfolk," 69.

64. Ann Elizabeth McCleary, "Shaping a New Role for the Rural Woman: Home Demonstration Work in Augusta County, Virginia, 1917–1940" (Ph.D. diss., Brown University, 1996), 39–41; *DVB*, 1:43–44; *Three Years of Extension Work in Agriculture and Home Economics in Virginia* (Richmond, 1919), 7–8, 54–69.

65. McCleary, "Shaping a New Role for the Rural Woman," 32–36.

66. Ibid., 40–42.

67. Ibid., 25–28.

68. Elna C. Green, *Southern Strategies: Southern Women and the Woman Suffrage Question* (Chapel Hill, 1997), 8–9, 155.

69. Ibid., 160; Brinson, "'Helping Others to Help Themselves,'" 27–29; Sara Hunter Graham, "Woman Suffrage in Virginia: The Equal Suffrage League and Pressure-Group Politics, 1909–1920," *VMHB* 101 (1993): 232, 236–237.

70. Marjorie Spruill Wheeler, *New Women of the New South: The Leaders of the Woman Suffrage Movement in the Southern States* (New York, 1993), 26–27; Richmond *Evening Journal*, 4 May 1915, p. 4 (quotation).

71. Wheeler, *New Women of the New South*, 42, 55–57.

72. Green, *Southern Strategies*, 66–69.

73. Ibid., 158–160, 210; Jennifer Davis McDaid, "All Kinds of Revolutionaries: Pauline Adams, Jessie Townsend, and the Norfolk Equal Suffrage League," *Virginia Cavalcade* 49 (2000): 84–93; Graham, "Woman Suffrage in Virginia," 230.

74. Green, *Southern Strategies*, 51–55, 80, 82, 85, 87, 105–106, 165–166; Molly Elliot Seawell, "Two Suffrage Mistakes," *North American Review* 199 (1914): 366–382 (quotation on 368); Philip Alexander Bruce, *History of the University of Virginia, 1819–1919* (1921), 4:63–65.

75. Wheeler, *New Women of the New South*, 77, 104–106; Green, *Southern Strategies*, 167.

76. Wheeler, *New Women of the New South*, 74–75, 77; Green, *Southern Strategies*, 162–164, 168–169; *Washington Post*, 9 Mar. 1912, p. 11 (quotation).

77. Wheeler, *New Women of the New South*, 74–75, 77; Green, *Southern Strategies*, 163–164, 168–169; *Richmond Times-Dispatch*, 20 Jan. 1912, p. 5 (quotation); *Journal of the House of Delegates of Virginia, Session which Commenced … on … January 10, 1912* (Richmond, 1912), 364; Graham, "Woman Suffrage in Virginia," 238.

78. Jennifer Davis McDaid, "'Our Share in the War Is No Small One': Virginia Women and World War I," *Virginia Cavalcade* 50 (2001): 119–121, 123.

79. Ibid., 119, 120, 123; Heinemann et al., *Old Dominion, New Commonwealth*, 291.

80. McDaid, "'Our Share in the War Is No Small One,'" 115–117; Anna Elizabeth McFadden (first quotation), Edna Breareley Bishop, and Verna Mae Smith (second quotation), all in Military Service Records, World War I History Commission Records, RG 66, LVA.

81. Green, *Southern Strategies*, 160, 174–175; Graham, "Woman Suffrage in Virginia," 244–247.

82. Green, *Southern Strategies*, 175–176; Lorraine Gates Schuyler, *The Weight of Their Votes: Southern Women and Political Leverage in the 1920s* (Chapel Hill, 2006), 53.

83. Green, *Southern Strategies*, 175–176; Schuyler, *The Weight of Their Votes*, 32, 50, 53, 132.

84. Green, *Southern Strategies*, 176.

85. *Winchester Evening Star*, 27 Aug., p. 1, 2 Oct. 1920, p. 1; *Roanoke Times*, 2 Oct. 1920, pp.

2–3; *Richmond Times-Dispatch*, 3 Oct. 1920, p. 20; Schuyler, *The Weight of Their Votes*, 75, 262; Ida Mae Thompson to Mrs. Lee, 28 July 1921, Adèle Goodman Clark Papers, M9, Series 5 (Virginia League of Women Voters), VCU (quotation).

86. Schuyler, *The Weight of Their Votes*, 91, 145–146; Richmond *News Leader*, 18 Sept. 1920, p. 1 (quotation).

87. Schuyler, *The Weight of Their Votes*, 93, 115–117; for Elizabeth Lewis Otey, see Henry W. Anderson, *Freedom in Virginia: An Address by Henry W. Anderson . . . Delivered before the Republican State Convention at Norfolk, July 14, 1921* [Norfolk], 1921), 39 (first quotation); for Lillie Davis Custis (Mrs. George Custis), see *Richmond Times-Dispatch*, 22 Oct. 1921, p. 5 (second quotation) and Onancock *Accomack News*, 28 Oct. 1921, p. 1; official election returns in *Annual Report of the Secretary of the Commonwealth . . . for the Year Ending September 30, 1921* (Richmond, 1922), 419–424.

88. Lebsock, *"A Share of Honour,"* 136–137; *DVB*, 2:506–507, 3:457–459; "Shall I Run for Congress?," *Atlantic Monthly* 130 (1922): 713–714 (quotations).

89. Sandra Gioia Treadway, "Sarah Lee Fain: Norfolk's First Woman Legislator," *Virginia Cavalcade* 30 (1981): 125–133; *DVB*, 2:86–87, 505–506.

90. Schuyler, *The Weight of Their Votes*, 172, 208; *Acts . . . of the General Assembly of the State of Virginia Session Which Commenced . . . on . . . January 1, 1922* (Richmond, 1922), 491–492, 860, 861.

91. Schuyler, *The Weight of Their Votes*, 208.

92. Ibid., 185; *DVB*, 3:258–262, 348–350.

93. "Emily Wayland Dinwiddie (1879–1949)," *Encyclopedia Virginia*, http://www.encyclopediavirginia.org/Dinwiddie_Emily_Wayland_1879-1949.

94. Schuyler, *The Weight of Their Votes*, 158.

95. Pippa Holloway, *Sexuality, Politics, and Social Control in Virginia, 1920–1945* (Chapel Hill, 2006), 43–47.

96. Ibid., 5, 19, 25–27; Gregory Michael Dorr, *Segregation's Science: Eugenics and Society in Virginia* (Charlottesville, 2008), 96–97, 109–111, 119.

97. Holloway, *Sexuality, Politics, and Social Control in Virginia*, 27–30, 57; *DVB*, 2:372–373; *Carrie Buck, by R. G. Shelton, Her Guardian and Next Friend* v. *Dr. J. H. Bell, Superintendent of the Colony for Epileptics and Feeble-Minded* (1925) 143 (Virginia Reports) 310–324 (quotation on 315). See also, Paul A. Lombardo, *Three Generations, No Imbeciles: Eugenics, the Supreme Court, and Buck v. Bell* (Baltimore, 2008).

98. Holloway, *Sexuality, Politics, and Social Control in Virginia*, 32, 57; Peter Wallenstein, *Tell the Court I Love My Wife: Race, Marriage, and Law—An American History* (New York, 2002), 139–140; J. Douglas Smith, *Managing White Supremacy: Race, Politics, and Citizenship in Jim Crow Virginia* (Chapel Hill, 2002), 220–221; "Walter Ashby Plecker (1861–1947)," *Encyclopedia Virginia*, http://www.encyclopediavirginia.org/Plecker_Walter_Ashby_1861-1947 (accessed 30 Apr. 2012).

99. Heinemann et al., *Old Dominion, New Commonwealth*, 299; McCleary, "Shaping a New Role for the Rural Woman," 399.

100. McCleary, "Shaping a New Role for the Rural Woman," 22–28, 48, 49.

101. Ibid., 68, 121, 260; Virginia Polytechnic Institute *Extension Division News* 12 (Feb. 1930): 1, 5 (quotation).

102. McCleary, "Shaping a New Role for the Rural Woman," 101–102, 157–168; Virginia Polytechnic Institute *Extension Division News* 10 (Oct. 1928): 1, 4.

103. Kathleen C. Hilton, "'Both in the Field, Each with a Plow': Race and Gender in USDA Policy, 1907–1929," in *Hidden Histories of Women in the New South*, ed. Virginia Bernhard et al. (Columbia, Mo., 1994): 114–133; Cynthia Neverdon-Morton, *Afro-American Women in the South and the Advancement of the Race* (Knoxville, 1989), 118–119; *Southern Workman* 46 (1917): 201–202; *Norfolk Journal and Guide*, National edition, 10 Mar. 1945, p. 12 (quotation).

104. Bennett, "'A Responsibility on Women That Cannot Be Delegated to Father, Husband, or Son,'" 83–95; Green, *This Business of Relief*, 202.

CHAPTER 6

1. Ronald L. Heinemann, *The Depression and New Deal in Virginia: The Enduring Dominion* (Charlottesville, 1983), 7–10; Elna C. Green, *This Business of Relief: Confronting Poverty in a Southern City, 1740–1940* (Athens, Ga., 2003), 179.

2. Heinemann, *Depression and New Deal in Virginia*, 4, 19.

3. Green, *This Business of Relief*, 188; Heinemann, *Depression and New Deal in Virginia*, 14–15, 155.

4. Hazel Hall youth study, interviewed by Maude R. Chandler, 10 June 1940 (LH00986); Dulcie Jenkins, interviewed by Margaret A. Jeffries, [1939?] (LH00950); Susie Fugate, interviewed by Maude R. Chandler, 12 June 1940 (LH00987), all in Virginia Writers' Project Life Histories, Acc. 36002, LVA.

5. Jeffrey S. Cole, "The Impact of the Great Depression and New Deal on the Urban South: Lynchburg, Virginia, as a Case Study, 1929–1941" (Ph.D. diss., Bowling Green State University, 1998), 135–137; *Fifteenth Census of the United States, 1930, Population: Occupations, by States* (Washington, D.C., 1933), 4:1672.

6. Green, *This Business of Relief*, 198; Nancy J. Martin-Perdue and Charles L. Perdue, Jr., eds., *Talk About Trouble: A New Deal Portrait of Virginians in the Great Depression* (Chapel Hill, 1996), 198–199.

7. Heinemann, *Depression and New Deal in Virginia*, 37; Earl Lewis, *In Their Own Interests: Race, Class, and Power in Twentieth-Century Norfolk, Virginia* (Berkeley, Calif., 1991), 112–113; *Danville Register*, 29 Mar. 1933, p. 4 (quotation).

8. Beulah Handly, interviewed by Anne Davidson, 21 Jan. 1939, pp. 1, 9 (LH01326), Virginia Writers' Project, Acc. 36002, LVA.

9. Ibid., 9–10.

10. Mr. and Mrs. John Scott (pseudonym for Smithers), interviewed by Essie Wade Smith, [1939?], pp. 1, 7 (quotation) (LH00259), Virginia Writers' Project, Acc. 36002, LVA.

11. Jo S. Perry and Mary Catherine Powers Bray, interviewed by Ann McCleary, 6 Oct. 1995, Home Demonstration Resources, Helen Wolfe Evans Papers, Acc. 42286, Personal Papers Collection, LVA.

12. Sandra F. Waugaman and Danielle Moretti-Langholtz, *We're Still Here: Contemporary Virginia Indians Tell Their Stories* (Richmond, 2000), 56–61.

13. Ann Elizabeth McCleary, "Shaping a New Role for the Rural Woman: Home Demonstration Work in Augusta County, Virginia, 1917–1940" (Ph.D. diss., Brown University, 1996), 261–264, 278, 282.

14. Ibid., 283–297.

15. Edith Blanche Brown, interviewed by Margaret Jeffries, 24 June 1940 (LH00591); Mary B. Garrett, social-ethnic study, interviewed by Gertrude Blair, [1939?] (LH00802); Gladys Moore, interviewed by John W. Garrett, 20 Dec. 1939 (LH00894); Faye J. Lipes, interviewed by Leila

Blanche Bess, 12 Feb. 1940 (LH00679); Violet Roach-Crowder, interviewed by Leila Blanche Bess, 18 Mar. 1940 (LH00687), Mary Broyhill, interviewed by John W. Garrett, 7 Feb. 1940 (LH00880); Daisy Collins, interviewed by John W. Garrett, 9 Feb. 1940 (LH00878), all in Virginia Writers' Project Life Histories, Acc. 36002, LVA .

16. Edith Blanche Brown, interviewed by Margaret Jeffries, 24 June 1940, pp. 1, 3 (quotation) (LH00591), Virginia Writers' Project Life Histories, Acc. 36002, LVA.

17. Mary Broyhill, interviewed by John W. Garrett, 7 Feb. 1940, pp. 3–8 (LH00880), Virginia Writers' Project Life Histories, Acc. 36002, LVA.

18. Mary B. Garrett, social-ethnic study interviewed by Gertrude Blair, [1939?], p. 2 (LH00802), Virginia Writers' Project Life Histories, Acc. 36002, LVA.

19. Nancy Carter, interviewed by Everett Anderson, 14 Feb. 1939, pp. 2–3 (quotation) (LH01208), Virginia Writers' Project Life Histories, Acc. 36002, LVA.

20. Quoted in Richard Love, "The Cigarette Capital of the World: Labor Race, and Tobacco in Richmond, Virginia, 1880–1980" (Ph.D. diss., University of Virginia, 1998), 1.

21. Cole, "The Impact of the Great Depression and New Deal on the Urban South," 131–133; Julia C., social-ethic study, interviewed by Mack T. Eads, [1938?], quotation on p. 8 (LH01204), Virginia Writers' Project Life Histories, Acc. 36002, LVA.

22. Matilda Lindsay, "Women Hold the Key to Unionization of Dixie," *Machinists' Monthly Journal* 41 (1929): 638–639; Danville *Bee*, 10 Feb. 1930, p. 1, 23 Apr. 1930, pp. 1, 3, 29 Sept. 1930, pp. 1, 6.

23. Ronald L. Heinemann, John G. Kolp, Anthony S. Parent, Jr., and William G. Shade, *Old Dominion, New Commonwealth: A History of Virginia, 1607–2007* (Charlottesville, 2007), 318.

24. Martin-Perdue and Perdue, *Talk About Trouble*, 288–289; Roxy Prescott Dodson, interviewed by Bessie A. Scales, 30 July–5 Aug. 1940, quotation on pp. 3–4 (LH00115), Virginia Writers' Project Life Histories, Acc. 36002, LVA.

25. *Roanoke Times*, 20 Mar. 1930, p. 2.

26. Cole, "The Impact of the Great Depression and New Deal on the Urban South," 149–151; *Washington Post*, 11 June 1937, p. 30.

27. Heinemann, *Depression and New Deal in Virginia*, 166.

28. Love, "The Cigarette Capital of the World," 181–189.

29. Ibid., 190–206.

30. Etta Belle Walker Northington, *A History of the Virginia Federation of Women's Clubs, 1907–1957* (Richmond, 1958), 22–23; Sandra Gioia Treadway, *Women of Mark: A History of the Woman's Club of Richmond, Virginia, 1894–1994* (Richmond, 1995), 80–81.

31. *Virginia Business and Professional Woman* 1 (Dec. 1938): 6.

32. *Roanoke Times*, 28 Sept. 1930, p. 8.

33. McCleary, "Shaping a New Role for the Rural Woman" 400–401.

34. Amy J. Tillerson, "Negotiating Intersections of Gender, Social Class, and Race: Black Women in Prince Edward County, Virginia, Activists and Community Builders, 1930–1965" (Ph.D. diss., Morgan State University, 2006), 111–115; Kara Miles Turner, "'It Is Not at Present a Very Successful School': Prince Edward County and the Black Educational Struggle, 1865–1995" (Ph.D. diss., Duke University, 2001), 96–100.

35. Gertrude Woodruff Marlowe, *A Right Worthy Grand Mission: Maggie Lena Walker and the Quest for Black Economic Empowerment* (Washington, D.C., 2003), 247–250.

36. *Roanoke Times*, 6 Nov. 1937, p. 4.

37. Green, *This Business of Relief*, 185.

38. *Roanoke Times*, 6 Mar. 1932, p. 18.

39. Heinemann et al., *Old Dominion, New Commonwealth*, 316–317.

40. "Reports of State Directors, Division of Women's and Professional Projects, Works Progress Administration," 4–6 May 1936, pp. 1 (quotation), 4, Works Progress Administration file, Helen Wolfe Evans Papers, Acc. 42286, Personal Papers Collection, LVA.

41. Ibid., 2.

42. Green, *This Business of Relief*, 199–200; Heinemann, *Depression and New Deal in Virginia*, 91.

43. Heinemann et al., *Old Dominion, New Commonwealth*, 316; Heinemann, *Depression and New Deal in Virginia*, 74.

44. *Richmond Times-Dispatch Sunday Magazine*, 24 Nov. 1935, pp. 8 (quotations)–9.

45. "Reports of State Directors, Division of Women's and Professional Projects, Works Progress Administration," 4–6 May 1936, p. 3, Works Progress Administration file, Helen Wolfe Evans Papers, Acc. 42286, LVA.

46. Green, *This Business of Relief*, 199–200; Lorena Hickok to Harry L. Hopkins, 5 Feb. 1934, in *One Third of a Nation: Lorena Hickok Reports on the Great Depression*, ed. Richard Lowitt and Maurine Beasley (Urbana, Ill., 1981), 173 (quotation).

47. Heinemann et al., *Old Dominion, New Commonwealth*, 316–317.

48. Lewis, *In Their Own Interests*, 154; Norfolk *Journal and Guide*, National edition, 22 Jan. 1938, p. 20, 12 Mar. 1938, p. 12.

49. Reports of State Directors, Division of Women's and Professional Projects, Works Progress Administration," 4–6 May 1936, p. 3, Works Progress Administration file, Helen Wolfe Evans Papers, Acc. 42286, LVA.

50. Heinemann, *Depression and New Deal in Virginia*, 75, 83; Green, *This Business of Relief*, 199, 201; Martin-Perdue and Perdue, *Talk About Trouble*, 199–200 (quotation).

51. [Josephine Halloran], Secretary of the Richmond League of Women Voters, to Sen. Harry Byrd, 2 Feb. 1935, 1935 Minutes, League of Women Voters of the Richmond Area Archives, M18, VCU.

52. *Richmond Times-Dispatch*, 21 Nov. 1937, p. 8.

53. *DVB*: 3:258–261, 349–350.

54. Northington, *A History of the Virginia Federation of Women's Clubs*, 24, 152–154, 158–159, 167–169; Charlotte Allen, comp., "A Record of Twenty-Five Years, an Interpretation: Virginia Federation of Business and Professional Women, 1919–1944" (Richmond, 1946), esp. 45–56; *Virginia Club Woman* 6 (Jan.–Feb. 1934): 2; ibid., 11 (Feb. 1939): 11, 13 (quotation); *Washington Post*, 22 July 1937, p. 11.

55. Pippa Holloway, *Sexuality, Politics, and Social Control in Virginia, 1920–1945* (Chapel Hill, 2006), 89–109, 123; *Southern Workman* 50 (1921): 51–53, 203. It is important to note that the veneral disease programs may have been useful for eradicating syphilis, but these programs focused mainly on African Americans, because of the latent stereotypes of sexuality held by elite whites, and on working-class workers, for much of the same reason.

56. Mrs. Fred M. Alexander, "The Dilemma of Youth," *Virginia Club Woman*, 9 (Feb. 1939): 9 (quotation); *DVB*, 1:56–57.

57. Suzanne Lebsock, *"A Share of Honour": Virginia Women, 1600–1945* (Richmond, 1984), 142; Treadway, *Women of Mark*, 86.

58. John A. Salmond, *Miss Lucy of the CIO: The Life and Times of Lucy Randolph Mason, 1882–1959* (Athens, Ga., 1988), 60–61, 73–74, 87.

59. Peter Wallenstein, *Cradle of America: Four Centuries of Virginia History* (Lawrence, Kan., 2007), 311; Larissa M. Smith, "Where the South Begins: Black Politics and Civil Rights Activism in Virginia, 1930–1951" (Ph.D. diss., Emory University, 2001), 91–99, 107; the Alice Jackson Stuart Papers are located at UVA.

60. Smith, "Where the South Begins," 140–165; Wallenstein, *Cradle of America*, 332–333; for Aline Elizabeth Black, see also *DVB*, 1:510–511.

61. Peter Wallenstein, *Blue Laws and Black Codes: Conflict, Courts, and Change in Twentieth-Century Virginia* (Charlottesville, 2004), 91–92. For more information on the Richmond lawsuit, see Megan Taylor Shockley, *"We, Too, Are Americans": African American Women in Detroit and Richmond, 1940–54* (Urbana, Ill., 2004), 52–53. Teachers in Roanoke, Danville, Lynchburg, Portsmouth, Princess Anne County (later Virginia Beach), and other localities across the state petitioned school boards and filed suits when necessary to achieve salary equalization; see Smith, "Where the South Begins," 165–167.

62. Heinemann et al., *Old Dominion, New Commonwealth*, 324–328, 332.

63. Norfolk *Virginian-Pilot*, 28 May 1942, pp. 14, 20.

64. Ibid.; *Richmond News Leader* 7 Aug. 1942, p. 3; Norfolk *Virginian-Pilot*, 22 Aug. 1942, p. 5; *Richmond Times-Dispatch* 27 Aug. 1942, p. 4, 12 Sept. 1942, p. 4, 22 Aug. 1943, p. 2H (quotations); Mattie E. Treadwell, *The Women's Army Corps* (Washington, D.C., 1954), 55, 58, 139, 172–173, 181–184, 192.

65. Mrs. O. F. Northington, "Club Activities Face New Program," *Virginia Club Woman* 15 (Oct. 1942): 6.

66. Northington, *History of Virginia Federation of Women's Clubs*, 217.

67. "With the Clubs," *Virginia Business and Professional Woman* 5 (Oct. 1942): 8; "Report of the Work of our Clubs," ibid., 6 (June 1943): 4–5.

68. "Something Special Every Day," *The Minute Man*, 1 Dec. 1942, pp. 35–36, Correspondence and Data Files, Subseries A, Reference Notes and Newspaper Clippings, World War II History Commission, RG 68, LVA; *Washington Post*, 16 Nov. 1942, B2, 9 Dec. 1942, B8; Norfolk *Journal and Guide*, National edition, 28 Nov. 1942, p. 8.

69. Mrs. Claud E. Eley, "Seventh District," *Virginia Club Woman*, 13 (Apr. 1941): 24–25.

70. Mrs. John W. Dickenson, "Days of Decision," *Virginia Club Woman*, 17 (Feb. 1945): 9.

71. Ibid.

72. For a complete discussion of "responsible patriotism," and its origins in national black women's organizations, see Shockley, *"We, Too, Are Americans,"* introduction and chapter 1. Norfolk *Journal and Guide*, National edition, 2 Jan. 1943, p. 16 (quotation), 28 Nov. 1942, p. 20.

73. Shockley, *"We, Too, Are Americans,"* 35.

74. Helen Jones Campbell, comp., "York County, Virginia, in World War II, Together with Rosters of Her Service Men in Other Wars" (unpublished manuscript commissioned by the York County Board of Supervisors, 1950), 108–110, Correspondence and Data Files, Subseries D, Misc. Material, Unpublished Manuscripts, World War II History Commission, RG 68, LVA.

75. Shockley, *"We, Too, Are Americans,"* 36.

76. Ibid., 41; Ada C. Burroughs, "Historical Record, Leight Street USO Area Office . . . October 1, 1947–December 31, 1947," Correspondence and Data Files, Subseries D, Misc. Material, USO Histories, World War II History Commission, RG 68, LVA (quotation).

77. Shockley, *"We, Too, Are Americans,"* 48–49.

78. Ibid., 50–51, 62.

79. Edwin C. Griffith, "Virginia Manufacturers at War" (unpublished manuscript commissioned by World War II History Commission), 58, 70, 97, Correspondence and Data Files, Subseries D, Misc. Material, Unpublished Manuscripts, World War II History Commission, RG 68, LVA.

80. Quoted in Griffith, "Virginia Manufacturers at War," 59.

81. Ibid., 121.

82. Quoted in ibid., 111.

83. Ashley M. Neville and Debra A. McClane, "The World War II Ordnance Department's Government-Owned Contractor-Operated (GOCO) Industrial Facilities: Radford Ordnance Works Historic Investigation," U.S. Army Matériel Command Historic Context Series, Report of Investigations No. 6A (1996), 11–12, 85–86; Griffith, "Virginia Manufacturers at War," 135, 190.

84. Lewis, *In Their Own Interests*, 178; Norfolk *Journal and Guide*, National edition, 7 Mar. 1942, p. 2, 1 Aug. 1942, p. 3; Shockley, *"We, Too, Are Americans,"* 68–70.

85. Shockley, *"We, Too, Are Americans,"* 69–70; Elizabeth Smith to Fourth District, U.S. Civil Service Commission, 24 Sept. 1942, Fair Employment Practices, War Dept., Richmond Quartermaster Depot File, Central Files of Committee on Fair Employment Practices (1941–1946), Region 4, Records of the Committee on Fair Employment Practice, RG 228, NARA, College Park, Md. (quotations).

86. Shockley, *"We, Too, Are Americans,"* 70; Ora Cogbill Branch to President Franklin D. Roosevelt, 10 Sept. 1942, Fair Employment Practices, War Dept., Richmond Quartermaster Depot File, Central Files of Committee on Fair Employment Practices (1941–1946), Region 4, Records of the Committee on Fair Employment Practice, RG 228, NARA, College Park, Md. (quotations).

87. Shockley, *"We, Too, Are Americans,"* 70–71.

88. Lewis, *In Their Own Interests*, 179; Norfolk *Journal and Guide*, Home edition, 19 Sept. 1942, pp. 1–2.

89. Griffith, "Virginia Manufacturers at War," 192; Norfolk *Journal and Guide*, Home edition, 19 Sept. 1942, pp. 1–2; Norfolk *Journal and Guide*, National edition, 3 Oct. 1942, pp. 1–2, 17 Oct. 1942, p. 12, 1 May 1943, p. 6.

90. Shockley, *"We, Too, Are Americans,"* 72–73, 66; Griffith, "Virginia Manufacturers at War," 99 (quotation).

91. Griffith, "Virginia Manufacturers at War," 58; Shockley, *"We, Too, Are Americans,"* 93–96; *Richmond News Leader*, 23 May 1944, p. 18 (quotation).

92. Griffith, "Virginia Manufacturers at War," 58.

93. Shockley, *"We, Too, Are Americans,"* 96–97; Lucille Harris remarks in "Annual Descriptive Report for the Year 1945," 27, Annual Report Industrial-Department, 1941–1945, General Files, Richmond YWCA Archives, M177, VCU (quotation).

94. Shockley, *"We, Too, Are Americans,"* 97–98; Sarah Jackson remarks in "Annual Descriptive Report for the Year 1945," 31, Annual Report Industrial-Department, 1941–1945, General Files, Richmond YWCA Archives, M177, VCU (quotation).

95. Smith, "Where the South Begins," 208–212, 216.

96. Mrs. O. F. Northington, "Annual Address by Federation President at Closing Session of Convention, April 12th," *Virginia Club Woman* 17 (Apr. 1945): 4 (quotations), 30.

97. Mrs. Claude Eley, "Whither Are We Going?" *Virginia Club Woman* 20 (Oct. 1947): 4.

98. Cornelia S. Adair, "Our Privileges And Responsibilities As A Citizen," *Virginia Club Woman* 20 (Oct. 1947): 10, 19; *DVB*, 1:15–17; Norfolk *Journal and Guide*, Peninsula edition, 11 Mar. 1950, p. 2.

99. Norfolk *Journal and Guide*, Home edition, 20 May 1944, pp. 1–2 (quotation), 7 Oct. 1944, p. 1; Norfolk *Journal and Guide*, National edition, 21 May 1949, p. 19, 25 Feb. 1950, p. 20; *Washington Post*, 29 May 1951, p. 2; Wallenstein, *Cradle of America*, 368.

100. Norfolk *Journal and Guide*, Peninsula edition, 18 Sept. 1948, p. 3, 18 Feb. 1950, p. 3, 4 Nov. 1950, p. 22, 13 May 1961, p. 6, 27 Oct. 1962, p. 7.

101. Norfolk *Journal and Guide*, Peninsula edition, 17 May 1952, p. 2; Norfolk *Journal and Guide*, Virginia-Carolina edition, 3 Oct. 1953, pp. 3, 11.

102. Norfolk *Journal and Guide*, Home edition, 4 Mar. 1950, p. 4, 17 Oct. 1953, p. 5, 3 Oct. 1953, p. 3. In the 1940s and 1950s, the Norfolk *Journal and Guide* detailed many organizational meetings of women's groups that focused simply on voting.

103. *Arlington Daily Sun*, 11 July 1947, p. 1 (first and second quotations); *Washington Post*, 19 July 1947, B1 (third quotation), 22 July 1947, B1; for Cooper, see *DVB*, 3:443–445.

104. "Women's Election World-Wide News," *Virginia Club Woman*, 21 (Oct. 1948): 8 (quotations); *Washington Post*, 3 Sept. 1950, S1. For women as town council members, see the annual *Report of the Secretary of the Commonwealth to the Governor and General Assembly of Virginia* during the 1950s. For White, see *Gloucester-Mathews Gazette-Journal*, 24 Feb. 1983, A8.

105. Mrs. H. Stanley Bailey, "From the President's Desk: Clubwomen and Elections to Come," *Virginia Club Woman* 25 (Nov. 1952): 5 (quotations); *DVB*, 1:286–287.

106. Bailey, "From the President's Desk: Clubwomen and Elections to Come," 5 (quotations); *Richmond Times-Dispatch*, 13 Jan. 1954, p. 16.

107. Shockley, "We, Too, Are Americans," 202–203; *Richmond Afro-American*, 6 July 1946, pp. 1, 19, 29 June 1946, pp. 1–2, 14 Sept. 1946, pp. 1, 6 (quotation).

108. Shockley, "We, Too, Are Americans," 203–204; *Richmond Afro-American*, 25 Jan. 1947, pp. 1–2 (quotation), 29 Mar. 1947, p. 20.

109. Shockley, "We, Too, Are Americans," 204; Norfolk *Journal and Guide*, Home Edition, 11 Feb. 1950, pp. 1–2.

110. Petersburg *Progress-Index*, 10 Oct. 1929, pp. 1–2; Louis Brownlow, "Public Safety," *Eighth Yearbook of the City Managers' Association* (1922), 180–181.

111. Southern Regional Council *New South* 4 (Sept. 1949): 1.

112. Norfolk *Journal and Guide*, Peninsula edition, 17 Dec. 1949, pp. 1–2; Norfolk *Journal and Guide*, Home edition, 22 Nov. 1952, p. 1, 4 June 1955, p. 16; Norfolk *Journal and Guide*, Virginia-Carolina edition, 22 Nov. 1952, p. 6.

113. Sandra K. Wells and Betty Sowers Alt, *Police Women: Life With the Badge* (Westport, Conn., 2005), 58–60; W. Marvin Dulaney, *Black Police in America* (Bloomington, Ind., 1996), 111–112.

114. Shockley, "We, Too, Are Americans," 182; *Richmond Afro-American*, 27 Sept. 1947, pp. 1, 13, 10 Jan. 1948, p. 9.

115. *DVB*, 2:92–94; Norfolk *Journal and Guide*, Peninsula edition, 4 Feb. 1950, p. 7, 11 Feb. 1950, p. 1; Norfolk *Journal and Guide*, Home edition, 18 Feb. 1950, p. 4.

116. Norfolk *Virginian-Pilot*, 5 Jan. 1950, p. 26.

117. *Washington Post*, 28 Feb. 1950, B13; Norfolk *Journal and Guide*, National edition, 4 Mar. 1950, p. 2.

118. Norfolk *Journal and Guide*, Home edition, 14 Jan. 1950, p. 2.

119. Smith, "Where the South Begins," 228–232, 276, 288, 291–295.

120. Ibid., 222–226; Stefanie Lee Decker, "The Mask of the Southern Lady: Virginia Foster Durr, Southern Womanhood and Reform" (Ph.D. diss., Oklahoma State University, 2007), 133–134, 143–144; Norfolk *Journal and Guide*, Home edition, 29 Nov. 1947, p. 1.

121. Norfolk *Journal and Guide*, Home edition, 29 Nov. 1952, p. 6, 26 Dec. 1953, p. 7, 12 Nov. 1955, p. 28.

122. Norfolk *Journal and Guide*, Home edition , 18 Feb. 1950, p. 8; Norfolk *Journal and Guide*, Peninsula edition, 18 Mar. 1950, p. 7 (quotation).

123. Norfolk *Journal and Guide*, Virginia-Carolina edition, 22 Nov. 1952, p. 4, 19 Dec. 1953, p. 9; Norfolk *Journal and Guide*, National edition, 5 May 1951, p. 11; "What about Comic Books, Ask Juniors," *Virginia Club Woman* 27 (Dec. 1954): 7 (quotations).

124. Smith, "Where the South Begins," 241–243; Ronald L. Heinemann, *Harry Byrd of Virginia* (Charlottesville, 1996), 274–277.

CHAPTER 7

1. Ronald L. Heinemann, John G. Kolp, Anthony S. Parent, Jr., and William G. Shade, *Old Dominion, New Commonwealth: A History of Virginia, 1607–2007* (Charlottesville, 2007), 350–355.

2. Amy J. Tillerson, "Negotiating Intersections of Gender, Social Class, and Race: Black Women in Prince Edward County, Virginia, Activists and Community Builders" (Ph.D. diss., Morgan State University, 2006), 160–167. The conditions faced by Prince Edward County students were not an anomaly. Lauranett L. Lee's *Making the American Dream Work: A Cultural History of African Americans in Hopewell, Virginia* (Hampton, 2008) contains interviews with African Americans that describe the desegregated schools and the lengths to which the black community tried to ameliorate the conditions, as well as the ways in which African Americans fought for equality.

3. Bob Smith, *They Closed Their Schools: Prince Edward County, Virginia, 1951–1964* (Chapel Hill, 1965), 48, 58–59. Several recent dissertations have focused on providing detailed accounts of the Prince Edward County desegregation crisis, including Amy Tillerson, "Negotiating Intersections of Gender, Social Class, and Race"; Jill L. Ogline, "A Mission to a Mad County: Black Determination, White Resistance, and Educational Crisis in Prince Edward County, Virginia" (Ph.D. diss., University of Massachusetts, Amherst, 2007); and Kara Miles Turner, "'It Is Not at Present a Very Successful School': Prince Edward County and the Black Educational Struggle" (Ph.D. diss., Duke University, 2001).

4. For a complete contemporary account of Massive Resistance, see Benjamin Muse's *Virginia's Massive Resistance* (Bloomington, Ind., 1961). The book is entirely unsympathetic to segregationists, but its "bias" makes for a compelling read. This information is on 28–32.

5. Ogline, "A Mission to a Mad County," 64.

6. Jane Dailey, "Sex, Segregation, and the Sacred after Brown," *Journal of American History* 91 (June 2004): 133–136.

7. Muse, *Virginia's Massive Resistance*, 33.

8. James Howard Hershman, Jr., "A Rumbling in the Museum: The Opponents of Virginia's Massive Resistance" (Ph.D. diss., University of Virginia, 1978), 132.

9. Quoted in Muse, *Virginia's Massive Resistance*, 87.

10. Quoted in ibid.

11. Catherine Drew Gilpin to President Dwight D. Eisenhower, 12 Feb. 1957 (misdated 1956), White House Central Files, Dwight D. Eisenhower Presidential Library and Museum, Abilene, Kan.; digital image and transcript available at Faust's entry in LVA's Virginia Women in History website, http://www.lva.virginia.gov/public/vawomen/2009/honoree.asp?bio=5 (accessed 1 June 2012). Catherine Drew Gilpin, better known as Drew Gilpin Faust, became president of Harvard University in 2007.

12. Hershman, "A Rumbling in the Museum," 285; Radford *News Journal*, 22 May 1958, p. 1.

13. Hershman, "A Rumbling in the Museum," 187–188; Norfolk *Virginian-Pilot*, 6 Sept. 1956, p. 9 (quotation).

14. Andrew B. Lewis, "Emergency Mothers: Basement Schools and the Preservation of Public Education in Charlottesville," in *The Moderates' Dilemma: Massive Resistance to School Desegregation in Virginia*, eds. Matthew D. Lassiter and Andrew B. Lewis (Charlottesville, 1998), 76; Elizabeth Cooper and Jane Cooper Johnson, interview by Ronald E. Carrington, 21 Mar. 2003, Voices of Freedom Collection, VCU Digital Archives, http://dig.library.vcu.edu/cdm/singleitem/collection/voices/id/1 (accessed 1 June 2012); Frank Warren Cool III, "A Study of the Norfolk Public School Desegregation Process" (Ed.D. diss., Virginia Polytechnic Institute and State University, 1983), 33.

15. Hershman, "A Rumbling in the Museum," 64; "Public Opinion and the School Decision," Southern Regional Council *New South* 10 (May 1955): 10–11 (quotation).

16. Hershman, "A Rumbling in the Museum," 64–66, 122–123; Norfolk *Journal and Guide*, Home edition, 24 Dec. 1955, p. 14.

17. Hershman, "A Rumbling in the Museum," 122–123; Annual Reports of the League of Women Voters of Virginia, 1955–1956 (insert), 1957, p. 5 (Public Relations), 1958, p. 6 (State Program), 1963–1964, p. 15 (State Program), all in Administrative Records, Subseries 19, Reports, League of Women Voters of Virginia Records, Acc. 39487, Organization Records Collection, LVA.

18. Lewis, "Emergency Mothers: Basement Schools and the Preservation of Public Education in Charlottesville," 72–103.

19. Kathleen Murphy Dierenfield, "One 'Desegregated Heart': Sarah Patton Boyle and the Crusade for Civil Rights in Virginia," *VMHB* 104 (1996): 254–281; *DVB*, 2:176–178.

20. Ogline, "A Mission to a Mad County," 115–119, 148, 464; Amy E. Murrell, "The 'Impossible' Prince Edward Case: The Endurance of Resistance in a Southside County, 1959–1964," in Lassiter and Lewis, *The Moderates' Dilemma*, 148.

21. Murrell, "The 'Impossible' Prince Edward Case," in Lassiter and Lewis, *The Moderates' Dilemma*, 152; *Farmville Herald*, 26 June 1959, 1A, 7A (quotations).

22. Murrell, "The 'Impossible' Prince Edward Case," in Lassiter and Lewis, *The Moderates' Dilemma*, 158–159; *Farmville Herald*, 22 Jan. 1960, 1C.

23. Tillerson, "Negotiating Intersections of Gender, Social Class, and Race," 280–287; Ogline, "A Mission to a Mad County," 148–149.

24. Ogline, "A Mission to a Mad County," 148–150, 152; Tillerson, "Negotiating Intersections of Gender, Social Class, and Race," 282–284.

25. Jill Ogline Titus, *Brown's Battleground: Students, Segregationists, and the Struggle for Justice in Prince Edward County, Virginia* (Chapel Hill, 2011), 51–53; Tillerson, "Negotiating Intersections of Gender, Social Class, and Race," 296–297, 305.

26. Ogline, "A Mission to a Mad County," 163–184, 275, 313–318.

27. Vivian C. Mason interview embedded in William G. Thomas III, "Television News and the Civil Rights Struggle: The Views in Virginia and Mississippi," *Southern Spaces*, 3 Nov. 2004, http://www.southernspaces.org/2004/television-news-and-civil-rights-struggle-views-virginia-and-mississippi (accessed 29 May 2012).

28. Testimony of Joyce M. Russell Terrell, "Veterans Roll Call," Veterans of the Civil Rights Movement website, http://www.crmvet.org/ (accessed 29 May 2012); see also, Joyce Russell Terrell, *A Blues Song of My Own* (Signal Mountain, Tenn., 2009).

29. Elizabeth Cooper and Jane Cooper Johnson, interview by Ronald E. Carrington, 21 Mar. 2003, Voices of Freedom Collection, VCU Digital Archives, http://dig.library.vcu.edu/cdm/singleitem/collection/voices/id/1 (accessed 6 June 2012), first quotation at 8:33, second quotation at 10:00, third quotation at 11:46, fourth quotation at 12:38, fifth quotation at 12:46, sixth quotation at 14:07, seventh quotation at 14:52; eighth quotation at 15:05.

30. General overview in "Virginia's 'Massive Resistance' to School Desegregation," Digital Resources for United States History by the Virginia Center for Digital History at the University of Virginia, http://www2.vcdh.virginia.edu/xslt/servlet/XSLTServlet?xml=/xml_docs/solguide/Essays/essay13a.xml&xsl=/xml_docs/solguide/sol_new.xsl&section=essay (accessed 29 May 2012). For more information about trouble in the 1970s, see Peter Wallenstein, *Cradle of America: Four Centuries of Virginia History* (Lawrence, Kan., 2007), 356–357.

31. Edwilda Gustava Allen Isaac, interview by George Gilliam and Mason Mills, 2000, transcript of interview used in the film *Massive Resistance* (2000) at "Television News of the Civil Rights Era, 1950–1970," Virginia Center for Digital History at the University of Virginia, http://www2.vcdh.virginia.edu/reHIST604/people2b.html (accessed 29 May 2012).

32. Danville *Bee*, 17 July 1963, pp. 1A, 8A; Lawrence M. Clark, interview by Emma C. Edmunds, 2 Oct. 1998, transcript available at Mary Blount Library, Averett University, and online at "Mapping Local Knowledge: Danville, Virginia 1945–1975," Virginia Center for Digital History at the University of Virginia http://www.vcdh.virginia.edu/cslk/danville/interviews.html (accessed 29 May 2012).

33. Peter Wallenstein, *Blue Laws and Black Codes: Conflict, Courts, and Change in Twentieth-Century Virginia* (Charlottesville, 2004), 118–137.

34. Simon Hall, "Civil Rights Activism in 1960s Virginia," *Journal of Black Studies* 38 (2007): 252–253; Wallenstein, *Cradle of America*, 363; *Life*, 7 Mar. 1960, p. 42–43.

35. Lynchburg *Daily Advance*, 15 Dec. 1960, pp. 25, 47, 16 Dec. 1960, pp. 21, 37, 5 Jan. 1961, pp. 19, 26; Lynchburg *News and Advance*, 14 Jan. 2009, B1, B3.

36. Women all over the commonwealth were instrumental in civil rights actions in this era. In Fredericksburg, for example, Nan Grogan Orrock organized Mary Washington students to participate in YWCA-sponsored integration actions. She was a founding member of the Virginia Students Civil Rights Commission and helped to build boycotts and other actions in rural areas. A bit farther south of Fredericksburg, Nellie McLeod and Priscilla McLeod Robinson were mother-daughter members of the Petersburg Improvement Association. They both worked in pickets and sit-ins throughout the city with hundreds of other civil rights activists. Not only did these two protest in actions designed to overturn Jim Crow accommodations, they were also the first litigants in the Chesterfield County school desegregation case. See individual testimonies at "Veterans Roll Call," Veterans of the Civil Rights Movement website, http://www.crmvet.org/ (accessed 29 May 2012). More information can be found about the Farmville protests in Ogline, "Mission to a Mad County."

37. Alicia Petska, "Civil Rights in Central Virginia: From Student to Activist," published online by the Lynchburg *News and Advance*, 14 Jan. 2009, http://www2.newsadvance.com/news/2009/jan/14/civil_rights_in_central_virginia_from_student_to_a-ar-217264/ (accessed 29 May 2012). Also see Sara M. Evans, ed., *Journeys That Opened up the World: Women, Student Christian Movements, and Social Justice, 1955–1975* (New Brunswick, N.J., 2003), 66–83.

38. Len Holt, *An Act of Conscience* (Boston, 1965), 74–82, 106, 205–207; Dorothy Miller, *Danville, Virginia* (Atlanta, 1963), 4 (first quotation)–5; Chap. 358, "An Act to revise, rearrange, amend and recodify the general laws of Virginia relating to crimes and offenses generally…."

Acts and Joint Resolutions of the General Assembly of the Commonwealth of Virginia, Extra Session 1959, Regular Session 1960 (Richmond, 1960), 491 (second quotation).

39. Holt, *An Act of Conscience*, 4 (quotation), 88–95.

40. *Richmond Afro-American*, 22 June 1963, p. 1 (first quotation), 29 June 1963, p. 7 (second quotation).

41. Holt, *An Act of Conscience*, 6–9, 22–25 (quotations on 24–25), 52–53.

42. Ibid., 36–37.

43. Ibid., 100, 107–108 (quotation).

44. Thomas, "Television News and the Civil Rights Struggle," http://www.southernspaces.org/2004/television-news-and-civil-rights-struggle-views-virginia-and-mississippi (accessed 29 May 2012); Holt, *An Act of Conscience*, 209.

45. Holt, *An Act of* Conscience, 19; *DVB*, 3:183–185; Dorothy O. Harris, interview by Emma C. Edmunds, 4, 11 Apr. and 9 May 2003, and James Ulysses Griffin Hughes, interview by Emma C. Edmunds, 6 Aug. 2003, transcripts available at Mary Blount Library, Averett University, and online at "Mapping Local Knowledge: Danville, Virginia 1945–1975," Virginia Center for Digital History at the University of Virginia, http://www.vcdh.virginia.edu/cslk/danville/interviews.html (accessed 29 May 2012); Miller, *Danville, Virginia*, 6 (quotation).

46. Holt, *An Act of Conscience*, 124.

47. Cecilia A. Moore, "'To Serve through Compelling Love': The Society of Christ Our King and the Civil Rights Movement in Danville, Virginia, 1963," *U.S. Catholic Historian* 24 (2006): 83–103 (esp. 99–100).

48. Holt, *An Act of Conscience*, 217–218; *DVB* 1:45–46.

49. Holt, *An Act of Conscience*, 220–221; 1963 Danville Civil Rights Case Files, 1963–1973, Acc. 38099, LVA. Of the 253 individual case files in this collection, almost half belonged to women. Also see the Danville (VA) Movement, 1963, section of the Civil Rights Movement Veterans website at http://www.crmvet.org (accessed 29 May 2012).

50. *DVB*, 2:449–450; *Richmond News-Leader* 29 Nov. 1963, p. 1, 23 Mar. 1964, pp. 1, 3, 3 Apr. 1964, p. 25; Norfolk *Ledger-Star*, 25 Jan. 1966, pp. 1, 4 (quotations).

51. *DVB*, 2:449–450; *Richmond Times-Dispatch*, 13 Nov. 1964; Norfolk *Ledger-Star*, 25 Jan. 1966, pp. 1, 4; Norfolk *Virginian-Pilot*, 8 Apr. 1967, pp. 1 (quotation), 13.

52. For more information on *Loving v. Virginia*, see Peter Wallenstein, *Tell the Court I Love My Wife: Race, Marriage, and Law—An American History* (New York, 2002); Phyl Newbeck, *Virginia Hasn't Always Been for Lovers: Interracial Marriage Bans and the Case of Richard and Mildred Loving* (Carbondale, Ill., 2004); Newport News *Daily Press*, 11 June 2006, B7.

53. For information on the demise of the Byrd machine, see the last chapter of Heinemann et al., *Old Dominion, New Commonwealth*.

54. Jo Freeman, "How 'Sex' Got Into Title VII: Persistent Opportunism as a Maker of Public Policy," *Law and Inequality: A Journal of Theory and Practice* 9 (1991): 163–184.

55. Historians consider this movement the "second wave" of feminism to distinguish it from the earlier "first wave" feminist movement that focused on woman suffrage. For more information about the feminist movement in the country, see Jane Gerhard, *Desiring Revolution: Second-Wave Feminism and the Rewriting of American Sexual Thought, 1920 to 1982* (New York, 2001); Alice Echols, *Daring to Be Bad: Radical Feminism in America, 1967–1975* (Minneapolis, 1989); Ruth Rosen, *The World Split Open: How the Modern Women's Movement Changed America* (New York, 2000); Benita Roth, *Separate Roads to Feminism: Black, Chicana, and White Feminist Movements in America's Second Wave* (Cambridge, Eng., 2004); Estelle B.

Freedman, *No Turning Back: The History of Feminism and the Future of Women* (New York, 2002); Sara M. Evans, *Tidal Wave: How Women Changed America at Century's End* (New York, 2003).

56. Report of the Inter-Organizational Luncheon, 27 June 1964, p. 1, Status of Women, 1964–1966, Subject Files, Subseries 10, Women, League of Women Voters of Virginia Records, Acc. 39487, Organization Records Collection, LVA; Norfolk *Virginian-Pilot*, 28 June 1964, A25 (quotation).

57. Report of the Inter-Organizational Luncheon, 27 June 1964, p. 2.

58. Ibid.; Norfolk *Virginian-Pilot*, 28 June 1964, A25.

59. Norfolk *Virginian-Pilot*, 28 June 1964, A25 (quotation).

60. Virginia Council on the Status of Women, *History, 1965–1987* (Richmond, 1987); *DVB*, 3:415–416; *Roanoke Times and World-News*, 21 Aug. 1990, A6; the *Code of Virginia* (2.2-2630–2631) regarding the council can be accessed at the online Legislative Information System of the General Assembly, http://leg1.state.va.us/cgi-bin/legp504.exe?000+cod+TOC (accessed 29 May 2012).

61. Virginia National Organization for Women, "The Equal Rights Amendment Supporter's Handbook" (n.d.), pp. 2–3, Virginia ERA Ratification Council, Jean D. Hellmuth Papers, 1976–1992, M304,VCU.

62. "Labor-Sponsored Rally," *E.R.A. Time*, 18 Jan. 1978, p. 2, ERA Extension 1978 folder, and "Calendar of Events for Equality," Virginia Equal Rights Amendment Ratification Council, for 1980, Activities 1981 Folder," both in Jean D. Hellmuth Papers, 1976–1992, M304, VCU; "The Virginia General Assembly and the Equal Rights Amendment," *The Virginia Voter*, Piggyback Edition, No. 31 (Mar. 1979), p. 1, Virginia Voter 1979–1980 Folder, League of Women Voters of the Richmond Area Archives, M18, VCU; *Richmond Times-Dispatch*, 11 Jan. 1979, A7; *Washington Post*, 7 Feb. 1979, C3.

63. Event advertisements, Virginia ERA Ratification Council Advertisements folder, and Virginia ERA Ratification Council Executive Meeting, 10 Jan. 1982, Agenda folder, both in Jean D. Hellmuth Papers, 1976–1992, M304, VCU; "The Virginia General Assembly and the Equal Rights Amendment," *The Virginia Voter*, Piggyback Edition, No. 31 (Mar. 1979), p. 1, Virginia Voter 1979–1980 Folder, League of Women Voters of the Richmond Area Archives, M18, VCU; Mary M. Bezbatchenko, "Virginia and the Equal Rights Amendment" (M.A. thesis, Virginia Commonwealth University, 2007), iii, 86–87; *Richmond News Leader*, 27 Jan. 1978, p. 4 (quotation).

64. Bezbatchenko, "Virginia and the ERA," 72; *Washington Post*, 26 Jan. 1976, B1, B2 (quotation).

65. "Impatiens Plant Mourns ERA Bill," undated clipping [*Richmond News-Leader*], Newspaper and Magazine Clippings, 1974–1979, Zelda Kingoff Nordlinger Papers, Acc. 31719, Personal Papers Collection, LVA.

66. Virginia ERA Ratification Council Executive Meeting, 10 Jan. 1982, Virginia ERA Ratification Council Agendas folder, Jean D. Hellmuth Papers, 1976–1992, M304, VCU.

67. *Richmond News Leader*, 6 Feb. 1973, p. 11.

68. Adèle Clark, "Opposition to ERA(SE) Set Forth by Reader," letter to the editor in undated and unidentified newspaper (labeled by Nordlinger as Feb. 1974), Newspaper and Magazine Clippings, 1974–1979, Zelda Kingoff Nordlinger Papers, Acc. 31719, LVA.

69. Bezbatchenko, "Virginia and the ERA," 25–32, 42–43; Virginia ERA Central, "Homosexual 'Marriages'????" (n.d.), ERA Effects Family Law folder, ERA Issues, 1972–1980, Virginia Equal Rights Amendment Ratification Council Papers, 1970–1982, Acc. 31486, Organization Records Collection, LVA (quotation).

70. Bezbatchenko, "Virginia and the ERA," 47–49, 86, 96–97. Geline Williams, whose mother John-Geline MacDonald Bowman had been president of the Virginia Federation of Business and Professional Women's Clubs and of the National Federation of Business and Professional Women's Clubs, had a storied career herself. Williams served as mayor of Richmond from 1988 to 1990. (For more information on John-Geline Bowman, see *DVB*, 2:153–155).

71. Bezbatchenko, "Virginia and the ERA," 74–75, 100–102.

72. Charlottesville *Daily Progress*, 17 Feb. 1982, p. 1.

73. *Washington Post*, 6 Nov. 1977, B1, B3, 9 Nov. 1977, A1, A15, 10 Nov. 1977, C1 (quotation), C3; Patricia Winton and Mary Ann Bergeron, "Virginia NOW Fundraising Letter," n.d., Patricia Winton Goodman, Press Release, n.d., Virginia NOW Political Action Committee, "Statement of Organization," 6 Jan. 1979, and Report of Campaign Contributions and Expenditures, 6 Nov. 1979, all in Virginia Chapter of the National Organization for Women Records, Acc. 43458, Organization Records Collection, LVA.

74. Bezbatchenko, "Virginia and the ERA," 83–85.

75. Virginia Federation of Business and Professional Women's Clubs, *75th Anniversary History Book* (1994), 44, Alexandria Business and Professional Women's Club Records, Acc. 41929, Organization Records Collection, LVA.

76. Blacksburg-Christiansburg *News Messenger*, 4 Nov. 1981, pp. 1–2; *Washington Post*, 6 Nov. 1981, B1 (quotations), B4.

77. The Virginia NOW records list many fund-raisers and disbursements for the PAC through the 1990s, Virginia Chapter of the National Organization for Women Records, Acc. 43458, LVA.

78. *Richmond Times-Dispatch*, 26 Oct. 1969, B13.

79. Kenneth Skipper, "The Origins of the Modern Religious Lobby in Virginia, 1968–1980" (M.A. thesis, Clemson University, 2009), 50–51.

80. Ibid., 46–50; brief history on the Virginia Society for Human Life website, http://www.vshl.org/about_us.html (accessed 29 May 2012); "CCC Honors Local Volunteers," *Henrico Citizen*, 17 May 2012, online at http://www.henricocitizen.com/index.php/news/article/ccc_honors_local_volunteers0517 (accessed 29 May 2012); *Washington Post*, 9 Jan. 1977, B2, 29 Nov. 1977, C1 (quotation), C7, 16 Feb. 1978, B3, 28 July 1978, C1–C2.

81. Skipper, "The Origins of the Modern Religious Lobby in Virginia," 34, 54.

82. Ibid., 57–58; *Washington Post*, 9 Sept. 1980, B3 (quotations).

83. Phyllis Leffler, "Mr. Jefferson's University: Women in the Village!" *VMHB* 115 (2007): 56–107; Board of Visitors Minutes, 8 Apr. 1967, 15 Feb. 1969 (third quotation), UVA Board of Visitors Minutes, 1817–2002, UVA (access available through UVA's online catalog, http://search.lib.virginia.edu/catalog, accessed 29 May 2012); *Cavalier Daily*, 11 Apr. 1967, p. 1 (first and second quotations); *Washington Post*, 9 Sept. 1969, B4, 10 Feb. 1970, C3; Charlottesville *Daily Progress*, 13 Sept. 1974, B1.

84. Schuyler VanValkenburg, "Defying Labels: Richmond NOW's Multi-Generational Dynamism" (M.A. thesis, Virginia Commonwealth University, 2010), 18, 32–33; "Women Take Last Fort," unidentified newspaper clipping and photo, n.p., n.d., Biographical Information, Zelda Kingoff Nordlinger Papers, Acc. 31719, LVA.

85. Nordlinger to Mr. Lauren Selden, 27 Aug. 1970, Correspondence, 1970, Zelda Kingoff Nordlinger Papers, Acc. 31719, LVA.

86. Nordlinger to June Wakeford, 14 Sept. 1970, Nordlinger to WRVA Radio News, 7 Dec. 1970, Nordlinger to WTVR, WTEX, WWBT, all 7 Dec. 1970, Nordlinger to Sgt. D. R. Duling, 8 Dec.

1970, in Correspondence, 1970; Nordlinger to Flora Crater, 25 Feb. 1971, Nordlinger to WOMEN, 28 Feb. 1971, in Correspondence, 1971, all in Zelda Kingoff Nordlinger Papers, Acc. 31719, LVA; VanValkenburg, "Defying Labels," 20–21.

87. Nordlinger to The Spokeswoman, 26 Jan. 1972, Correspondence, 1972, Zelda Kingoff Nordlinger Papers, Acc. 31719, LVA.

88. Alice C. Cook, telephone interview by Matthew Gottlieb, 8 June 2012, notes in *Changing History: Virginia Women through Four Centuries* files, LVA (quotation); Norfolk *Virginian-Pilot*, 21 Aug. 1973, B1; *Altoona (Pa.) Mirror*, 21 Sept. 1978, p. 23; Susan H. Godson, *Serving Proudly: A History of Women in the U.S. Navy* (Annapolis, 2001), 245–246, 384n137.

89. EEOC Settlement of *Zelda Nordlinger* v. *Southwestern General Life Insurance Co.*, 16 Nov. 1977, Suits and Complaints, Zelda Kingoff Nordlinger Papers, Acc. 31719, LVA.

90. Nordlinger to Ms. Tony Radler, WRVA Radio, 14 Oct. 1971, Correspondence, 1971, Zelda Kingoff Nordlinger Papers, Acc. 31719, LVA.

91. *Richmond Mercury*, 14 Nov. 1973, pp. 1, 3–5.

92. Arlington NOW 1990 Annual Report, 27 Mar. 1991, Virginia Chapter of the National Organization for Women Records, Acc. 43458, LVA.

93. Although much more research needs to be done on southern race relations within the second-wave feminist movement, Janet Allured's "The Louisiana AFL-CIO and the Second Wave in Louisiana," presented at the Southern Association for Women Historians Eighth Southern Conference on Women's History, Columbia, S.C., June 2009, suggests that black women had more-pressing concerns with economic equality and issues that were not as much a concern to middle-class white women.

94. As quoted by Nordlinger in her letter to Mary Nell Duggan, 14 Oct. 1971, Correspondence, 1971, Zelda Kingoff Nordlinger Papers, Acc. 31719, LVA.

95. *Richmond Times-Dispatch*, 16 April 1971, B10.

96. LaVerne Byrd Smith, interview by Ronald E. Carrington, 21 Mar. 2003, Voices of Freedom Collection, VCU Digital Archives, interview and transcription available at http://dig.library. vcu.edu/cdm/ref/collection/voices/id/9 (accessed 29 May 2012).

97. *DVB*, 2:449–450; Norfolk *Virginian-Pilot*, 16 July 1975, B3, 7 Sept. 1979, D3, 3 July 1982, B2; Norfolk *Ledger-Star*, 9 Mar. 1976, B1, 13 Aug. 1979, A6.

98. "Virginia Action Begins Organizing Process," *Virginia Action* 1 (Aug. 1981): 2, Virginia Chapter of the National Organization for Women Records, Acc. 43458, LVA.

99. Ibid., 2–3.

100. "Brown Lung Association fights for changes in workers' compensation laws," *Virginia Action* 1 (Aug. 1981): 8–9 (quotations), Virginia Chapter of the National Organization for Women Records, Acc. 43458, LVA; *Washington Post*, 28 Nov. 1980, A1, A20, 14 Jan. 1981, C1, C3; Chap. 82, "An Act to amend and reenact 65.1-52 of the Code of Virginia, relating to the occupational disease statute of limitations for workmen's compensation benefits," approved 12 Mar. 1982, *Acts of the General Assembly of the Commonwealth of Virginia 1982 Regular Session . . .* (Richmond, 1982), 1:194–195.

101. Peter Matthiessen, *In the Spirit of Crazy Horse* (New York, 1983), 34–35, 54–55; *Washington Post*, 4 Nov. 1972, A1, A8, 9 Nov. 1972, C1, C3; Laura Waterman Wittstock and Elaine J. Salinas, "A Brief History of the American Indian Movement," on the AIM Grand Governing Council website, http://www.aimovement.org/ggc/history.html (accessed 29 May 2012).

102. Samuel R. Cook, *Monacans and Miners: Native American and Coal Mining Communities in Appalachia* (Lincoln, Neb., 2000), 125.

103. Danielle Moretti-Langholtz, "Other Names I Have Been Called: Political Resurgence Among Virginia Indians in the Twentieth Century" (Ph.D. diss., University of Oklahoma, 1998), 193–194; Fredericksburg *Free Lance-Star*, 11 June 1997, A1, A10, 12 June 1997, A1, A12; G. Anne Nelson Richardson biography at Virginia Women in History, 2006, LVA, http://www.lva. virginia.gov/public/vawomen/2006/richardson.htm (accessed 29 May 2012).

104. Sandra F. Waugaman and Danielle Moretti-Langholtz, *We're Still Here: Contemporary Virginia Indians Tell Their Stories* (Richmond, 2000), 25–28, 45, 83–84.

105. Ibid., 87 (quotation); Helen Red Wing Vinson (sister), "Who is Mary Laughing Dove," Manataka American Indian Council website, http://www.manataka.org/page497.html (accessed 29 May 2012).

106. *Richmond Times Dispatch*, 21 Oct. 1984, L6.

107. Peter Wallenstein, "'These New and Strange Beings': Women in the Legal Profession in Virginia," *VMHB* 101 (1993): 211–223.

108. *Washington Post*, 24 Feb. 1980, A1, A6.

109. *Washington Post*, 13 Oct. 1984, C1, C7, 26 Oct. 1984, B3 (quotation).

110. Election Alert Memorandum, Georgia Fuller to Virginia NOW, 3 Oct. 1989, Virginia Chapter of the National Organization for Women Records, Acc. 43458, LVA.

111. Fredericksburg *Free Lance-Star*, 20 Apr. 1992, C3; Norfolk *Virginian-Pilot*, 11 Jan. 1994. These efforts seemed particularly visible late in the 1980s and early in the 1990s. Evidence of these activities are scattered throughout chapter newsletters, including *NOW Fredericksburg Area Newsletter* (Sept. 1989) and the Pro-Choice Community Outreach Kit (prepared by Alexandria NOW), Virginia Chapter of the National Organization for Women Records, Acc. 43458, LVA. Many more of these newsletters, primarily from Alexandria, Arlington, Fredericksburg, Norfolk, and Richmond can be found in the Virginia NOW Records at LVA.

112. Norfolk *Virginian-Pilot*, 11 Jan. 1994, D1 (first quotation); *Washington Post*, 21 Feb. 1997, A1; News Release, 22 Jan. 2003, (second quotation), Virginia Chapter of the National Organization for Women Records, Acc. 43458, LVA.

113. *Washington Post*, 7 Aug. 1992, E3; *Elizabeth Howze* v. *Virginia Polytechnic and State University, et al.*, 901 F. Supp. 1091 (W.D., Va., 1995), [1092], quotation; Donna Euben, "A Legal Primer for New and Not-So-New Administrators," presented on 24 Oct. 2005 at 15th Annual Legal Issues in Higher Education Conference, Burlington, Vt., http://www.aaup.org/AAUP/ programs/legal/topics/primer.htm (accessed 29 May 2012).

114. *Washington Post*, 1 Oct. 1993, D1, D5.

115. U.S. Census Bureau, *Virginia: 2000: Summary Social, Economic, and Housing Characteristics*, PHC-2-48 (2003), 79, http://www.census.gov/prod/cen2000/phc-2-48.pdf (accessed 1 June 2012); *2003 Catalyst Census of Women Board Directors: A Call to Action in a New Era of Corporate Governance* (New York, 2003), 34; *Washington Post*, 4 Dec. 2003, E3.

116. For Collins, see *DVB* 3:381–382; "Elizabeth James Morris Downes (1886–1968)," *Encyclopedia Virginia*, http://www.encyclopediavirginia.org/Downes_Elizabeth_James_ Morris_1886-1968; for Bouey, see *DVB* 2:118–119.

117. Pamela R. Durso and Keith E. Durso, "'Cherish the Dream God Has Given You': The Story of Addie Davis," in *Courage and Hope: The Stories of Ten Baptist Women Ministers*, ed. Pamela R. Durso and Keith E. Durso (Macon, Ga., 2005), 18–30; *Richmond Times-Dispatch*, 13 May 1965, p. 6.

118. Larry Ray Hygh, Jr., "A Qualitative Leadership Study of the Four Female African American Bishops of the United Methodist Church" (Ed.D. diss., Pepperdine University, 2008), 31–35; Isabel Wood Rogers biography, Virginia Women in History, 2008, LVA, http://www.

lva.virginia.gov/public/vawomen/2008/honorees.asp?bio=5 (accessed 1 June 2012); Pauline Dubkin Yearwood, "Amy M. Schwartzman: Speaking Out on Critical Issues," *Jewish Woman Magazine* 8 (Fall 2005): 18–19, http://www.jwi.org/Page.aspx?pid=639 (accessed 1 June 2012); Frederica Harris Thompsett, "Women in the American Episcopal Church," in *Encyclopedia of Women and Religion in Northern America*, eds. Rosemary Skinner Keller, Rosemary Radford Roether, and Marie Cantlon (Bloomington, Ind., 2006), 1:278; "Episcopal Church consecrates first indigenous woman to episcopate," 10 Apr. 2002, Episcopal News Service, http://archive. episcopalchurch.org/3577_20502_ENG_HTM.htm (accessed 1 June 2012).

119. Yvonne Bond Miller biography at Virginia Women in History, 2012, LVA, http:// www.lva.virginia.gov/public/trailblazers/2012/?bio=miller (accessed 1 June 2012); for more information on Wensel and the campaign against Byrd, see George Lewis, "'Any Old Joe Named Zilch'?: The Senatorial Campaign of Dr. Louise Oftedal Wensel," *VMHB* 107 (1999): 287–316; for Barger, see *DVB*, 1:341–342; Mary Sue Terry biography at Virginia Women in History, 2009, LVA, http://www.lva.virginia.gov/public/vawomen/2009/honoree.asp?bio=6 (accessed 1 June 2012); "Leslie Byrne (1946–)," *Encyclopedia Virginia* at http://encyclopediavirginia.org/ Byrne_Leslie_1946- (accessed 1 June 2012); "Davis, Jo Ann (1950–2007), *Biographical Directory of the United States Congress, 1774–Present*, http://bioguide.congress.gov/scripts/biodisplay. pl?index=D000597 (accessed 1 June 2012); "Drake, Thelma D. (1949–), *Biographical Directory of the United States Congress, 1774–Present*, http://bioguide.congress.gov/scripts/biodisplay. pl?index=D000605 (accessed 1 June 2012).

120. *Richmond Times-Dispatch*, 16 Apr. 1971, B10.

121. Memorandum, Georgia E. Fuller, Committee Opportunities and Appointments, 3 April 1990, Virginia Chapter of the National Organization for Women Records, Acc. 43458, LVA.

122. Two books deal exclusively with the VMI case and its aftermath: Laura Fairchild Brodie, *Breaking Out: VMI and the Coming of Women* (New York, 2000), and Philippa Strum, *Women in the Barracks: The VMI Case and Equal Rights* (Lawrence, Kan., 2002).

123. *Yes Virginia …* (Virginia NOW newsletter), [1979]; Leslie Alden, "Legislative Summary, Virginia General Assembly 1980," 29 Apr. 1980, both in Virginia Chapter of the National Organization for Women Records, Acc. 43458, LVA.

124. Memorandum, Mary A. Marshall to Virginia Women's Organizations, 21 Feb. 1981, Virginia Chapter of the National Organization for Women Records, Acc. 43458, LVA.

125. *Washington Post*, 26 June 1993, D5, 8 Nov. 1993, D1, D7, 11 Nov. 1993, A1, A36.

126. *Washington Post*, 19 Jan. 1994, D1, D3, 23 Jan. 1994, A1; Marybeth H. Lenkevich, "Admitting Expert Testimony on Battered Woman Syndrome in Virginia Courts: How Peeples Changed Virginia Self-Defense Law," *William and Mary Journal of Women and the Law* 6 (1999): 298–299.

127. *Now and Then Times* (Nov. 1983); "From the President's Desk," *NOW Spring Edition*, Richmond pamphlet (Apr./May 1983), p. 1; Workshops list, Virginia NOW State Conference Program, 1990; "Viewpoints," *Newsletter of Montgomery Co. NOW* (spring 1999), all in Virginia Chapter of the National Organization for Women Records, Acc. 43458, LVA.

128. "Action on Fairfax Co. Battered Women's Shelter Continues," *Alexandria NOW Newsletter* (Apr. 1991), pp. 1–2; Amy Tracy, "President's Corner," *Alexandria NOW Newsletter* (May 1991), p. 1, both in Virginia Chapter of the National Organization for Women Records, Acc. 43458, LVA.

129. *Alexandria, Arlington, Northern Virginia Chapter News* (Dec. 1999/Jan. 2000); *Alexandria, Arlington, Northern Virginia Chapter News* (Sept. 1996); "Viewpoints" *Newsletter of Montgomery Co. NOW* (spring 1999); Jessie Gilliam to Virginia NOW and Ms. Hays-Hamilton,

29 Nov. 1997, all in Virginia Chapter of the National Organization for Women Records, Acc. 43458, LVA. These are just representative samples—NOW newsletters include information about student activities on campus as well as collaborations with YWCAs and other organizations, so they are very valuable sources.

130. As the director of Women's Studies at Longwood and the sponsor of WILL, Megan Shockley was involved in helping the students with this production, although they did everything themselves. The students had to re-order the chocolate lollipops because they ran out so quickly.

131. Evidence of these events can be found in every college newspaper in the state, public and private. Events are usually held in April, as the weather turns warmer, and normally feature a march and a speak-out against violence. Organizers of Longwood's events often invited people to speak about their own experiences with violence, and people would often get up spontaneously to tell their stories.

132. Megan Taylor Shockley, "Southern Women in the Scrums: The Emergence and Decline of Women's Rugby in the American Southeast, 1974–1980s," *Journal of Sport History* 33 (2006): 127–155; Beth Marschak and Alex Lorch, *Lesbian and Gay Richmond* (Charleston, S.C., 2008), 63–67, 80.

133. *Richmond News Leader*, 10 Dec. 1990, p.16.

134. LaShonda Mims argues that the creation of lesbian bar culture was an important step not only in creating community but also in forging bonds that would assist in later activist efforts in "Sorry Gentleman, but Diana's is for Women Only," paper presented at the Southern Association for Women Historians Eighth Southern Conference on Women's History, Columbia, S.C., June 2009.

135. William A. Henry III, "Gay Parents: Under Fire and On the Rise," *Time*, 20 Sept. 1993, 66–68, 71 (second quotation on 67); *Richmond Times-Dispatch*, 23 May 1993, A1; *Washington Post*, 28 Feb. 1996, D6 (first quotation).

136. Marschak and Lorch, *Lesbian and Gay Richmond*, 100.

137. *Bottoms* v. *Bottoms* (1995), 249 (Virginia Reports) 410–422; *Washington Post* 28 Feb. 1996, D6; Norfolk *Virginian-Pilot*, 1 Sept. 1996, J5.

138. *Washington Post*, 6 Dec. 2001, B1; Linda Kaufman, "About Fairness and My Family," *Washington Post*, 30 Mar. 2003, B7 (quotations).

139. Linda Kaufman Wire Art website, http://www.lkwireart.com (accessed 1 June 2012).

140. Official Results of the State Board of Elections, Commonwealth of Virginia, 7 Nov. 2006, http://www.sbe.virginia.gov/electionresults/2006/nov/htm/index.htm (accessed 1 June 2012); *Richmond Times-Dispatch*, 8 Nov. 2006, A1, A26.

EPILOGUE

1. *Washington Post*, 20 Feb. 2009, B1.

2. Comments at http://www.washingtonpost.com/wp-dyn/content/article/2009/02/19/AR2009021901780_Comments.html# (accessed 2 Sept. 2009, but no longer available).

3. *Richmond Times-Dispatch*, 29 Oct. 2009, B1; comments at http://www2.timesdispatch.com/rtd/news/columnists_news/article/MIKE29_20091028-221803/302244/ (accessed 1 Dec. 2009, but no longer available).

4. See, for instance, the superb online archive of that name at Virginia Commonwealth University, http://www.library.vcu.edu/newdominion/ (accessed 3 Sept. 2009, but no longer available).

5. National Women's Law Center Position Paper, "The Paycheck Fairness Act Would Help Close the Wage Gap for Virginia Women," http://www.nwlc.org/sites/default/files/pdfs/VirginiaWageGap2009.pdf (accessed 17 May 2012).

6. Ibid.; *Richmond Times-Dispatch*, 5 Apr. 2009, A1, A8; Bureau of Labor Statistics, "Local Area Unemployment Statistics," http://data.bls.gov/ (accessed on 17 May 2012); Heidi Hartmann and Jeff Hayes, "The Job Loss Tsunami of the Great Recession: Wave Recedes for Men, Not Women," July 2011, http://www.iwpr.org/publications/pubs/the-job-loss-tsunami-of-the-great-recession-wave-recedes-for-men-not-for-women (accessed 17 May 2012); "Slow and Positive Job Growth for Women and Men Continues in April," May 2012, http://www.iwpr.org/publications/pubs/slow-and-positive-job-growth-for-women-and-men-continues-in-april/at_download/file (accessed 17 May 2012).

7. For national statistics, see "Higher Education: Institutions and Enrollment, 1980 to 2008," in 2011 Statistical Abstract of the United States, compiled by the U.S. Census Bureau, http://www.census.gov/compendia/statab/2011/tables/11s0274.pdf (accessed 17 May 2012); for Virginia, see http://research.schev.edu/enrollment/E2_Report.ASP (accessed 8 Sept. 2009).

8. Ray Bonis, Jodi Koste, and Curtis Lyons, *Virginia Commonwealth University* (Charleston, S.C., 2006), 27; *Women Graduates, 1921–1925, University of Virginia* (Charlottesville, 1926), 11.

9. "Virginia Quick Facts," Records of the U.S. Census, http://quickfacts.census.gov/qfd/states/51000.html (accessed 17 May 2012); for Fearnow, see *Richmond News Leader*, 23 Oct. 1956, p. 6, and *Richmond Times-Dispatch*, 22 July 1996, E7; Betty Sams Christian biography at Virginia Women in History, 2012, LVA, http://www.lva.virginia.gov/public/vawomen/2012/?bio=christian (accessed 17 May 2012); for Johnson, see Paula C. Squires, "The Virginia 100 Index," *Virginia Business* 22 (June 2007): 16; for Dhillon, see *Washington Post*, 14 Mar. 2006, B6; Elisabeth Frater, *Breaking Away to Virginia and Maryland Wineries* (Sterling, Va., 2000), 59–61.

10. Sandra Gioia Treadway, "Pioneers to Power Brokers: Women Office Holders in Twentieth Century Virginia," paper presented at the Southern Association for Women Historians plenary session, annual meeting of Southern Historical Association, New Orleans, La., 11 Oct. 2008; Center for American Women and Politics, "State Fact Sheet–Virginia," http://www.cawp.rutgers.edu/fast_facts/resources/state_fact_sheets/VA.php (accessed 5 Apr. 2012); *Richmond Times-Dispatch*, 17 Feb. 2011, B2; "Virginia NOW PAC Endorses Charniele Herring," 15 Dec. 2008, http://archive.bluecommonwealth.com/node/1591 (accessed 5 Apr. 2012); "Delegate Charniele Herring (D-46th) Appointed Democratic Minority Whip," press release, VA House Democrats, 13 Dec. 2011, http://www.vahousedems.com/p/salsa/web/press_release/public/?press_release_KEY=795 (accessed 17 May 2012).

11. Center for American Women and Politics, "State Fact Sheet–Virginia," http://www.cawp.rutgers.edu/fast_facts/resources/state_fact_sheets/VA.php (accessed 5 Apr. 2012).

12. "2007 Domestic Violence Services: Adults and Children" and "2007 Domestic Violence Services: Crisis and Advocacy," reports by Virginia Sexual and Domestic Violence Action Alliance, http://www.vsdvalliance.org (accessed 17 May 2012); Public Policy Priorities Brochure 2005–2010, http://www.ncadv.org/files/virginia.pdf (accessed 2 Sept. 2009); *Protective Orders in Virginia*, 2011, http://www.vsdvalliance.org/secPublications/PO%20Booklet-2011FINAL.pdf (accessed 5 April 2012).

13. NOW reports on reproductive choice, home page, http://virginianow.wordpress.com/ (accessed 17 May 2012); *Richmond Times-Dispatch*, 31 Mar. 2009, and reader's comment (first quotation), http://www2.timesdispatch.com/rtd/news/state_regional/state_

regional_govtpolitics/article/KAIN31S_20090330-222411/244755/ (accessed 2 Dec. 2009); "Virginians: "Trust Women, Respect Choice" License Plates on Sale in Virginia!," http://www. plannedparenthood.org/health-systems/trust-women-respect-choice-plates-va-31162.htm (accessed 5 Apr. 2012); Chap. 776, "An Act to authorize the issuance of speical license plates; fees," approved 21 Apr. 2010, *Acts of the General Assembly of the Commonwealth of Virginia, 2010 Regular Session* (Richmond, 2010), 2:1404 (second quotation).

14. *Richmond Times-Dispatch*, 22 Mar. 2012, A11; Norma Gattsek, "Mandating Rape in Virginia," 16 Feb. 2012, *Feminist Majority Foundation Blog*, http://feminist.org/blog/ index.php/2012/02/16/mandating-rape-in-virginia/ (accessed 5 Apr. 2012); http://www. womensstrikeforce.com/ (accessed 21 May 2012).

15. Equality Virginia Media Center, http://equalityvirginia.org/site/how-you-can-help/ media-center.html (accessed 2 Sept. 2009, but no longer available), "Tell the Governor to Oppose the Conscience Clause Bills," http://equalityfederation.salsalabs.com/o/35035/p/dia/action/ public/?action_KEY=855 (accessed 5 Apr. 2012); *Richmond Times-Dispatch*, 15 Dec. 2011, A1, A9.

16. U.S. Census, 1990, http://censtats.census.gov/cgi-bin/pl94/pl94data.pl (accessed 5 Apr. 2012); U.S. Census, American Fact Finder, "Profile of General Population and Housing Characteristics: 2010," http://factfinder2.census.gov/faces/nav/jsf/pages/index.xhtml (accessed 5 Apr. 2012).

17. Kristen Ball, "Latin Ballet Heats Up Virginia," *Soul of Virginia* 3 (spring 2006): 23, and http://www.latinballet.com (accessed 21 May 2012); Report of the Latina discussion group, Creciendos Juntos, http://www.cj-network.org/cjloclatfocusedin/LatinaGroup.doc (accessed 21 May 2012); "Fairfax County Board of Supervisors to Recognize Citizens," 2004 News Release, http://www.fairfaxcounty.gov/news/2004/04165.htm (accessed 21 May 2012); *Washington Post*, 19 Oct. 2006, Fairfax Extra, pp. 20–22; "Cora Foley, 'Lady Fairfax,'" *Asian Fortune News*, 2 May 2010, http://www.asianfortunenews.com/site/article_0610.php?article_id=11 (accessed 21 May 2012).

18. Board of Directors, Democratic Latino Organization of Virginia, http://www.dlov. net (accessed 2 Dec. 2009); Republican National Hispanic Assembly of Virginia, http:// rnhava-slate.tripod.com (accessed 29 July 2011); *Richmond Times-Dispatch*, 17 Nov. 2003; B1, B4; Records of the Latino Liason, Timothy M. Kaine Executive Papers (2004–2009), Acc. 44808, LVA; "Governor Kaine Announces Latino Liaison," press release, 13 Apr. 2009, http://wayback. archive-it.org/263/20090414121354/http://www.governor.virginia.gov/MediaRelations/ NewsReleases/viewRelease.cfm?id=923 (accessed 17 May 2012); Colaborandos Juntos website, www.colaborandojuntosva.com (accessed 2 Dec. 2009); OCA Northern Virginia Chapter, http:// www.ocanova.org/11.html (accessed 2 Dec. 2009); Virginia Asian Advisory Board, http://www. vaab.virginia.gov/about.cfm (accessed 2 Dec. 2009).

SUGGESTED READINGS

CHAPTER 1

Brown, Kathleen M. *Good Wives, Nasty Wenches, and Anxious Patriarchs: Gender, Race, and Power in Colonial Virginia.* Chapel Hill: Published for the Omohondro Institute of Early American History and Culture, Williamsburg, Virginia, by the University of North Carolina Press, 1996.

Carr, Lois Green, and Lorena S. Walsh, "The Planter's Wife: The Experience of White Women in Seventeenth-Century Maryland." *William and Mary Quarterly*, 3rd ser., 34 (1977): 542–571.

Clinton, Catherine, and Michele Gillespie, eds. *The Devil's Lane: Sex and Race in the Early South.* New York: Oxford University Press, 1997.

Gundersen, Joan R. *To Be Useful to the World: Women in Revolutionary America, 1740–1790,* rev. ed. Chapel Hill: University of North Carolina Press, 2006.

Kerrison, Catherine. *Claiming the Pen: Women and Intellectual Life in the Early American South.* Ithaca, N.Y.: Cornell University Press, 2006.

Kierner, Cynthia A. *Beyond the Household: Women's Place in the Early South, 1700–1835.* Ithaca, N.Y.: Cornell University Press, 1998.

Meacham, Sarah Hand. *Every Home a Distillery: Alcohol, Gender, and Technology in the Colonial Chesapeake.* Baltimore: Johns Hopkins University Press, 2010.

Morgan, Jennifer L. *Laboring Women: Reproduction and Gender in New World Slavery.* Philadelphia: University of Pennsylvania Press, 2004.

Pagan, John Ruston. *Anne Orthwood's Bastard: Sex and Law in Early Virginia.* New York: Oxford University Press, 2003.

Shammas, Carole, "Black Women's Work and the Evolution of Plantation Society in Virginia." *Labor History* 26 (1985): 5–28.

Smith, Daniel Blake. *Inside the Great House: Planter Life in Eighteenth-Century Chesapeake Society.* Ithaca, N.Y.: Cornell University Press, 1980.

Snyder, Terri L. *Brabbling Women: Disorderly Speech and the Law in Early Virginia.* Ithaca, N.Y.: Cornell University Press, 2003.

Spruill, Julia Cherry. *Women's Life and Work in the Southern Colonies.* Chapel Hill: University of North Carolina Press, 1938.

Sturtz, Linda L. *Within Her Power: Propertied Women in Colonial Virginia.* New York: Routledge, 2002.

Townsend, Camilla. *Pocahontas and the Powhatan Dilemma.* New York: Hill and Wang, 2004.

Treckel, Paula A. "'The Empire of My Heart': The Marriage of William Byrd II and Lucy Parke Byrd." *Virginia Magazine of History and Biography* 105 (1997): 125–156.

CHAPTER 2

Allgor, Catherine. *A Perfect Union: Dolley Madison and the Creation of the American Nation.* New York: Henry Holt and Company, 2006.

Berkin, Carol. *Revolutionary Mothers: Women in the Struggle for America's Independence.* New York: Vintage Books, 2005.

Brady, Patricia. *Martha Washington: An American Life.* New York: Viking, 2005.

Buckley, Thomas E., S.J., *The Great Catastrophe of My Life: Divorce in the Old Dominion.* Chapel Hill: University of North Carolina Press, 2002.

Gordon-Reed, Annette. *The Hemingses of Monticello: An American Family.* New York: W. W. Norton & Co., 2008.

Hamilton, Phillip. *The Making and Unmaking of a Revolutionary Family: The Tuckers of Virginia, 1752–1830.* Charlottesville: University of Virginia Press, 2003.

Kerber, Linda K. *Women of the Republic: Intellect and Ideology in Revolutionary America.* Chapel Hill: Published for the Institute of Early American History and Culture, Williamsburg, Virginia, by the University of North Carolina Press, 1980.

Kierner, Cynthia A. *Martha Jefferson Randolph, Daughter of Monticello: Her Life and Times.* Chapel Hill: University of North Carolina Press, 2012.

———. *Scandal at Bizarre: Rumor and Reputation in Jefferson's America.* New York: Palgrave Macmillan, 2004.

Lewis, Jan. *The Pursuit of Happiness: Family and Values in Jefferson's Virginia.* Cambridge, Eng.: Cambridge University Press, 1983.

Norton, Mary Beth. *Liberty's Daughters: The Revolutionary Experience of American Women, 1750–1800.* Boston: Little, Brown, 1980.

_____. "'What an Alarming Crisis Is This': Southern Women and the American Revolution." In *The Southern Experience in the American Revolution.* Edited by Jeffrey J. Crow and Larry Tise, 203–234. Chapel Hill: University of North Carolina Press, 1978.

Pybus, Cassandra. *Epic Journeys of Freedom: Runaway Slaves of the American Revolution and their Global Quest for Liberty.* Boston: Beacon Press, 2006.

Stanton, Lucia. *Free Some Day: The African American Families of Monticello.* Charlottesville: The Thomas Jefferson Foundation, Inc., 2000.

———. *"Those Who Labor for My Happiness": Slavery at Thomas Jefferson's Monticello.* Charlottesville: University of Virginia Press, 2012.

Treadway, Sandra Gioia. "Anna Maria Lane: An Uncommon Soldier of the American Revolution." *Virginia Cavalcade* 37 (1988): 134–143.

Zagarri, Rosemarie. *Revolutionary Backlash: Women and Politics in the Early American Republic.* Philadelphia: University of Pennsylvania Press, 2007.

CHAPTER 3

Bardaglio, Peter W. *Reconstructing the Household: Families, Sex, and the Law in the Nineteenth-Century South.* Chapel Hill: University of North Carolina Press, 1995.

Breen, Patrick H. "The Female Antislavery Petition Campaign of 1831–32." *Virginia Magazine of History and Biography* 110 (2002): 377–398.

Camp, Stephanie M. H. *Closer to Freedom: Enslaved Women and Everyday Resistance in the Plantation South*. Chapel Hill: University of North Carolina Press, 2004.

Clinton, Catherine. *The Plantation Mistress: Woman's World in the Old South*. New York: Pantheon Books, 1982.

Delfino, Susanna, and Michele Gillespie, eds. *Neither Lady nor Slave: Working Women of the Old South*. Chapel Hill: University of North Carolina Press, 2002.

Jabour, Anya. *Marriage in the Early Republic: Elizabeth and William Wirt and the Companionate Ideal*. Baltimore: Johns Hopkins University Press, 1998.

_____. *Scarlett's Sisters: Young Women in the Old South*. Chapel Hill: University of North Carolina Press, 2007.

Johansen, Mary Carroll. "All Useful, Plain Branches of Education: Educating Non-Elite Women in Antebellum Virginia." *Virginia Cavalcade* 49 (2000): 76–83.

Lebsock, Suzanne. *The Free Women of Petersburg: Status and Culture in a Southern Town, 1784–1860*. New York: Norton, 1985.

McMillen, Sally. *Motherhood in the Old South: Pregnancy, Childbirth, and Infant Rearing*. Baton Rouge: Louisiana State University Press, 1990.

Rothman, Joshua D. *Notorious in the Neighborhood: Sex and Families Across the Color Line in Virginia, 1787–1861*. Chapel Hill: University of North Carolina Press, 2003.

Stevenson, Brenda E. *Life in Black and White: Family and Community in the Slave South*. New York: Oxford University Press, 1996.

Varon, Elizabeth R. *We Mean To Be Counted: White Women and Politics in Antebellum Virginia*. Chapel Hill: University of North Carolina Press, 1998.

White, Deborah Gray. *Ar'n't I a Woman?: Female Slaves in the Plantation South*. New York: Norton, 1985.

Wood, Kirsten E. *Masterful Women: Slaveholding Widows from the American Revolution through the Civil War*. Chapel Hill: University of North Carolina Press, 2004.

CHAPTER 4

Campbell, Edward D. C., Jr., and Kym S. Rice, eds. *A Woman's War: Southern Women, Civil War, and the Confederate Legacy*. Richmond: The Museum of the Confederacy, and Charlottesville: University Press of Virginia, 1996.

Censer, Jane Turner. *The Reconstruction of White Southern Womanhood, 1865–1895*. Baton Rouge: Louisiana State University Press, 2003.

Chesson, Michael B. "Harlots or Heroines?: A New Look at the Richmond Bread Riot." *Virginia Magazine of History and Biography* 92 (1984): 131–175.

Edwards, Laura F. *Scarlett Doesn't Live Here Anymore: Southern Women in the Civil War Era*. Urbana and Chicago: University of Illinois Press, 2000.

Farmer, Mary J. "'Because They Are Women': Gender and the Virginia Freedmen's Bureau's 'War on Dependency.'" In *The Freedmen's Bureau and Reconstruction: Reconsiderations*. Edited by Paul A. Cimbala and Randall M. Miller, 161–192. New York: Fordham University Press, 1999.

Farmer-Kaiser, Mary. *Freedwomen and the Freedmen's Bureau: Race, Gender, and Public Policy in the Age of Emancipation*. New York: Fordham University Press, 2010.

Faust, Drew Gilpin. *Mothers of Invention: Women of the Slaveholding South in the American Civil War*. Chapel Hill: University of North Carolina Press, 1996.

Krowl, Michelle A. "African American Women and the United States Military in Civil War Virginia." In *Afro-Virginian History and Culture*. Edited by John Saillant, 173–210. New York: Garland Publishing, 1999.

Janney, Caroline E. *Burying the Dead but Not the Past: Ladies' Memorial Associations and the Lost Cause*. Chapel Hill: University of North Carolina Press, 2008.

Morgan, Lynda J. *Emancipation in Virginia's Tobacco Belt, 1850–1870*. Athens: University of Georgia Press, 1992.

Morsman, Amy Feely. *The Big House after Slavery: Virginia Plantation Families and Their Postbellum Domestic Experiment*. Charlottesville: University of Virginia Press, 2010.

Varon, Elizabeth R. *Southern Lady, Yankee Spy: The True Story of Elizabeth Van Lew, A Union Agent in the Heart of the Confederacy*. New York: Oxford University Press, 2003.

CHAPTER 5

Brown, Elsa Barkley. "Womanist Consciousness: Maggie Lena Walker and the Independent Order of Saint Luke." *Signs* 14 (Spring 1989): 610–633.

Censer, Jane Turner. *The Reconstruction of White Southern Womanhood, 1865–1895*. Baton Rouge: Louisiana State University Press, 2003.

Coski, John M., and Amy R. Feely. "A Monument to Southern Womanhood: The Founding Generation of the Confederate Museum." In *A Woman's War: Southern Women, Civil War, and the Confederate Legacy*. Edited by Edward D. C. Campbell, Jr., and Kym S. Rice, 131–163. Richmond: The Museum of the Confederacy, and Charlottesville: University Press of Virginia, 1996.

Cox, Karen L. *Dixie's Daughters: The United Daughters of the Confederacy and the Preservation of Confederate Culture*. Gainesville: University of Florida Press, 2003.

Dailey, Jane. *Before Jim Crow: The Politics of Race in Postemancipation Virginia*. Chapel Hill: University of North Carolina Press, 2000.

Dorr, Lisa Lindquist. *White Women, Rape, and the Power of Race in Virginia, 1900–1960*. Chapel Hill: University of North Carolina Press, 2004.

English, Beth. "'I have ... a Lot of Work to Do': Cotton Mill Work and Women's Culture in Matoaca, Virginia, 1888–95." *Virginia Magazine of History and Biography* 114 (2006), 356–383.

Green, Elna C. *Southern Strategies: Southern Women and the Woman Suffrage Question*. Chapel Hill and London: University of North Carolina Press, 1997.

_____. *This Business of Relief: Confronting Poverty in a Southern City, 1740–1940*. Athens: University of Georgia Press, 2003.

Holloway, Pippa. *Sexuality, Politics, and Social Control in Virginia, 1920–1945*. Chapel Hill: University of North Carolina Press, 2006.

Marlowe, Gertrude Woodruff. *A Right Worthy Grand Mission: Maggie Lena Walker and the Quest for Black Economic Empowerment*. Washington, D.C.: Howard University Press, 2003.

Schuyler, Lorraine Gates. *The Weight of Their Votes: Southern Women and Political Leverage in the 1920s*. Chapel Hill: University of North Carolina Press, 2006.

Treadway, Sandra Gioia. *Women of Mark: A History of the Woman's Club of Richmond, Virginia, 1894–1994*. Richmond: Library of Virginia, 1995.

Wallenstein, Peter. *Blue Laws and Black Codes: Conflict, Courts, and Change in Twentieth-Century Virginia*. Charlottesville: University of Virginia Press, 2004.

———. *Tell the Court I Love My Wife: Race, Marriage, and Law—An American History*. New York: Palgrave Macmillan, 2002.

Wheeler, Marjorie Spruill. *New Women of the New South: The Leaders of the Woman Suffrage Movement in the Southern States*. New York and Oxford, Eng.: Oxford University Press, 1993.

CHAPTER 6

Green, Elna C.. *This Business of Relief: Confronting Poverty in a Southern City, 1740–1940*. Athens: University of Georgia Press, 2003.

Heinemann, Ronald L. *The Depression and New Deal in Virginia: The Enduring Dominion*. Charlottesville: University Press of Virginia, 1983.

Holloway, Pippa. *Sexuality, Politics, and Social Control in Virginia, 1920–1945*. Chapel Hill: University of North Carolina Press, 2006.

Lewis, Earl. *In Their Own Interests: Race, Class, and Power in Nineteenth and Twentieth-Century Norfolk, Virginia*. Berkeley: University of California Press, 1991.

Martin-Perdue, Nancy J., and Charles L. Perdue, Jr., eds. *Talk About Trouble: A New Deal Portrait of Virginians in the Great Depression*. Chapel Hill: University of North Carolina Press, 1996.

Salmond, John A. *Miss Lucy of the CIO: The Life and Times of Lucy Randolph Mason, 1882–1959*. Athens: University of Georgia Press, 1988.

Shockley, Megan Taylor. *"We, Too, Are Americans": African American Women in Detroit and Richmond, 1940–54*. Urbana and Chicago: University of Illinois Press, 2004.

Wallenstein, Peter. *Blue Laws and Black Codes: Conflict, Courts, and Change in Twentieth-Century Virginia*. Charlottesville: University of Virginia Press, 2004.

Waugaman, Sandra F., and Danielle Moretti-Langholtz. *We're Still Here: Contemporary Virginia Indians Tell Their Stories*. Richmond: Palari Publishing, 2000.

CHAPTER 7

Brodie, Laura Fairchild. *Breaking Out: VMI and the Coming of Women*. New York: Vintage Books, 2001.

Dailey, Jane. "Sex, Segregation, and the Sacred after Brown." *Journal of American History* 91 (2004): 119–144.

Dierenfield, Kathleen Murphy, "One 'Desegregated Heart': Sarah Patton Boyle and the Crusade for Civil Rights in Virginia." *Virginia Magazine of History and Biography* 104 (1996): 251–284.

Hall, Simon. "Civil Rights Activism in 1960s Virginia." *Journal of Black Studies* 38 (2007): 251–267; originally published online, 19 March 2007.

Leffler, Phyllis. "Mr. Jefferson's University: Women in the Village!" *Virginia Magazine of History and Biography* 115 (2007): 56–107.

Lewis, Andrew B. "Emergency Mothers: Basement Schools and the Preservation of Public Education in Charlottesville." In *The Moderates' Dilemma: Massive Resistance to School Desegregation in Virginia*. Edited by Matthew D. Lassiter and Andrew B. Lewis, 72–103. Charlottesville and London: University Press of Virginia, 1998.

Marschak, Beth, and Alex Lorch. *Lesbian and Gay Richmond*. Charleston, S.C.: Arcadia Publishing, 2008.

Murrell, Amy E. "The 'Impossible' Prince Edward Case: The Endurance of Resistance in a Southside County, 1959–1964. " In *The Moderates' Dilemma: Massive Resistance to School Desegregation in Virginia*. Edited by Matthew D. Lassiter and Andrew B. Lewis, 134–167. Charlottesville and London: University Press of Virginia, 1998.

Newbeck, Phyl. *Virginia Hasn't Always Been for Lovers: Interracial Marriage Bans and the Case of Richard and Mildred Loving*. Carbondale: Southern Illinois University Press, 2004.

Shockley, Megan Taylor "Southern Women in the Scrums: The Emergence and Decline of Women's Rugby in the American Southeast, 1974–1980s." *Journal of Sport History* 33 (2006): 127–155.

Strum, Philippa. *Women in the Barracks: The VMI Case and Equal Rights*. Lawrence: University Press of Kansas, 2002.

Thomas, William G., III. "Television News and the Civil Rights Struggle: The Views in Virginia and Mississippi." *Southern Spaces*, 3 November 2004, http://southernspaces. org/2004/television-news-and-civil-rights-struggle-views-virginia-and-mississippi (accessed 16 July 2012).

Titus, Jill Ogline. *Brown's Battleground: Students, Segregationists, and the Struggle for Justice in Prince Edward County, Virginia*. Chapel Hill: University of North Carolina Press, 2011.

Wallenstein, Peter. *Blue Laws and Black Codes: Conflict, Courts, and Change in Twentieth-Century Virginia*. Charlottesville: University of Virginia Press, 2004.

————. *Tell the Court I Love My Wife: Race, Marriage, and Law—An American History*. New York: Palgrave Macmillan, 2004.

————. "'These New and Strange Beings'; Women in the Legal Profession in Virginia, 1890–1990." *Virginia Magazine of Biography and History* 101 (1993): 193–226.

Whitlock, Rosemary Clark. *The Monacan Indian Nation of Virginia: The Drums of Life*. Tuscaloosa: University of Alabama Press, 2008.

BIOGRAPHIES AND MEMOIRS
These titles are arranged alphabetically by subject, rather than by author.

Boyle, Sarah Patton. *The Desegregated Heart: A Virginian's Stand in Time of Transition*. Edited by Jennifer Ritterhouse. Charlottesville: University Press of Virginia, 2001.

Zwonitzer, Mark, with Charles Hirshberg. *Will you Miss Me When I'm Gone?: The Carter Family and Their Legacy in American Music*. New York: Simon & Schuster, 2002.

Bego, Mark. *I Fall to Pieces: The Music and the Life of Patsy Cline*. Holbrook, Mass.: Adams Publishing, 1995.

Coolidge, Ellen Wayles. *Thomas Jefferson's Granddaughter in Queen Victoria's England: The Travel Diary of Ellen Wayles Coolidge, 1838–1839*. Edited by Ann Lucas Birle and Lisa A. Francavilla. Charlottesville: University of Virginia Press, 2011.

Goodman, Susan. *Ellen Glasgow: A Biography*. Baltimore: Johns Hopkins University Press, 1998.

Cella, C. Ronald. *Mary Johnston*. Boston: Twayne Publishers, 1981.

Keckley, Elizabeth. *Behind the Scenes, or, Thirty Years a Slave, and Four Years in the White House*. New York: G. W. Carleton & Co., Publishers, 1868.

Phipps, Sheila R. *Genteel Rebel: The Life of Mary Greenhow Lee*. Baton Rouge: Louisiana State University Press, 2004.

Allgor, Catherine. *A Perfect Union: Dolley Madison and the Creation of the American Nation*. New York: Henry Holt and Company, 2006.

Salmond, John A. *Miss Lucy of the CIO: The Life and Times of Lucy Randolph Mason, 1882–1959*. Athens: University of Georgia Press, 1988.

Hatfield, Sharon. *Never Seen the Moon: The Trials of Edith Maxwell*. Urbana and Chicago: University of Illinois Press, 2005.

Townsend, Camilla. *Pocahontas and the Powhatan Dilemma*. New York: Hill and Wang, 2004.

Kierner, Cynthia A. *Martha Jefferson Randolph, Daughter of Monticello: Her Life and Times*. Chapel Hill: University of North Carolina Press, 2012.

_____, and Sandra Gioia Treadway. *Virginia Women: Their Lives and Times*. Athens: University of Georgia Press, forthcoming.

Tribe, Ivan M. *The Stonemans: An Appalachian Family and the Music That Shaped Their Lives*. Urbana and Chicago: University of Illinois Press, 1993.

Seager, Robert. *And Tyler Too: A Biography of John and Julia Gardiner Tyler*. New York: McGraw-Hill Book Company, Inc., 1963.

Varon, Elizabeth R. *Southern Lady, Yankee Spy: The True Story of Elizabeth Van Lew, A Union Agent in the Heart of the Confederacy*. New York: Oxford University Press, 2003.

Marlowe, Gertrude Woodruff. *A Right Worthy Grand Mission: Maggie Lena Walker and the Quest for Black Economic Empowerment*. Washington, D.C.: Howard University Press, 2003.

Brady, Patricia. *Martha Washington: An American Life*. New York: Viking, 2005.

DIGITAL RESOURCES

African American Trailblazers in Virginia History. Library of Virginia
http://www.lva.virginia.gov/public/trailblazers/

Breaking and Making Tradition: Women at the University of Virginia. Larissa Mehmet, curator, University of Virginia
http://www2.lib.virginia.edu/exhibits/women/

Captain Sally Tompkins, Angel of the Confederacy, 1861–1865. Ronald Maggiano, ed. George Mason University
http://mason.gmu.edu/~rmaggian/hist697/finalproject/sallytompkins.html

Carver-VCU Partnership Oral History Collection. Virginia Commonwealth University Libraries, Digital Collections
http://dig.library.vcu.edu/cdm/landingpage/collection/car

Civil Rights Movements Veterans
http://www.crmvet.org/index.htm

Suggested Readings

Discovering American Women's History Online
http://digital.mtsu.edu/cdm/states/collection/women

Documenting the American South. University of North Carolina at Chapel Hill
http://docsouth.unc.edu/

The Dolley Madison Digital Edition. Holly C. Shulman, ed. University of Virginia Press/ Rotunda
http://rotunda.upress.virginia.edu/dmde/

Encyclopedia Virginia. Virginia Foundation for the Humanities
http://www.encyclopediavirginia.org/

Family Letters Digital Archive. Thomas Jefferson Memorial Foundation, Inc.
http://retirementseries.dataformat.com/Search.aspx

Freedmen and Southern Society Project
http://www.history.umd.edu/Freedmen/

The Freedmen's Bureau online
http://www.freedmensbureau.com/

Hearts at Home: Southern Women in the Civil War. Ervin Jordan and Michele Ostrow, curators. University of Virginia
http://explore.lib.virginia.edu/exhibits/show/hearts

Mapping Local Knowledge, Danville, Va., 1945–1970. Emma C. Edmunds, ed.
http://www.vcdh.virginia.edu/cslk/danville/index.html

Nettleton Civil War Collection, Correspondence Between Adelaide E. Case and Charles N. Tenney, 1861–1863. University of Virginia
http://etext.virginia.edu/civilwar/nettleton/Letters.html

Television News of the Civil Rights Era. William G. Thomas, ed.
http://www2.vcdh.virginia.edu/civilrightstv/

The Valley of the Shadow: Two Communities in the American Civil War. Edward L. Ayers, ed.
http://valley.lib.virginia.edu/

Virginia Women in History. Library of Virginia
http://www.lva.virginia.gov/public/vawomen/

Voices of Freedom. Virginia Commonwealth University Libraries, Digital Collections
http://dig.library.vcu.edu/cdm/landingpage/collection/voices

Working Out Her Destiny: Women's History in Virginia. Library of Virginia
http://www.lva.virginia.gov/exhibits/destiny/index.htm

INDEX

LIBRARY OF CONGRESS CATALOGING-IN-PUBLICATION DATA

Kierner, Cynthia A., 1958-
  Changing history : Virginia women through four centuries / Cynthia A. Kierner, Jennifer R. Loux, Megan Taylor Shockley.
    p. cm.
  Includes bibliographical references and index.
  ISBN 978-0-88490-212-6 (alk. paper)
  1. Women--Virginia--Social conditions. 2. Women--Virginia--History. 3. Feminism--Virginia--History. I. Loux, Jennifer R. (Jennifer Renee), 1975- II. Shockley, Megan Taylor. III. Title.
  HQ1438.V5K54 2013
  305.4209755--dc23

                                                                    2012038364

Changing History: Virginia Women through Four Centuries was designed by Christine Sisic of the Library of Virginia. Page layout was produced by Sisic using an Apple MacPro and Adobe InDesign CS5.5. Text was composed in Thesis. Printed on acid-free Anthem Matte, 80-lb. text by Sheridan Books, Inc., Chelsea, Michigan.

Jacket design by Christine Sisic, *Graphic Designer*, Library of Virginia. Cover image by Savannah Yuan, *Graphic Design Intern*, Library of Virginia.